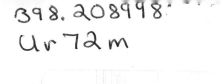

*Metaphysical Community*

# Metaphysical Community

## The Interplay of the Senses and the Intellect

Greg Urban

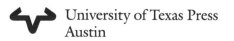
University of Texas Press
Austin

First edition, 1996

Requests for permission to reproduce material from this work should
be sent to Permissions, University of Texas Press, Box 7819, Austin, TX
78713-7819.

Excerpts from Bob Ortega's "A Tiny Town in Texas Is Flooded with
Pilgrims Seeking a Miracle" reprinted by permission of *The Wall Street
Journal*, © 1993 Dow Jones & Company, Inc. All Rights Reserved
Worldwide.

Plate 2 reproduced from *Walker's Mammals of the World* (4th edition,
Ronald M. Nowak and John L. Paradiso, eds., © 1983 by permission of
Ronald M. Nowak and The Johns Hopkins University Press.

∞The paper used in this publication meets the minimum requirements
of American National Standard for Information Sciences — Permanence
of Paper for Printed Library Materials, ANSI Z39.48-1984.

Library of Congress Cataloging-in-Publication Data
Urban, Greg, 1949–
    Metaphysical community : the interplay of the senses and the
intellect / by Greg Urban. — 1st ed.
       p.    cm.
    Includes bibliographical references and index.
    ISBN 0-292-78528-3 (alk.) 0-292-78529-1 (alk :pbk)
    1. Indians of South America — Brazil — Posto Indigena de
Ibirama — Folklore.   2. Indian philosophy — Brazil — Posto
Indigena de Ibirama.   3. Indians of South America — Brazil — Posto
Indigena de Ibirama — Psychology.   4. Oral tradition — Brazil —
Posto Indigena de Ibirama.   5. Discourse analysis, Narrative —
Brazil — Posto Indigena de Ibirama.   6. Posto Indigena de Ibirama
(Brazil) — Social life and customs.
    I. Title.
    F2519.1.I25U73    1996
    398.2'0899808164 — dc20                                95-21525

This book has been supported by a grant from the National
Endowment for the Humanities, an independent federal agency.

*. . . here we are treading on sacred, numinous*
*ground — and I beg the printer not to put luminous . . .*

— JULIO CORTÁZAR (1973: 290)

# Contents

List of Illustrations          ix

Preface                        xi

Acknowledgments                xv

1. A Tapir's Heart             1

2. We the Living               28

3. The Hole in the Sky         66

4. A Lock of Hair in a Ball of Wax    99

5. The Jaguar's Spots          134

6. This Is Your Making         172

7. Rocks That Talk             215

8. Between Myth and Dream      241

Notes                          259

References                     267

Index                          279

# Illustrations

## Figures

*1.* Wãñpõ's House, May 2, 1982, circa 4 : 00 P.M.  75

*2.* Wãñpõ's House, May 2, 1982, circa 4 : 00 P.M.: Intelligible
Relations Made Sensible  77

*3.* Wãñĕkĭ's Sketch of the Village (1975)  82

*4.* Nil's Sketch of the Village (1975)  83

*5.* Jules Henry's Representation of Communal Level Differences  140

*6.* Amplitude over Time for Three Sung Occurrences of *ñõ*  201

## Plates

*1.* Photograph of Textual Artifact — a Field Notecard Recording
Wãñĕkĭ's Tapir Dream  2

*2.* Photograph of Two Brazilian Tapirs (*Tapirus terrestris*)  3

*3.* Eduardo de Lima e Silva Hoerhan  30

*4.* Wòmle, Member of the P. I. Ibirama Community  31

*5.* Kàmlĕn — Great Shaman — circa 1920  34

*6.* Wãñpõ's House in 1974  68

*7.* Center of Dance Plaza, August 1975  84

*8.* Kũñĕpã Paints with Designs, October 1974  136

*9.* Men Dancing at *Ãgyĭn* Ceremony, August 1975  138

*10.*  Kàyèta Dancing at *Āgyïn* Ceremony, August 1975          139

*11.*  Studio Portrait of an Unidentified Man (possibly Kowi),
     circa 1920                                              145

*12.*  Photograph of Jaguar (*Panthera onca*)                  157

*13.*  Photograph of Brazilian Howler Monkey (*Alouatta fusca*)  227

# Preface

This is a study of one small corner of our planet: an Amerindian community in the interior of Brazil. What possible significance can it hold for the planet as a whole? What light can it shed on the large intellectual issues of modern times? The answer is this: If truth is carried in discourse, and if discourse is complexly embedded in the human populations in which it circulates, then to study the nature of truth and knowledge, we need to study the ways in which discourse — and hence truth — varies from one part of our globe to the next.

This is why anthropology has become so central to philosophical and more broadly intellectual concerns in the late twentieth century. Long before it became fashionable to do so, anthropologists immersed themselves in the truth systems of populations remote from their own. Initially, this did not impel them to question their own truth discourses, as they were able to rank knowledge systems evolutionarily, placing their own at the pinnacle. But there was always a measure of self-doubt involved in this, a nervous assertion of superiority, and the nervousness was only exacerbated by the rise of intensive field research — prolonged immersion in communities that were the most different from their own — such as Bronislaw Malinowski described in his *Argonauts of the Western Pacific*, often heralded as the first modern ethnography.

The nervousness took articulate shape in the concept of cultural relativism, so eloquently espoused in recent times by Clifford Geertz (1984), notably in his "Anti Anti-relativism." The key dictum is this: You should endeavor to understand an element of culture — a belief, for example — in the context in which it occurs. You look for its motivation in its relationship to the other beliefs and practices surrounding it. However, it is one thing to contemplate relativism at a distance, quite another to experience truth discourses up close, when something you initially described to yourself as a quaint "myth" suddenly takes on — at a gut level — a profound meaning in your own life. You question the absolute certainty of your old knowledge, just as you catch a glimpse of the meaningfulness of your new "knowledge."

Anthropology, with its self-doubt grounded in personal research experience, might never have assumed broader significance had it not evolved alongside the internally generated self-doubt of twentieth-century philosophy. Kantian foundations — which figure into the terminology of this book — began to crumble with the very attempts made to secure them. The rise of logical empiricism promised a way of anchoring not only mathematics but also all of truth itself. But the questions it opened up, about the relationship between statements and the external world, proved more refractory than the initial claims of Frege and Russell led everyone to assume. Efforts in analytical philosophy continue to this day — Saul Kripke's "possible world" approach comes to mind — the goal being to ground truth in a reflexive formal apparatus, or, minimally, to explore the limitations of such a grounding.[1]

Another line of thought opened up with Wittgenstein, whose own self-doubt about logical foundations led him to examine ordinary language usage. Wittgenstein turned away from meanings and toward speaking habits, though he did not investigate those habits ethnographically. Just how do people use words? How does that use seem to result in problems of meaning? This line of thinking was picked up by John Austin, who observed that people do much more with words than merely talk about the world. His distinction between "constativity" (talking about the world) and "performativity" (doing something in the world) might lead you to wonder in what measure truth in discourse is parasitic upon doing things with discourse. In what measure are claims of truth ways of accomplishing practical, rather than purely theoretical, ends?

This was probably not the historical trajectory that led to poststructuralism and deconstructionism. The latter seem more obviously to have grown out of linguistic and anthropological insights — the work of the Swiss linguist Ferdinand de Saussure and the French anthropologist Claude Lévi-Strauss, in particular. But both might have grown out of the questions raised and unanswered by logical empiricism, and, in any case, both reflect the same kind of doubt about the fit between discursive truths and the world.

You can readily appreciate the ontological priority that Foucault gave to power, with truth at power's behest. If performativity is the matrix of constativity, and if, further (though this be a big "if"), overtly constative statements are disguised as performative ones, then truth seems to be a function of social relations. Furthermore, if statements cannot be directly linked to the world in an unproblematic fashion, then it appears (as it did to Derrida) that all is interpretation. And if all is interpretation, then we are in the realm of play, a decidedly postmodern conceit. The play of signifiers renders nugatory any scientific ethnographic pursuit.

This is the starting point for the present book. In agreement with the deconstructionists, this book denies any direct connection between statements and the world. However, the absence of direct connection does not imply no connection at all, as if discourse and truth systems were cut loose, free-floating. The disproof of the detached character of discourse, and hence truth, is to be found in the notion of circulation, which is the basis of all culture, and which grounds the possibility of locally shared frameworks of interpretation.

How is circulation possible? It is only possible if discourse is simultaneously two things, not just one. Discourse is about the world (it is the bearer of truth, statements, meanings), but discourse is also in the world. It has a thing-like quality, and it is that quality that makes circulation (and hence culture) possible. Discourse is an object of the senses as well as of the intellect. However, its status as simultaneously in and about the world does not mean that the connection between the two is straightforward or unproblematic. Token-reflexive paradoxes — for example, "this sentence is false" — had long ago warned us of this fact.

Rather than closing off the possibilities of a scientific ethnography, however, the problematic character of relationships between statements and the world only makes it more urgent. Indeed, it is for this reason that, among the human sciences, anthropology today looms so large. What can we learn about the relationships between truth systems and the world through ethnographic study? What does the distanced, truth-laden, interpretive side of discourse have to do with its up-close, sensible, practical side? For not just any truth systems circulate. The meaningful side of discourse is not perfectly free-floating with respect to the experienceable world. To be carried along in the processes of discourse replication, statements must have (or so this book contends) something to do with the world. But what? That is a mystery that ethnography in general, and this ethnography in particular, seeks to solve.

Perhaps it would not be amiss to suggest one way of reading this book, since you might otherwise only conceptualize it in terms of classical anthropological categories such as autodesignation, space, kinship, communal organization, ritual. Let me propose that it is also possible to read this book in terms of the problematic of knowledge. You will, no doubt, appreciate that the tripartite structure of Chapter 1 (text explication, fieldwork description, theoretical formulation) models the theme of intelligibility and sensibility and their interrelations, which I see as central to the issue of public circulation. You might not so readily appreciate, however, that Chapter 2 — concerned with autodesignation — is also about the classical problem of logical empiricism — proper names and their connection to the world. Not only does the chapter move from proper names to pronouns, but it tries to break apart the linkage problem by exploring the issue of circulation.

Chapter 3 takes up more centrally the issue of the attachment (or detachment) of circulating discourse to sensible space, showing that narratives that circulate most readily in the community under consideration are not ones whose immediate referents are present to the senses. Perhaps it is the very distance they maintain with respect to the senses that facilitates their circulation. Chapters 4 and 5 address more obviously Foucaultian issues — how social relations form the matrix for social circulation, but are themselves simultaneously the products of that circulation — both as the referential objects of terms (such as kinship or moiety terms) and as the precipitates of circulation, the fit being far from perfect. Here is the problematic of discourse and power/social relations.

Chapter 6 plunges into the sensuous interface of ritual, where discourse is itself most obviously a palpable thing, publicly accessible to the senses simultaneously as it circulates in a sensible ambience. This sets the stage for considering the broader problematic of interconversion between sensibility and reference, which forms the theme of the final two chapters. You can read them (and I encourage you to do so) as an attempt to deal with the old problem of reference — originally understood as the relationship between statements and the world, or even between individual terms (such as proper names and pronouns) and the world, conceptualized as a straightforward linkage problem. Here the problem is refigured more complexly in terms of the interconversions undergone by discourse as it publicly circulates, migrating from the pole of representation to that of thing, with the representation also sometimes projected into the world of things through enactments, an echo of the old constative-as-disguised-performative problem.

A note of apology to my colleagues: There are far fewer citations and discussions of contemporaneous works in this text than the subject matter seems, to our specialists' eyes, to merit. However, I have attempted to keep the text as uncluttered, and hence readable, as possible, believing that our work is relevant to a broader audience. There are resonances between our concerns and those of scholars not just in the humanities or social sciences more generally, but even in the biological and physical sciences. The processes of discourse circulation and replication are nothing if not mysterious, as inscrutable as the orbits of planets or the reproduction of life; indeed, they may be among the last and greatest mysteries of our time. It behooves us to render our investigations of them more broadly accessible.

Philadelphia
January 21, 1995

# Acknowledgments

Nearly every morning from June 1993 through May 1994, I awoke in my Austin home, looked to the east — in what became an amusing ritual — and thanked the John Simon Guggenheim Memorial Foundation for the opportunity to write this book. I'll take the opportunity here to publicly acknowledge their support, as well as that of the University of Pennsylvania, which funded a glorious year — my first ever since receiving my Ph.D. too long ago — to do nothing but write. What you have before you is the result.

I am grateful to people too numerous to mention for their support and help. Several individuals read this manuscript in its entirety at different stages, among them Laura Graham, Benjamin Lee, Charles Briggs, Kristin Smith, Aaron Fox, and Susan Lepselter. Henry Selby also read a large chunk. Naomi Lindstrom suggested that I read Julio Cortázar, from whom I have borrowed the book's epigraph.

Chapters 1, 2, and 7 were the focus of an intensive discussion at a Center for Transcultural Studies (Chicago) seminar in the summer of 1994. Chapter 2 was first presented at the University of Texas at Austin in the spring of 1993. Chapter 4 was read and discussed at the University of Pennsylvania Anthropology Colloquium in the fall of 1994, and Chapter 7 at the Ethnohistory Colloquium in January of 1995, although an initial version was read at the annual meeting of the American Anthropological Association in November of 1991, at a session on dreams I co-organized with Laura Graham. Matthew Tomlinson supplied invaluable editorial help. Steve Feld and Alison Leitch gave invaluable moral support.

I am deeply grateful to the late Eduardo de Lima e Silva Hoerhan for his friendship, and for the old photos he gave to me, some of which are reproduced herein. This book would not have been possible without the active participation of the late Wãñpõ, Wãñẽkï, and Nil of the indigenous post [P. I.] Ibirama, as well as that of Nãnmla, Yòko, and many others. I hope that in some measure it contributes to their own efforts to pass on their knowledge. My wife, Patricia Kent, who figures in the ensuing narrative, actively cooperated in the first phase of field research, and has co-authored

Chapter 7 with me. Thank you, all of you, including those I have neglected to mention.

A note on the experience of writing this book—I now appreciate in a personal way the meaning of Claude Lévi-Strauss's famous assertion "myths think themselves through men." This book seemed, almost magically, to write itself through me. Perhaps this is because the thoughts behind it have been swirling for so long in my brain; perhaps it is acknowledgment of the role others have played in its creation; or perhaps, again (and not contradicting the earlier possibilities), it is evidence of how culture works—this book being one small fragment of that vast culture that flows through all of us.

# *Chapter 1.* A Tapir's Heart

*He was working in his garden,*
*and had picked up a large rock,*
*to roll down the hill,*
*to get it out of the way.*
*The rock spoke up,*
*saying that he shouldn't remove him from his bed,*
*why was he tearing apart his house?*
*When the rock first spoke, it looked like the same rock,*
*but then it appeared just like a person.*

— Waneki (August 22, 1975)

Poor empiricism! You are under attack and perhaps even on the wane within some neighborhoods of our intellectual community. In casual speech you are used, in parts of the humanities and social sciences, as a mark of derision — a "rank empiricist." The foundations of your house, once so regally splendid, have steadily eroded in the late twentieth century, the cracks and fissures and crumbling mortar becoming apparent upon inspection through the lens of cultural meanings. Why is this so? In the first place, people find that they cannot derive meanings from experience in any simple way. There seems to be no obvious one-to-one mapping. And, in the second place, the meanings attributed to experiences vary from one culture to the next. What are we to make of this, if not your unsustainability, your decrepitude?

Anti-empiricism has reached such a feverish pitch in some quarters that ethnography itself is open to question. Originally an endeavor to investigate the nonempirical or variable foundations of meaning in culture — one thinks here of Boas's observations about the color of sea water and of his formulation of "the seeing eye as organ of tradition,"[1] or of Durkheim's argument that social classifications formed the basis for the Aristotelian categories of knowledge — ethnography has now become suspect for its own empirical pretentions. Do the meanings ethnographers infer from their field experiences derive from the object of those experiences, that is, from another culture? Or are they superimposed from the ethnographer's own culture? Is the Other a construct of our cultural imagination, having little or nothing to do with the people who are Othered? Or does the Other have some substance?

One despairs here at the recognition of irreconcilable dualisms. Either experience is determinate of knowledge or it is neutral, its significance a result of cultural superimpositions. But between these two positions lies a third, which has to do with the empirical foundations of cultural meaning, not in extracultural experiences but in experiences of the very sign vehicles by which cultural meanings are circulated and shared; that is, by which they become properly cultural in the first place. And the most important of those vehicles is discourse.

The textual artifact in Plate 1 is such an empirical object. It is a photograph of field notes typed by Patricia Kent in 1975, while she and I resided in a tiny, bat-infested wooden house at P. I. [Indigenous Post] Ibirama,[2] a government-run indigenous reserve in the southern Brazilian state of Santa Catarina. The original notes were part of an ethnographic encounter, situated within space and time. As I examine them today, nearly two decades

```
tk                                  Cosmology: Dreams:
                                    Hunting the Tapir's ngiyudn
                                                            p. 1
        9-15-75 (M.T.)
              he was hunting with Kaña'+ and Maip5. Maip. said that it was
        a tapir that the dogs were chasing. they stayed waiting on a trail,
        and soon the tapir came running down the trail. they hit it with
        an ax, and it fell over, still a little bit alive. so Maip. got
        a vine, and said that they should tied it up. then they started
        to pull it along by the vine. they stopped and the tapir was lying
        belly-up, waving his legs in the air. Mainki was feeling sorry
        for the animal, because he was still alive. K. said for him to
        help pull, but M. said that he wouldn't help. so K. said that
        he would pull it by himself. so they went on for aways. they
        decided to take off the skin. they started taking off the skin,
        but the tapir was still alive, and waving its legs. M. was
        saying that they should leave it there and go on, because it
        could harm them.  but Maip. said that he wanted to get a piece
        of meat to bring home. then they decided to take out the guts,
        and cut open the belly.  they took out all of the innards except
        for the heart, which was still beating. at each beat of the
        heart, the tapir's head would move yto one side and then back again
        at the nest beat.  M. again said that they should leave this
```

*Plate 1.* Photograph of textual artifact — a field notecard recording Wáñēki's tapir dream. The card was typed at P. I. Ibirama in 1975 and transported across space and time, carrying the narrative to the author in 1993. Notice that a "tapir" is present in this object in only ghostlike, textual fashion. Compare Plate 2.

*Plate 2.* Photograph of two Brazilian tapirs (*Tapirus terrestris*), mature (*back-ground*) and immature (*foreground*). Compare this representation with the textual "tapir" of Plate 1. The immature (less than six months old) tapir exhibits the characteristic stripes, which disappear later in life. These stripe designs (or *mēkalem*), according to the P. I. Ibirama origin myth, were painted by the ancestors on the first tapir at the time of its creation (see Chapter 5). Plate 2 reproduced from *Walker's Mammals of the World* (4th edition, Ronald M. Nowak and John L. Paradiso, eds., 1983) by permission of Ronald M. Nowak and The Johns Hopkins University Press.

later and more than four thousand miles removed, I recognize them as part of a present empirical world, and also as my link by an invisible thread to a remote and forgotten corner of the planet, to a world gone by, the notes' still faintly musty and smoky smell rekindling old sensory experiences.

I give below a different representation of Plate 1, as well as of the two cards that follow it in the file:

9-15-75 (W. T.)
He was hunting with Kañã'ï and Wãñpõ.
Wãñpõ said that it was a tapir that the dogs were chasing.
They stayed waiting on a trail,
and soon the tapir came running down the trail.
They hit it with an ax,

and it fell over, still a little bit alive.
So Wãñpõ got a vine,
and said that they should tie it up.
Then they started to pull it along by the vine.
They stopped and the tapir was lying belly-up,
waving his legs in the air.
Wãñeki̇̆ was feeling sorry for the animal,
because he was still alive.
Kañã'ï said for him to help pull,
but Wãñeki̇̆ said that he wouldn't help.
So Kañã'ï said that he would pull it by himself.
So they went on for a ways.
They decided to take off the skin.
They started taking off the skin,
but the tapir was still alive,
and waving its legs.
Wãñeki̇̆ was saying that they should leave it there and go on,
because it could harm them.
But Wãñpõ said that he wanted to get a piece of meat to bring home.
Then they decided to take out the guts and cut open the belly.
They took out all of the innards except for the heart,
which was still beating.
At each beat of the heart,
the tapir's head would move to one side
and then back again at the next beat.
Wãñeki̇̆ again said that they should leave this animal and go on,
because it was going to harm them.
But Kañã'ï said that his wife was waiting for him
and would want some meat.
Wãñpõ said that tapir meat was even better than pork.
Then Wãñeki̇̆ was looking at the tapir's heart,
which was the only organ left inside the body,
when it all of a sudden appeared as though the heart had looked up at him
and then down again.
Wãñeki̇̆ became afraid,
and told the others.
Wãñpõ said that he didn't even want to hear about that stuff,
and cut himself a piece of meat to take home,
as did Kañã'ï
Wãñeki̇̆ didn't want any, though.
They all started walking away,
and Wãñeki̇̆ turned around to look at the tapir,
which was standing up,

and shaking its head at him.
The others also turned to look,
but didn't say anything.

I cannot doubt that Plate 1 is a photograph of a physical object of experience that is here before me — a tangible, visible entity providing the public[3] access through the senses that empiricism regards as fundamental to knowledge. And you will probably agree that my re-presentation of this physical object in the lines above resulted in a different object, but one that is a more or less regular physical transformation of the first. What you will regard as crucial, however, is that this physical object is not only *sensible* — dark shapes leaping out at the eye against a light background. It is also *intelligible*. That is, you know that those shapes are the bearers of meanings, and you recognize in the meanings something resembling a story, a narrative of an occurrence.

As soon as one steps into the realm of intelligibility, the problem of the specific language (English) by which these meanings are carried becomes crucial. Language is brought to bear on and presupposed in the ability to experience an object as meaningful. It is that quintessential pre-empirical backdrop of a present sensory encounter from whose vantage point one can criticize the empiricist project. But, if you accept that criticism, there is another issue. Speaking English is by itself not sufficient to allow you to recover the specific meanings associated with this physical object of experience. You must have a sensory encounter with the object. There is, in other words, an empirical condition for access to these meanings, even if there is also a pre-empirical one in the language you speak.

I have argued in an earlier work that the cultural specificities of grammar must have some basis in experiences analogous to our encounter with the physical object, the text artifact, depicted above. The Saussurean system we call language only appears to be pre-empirical. In fact, it is built up out of repeated encounters with discourse as a physical object, discourse such as is reflected in the text artifacts above, or in instances of actual speech. This long history of encounters — beginning with earliest childhood and continuing up to the present — provides the empirical, experiential basis for a culturally specific, as opposed to a universal, grammar. But the historical empirical foundations of the culturally specific grammar do not detract from the important insight that one does bring to bear in momentaneous encounters with specific text artifacts or bits of discourse, insight that existed prior to the artifacts. That insight is pre-empirical or pre-experiential in this special sense. One superimposes it on the text artifact that is the object of immediate scrutiny. You can think of meaning in this way as half subjective, deriving in part from something that is not there for you to behold at the moment.

But if meaning is half subjective, it is also, importantly, half objective. You know this because the specific text artifact might have been different. Depending upon the nature and degree of difference, the meanings would have been different as well. The objective characteristics of the sign vehicle matter; they fight back against solipsistic tendencies; they are the reason for doing ethnography in the first place — an endeavor that might otherwise degenerate into pure projection, as some critics have charged. Discourse, as a socially circulating empirical phenomenon, keeps the ethnographer honest. It ensures that he or she is retrieving something from the realm of the senses.

If grammar is a pre-experiential foundation for experience of the text artifact — at least in the limited sense discussed above — you might wonder whether it is the only such pre-experiential foundation. Is knowledge of grammar alone sufficient to furnish an understanding of the text artifact? Or, put differently, how much do you understand about the meaning associated with this text artifact as it currently stands? What more would you need in order to grasp the significance of it for the particular social encounter out of which it grew, and, perhaps also, for related social encounters?

One issue here is what has been termed in the literature "metadiscursive framing" — how this discourse itself is represented through other signs. I have already framed it, in some measure, by referring to it as "resembling a story, a narrative of an occurrence." That framing places the instance of discourse, and the meanings associated with it, relative to others, but I could get more specific, as did the participants in the encounter that produced the artifact, by framing it as a dream narrative, and you would have been cued in by an encounter with the remainder of the text artifact:

> [Then he woke up.
> he told his wife about this dream;
> she said that it was a bad dream,
> and it was a good thing that he had told her about it.
> It was a bad dream, because the animal never died,
> it must not have been a tapir,
> but something else,
> maybe a *gàyun* (spirit).
> He is also going to tell this dream to Wãñpõ.]

The story takes on a different meaning, framed metadiscursively as a dream. From discourse-internal properties, an educated Westerner might otherwise read this as a type of fiction, because, in part, the metadiscursive interpretation of narratives of realistic events does not permit statements of the sort: "Then Wãñẽkï was looking at the tapir's heart, which was the only organ left inside the body, when it all of a sudden appeared as though the heart had looked up at him and then down again."

Of course, you probably already guessed that we were out of the realm of documentary narrative with the statement: "They took out all the innards except for the heart, which was still beating," and, if not at this point, then when the animal's head moved back and forth in time with the heart. The narrative simply does not make sense to us — and the "us" I am referring to here is educated Westerners — as an account of what empiricism regards as ordinary experience, since it is out of accord with other discourse describing biological functioning. We cannot imagine that a heart would continue beating once the other organs were removed, let alone that the animal's head would be moving in time to the beats, unless, of course, this were a description of a scientific experiment involving electrical stimulation — a possibility ruled out by earlier portions of the narrative. But until this point, the narrative might have passed as documentary, a recounting of personal experience told secondhand.

Whatever the specific text-internal cues — and there may be, in some stretches of discourse, none — the principal determinant of metadiscursive framing is discourse external to the stretch in question, which is nevertheless "about" that stretch. Such is the case with "he told his wife about this dream" and "he is also going to tell this dream to Wãñpõ." The word "this" points to the stretch of discourse physically preceding it. It creates a relationship between that stretch of discourse and the word "dream." The word "dream" in turn tells the listener or reader how to interpret the relationship between that preceding stretch of discourse and the experienceable, phenomenal world. The tapir narrative is a narrativization of dream experience.

So here you have one fragment of discourse ("this dream") which is about another, longer fragment of discourse ("He was hunting with Kañã'i . . ."). Both fragments are half subjective, requiring the pre-experiential or pre-empirical cultural foundations we have been discussing, and yet also half objective, that is, not derivable from the earlier discourse alone but dependent upon an empirical encounter with the sign vehicles in question — the tangible, publicly accessible objects of experience that carry them along. At the same time, the two bits of discourse are related because the one (the metadiscourse) is about the other (the narrative). The problem here, consequently, is analogous to that of the relationship between an instance of discourse and some nondiscursive object of experience to which it might pertain.

What are we to make of this? Let's pursue the question of what it might mean to frame the narrative as a dream. For an educated Westerner, this framing will relate to how you are to understand the connection between the narrative and the rest of reality. And it will mean that you are able to dismiss it with respect to the broader empirical project: the delineation of a public world of common experience, reality, and truth.

Metadiscursive framing accomplishes this by separating the dream narrative from genres of documentary discourse, asserting a boundary between them, and denying the significance of the former for the latter, while asserting the explanatory power of the documentary genres with respect to the dream narrative. But is the label "dream" sufficient to accomplish this? You must conclude that no, the label merely summarizes broader patterns of interpreting or talking about the discourse. It is those broader patterns that are crucial to the epistemological position of the dream narrative with respect to the empirical project.

In modern Europe and America, the dream is of little or no public interest. It is not thought to pertain to anything outside the individual. It is inconceivable, for example, that a dream narrative from an American president should become the focus of national interest. The interpretive or metadiscursive patterns associated with dream narratives define them as irrelevant to the empirical project. Although dreams are experiences, they are not the kind of experiences capable of revealing anything fundamental about the universe or about the inner workings of things.

In contrast, the interpretive patterns in the P. I. Ibirama community from which the above-recounted dream narrative emerged define the experiences to which that discourse pertains as of definite public interest. Correspondingly, the dream narratives are actively circulated, providing evidence about an external reality to which the community as a whole is attuned and in which they have an abiding interest. Dreams are not defined as simply individual fantasy material without import for the collective endeavor. Rather, they provide entry into a realm beyond or behind surface appearance, the waking, visual shapes being only one manifestation of essences or, to borrow Kant's terminology, noumena as opposed to phenomena, but not the only manifestation and perhaps not even the most important one.

This is apparent from the brief snippet of interpretation reported above: The dreamer's wife tells him, after he has awakened, that the animal "must not have been a tapir, but something else, maybe an *gàyun* (spirit)." In her reported interpretation, she claims that a part of reality has been revealed to the dreamer — spirits or forces that animate the world but that are not apparent to the waking eye in everyday circumstances. Yet because they animate the world, they are of public interest, relevant to the commonweal.

This does not mean that metadiscourses in this community always encourage people to make their dreams public — "it was a good thing he had told her about it." Examination of other instances of interpretation that are part of the same discursive field show that the dreamer is sometimes coached to withhold dream experiences from the public: "His wife says that he shouldn't tell anybody about his dreams, because perhaps he would become a shaman as a result . . ." But here the motivation for withholding the dream narrative is not its irrelevance to the broader public. On the contrary, the withholding may allow the dreamer to achieve special knowledge or understanding or experience that puts him in a privileged position relative to the public.

Almost the opposite situation obtains in the case of Western interpretive patterns, including psychoanalysis. Here, dreams are considered irrelevant to the public; they do not provide access to a realm of common interest, for which, on the contrary, everyday waking experience — and especially visually confirmable experience — is paramount. This is why we want to hear a leader's waking thoughts about the world, but we never discuss his or her dreams. For psychoanalysis, dreams are important for what they reveal about individuals, but not for what they reveal about reality. Like fiction, they do not reflect a different facet of a complex reality, but rather fantasy or imagination or unreality.

What accomplishes this is the metadiscursive framing or interpretation of the discourse in question. Such framing determines how a given instance of discourse is to be understood, and, in interpreting an instance, it also shapes and builds up an understanding of the world, of reality. As a provisional definition, we might say that reality is that which is of public interest, of concern to the commonweal, where we understand interest to be reflected in socially circulating discourse construed metadiscursively as descriptive and nonmetaphorical.

This is by no means a denial of empiricism, since the community is interested in things that affect it, and the peculiar focus of Western empiricism — waking experience of things — does in part take into account what affects the community. But you can imagine communities differing as to whether the Western understanding takes into account all of what is of public interest. The above example, of course, suggests that it does not, that at least in that one instance metadiscursive patterns construct a public external world that includes, but is not limited to, what is accessible through Western empiricism.

Of course, this does not mean that every discourse that publicly circulates is a discourse of reality. Metadiscourses can define public functions for discourse other than the disclosure of reality. In the educated West, for example, we have entertainment and aesthetics separated from the disclosure of reality. This may be part of the continuing attempt to restrict the valid empirical encounter, which in other metadiscursive traditions is opened up, but it is not unreasonable to suppose that there are, everywhere, some exclusions of this sort.

From the proposition that reality is constructed by the community, however, it does not follow that anything goes, that the floodgates are left open, that the we-are-only-superimposing critique of ethnography obtains. You find instead an empirical constraint on the metadiscourse that defines the relationship between discourse and reality; it itself must socially circulate; it must be encoded in publicly accessible, sensible sign vehicles. And not just anything will circulate. The discourse that does achieve a wider currency does so because of its effectiveness in helping a community to exist in the world. The discourse is like a membrane or thin film that is simultaneously in the world and yet a filter through which the perceptible world is passed and its underlying realities understood.

Because a key feature of publicly occurring sign vehicles is not just that they are sensible but also that they are intelligible — and intelligibility requires the superimposition of a whole history of encounters with discourse onto a present instance — metadiscourses may vary in how they structure what is of public concern. But not just anything will convince a public about what it is that affects it. Indeed, you have to leave open the possibility that some metadiscursive formulations may be universally more convincing than others. The ethnographic experience makes one aware that the Western framing of empirical knowledge is one among alternatives, but you cannot deny that that alternative may have, ultimately, a broader public appeal than others, as the international public sphere widens its scope of operation. Ironically, or perhaps not so ironically, this is a matter for empirical investigation.

Our journey to Brazil began in Chicago. It was the summer of 1973 — and in those days there seemed to be perpetual summer. We were glued to our television sets as the drama of Watergate unfolded before our eyes — obsessed with names like Haldeman, Erlichman, and John Dean, that now only vaguely recall the sentiments in which they were then steeped.

The University of Chicago had been the site of student protests in the late 1960s, and protests continued into the 1970s, but we were dazzled as well by the acorporeal intellectuality that flourished there, like a garden of ideas overdosed on fertilizer; the incomprehensible lectures of the famous philosopher Paul Ricouer, whose almost comical French accent enabled us to pick out only fragmentary, but no less epiphanic, utterances (the four questions of Immanuel Kant — What can I know? What must I do? What may I hope? What is man? — were barely discernible), contrasting (somewhat later) with the logical lucidity of Donald Davidson, the final effect of which was no more, for all its apparent rigor, comprehensible. Nevertheless, the proximity to ultimate understandings seemed palpable, although it vanished like some vaporous apparition when we tried to reassemble it in smoke-filled rooms and coffee shops with odd names like The Bandersnatch.

In the anthropology department itself, Clifford Geertz had come and gone, but traces of his presence were everywhere, the culture concept mingling with structural functionalism, brought to life by visits from Meyer Fortes and Raymond Firth — giving the department a British club atmosphere the density of pipe smoke — and by senior students returning with stories from the mysterious "field" (a narrative space kept alive in this little discourse community by informal encounters, in our case, those wonderful evenings with Anthony and Judy Seeger, then just back from Brazil). And structuralism was the rage, though it flowed into Marxism, culturalism, and the rest more like a lava lamp bubble, the whole configuration constantly oozing and shifting, and managing thereby to hold us transfixed.

My wife and I had already been to Rio for the summer of 1972. Flying in again in May of 1974 was no less magical. We were aware that impeachment proceedings against President Nixon were set to begin back in the United States, but the aerial view of Copacabana Beach nestled into the Serra Geral mountains; the tropical vegetation; the heavy, bus-fumed air; the breakfasts of carefully cut oranges, papayas, and assorted fruits with toast, jams, and ludicrously rich Brazilian coffee served up on thick white tablecloths by waiters in crisp white dinner jackets; and the turtles and macaws in the lushly vegetated courtyard of the National Museum, where the anthropology department was housed — all marked this time and place as special, different from what we had left behind, like stepping into a Carmen Miranda movie, and we did indeed see Carmen Miranda look-alikes at tourist spots, especially at the Pão de Açucar, or Sugar Loaf, with stacks of fruit perched atop their heads, re-creating the movie images for those who came there to find them, in that global circulation that was coming to be culture.

But it was also the heyday of military repression in Brazil, and truckloads of young men — some mere boys — in army fatigues, carrying tommy guns, were stationed at street corners. The Brazilian Navy reportedly held target practice off Copacabana Beach. And the United States had not yet pulled out of Vietnam, so that the era of post–World War II supremacy was still manifest in our dealings; the open, breezy American style was not yet so openly identified with imperial aspirations the way it would be, and the way British accents and demeanors had been around the globe a generation or two earlier.

For us, however, there was the exoticism of Brazil, and it would only deepen, change its hue, but never again be so noteworthy, as we bid farewell to civilization, whose amenities seemed already significantly curtailed in Rio. From no hot water to no running water was a mere matter of degree. And only a few steps down from the omnipresent "Fusquinhas," or Volkswagen Beetles, scurrying about in tightly packed, but always improvised, clusters on Rio streets was the 1950 banana yellow army Jeep, originally part of the U.S. Geological Survey, which haltingly carried us into the hinterland, its gears held in place, we later found, by tin cans hammered in as bushings. (You may want to know, incidentally, that dried corn cobs make excellent battery caps, and Brazilian rot-gut rum, known as *cachaça*, has the viscosity of brake fluid.)

As you drive inland from the coast at Florianópolis, you ascend a lovely and ancient mountain range known as the Serra Geral, whose peaks rise above 3,000 feet. The range is a continuation of the mountains that stretch along the entire east coast of Brazil. About one hundred or one hundred and fifty miles inland, you reach their peaks, and the rivers flow in the op-posite direction, moving westerly toward the great drainages of the Ama-zon, farther north, and the Paraguay-Paraná to the south. The enormous plateau of central and southern Brazil is homeland to peoples who were among the last to be disturbed by Western civilization in the twentieth cen-tury. In the vast, and then still considerably uncharted, area from just south of the Amazon to the far south of Brazil were to be found seminomadic peoples and part-time agriculturalists speaking related languages grouped under the names Jê or Gê in the anthropological literature. The best guess of scientists is that peoples speaking these languages have probably occu-pied this remote upland region for several thousand years.

As the first drops of rain began falling that gray, overcast afternoon—which my field notes indicate was the 21st day of July in 1974—I had to remind myself why I was there. We had passed the last town before Indian country. It was known as Ibirama, a quaint German settlement with cobbled streets on which roamed horses and Volkswagen Beetles alike. From there the dirt road turned to mud with the first drops of rain. The gears on our jeep began failing one after the next, as we slipped and slid, the drizzle turning into a downpour. Fewer and fewer settler dwellings could be seen as afternoon turned into dusk. The only other traffic was going in the opposite direction—frighteningly huge, fully loaded lumber trucks descending at improbable speeds, causing us to swerve and nearly careen off the road into the Itajaí River some fifty or a hundred feet below. Lumber trucks? We knew that the great Araucaria forests of southern Brazil were rapidly vanishing, but where was this lumber coming from? Much of it was from outside the indigenous reserve that had been established at P. I. Ibirama. We would later confirm, however, that some of it was being sold by the Indians themselves to lumber companies that today have shifted their locus of activities farther north into the Amazon basin.

Was the trip going to be worth it? The road narrowed, with a steep slope on the left, a sharp drop-off to the river below on the right. At its narrowest point stood a lovely German-style cottage, with lush tropical gardens sur-rounding it. This was the home of Eduardo de Lima e Silva Hoerhan, leg-endary frontiersman, who as a young man had established the first peaceful contact with the indigenous group known variously as Bugres, Shokleng (or Xokleng), Botocudo of Santa Catarina, Aweikoma, and Kaingang of Santa Catarina. That year was 1914, and "Seu Eduardo"[4]—as he was known to locals—was still alive and lucid in 1974, though it would be months before we actually met him.

Thinking back on it today, the stories told by settlers and Indians alike seem fantastic. Seu Eduardo had a trained horse, which he rode into saloons, having it dance about on its hind legs as he shot off his revolvers. Seu Eduardo had killed the government Indian agent originally in charge of the "pacification" project. Seu Eduardo had murdered an Indian. Yet here was a cultured, intelligent man who spoke and wrote several languages, and was eager to converse about Freud and physics. He had grown up in Rio, in an upper-class world. He told us that he had been attracted to the frontier by the romantic image of the Indian popular in earlier twentieth-century Brazil. He announced one day to his mother that he was going off to pacify wild Indians in the wilderness of Santa Catarina. His mother said, as Seu Eduardo reported, and as I will never forget: "You will repent; you will cry tears of blood; you will eat bread that the devil has kneaded." On a lazy afternoon in 1975 he told us that it was all true, but that he had never repented. I did not appreciate then that I would never see that great friend and colleague again. By the time I returned to Brazil in 1981, he had already died. His house, once so vibrant with frontier life, had been abandoned and partially destroyed in a flood. The Santa Catarina frontier had come to a definite end.

As I write this, I know that the memory flashes by because of an association with his house, which marked the entrance to the indigenous reserve. We unwittingly drove past it for several kilometers until we rattled to a halt in front of a few wooden structures marking the outskirts of the Indian post—P. I. Ibirama. At that time, the government Indian agency was headquartered across the river, about a half mile up a steep hill. We crossed over the river on a suspension foot bridge. That night it was gloomily dark and raining steadily and hard. Fortunately, as the bridge swayed and we stumbled along, we could not see the innumerable broken and missing and severely rotted planks. An army colonel and his aide, there to hunt, would later fall through, plunging sixty or so feet into the waters below. That night we crossed safely, and were greeted by the acting post chief, Isaac Bavaresco. We would become close friends with Seu Isaac and his wife Dona Tina,[5] close enough to be shown Isaac's silver pistol and the scar from a bullet that had traversed his abdomen. That night we were thankful to be dry and safe and to have hot rice soup to eat.

The rains menaced us for two weeks, cracks of thunder and lightning breaking open the thick dark gray mist, that musty smell caused by mildew beginning to permeate our possessions. We were largely confined to the Indian post. The clay mud was so thick that we could not walk in our Brazilian sandals, known locally as "Hawaiians." Even our bare feet sank to the calves in mud. It seemed that we would never meet the Indians. As Lévi-

Strauss had said: "Anthropology is a profession in which adventure plays no part; merely one of its bondages, it represents no more than a dead weight of weeks or months wasted en route; hours spent in idleness when one's informant has given one the slip" (1968 [1955]: 17). We spent our time in idleness, waiting for the rains to stop.

Why were we there? Presumably, to continue the investigation of Jê social institutions begun by David Maybury-Lewis (1979) in the 1960s, under the auspices of the Harvard Central Brazil Project. Maybury-Lewis (1965, 1967) himself had lived with the Xavante, a group belonging to what is thought of as the central branch of the Jê family. Among his students, Jean Carter Lave and Delores Newton had gone to live with the Krĩkatí, Julio Cezar Melatti with the Krahó, Roberto da Matta with the Apinayé, and Joan Bamberger and Terence Turner with the Northern Kayapó, all groups that were part of the northern branch of the Jê family.

My wife and I had studied Jê ethnology at the University of Chicago under Terence Turner, and so considered ourselves grandstudents of David Maybury-Lewis, whose book *Akwẽ-Shavante Society* formed the basis for Turner's year-long course. It was the 1970–1971 academic year, and I recall Turner's deep, barrel-chested voice resonating throughout that drafty Classics classroom, light filtering through leaded gothic windows as we squirmed to find comfortable positions in ancient, straight-backed wooden chairs with attached writing arms. Despite our physical discomfort, Turner kept us rapt as we pored over genealogies, inspected residence charts, pondered the symbolic meanings of rituals, and examined photographs for a you-are-there sense of central Brazil.

Despite the immense contribution of the Harvard Central Brazil Project, it became apparent that little was known about the southern branch of the Jê family, in the then-modern social organizational sense, although Jules Henry (1941) had spent time between 1932 and 1934 at P. I. Ibirama, and Herbert Baldus (1952, 1955) had worked with the Kaingang. The group settled at P. I. Ibirama was one of three that flourished in the late nineteenth and early twentieth centuries. Eduardo Hoerhan established contact with the group in 1914. The remnants of a second group — largely decimated by raids from the P. I. Ibirama community as well as Brazilian "Indian hunters," known locally as *bugreiros* — was settled several years later near São João dos Pobres farther to the north and west. The third group was never successfully contacted. They continued to make news, raiding settlers in the area, until the 1950s, when they abruptly disappeared. In the early 1970s, the Brazilian anthropologist Sílvio Coelho dos Santos mounted an expedition to contact the survivors, then thought to be wandering in the Serra do Taboleiro south of Florianópolis. This is what had attracted our attention to the area in the first place. The group was never contacted, however, and if any Indians were still occupying the area, there could not have been more than a family or two. The area was simply too small to support a community of several hundred. So, we ended up at P. I. Ibirama.

The rains finally did subside. We went to visit some of the indigenous households, and were profoundly disappointed, for reasons that now seem worth recalling. If Rio was a self-consciously exotic city — constructing itself at least in part after the movie images tourists wanted to see firsthand — the community at P. I. Ibirama was outwardly unexotic, maybe even anti-exotic. The indigenous population wished not to attract attention to itself as a distinctive cultural entity, but to blend in, to become invisible. Men had given up using the lip-plugs that had so marked them in earlier generations, though the holes in the lower lips of many older men were still plainly visible. Most members of the community dressed not much differently from the local Brazilian settlers, and their houses resembled settler dwellings, stretched out over about ten kilometers on either side of a road that traversed the reserve.[6] In addition, many younger people were already fluent in Portuguese. When we first met Wãñĕkï, whose dream narrative opens this chapter, he was wearing a Columbia University sweatshirt and a baseball cap. We despaired of finding a distinctive and actively flourishing Amerindian culture.

All that would change over the course of the year. When we finally did observe the widow's seclusion ceremony, and the subsequent festival for reintegrating the widow, there was before us a plainly palpable indigenous culture. Men doffed their Brazilian clothes and donned their traditional costumes, painted their bodies, danced and sang in unmistakably indigenous ways. But none of this was for public consumption outside the reserve. No Brazilians were invited and only a handful of Kaingang showed up. The outward display of indigenousness had not yet become popular — as it has in the 1980s and 1990s among the Kayapó, Eastern Timbira, Xavante, and other groups. The latter have recognized their media image as a resource in political struggles. This was not true at P. I. Ibirama in the mid 1970s.

There the contrast between what I call the sensible and the intelligible slowly clarified, like shapes at dawn solidifying out of the darkness. While by outward, perceptible signs the indigenous population blended into its Brazilian settler surroundings, there was an inward, actively circulating discourse imbuing the world with a wholly different significance. There were stories of a land above the sky, through which men entered by means of a hole in the sky vault. There were reports of a land of the dead, where ants appeared as jaguars, and people nourished themselves on dirt. And there was the world of dreams, in which individuals encountered spirits behind the surface of everyday waking reality, like walking through a mirror in Jean Cocteau's *Orphée*. This was not the world of Brazilian settler culture.

During our stay, relations between the community and the Brazilian government via the government Indian agent, the official representative of

FUNAI — the National Indian Foundation — were continuously turbulent, sometimes exploding. There were countless reasons for this, not least of which was the lack of funds to carry out promised projects. But the principal source of friction concerned lumber. Many members of the community wanted to sell off wood in exchange for various goods, including, in some cases, electric refrigerators, though there was at that time no electricity in indigenous houses. I was opposed to this, regarding the forest as a key component of the patrimony, though my arguments were invariably brushed aside, like an annoying fly.

In any case, the turbulence at the FUNAI post provided us with an incentive, after a few months, to take up residence in an unoccupied indigenous house, conveniently situated between the homes of two men whose voices emerge prominently in this book — Wãñêkï and Wãñpõ. We were accorded some privacy, as a married couple, a situation that would change completely when I returned alone in 1981–1982. Nevertheless, our house, along with those of Wãñêkï and Wãñpõ — and, I imagine, every other house on the reserve as well — was the locus of continual comings and goings, innumerable conversations and storytelling sessions, as our competence in the indigenous language improved. I cannot claim to have achieved fluency during this first year and a half, but I could get by well enough to obtain numerous tape recordings, which I studied in earnest upon our return to the United States in March of 1976, after spending several additional months among the Kaingang of Ivaí at P. I. Manoel Ribas in central Paraná, and returning to the United States via the Andes.

With a few dramatic exceptions, our life there was tranquil, even bucolic. We made weekly trips to town for supplies. The bottled gas we brought in enabled us to type and read in the evenings, and to operate a two-burner cooking stove, which greatly facilitated our lives, since I was hopeless at picking out good firewood. We spent our days conversing with visitors, asking questions, tape-recording, visiting other households, or just observing the general goings-on. We had a massive invasion of native rats after the ripening of the bamboo, events said by local Brazilians to happen once every twenty years. The rats would leap all about, jumping over our shoulders onto the table, scrambling for whatever food was available. Bats lived in our roof and would awaken us each morning as they returned from their night's labors, scrambling for position. Flocks of prattling parrots descended upon neighboring fruit trees — the resultant cacophony sometimes making it impossible to converse. Once an enormous spider — said to eat fledgling birds! — leaped out of a tree onto my shoulder as I walked through the forest. Another time a huge lizard, at least six feet long, appeared on the road before us as we rounded a bend while returning from town. It was all part of a normal state of affairs. The serene existence was belied only by the circulating discourse, which was filled with magical occurrences of an animated world, with endless historical narratives of times gone by, and with dark rumors of political intrigue and mounting tensions.

Every three or four months, we traveled to São Paulo or Rio to meet with anthropologists, stock up on supplies, and see movies. One sunny afternoon, we were approaching the reserve, seemingly in the middle of nowhere, when out of the bush popped a camouflaged figure wielding a tommy gun, motioning for us to stop. In Brazil you are required by law to carry in your car a reflecting triangle and fire extinguisher. He asked whether we had ours — we did not. Then he asked stone-facedly for identification and told us to wait, which we did, and he disappeared into the bush. In a few minutes, he returned with a friendly-looking commanding officer, who informed us that the area had been cordoned off as a means of preventing the further extraction of lumber. However, he knew that we were American anthropologists, and he allowed us to proceed. Later at a bar outside the reserve, federal police officers clashed with some members of the community. Shots were fired, but no one was seriously hurt. Some rumors would circulate that we had summoned the army. By the time of our departure, however, the situation had calmed.

As our departure neared, Wãñpõ proposed that we adopt one of his own young daughters, one whom he himself had adopted. By that time, we had already been given indigenous name sets — my names were Mõgñã (Sucks Honey), Kañã'ï, and Lugmũ, names that had once belonged to one of Wãñpõ's two fathers, who had been captured from a different group. Now the adoption would solidify our ties to him. After considerable soul-searching, we decided against it. The lovely Mu (pronounced [ᵐbu]) was a constant delight, but how would she have adapted to life in a small Chicago apartment, separated from everyone she knew? Clearly, the idea was crazy, and yet it seemed so natural at the time. And then there was our constant companion, a black-and-white spotted dog named *bolinha* (little ball). Wãñpõ wanted him, and we wanted to take him. In the end, Wãñpõ won out. I learned later that *bolinha* had died within a year — though, as Wãñpõ told me in 1981, his was a valiant death, resulting from a fight with another dog twice his size over a female.

Five years later I returned, this time alone. So much had outwardly changed. The government had constructed a dam, which was to flood a considerable portion of the reserve. Its purpose: to prevent flooding in the downstream city of Blumenau. Ironically, when the rains came, and the dam broke, it resulted in the worst flooding in their history. Nevertheless, many people had moved. The community had fissioned, one group moving off into a remote corner of the reserve known as the "Bugio" (Howler Monkey), where they were unattended by FUNAI. Wãñpõ had remained, but had moved his house to the other side of the road, further up the hill. And to my dismay I learned that our great friend and companion Wãñēkï had died. When I listen to tapes of him today, and read the transcripts, I marvel at his intellect, at his ability to cast the traditional mythology into a philosophical understanding of his existence. His was a great loss.

In retrospect, my life during that year there seems hectic. I was never alone, even while wretchedly ill and desiring privacy. I befriended a young man named Nānmla, whom I taught to write the indigenous language, and who helped me transcribe the numerous tapes I was amassing. This freed up my own time to wander around with my tape recorder and lavalier microphone, recording whatever interesting discourse or sounds I happened upon. A considerable portion of my time was spent with the oldest man in the community, Nil (pronounced [ⁿdíli]). We wandered the forests, he teaching me about the plants and animals, the stories, the meaning of the world around me.

You might be asking, What did Nil think of all this? Like Wāñpō and Wāñĕkï, but unlike younger members of the community, Nil, I believe, thought that it was self-explanatory, that it was about time someone appeared from the outside who genuinely wanted to learn the traditional culture. The Indian agents were not there to learn, but to tell everyone what to do. The lumbermen had eyes only for those vast stands of virgin forest, and they would disappear without a trace once those were gone. The school teachers wanted to fill the heads of children with Portuguese and knowledge of Brazilian culture. But Nil, like Wāñpō, Wāñĕkï, and many other members of the community, knew that there was something valuable in what he had learned, and he wished in turn to pass it on.

Laura Graham has eloquently documented, in her recent book *Performing Dreams: The Discourse of Immortality among the Xavante of Central Brazil*, the relationship she had with the old chief Warodi. Through the years of her field research, she grew to understand that Warodi not only tolerated her tape-recording of public performances, including oratory in the men's council; he actually wanted her to record all of this. He would instruct her to turn on the tape recorder or bring the video equipment. Shrewdly, he grasped her pragmatic role. Through her recordings and publications, his discourse would live on. And through that discourse, he would live on, and with him the Xavante culture in which he had been raised.

Perhaps not so media savvy, Nil nevertheless similarly grasped the significance of my presence there, and he was determined to pass on his own knowledge. Re-examining a tape recording I made of a ceremony in 1975, I found that the tape recorder had inadvertently eavesdropped on Nil. I was trying to record some singing, but there was his voice in the background. He was talking to some young boys, trying to teach them the origin myth, just as the elders had done to him some seventy years earlier. At this phase in his life, he never ever missed an opportunity to pass on his culture. My arrival had been fortuitous, but for him it seemed preordained, the opportunity he had been waiting for. Day after day I immersed myself in his world, and I began to see my own life in terms of it. "I descend dancing, confronting my destiny" is a refrain from the origin myth. By the time I left P. I. Ibirama in 1982, and left Nil for good — he would die soon thereafter, reportedly amidst visions of the jaguar spirit — I knew precisely what that line meant.

Now a decade has passed, and those mundane aspects of my life have given way to a deeper sense of the profoundly philosophical dimensions of the discourse I had recorded. The book you have before you represents my attempt to probe those philosophical dimensions, to inquire into the nature of social life and its discursively encoded meanings in this tiny and largely forgotten backwater of our planet, and to project that inquiry onto the large intellectual questions of our time.

Yet, I still remember the small incidents, as if they had just happened. There was old Patè, who talked me out of my new, sleek Adidas running shoes I had brought from the United States and saved for special occasions. Normally, I wore a pair of cheap, ill-fitting sneakers, keeping the Adidas up in the rafters, dry and safe, but unfortunately visible to visitors:

"You have two pairs of shoes," Patè had said.
"Yes," I replied.
"And I have none," he said.
"Yes," I agreed, beholding his hardened feet, toes splayed.
"Perhaps I could try these on?"
"Oh, they would not fit you," I tried.
"Let us see."

And, sure enough, they fit, and it was obvious that two pairs of shoes for one person was too many when the other person had none. The logic was impeccable, and I grasped it immediately.

And there was another indelibly etched incident. Miguel, who had been raised on the Paraguayan border, was hired by FUNAI to survey the remaining forest. To the dismay of many members of the community, he boasted openly of men he had killed. Like many other Brazilians, he carried a revolver with him. One day I entered the house of Yòko, a woman who usually cooked for me. It was dark, and my eyes were slow to adjust. Beneath my feet I felt a splot, and then gradually made out the shape of a fledgling bird, flapping and gasping its last breath. "Oh," Yòko said, "that is Miguel's bird. For sure he will be angry."

So I immediately went to the FUNAI post, relocated because of the dam, and found Miguel seated behind a table. I confessed that I had inadvertently stepped on his fledgling bird, and indicated that I was sorry. He said that if the bird died, he would kill me. I said: "But, Miguel, your bird is dead." In a rage, he stood up, knocking over the table, making a gesture I interpret in retrospect as reaching for his gun. He went across the room, located the weapon, then stared at me with laser eyes, scoring the veneer of my reality. For one brief moment, I thought he would shoot, and I wondered again, as I had in those days of my first arrival in 1974, what on earth I was doing there. I wanted my body to be returned to the United States. I wanted to be buried in Illinois. But to my relief he lurched forward, bumping me with his shoulder as he passed, like a boy trying to start a fight. He disappeared out the door and into the forest, not to return for several days.

My troubles were only beginning. Yòko had followed me and observed the incident. Later I overheard her angrily recount the story to the Brazilian Indian agent, the gentle and thoughtful Seu Dival, remarking in Portuguese: "He who threatens Lugmũ [i.e., me], threatens my people." I had never heard any member of the P. I. Ibirama community say a positive word about me publicly until that moment. Of course, looking back on it today, I recognize that I was only the seed around which a sudden political crystallization had taken place in an already saturated solution, but it was a novel experience to be that kind of seed. By evening, word of the incident had spread like a Southern California brush fire across the entire reserve. A number of men gathered to make plans. I listened. They were talking about killing Miguel. They made reference to his own repeated boasting of killing others — a definite mistake on his part. And they considered his threats to me an affront to themselves. They would make clubs. Each man would hit Miguel once, so that no one would know who had inflicted the death blow. I spoke up, trying to talk them out of it, imagining the headlines — ANTHROPOLOGIST LINKED TO MURDER OF INDIAN AGENT. As in the lumber incidents, however, my arguments were swatted aside.

Miguel did not return that night, nor the next. Several men reported seeing him circling my house, trying to kill me while I slept. I was sure this was fantasy, but worried about what might ensue. Wisely, Miguel slipped back to the post one night and was taken out in FUNAI's Toyota Land-Rover. The incident blew over, and life returned to normal. I would see Miguel again some months later, this time in the city of Curitiba in Paraná. He was contrite, saying that he had been distraught, under pressure, the bird had meant so much to him. He did not mean to threaten me. Please accept his apologies. I did.

And there was the time I was up on the mountain ridge with old Nil. We were walking along, discussing various plants and animals. Nil was teaching me a song. Suddenly, I lost my footing and went careening some twenty or thirty yards down the slope. Nil came up behind me, a look of terror on his face. He thought I had died or seriously injured myself. I was scraped up, and considerably embarrassed, but otherwise fine. When he saw this, he chuckled. Looking at my field notes, I see that at the time I hardly remarked the incident. Yet it stands out so lucidly in my memory.

As I think about it now, I am led to relisten to the tape. Nil and I are chatting away about each of the plants we see, their usages, the mythology surrounding them — a good example of the transmission of culture at work, and it is occurring through discourse. As he teaches me a name, he insists: "Say it again." I too ask him always to repeat the names, especially for the tape recorder. In the background, we hear insects, rustling brush as we walk, air rushing across the microphone. Later Nil is singing, and I encourage him. So he continues:

> kū nū là kònā yòke.... ..... ..... ....
> nā kònā yòke
> kàn kàlà .... ....
> kàn kàlà
> wèn wala
> wèn walā ....m

There is a rustling and scraping as I fall, and later Nil's chuckle, but otherwise no evidence on the tape of its significance for my memory. Someone who had not experienced this directly would be unable to recover it from the tape. Bishop Berkeley wondered about the tree falling in the wood. Here was the anthropologist falling in the wood, and though the event was barely salient at the time, yet it has grown in my mind and gone on to live in my own discourse, in my storytelling. I wonder if Nil subsequently told this tale. Did it live on for him? Did it entertain and regale those around him, as other stories about me had? How curious it is what gets encoded from the fleeting experiences making up these lives of ours.

No doubt you have observed already, from the structure of this chapter, the main theme of my book: the relationship between intelligibility and sensibility, between understanding and experience, between what I will call, following the philosophical tradition, noumena and phenomena. So the first part of this chapter examines the intelligibility of the world as disclosed through an ethnographic fragment, a bit of discourse that, like a time capsule, carried meanings into a future. The second part records ethnographic experiences from the time when this and other ethnographic fragments were collected. One is a kind of hermeneutic of texts; the other a narrativization of my memory, based upon sensible encounters with the world. The first retrieves meanings that were not within the purview of my experience at the time; the second records recollections of my experiences themselves. I propose here that it is the relationship between these two — a discourse about meaningful discourse and a discourse about experience — that forms the proper object of ethnographic inquiry.

You will notice that we are at one remove from sensibility, since the ethnographer's personal experiences are already here encoded in words. In sensibility itself, there is a primacy to perceptions and feelings. These fall outside discourse, or, rather, they precede their formulation in publicly accessible words, and hence they cannot be studied directly but only indirectly through the words in which they are encoded. I recall today with great vividness the visible shape of Miguel's corpulence, the expression on his face that day in 1982. I can summon the smell — smoke-permeated beeswax — so characteristic of the P. I. Ibirama houses, including that in which I saw the vague outlines of a fledgling bird flap and gasp its last breath as my eyes adjusted to the dark. In fact, I have here in my desk beside me a piece of beeswax, carefully wrapped in plastic, a physical object transported from its original context into this one. I take it out and unwrap it and hold it near my nose, and its smell reproduces those original sensations. Yet, as soon as I try to describe the sensations to you, I must put them into words. It thus seems that we are already in the realm of intelligibility. The method of juxtaposing the ethnographer's narrative of sense experience with the interpretation of ethnographically collected discourse provides us no out from the poststructural conundrums of our time, with which we are already too familiar.

And yet my argument here is that this juxtaposition is our best hope. Precisely because we can examine the intelligibility of ethnographically occurring discourse, and compare its intelligibility with that coming from a narrativization of what our own eyes see, what our own noses smell, what our own ears hear, we have a check on the solipsistic tendencies latent in so much poststructural writing. Our own narrativization of sense experience is challenged through a double-leveled ethnographic encounter, in a way that it was not, for example, for Foucault, who dealt with entirely historical discourse. The narrativization of a dream experience as an encounter with the spirit world that lurks behind or beneath the sensible veneer of the waking one is shocking for Western patterns of intelligibility. Precisely for that reason, it challenges those patterns of intelligibility, leading us toward, rather than away from, the sensible world. It asks us to see for ourselves.

I will argue that this same push toward the empirical world is operative at P. I. Ibirama as well. It is really a kind of skepticism. It results from the conflict between the intelligibility of the world as encoded in the discourse of another and the way the world is intelligibly formulated by one's self. Because of this skepticism, the recourse is always to a go-and-see-for-yourself attitude. I will try to argue that at P. I. Ibirama the desire is for a relatively unmediated experience with the sensible world. This is an epistemological desire, and it accounts for, among other things, the peculiar form that group ceremonies assume in this community. If individuals experience this tension between intelligibility and sensibility, if they organize at least some of their social activity around it — as I will try to show they do — then surely that tension must be incorporated into the core of any theory of culture.

In fact, however, I believe that it has not been so incorporated into recent cultural theory[7] — at least not in its poststructural and postmodern wing. Perhaps this is due to the hard struggle in that area to establish discourse as a proper object of investigation in the first place, as Foucault endeavored to do in *The Archaeology of Knowledge*. In trying to distinguish "the statement" — the central unit, in his view, of discourse — from the proposition, the sentence, and the speech act, he ends up making it into a single thing, an interesting thing to be sure — which "circulates, is used, disappears, allows or prevents the realization of a desire, serves or resists various interests, participates in challenge and struggle, and becomes a theme of appropriation or rivalry" (1972 [1969]: 105) — but a unitary thing, nonetheless. For this reason, he failed to see the inherently "duplex" character of discourse, as Jakobson (1957) and Silverstein (1976) dubbed it.[8] Discourse leads a double life. It is something that is half sensible and half intelligible, and the two halves sit uncomfortably together, as do experience and understanding, phenomena and noumena, more generally.

Furthermore, this duplex nature of discourse is what allows us to distinguish between, on the one hand, the internal intelligibility of the world to the self, constructed through inner speech, toward which one cannot be normally skeptical, and, on the other hand, the speech of others about the world, about which we are naturally skeptical. For we recognize the external discourse as external by virtue of its sensible character. This is why I began this chapter with ethnographically collected dream narratives. Because of the sensible character of the discourse in which these narratives are carried, we recognize the narratives themselves as external. Consequently, we can maintain a skeptical attitude with respect to them. It was not *really* a spirit of the tapir that Wãñẽkï encountered in his dream. Though the tapir stood up and shook its head, its innards having been extracted, this was only a dream. It was based on encounters with real tapirs (Plate 2).

We can see a sharp contrast by comparing my own descriptions of the ethnographic context in which these dreams were recorded with Wãñẽkï's narratives themselves. Mine is a world devoid of magic, emptied of mystery. What we have here is a waking reality — a man wearing a Columbia University sweatshirt and baseball cap, a pair of Adidas running shoes, dark gray mist cracked open by lightning, a flapping and gasping fledgling bird. This is a sensibility with which Western readers will be comfortable. No spirits are to be found there, lurking behind the surface appearance of an ordinary tapir. No rock I kicked would ever speak back. Indeed, no dream of my own would seem noteworthy in this context, except as an illumination of my inner state at the time. It would not illuminate that external world of hard things we call reality.

So discourse here is not a single thing, a unitary entity. It is both sensible and intelligible, and this enables us to distinguish between our own inner discourse and that of others, and it enables us in some measure to distinguish discourse that is about the nondiscursive world from discourse that is about discourse, hard as this may be on some occasions. But because discourse is complex and heterogeneous, it does not follow that it is hopelessly fragmented, that its pieces do not and cannot maintain relations with one another, or, at least, that we cannot attempt to define pathways of linkage between them. On the contrary, it is my goal to show that two of the fundamental principles of culture concern the interconversion between the two sides of discourse, its sensibility and its intelligibility. The principles are a product of a simple fact: People want to put the two sides of discourse together. They want a discourse that leads them into the world, that produces some benefit for them in their lives.

From the point of view of culture as an adaptive mechanism, we can see why this would be. If people did not want a discourse that would accurately disclose the world to them, their task of living in that world would be made more difficult. Culture must be adapted to the real world, and the analogues of the long-stranded deoxyribonucleic acid that encode information about the real world are the long-stranded discourses, which similarly can be replicated and passed down across the generations. Consequently, these discourses must in some measure, and in certain ways, aid in the maintenance of relations with that world. This is not a novel claim. But what is novel is the further claim that individuals are actively trying to fit the discourse they circulate with the sensible world they encounter, and this struggle to produce a fit leads to some fundamental principles of culture, namely, those involving the interconversion between the sensible and intelligible sides of discourse.

What are these principles of culture? One principle maintains that there is a tendency for people to enact what is otherwise only intelligible through discourse. That is, they try to make the intelligible sensible. We shall see this throughout the following chapters, but it is perhaps nowhere clearer than in the case of shamanism. By contacting the spirit world, much as Wãñêkï did in his dream of the tapir, shamans are said to be able to harness that spiritual power for mundane concerns, such as healing. In fact, shamans harness the power by imitating the physical, sensible characteristics of the spirit being—in the case I will discuss subsequently, the actual body posture and call of the howler monkey. To nonshamans, the howler monkey spirit is only intelligible, accessible through discourse. The shaman makes that intelligible spirit palpable, available for anyone to see or hear, by his physical behavior. We may think of this as the principle of enactment. What otherwise exists only in the realm of meaning is made tangible by enactment. Nike — goddess of victory in Greek mythology — originally owed her existence to the mythological discourse in which she circulated. A pure object of the intellect, she assumed sensible form in the fourth century B.C. marble sculpture, known as the Nike of Samothrace, which can be seen today in the Louvre, even as the original discursive memory of her has faded. Who now remembers that she escorted Heracles to Olympus?

The other main principle is this: As discourse meanings expand their social circulation, especially through transmission across the generations, the form of their expression tends to become fixed. In other words, meanings are made sensible here not by enactment, but by holding constant the physical form of their expression. This process of fixation can take many forms. One need only think of the significance attributed to writing in the West. In the P. I. Ibirama community, fixation takes the form of verbatim repetition, and is most highly developed in connection with performances of the origin myth. As in the case of enactment, people seem to be striving here for the conversion of an object of the intellect — an intelligible meaning, or noumenon — into a sensible thing of the world, a phenomenally real entity. But the phenomenally accessible entity in this case is the material form of the discourse. In holding it constant, people seem to feel that they can hold constant as well the mercurial meanings, which otherwise slip constantly from their grasp, disappearing into the shadows of the mind.

You will no doubt be surprised to learn, having spent so much time on this journey into epistemology and culture theory, that this book is concerned with social organization, as classically conceived — its lineage can be traced back to Lewis Henry Morgan's *Systems of Consanguinity and Affinity of the Human Family* and through Emile Durkheim, Edward B. Tylor, and the British social anthropologists, among them Meyer Fortes; it includes the research on marriage systems undertaken by Claude Lévi-Strauss and others, who founded anthropological structuralism. But the study of social organization has fallen into some disrepute in the 1990s, or at least it has languished as concern with the world system, globalization, media, and reflexivity has increased. I hope to breathe some new life into this earlier research, with discourse as my smelling salts.

I want to show that a focus on discourse opens up the older concept of social organization, exposing it as having two interestingly distinct sides. On the one hand, social organization is the objective field in which, through which, and by which discourse circulates. It is the medium — dare I say ether! — for the physical movement of discourse across space and time by means of replication. On the other hand, social organization is the interpretation of the social world through discourse. It is the meaningful apprehension of individuals as members of groups — such as lineages, clans, and moieties — and as partners in relationships, especially kinship relationships. It is part of the broader intelligibility by which sense perceptions are interpreted and the phenomenal world is made real.

My proposal in this book is to look at the relationship between these two sides, seeing social organization through the lens of the two great interconversion principles discussed earlier. Unfortunately, the endeavor to investigate this relationship runs against historical trends. The evolution of academic culture opened a chasm between the two that has not yet been bridged. The fault lines of this chasm could be detected already at the turn of the century — in the famous debate between A. L. Kroeber (1909) and W. H. R. Rivers (1914) over the nature of kinship terminologies. Kroeber argued that kinship terms were to be understood at the plane of intelligibility, as reflecting, in his words, "psychology, not sociology." Rivers reaffirmed sensibility, declaring that systems of kinship — and, in particular, the "classificatory" system originally posited by Lewis Henry Morgan — were to be understood with reference to what he called "social conditions." If Rivers's position was a denial of the intelligible side of social organization, Kroeber's was a denial of its sensible side.

Regrettably, the chasm between the two points of view was never construed as reflecting a problem intrinsic to social organization itself, and hence as in the utmost need of exploration. Instead, it was celebrated by warring camps not only as a difference in theoretical point of view, but as a natural divide between analytic approaches or disciplinary methods, two distinct continents on which researchers could scurry about, conducting their investigations without the need for intellectual commerce with their neighbors. Indeed, Talcott Parsons proposed a fourfold disciplinary division in the study of human beings, which, he thought, could be construed in terms of distinct "systems": the biological, personality, social, and cultural systems. The division was actually implemented, during the 1960s, at the University of Chicago.[9] As you will have guessed (if you did not already know), the cultural system dealt with meaning, intelligibility, or what Kroeber called "psychology." The social system, in contrast, focused on what Rivers called "social conditions," which were apart from or prior to their meaningful construal.

Some will wonder at the wisdom of exploring this chasm today. Perhaps it is best to let the dead lie undisturbed. Even if the classical conception of social organization could be resuscitated, why do so? What significance can it have for us now? I want to argue that not only is discourse a means of illuminating social organization, but that social organization also illuminates discourse. We have stripped the tapir's innards, but its heart is still beating, and we recognize here, as did Wañēkï, that the beast is not what it at first appeared to be. It is something far more mysterious, vastly more powerful, than the flesh-and-blood creature of our senses. The discourse of social organization not only creates social life. More important for our understanding of discourse, the social life that it creates is important for discourse. The discourse of social organization is a discourse that produces its own conditions of circulation as well as the conditions of circulation for all other discourse — a matrix of interactions in which culture is nourished and grows. Without it, there could be no circulation. With it, discourse flows, and the universe comes to life, not only as something the eye sees, but also as something the mind comprehends.

# *Chapter 2.* We the Living

Our epistemological story begins well before that stormy evening in 1974 when a yellow Jeep rattled to a halt at P. I. Ibirama, indeed, before any anthropologists or government agents armed with notebooks and surveying instruments had ventured into the area, before there was a P. I. Ibirama.[1] It begins in the late nineteenth century. Travelers and settlers, penetrating deeper and deeper into the forbidding wilderness of the Itajaí valley in east-central Santa Catarina, came up against a frighteningly sensible object, one that physically resisted their progress, plundered their supplies, and threatened their lives. The object seemed to them as much a part of the material world as the Serra Geral mountain range, the jaguars, and the araucaria pines. Although their ability to describe the object was limited, the newcomers bestowed upon it names such as Bugres, Botocudo of Santa Catarina, and Shokleng.

Gradually, specific information began to accumulate about the object, though it was often difficult to distinguish fact from fiction. Reports from those who clashed with the Indians pointed to regularities in the physical appearance of male members of the group—tonsured haircuts, slender wooden labrets protruding through holes pierced in the lower lip, ankle cords, waist cords, bodies otherwise naked—all of this plainly visible. Shipped back to coastal cities, material items retrieved from the forest were inspected under calmer circumstances, and these, too, suggested a distinctive entity—the bows and arrows, for example, reached two meters in length, with some arrows sporting metal tips. The observable traits distinguished this social object, this group, from others in the region.

How humorous it sometimes was to get the other point of view on this epistemological encounter, fraught with danger and foreboding! Nil, Wãñpõ, Wãñekï, and others had their own stories to tell. As we approach the 1914 meeting with Eduardo Hoerhan, the stories become luminously specific. Hoerhan had mentioned to us a tactic used by the government Indian agency—then known as the Indian Protection Service, or SPI[2]—to "attract" the Indians. The government agents set up gramophones in the forest. They used these to pipe out Strauss waltzes, hoping thereby to signal to the "mysterious other" their peaceable intentions, to show that they were men of refined sensibilities. It occurred to me to ask Nil and Wãñpõ whether they remembered this. Indeed, they did. The elders had said that, by means of these horrible, scratchy sounds, the "enemy" (*zug*, a term now virtually synonymous with "Whiteman") was transmitting diseases to the people. When anywhere in the vicinity, it was best to stopper your ears with beeswax.

In any case, back in Europe the ontological status of the social group as object in the world was debated. In Paris, Emile Durkheim prepared his celebrated treatise on the active role of collectivities in the lives of individuals — *The Elementary Forms of the Religious Life* would be published in 1912, two years before Eduardo Hoerhan (Plate 3) braved the arrows of Kowi, who together with Nil's father's brother, Wòmle (Plate 4), took "presents" from Eduardo, thereby establishing the first peaceful relations between Brazilian national society and the group that would become the P. I. Ibirama community. From the European perspective, the groups were real. They had a thing-in-the-world quality. Why not go a step further and assume that this phenomenally apparent object also had a noumenal status?

It is best to be explicit about my meaning here. When I refer to the group, I am referring to a bounded entity, a set consisting of individuals. The set is decidable. One can determine whether any given individual is a member or not. For Durkheim, the question was bigger and ultimately fuzzier. He conflated the reality-of-the-group problem with the role of culture more generally, and hence with what today is glossed as the problem of agency — whether culture plays an active role in the lives of individuals, or is merely a product of individual agency. My concern in this chapter is not with agency in general, but specifically with boundedness or sethood — whether the group as a collection of individuals is a real thing.

My answer with regard to the P. I. Ibirama community is negative. The externally describable group is not noumenally real because it is not construed through the native circulating discourse as a bounded thing.[3] I must confess a certain grudging reluctance to admit this conclusion, as a positive answer would have made sense from the perspective on social organization charted in Chapter 1. There, you will recall, I proposed that the discourse of social organization has a special status because it creates the conditions for the circulation of discourse more generally. From this vantage, surely, a discourse of the group as bounded entity is a logical starting point. After all, if individuals enacted the existence of a social group described in some bits of discourse that happened to circulate among them, a natural ground for the circulation of other discourse — the continuing interactions among those individuals — would be created. A culture could be nourished and grown in that ground. The boundary would also provide a natural means

*Plate 3.* Eduardo de Lima e Silva Hoerhan, government agent who established relations with Wòmle in 1914, dressed in almost native garb — the loincloth is not authentic — circa 1914. Photo courtesy of Eduardo de Lima e Silva Hoerhan.

of resisting discourse from the outside, which might threaten the natively grown variety.

My acceptance of this conclusion, however, was also the starting point for a recognition of just how significant discourse is for the understanding of social organization. An attempt to take ethnographically occurring discourse seriously on its own terms breaks down some of our most cherished presuppositions, but in doing so it also opens the way for new insights, and, I believe, a way to rebuild our understanding of social organization itself.

Before I get to these new insights, however, let me tell the story of European and Euro-American attempts to name "the people" — a term whose singularity is now, of course, also suspect — some of whom settled at P. I. Ibirama. It is a story unfolding chronologically in a series of names, each with its own pattern of circulation, its own purposes within European and Euro-American discourse traditions. It is the story of a quest to get closer to a native point of view, to understand the world as the natives understand it, to discover the name by which they refer to themselves. But it is a story, alas, with an unhappy ending. After more than a century, Europeans have

*Plate 4.* Wòmle, member of the P. I. Ibirama community who established relations with Eduardo de Lima e Silva Hoerhan in 1914. Studio portrait probably dating from 1915 to 1920. Photo courtesy of Eduardo de Lima e Silva Hoerhan.

been unsuccessful in finding the natives' term for themselves, and we shall have to ask why.

In Brazilian Portuguese, the term "Bugre" means "Indian" or "savage." It connotes brutishness, treachery, and untrustworthiness.[4] I still heard "Bugre"—the name apparently used commonly among settlers who swarmed like leaf cutter ants into the eastern Santa Catarina forests in the late nineteenth and early twentieth centuries—occasionally in the 1970s among settler families, then blissfully ignorant of political correctness. The term was descriptive, but only externally so. Since the group was hostile toward all outsiders until 1914, the settlers had no access to the insider's or native's point of view. Still, the term "Bugre" did pick out a phenomenal reality; it labeled a set of experiences, an encounter with a something or someone out there that offered resistance. The group was hostile and war-like, dangerous, and in this it contrasted with other groups that might otherwise appear like it—the neighboring Kaingang Indians, for instance, who were, however, already settled and docile. The label "Indians" was therefore insufficiently precise; the behavior and characteristics of this group were unique. The uniqueness lay in the group's ferocity. True, they were Indians, but they were of an experientially special variety. For this reason, the term "Bugre" stuck.

The term circulated at a comparatively early date in the scholarly literature. The title of an anonymous article published in Brazil in 1852 was "Vocabulário da Língua Bugre" (Vocabulary of the Bugre Language). By the 1890s, "Bugre" could be found in the titles of articles published in Germany, such as that by Meyer (1896) in the *Verhandlungen der Gesellschaft für Erdkunde zu Berlin* (Proceedings of the Geographical Society of Berlin). In the twentieth century's first decade, it appeared in at least two articles in the scientifically prominent *Zeitschrift für Ethnologie* (Gensch 1908 and Lissauer 1904a). This was years before Kowi and Wòmle courageously ventured out of the forest to accept gifts from the young Eduardo Hoerhan, who was as scary to them as the Bugres were to the settlers. The term vanished from the scholarly literature, like some fickle wraith, during the 1930s. Coincidentally, the threat to settlers posed by the Bugres had by this time diminished. The last remaining unpacified band of Bugres secreted itself into the southern Santa Catarina forests, never to reappear. As the danger passed, so too did this danger-connoting term.

Geographically, the circulation of "Bugre" was circumscribed—the term appeared in Brazil and Germany, the two countries in which there was, at the time, worry over the phenomenal existence of this society. Nor was the German worry purely scientific; many southern Brazilian settlers were from Germany. Indeed, the principal settlement in the region—the city of Blumenau, which even in the 1970s looked like a postmodern architectural oxymoron, a German town picked up and plunked down in a lush, subtropical rain forest—fell within the traditional hunting-and-gathering territory of the people dubbed "Bugres." As a boy, my friend and mentor Nil himself would go to its outskirts to sack settler dwellings and pillage their fields.

In any case, it is probably because of its negative emotional charge that the term "Bugre" failed to achieve a broader scientific currency. The term was pushed out by two others: "Botocudo" and "Shokleng." "Botocudo" debuted on the Brazilian scene in 1902 (see Amaral), spreading from there to Germany (Koenigswald 1908, Aldinger 1913). It had already been in use—since the early nineteenth century, at least—to designate an altogether different people, who inhabited the eastern Brazilian states of Espírito Santo, Bahía, and Minas Gerais. "Botocudo" originated from the Portuguese word *botoque*, used to describe the enormous—three to four inches in diameter!—wooden discs worn in holes pierced in the earlobes and lower lips by the aforementioned peoples. Extension of the term to the southern Brazilian case was by observable analogy: The Santa Catarina people, too, wore plugs in their lower lips. However, the Santa Catarina group lacked the earplugs of their namesakes. Moreover, the plugs were of a different type—not discs, but two-to-four-inch-long pieces of resinous, seemingly lacquered wood (several of which I have before me as I write), fashioned from knots of the araucaria pine. The father of my 1975 neighbor and good friend Wãñpõ is pictured in Plate 5, in a photo dating probably from around 1920. Perhaps you can make out the lip-plug he is wearing.

The term "Botocudo" flourished until the 1940s. After this, it dropped out of the scholarly literature, where it was replaced by "Shokleng." But it had by no means vanished without a trace. Curiously, using the now-accepted strategy for naming native peoples—asking them what they call themselves—the term can be elicited from present-day members of the P. I. Ibirama community. Of course, the questions "who are you" or "by what name do you call yourself" are not ones that spring up naturally within the P. I. Ibirama community. They are the product of special epistemological encounters between insiders and outsiders, between people who know who they are and others who want to find out.

I myself made various awkward, stumbling attempts to ask these ethnographic questions, which, initially at least, provoked puzzlement. What did I mean, "How do you call yourselves?" Certain answers crystallized, however, especially among younger people—who no doubt considered me foolish for asking—the most common being *índios* (i.e., "Indians"). When I indicated by my persistence that this was not specific enough, some people would assert, to my disappointment, that they were "Botocudos." I say disappointment because, like *índios*, "Botocudos" is not an etymologically native term, but one that comes from Portuguese. I was looking for something autochthonous. The term "Botocudo" could not have predated

*Plate 5.* Kàmlẽn — great shaman, father of my neighbor Wãñpõ, and father-in-law of Wãñẽkï — circa 1920. Notice the labret through his lower lip. Notice also the cloth concealing a missing right arm (see Chapter 7). Photo courtesy of Eduardo de Lima e Silva Hoerhan.

1914, when Kowi and Wòmle decided to accept Eduardo's gifts. It was undoubtedly introduced in the course of subsequent interactions with Portuguese speakers, the discourse of one cultural formation infiltrating another. Its currency thus reflects the internalization of an externally circulating discourse.

As is perhaps already clear, however, the P. I. Ibirama community has not rallied around the term "Botocudo" as a label for their ethnic identity. The term continues to be, rather, a contrived response to a strange and perhaps unnatural question, one that itself seeks to set limits, to impose ethnic boundaries, to constitute an object in the world. Looking back on it today, I can see how my questions carried with them a baggage of presuppositions about culture and social groups, erroneous presuppositions, to be sure, but ones that, without tapping into naturally circulating discourse, I might never have dispelled.[5]

No great sleuthing is required to solve the mystery of who introduced the term "Botocudo" into the native vocabulary. It was Eduardo de Lima e Silva Hoerhan. A startling fact, however, is that Hoerhan, who spoke the language and knew the people and their customs intimately, "could never discover an autodenomination for them," according to the celebrated German-born Brazilian ethnographer Curt Nimuendajú (Nimuendajú and Guérios 1948: 215). He therefore introduced the term "Botocudo." As we have seen, the word had already been in use in the scientific literature in both Brazil and Germany. It was preferable in Hoerhan's mind to the derogatory term "Bugre," used so dismissively by Brazilian settlers. Hoerhan hoped that the P. I. Ibirama community would become known in the outside world by the name "Botocudo"; he cajoled me into using it on more than one occasion during my first stay there in 1974–1976; and he encouraged members of the P. I. Ibirama community themselves to use it.

If the naming process at work here is one of precisely characterizing a phenomenon, the word "Botocudo" does have something to recommend it. It is more specific than "Bugre," and it is accurate. Male members of the community did, from an early age (two or three years), begin to wear lip-plugs. Indeed, the piercing of a young boy's lower lip became the focal event for a community-wide ceremony, which I will describe in Chapter 6. Since groupness assumes its most palpable form in coordinated communal activity, which at P. I. Ibirama focused in considerable measure upon the lip-plug, the designation has a certain appeal. While lip-plugs have now fallen into disuse, and the ceremony surrounding them has not been regularly practiced since the 1920s, the designation "Botocudo" is far from arbitrary. It has its roots in the sensible world. Moreover, unlike "Bugre," which defined the phenomenon in terms of its effects on the settlers, this designation seemed to define the phenomenon in terms of its own intrinsic characteristics.

In southern Brazil at the time, lip-plugs were worn neither by Brazilian settlers nor by other Amerindian populations. Most similar in other regards were the nearby people called in the literature Kaingang (or Caingang or Caingan or Coroados), whose language was closely related to that of the P. I. Ibirama community. But the Kaingang did not wear lip-plugs. Lip-plugs were found among the Tupi-speaking populations, known as Cairjós, who inhabited the eastern Santa Catarina area in the sixteenth century. But they had been extinct for nearly two centuries. Lip-plugs were also worn by the remnant Xetá people, or Noto-botocudos, but at the time their presence in southern Brazil went undetected. They would be contacted by SPI, the Indian Protection Service, only in the 1950s. Lip-plugs thus were an observable differentiating feature of the P. I. Ibirama population.

Lip-plugs also figure into the semantic meaning of a group-designating term within the active vocabulary of members of the P. I. Ibirama community—*glòkòzï-tō-plèy* (long, slender lip-plug). Not an autodenomination of the local community now resident at P. I. Ibirama, the term was and is in common use in the discourse of that community to refer to another band, usually considered by ethnologists to be part of the same group or people, that is, "Botocudos" or "Bugres" or "Shokleng." The ethnological terms encompassed not just the P. I. Ibirama community, but also the *glòkòzï-tō-plèy* community, and even a third—the one that, as you will recall, vanished in the 1950s, having never been successfully brought under government control. All of these peoples spoke mutually intelligible dialects. Indeed, the P. I. Ibirama community held joint lip-plug ceremonies with the group they called *glòkòzï-tō-plèy* as late as the turn of the century, according to their own oral histories. Unfortunately, these celebrations ended in internecine fighting and terrible devastation.

An example of the use of the name *glòkòzï-tō-plèy*, from an extended historical narrative about feuding, is as follows:

| | |
|---|---|
| 1. kũ tã ẽ no tẽ kazàn mũ | 1. And he readied his arrows: |
| 2. tõ glòkòzï-tõ-plèy han | 2. "It makes like a glòkòzï-tõ-plèy, |
| 3. kũ ti katã | 3. and when he comes, |
| 4. kũ yè nũ ti pènũ ke | 4. I will shoot and kill him," (he) said. |

This usage is typical. Here the reported speaker characterizes someone he has seen but does not know—"It makes like a *glòkòzï-tō-plèy*." The term *glòkòzï-tō-plèy* distances the person or persons referred to from the speaker. It makes them out to be mere objects as opposed to subjects. True human beings, true subjects, in contrast—and this is a fact that will emerge as important subsequently—are referred to by means of individual personal names. Use of the group-designating term here is a way of dehumanizing the referent, making the person appear subhuman or perhaps supernatural.

In any case, this and other instances of public discourse provide evidence that the lip-plug is an intelligible feature of the world, and that it is used in designating a social group. If we understand "Botocudos" to mean "wearers of lip-plugs," it is possible to find some precedent for this usage within the native community.

At the same time, however, it is important that *glòkòzï-tõ-plèy* was not an autodesignation. It was, rather, a term used to indicate the groupness of some others, actually distant relatives, with whom the P. I. Ibirama community was on hostile terms. It did not apply tribal-wide, across the three communities speaking mutually intelligible dialects, grouped under the name "Botocudos" by outsiders. The term "Botocudos" therefore does not translate an autodesignation. Rather, its use betrays a frustrated quest, on the part of Europeans and Euro-Americans, to get inside the intelligible world of the native community.

The term "Botocudos" died in the scholarly literature in the 1940s, even though it has continued in the native community as a response to questions by outsiders, such as myself, regarding autodesignation. In Western discourse, the heyday of the term "Botocudos" thus overlaps with the term "Bugres." The latter, however, rose to prominence earlier in the nineteenth century and peaked earlier in the twentieth century. The term "Botocudos" dominated scholarly discourse in both Germany and Brazil between 1900 and the 1940s.

If we think of "Bugres" and "Botocudos" as two points in the history of Western discourse, the latter following the former, we can extrapolate from these points to a longer historical line or trend in Western naming practices. In "Bugres" we have pure externality. The name is a symptom, an index of the effects the P. I. Ibirama community had on settlers in the region. Its descriptive value resided in its connotations of savagery and treacherousness. This is how the settlers experienced the group—dangerous, wild, unpredictable. The term "Botocudos" is still external, but it is less emotionally charged, more scientific, and it characterizes the community in terms of intrinsic features, rather than effects on outsiders. It also makes a gesture toward internally circulating discourse, since the native community itself draws upon lip-plug style as a distinguishing feature at least as regards another group. A linear regression on these two points, therefore, reveals the lineaments of a broader movement from the nineteenth into the twentieth century, a movement from outside to inside, from effects of the group on Westerners to its intrinsic properties, from distinguishing the group as a phenomenon to comprehending it as a noumenon.

The extrapolation from these two points continues with the term "Schokléng," which, however, was probably introduced into the literature by Father Francisco das Chagas Lima in 1842. As part of his report on the Campos of Guarapuava, Chagas Lima mentioned a group called "Xocrens,"[6] indicating that they were "little known." We cannot be certain that this is the same group that reappeared around the beginning of the twentieth century. What we do know is that the term "Xocrens" itself submerged, only to reappear at the turn of the century in Germany, in articles by Bleyer (1904) and Lissauer (1904b). In Brazil, the name was not picked up again until Egon Schaden reintroduced it in 1937. The linguist Guérios (1944, 1945) used the original spelling "Xocrén," which was modified by Francisco Schaden (1949, 1953, 1957, 1958) to "Xokleng," possibly in a Brazilianization of the German spelling. Sílvio Coelho dos Santos (1973) used this version of the name in virtually all of his works. In my own writing, I have Anglicized the current Brazilian spelling, using "Shokleng," in deference to the usage prevalent in Brazilian ethnology, even though it did not correspond at all to an autodesignation.

Among whom did the term circulate? I have suggested that it was not an autodesignation. But neither, apparently, was it a word that originated among the settlers or European observers. Bleyer (1904: 830–831), in using "Schokléng" in the title of his article, adds "as they are known by the Caingaeng(e)-Indians, their western neighbors," though he also affirms that this is as the people "themselves also so designate" — a fact that studies of discourse within the P. I. Ibirama community fail to confirm.

The idea that the term originated among the Kaingang has impressive support. Curt Nimuendajú noted that:

> Xokre(n)' refers not only to the Botocudos but to other hordes of properly Kaingang that remain hostile and secluded, or at least that have remained so until recently. Thus, our interpreters from Ivahy in 1911–1912 classified as Xokre(n)' the Kaingang of the Salto da Ariranha and the Serra Pitanga and the then hostile groups from São Paulo and Laranjinha. (Nimuendajú and Guérios 1948: 215)

Before the 1914 encounter between Wòmle and Eduardo, therefore, the Kaingang of Ivahy were already using the name "Shokleng." And they were using it to refer not just to the P. I. Ibirama community, but also to other groups that even today are called Kaingang.

Some linguistic evidence can also be found to support a Kaingang origin for the term "Schokléng" or "Shokleng." Ursula Wiesemann (1972: 26) proposes an etymology for the name within that language. She suggests that *kléng* is the morpheme for "child" or "children," cognate with *krē* in the Paraná dialect of Kaingang and with *klā* in the language of the P. I. Ibirama community. The initial syllable *scho* she equates with *jū* in the Paraná dialect, meaning "anger" or "wildness." Hence, "the children or people of anger" or the "wild people." The cognate morpheme in the P. I. Ibirama community is *ñū*, where the name should be, under this interpretation, *ñūklā*. Unfortunately, in the naturally occurring discourse at P. I. Ibirama, I have found no evidence at all for the existence of *ñūklā*, let alone as an autodesignation. Most nearly homophonous is a word for "spider," and this is certainly not the name by which they call themselves.

Why should I regard this term, then, as continuing the earlier extrapolation of a historical line leading from externality to internality? The answer has to do with the form of the world itself—the word is not European-sounding. To speakers of Portuguese or German or English the word is decidedly foreign. Coupled with its possible origin in an indigenous community, even if not the one in question, it seems closer to an autodenomination than either "Bugre" or "Botocudo." Whereas "Bugre" is purely externally descriptive, as I have argued, characterizing the impression this group made on settlers, the subsequent term "Botocudos" accurately delimits the empirical group as a phenomenon. Moreover, its semantic meaning ("wearers of lip-plugs") is analogous to a term used by the community in question to designate another subgroup. However, the internality here is only a question of meaning, of referential content, since the word "Botocudo" is in its physical form unrelated to anything in the native language. Its phonology and morphology are those of Portuguese. "Shokleng," in contrast, is arguably indigenous sounding. It is a term that might have been used by a related indigenous population to pick out the group in question, and its constituent parts could be cognates of words in the language in question, even though the whole word "Shokleng" does not occur. It therefore has a greater claim to internality than either of its predecessors. It is closer to the side of intelligibility. We can understand its wide currency in the scientific literature from the 1940s onward in these terms.

A designation that is similarly positioned with respect to externality and internality is "Kaingang of Santa Catarina." The phrase was employed by Jules Henry (1935, 1936a, 1936b, 1940, 1964 [1941], 1942, 1948), an American anthropologist trained at Columbia University, who had done research in the area between 1932 and 1934. Henry did use the term "Botocudo," probably at the prompting of Eduardo Hoerhan, in one publication, done under his original name, J. H. Blumensohn (1936), and published in Brazil. After that, however, he used "Kaingang." But the term "Kaingang" was already in currency, and continues in use today, to describe a number of native communities widely distributed throughout southern Brazil and speaking mutually intelligible dialects. The word has a cognate (*kõñgàg*) in the community in question, where, however, it means "man," and is not the autodesignation of the group; indeed, some members of the community use the term "Kaingang" to refer to the Indians who came with Eduardo Hoerhan to help in the "pacification" efforts. Their descendants still reside at P. I. Ibirama.

Unfortunately, the origin of the term "Kaingang" itself, as used to designate these other separate but related groups, remains shadowed in mystery, falling into the black hole of the mid-nineteenth century. I do not propose to solve the mystery, merely to supply a few clues. In the earliest accounts — those of Chagas Lima (1842), for example — the name "Kaingang" does not appear; we find references instead to "Cames," "Votorões," "Dorins," and, of course, "Xocrens," the last described as "little known." From the literature of the mid-nineteenth century — the period from 1812 until the 1880s, from the first Brazilian expeditions into the region until the settlement of these groups — we learn little in specific about designations, auto or otherwise, and the name "Kaingang" fails to appear. Settlers and travelers alike used the Portuguese word "Coroados" (tonsured ones), a reference to the hairstyles then in vogue, and being a phenomenal descriptor, much like "Botocudos."

Alfredo d'Escragnolle Taunay, in a manuscript that did not see the light of publication until 1918, although it was based on observations made in the 1880s, initially imagined that he had been the first to "discover" (in his words, but should we instead use "invent"?) the term. He reports that

> . . . despite my questioning, no one knew of another autochthonous name [besides Coroados], and I was extremely pleased when, in the city of Guarapuáva, where I arrived on the seventh of April of 1886, I heard for the first time from the mouth of an Indian, who was on the acculturated side, the word kaingáng, as a name for the tribe in general. . . . (Taunay 1918: 573)

He goes on to explain, however, that he found in Curitiba a *Catalogue of Objects of the Paraná Museum Remitted to the Anthropological Exposition of Rio de Janeiro*, which dated from 1882 and had a memoir from Father Luiz de Cimitille and a vocabulary from Telemaco Morosini Borba, known subsequently for his ethnographic observations published as *Actualidade Indígena* in 1908. Both authors used the term "Kaingang." Somewhat disappointed that he could not receive exclusive credit, Taunay (1918: 574) conceded "that we three were the first to call the primitive inhabitants of that vast region by their true name."

But was it *their* "true name"? I note Taunay's remark, "despite my questioning." Such questioning, no doubt, was not something the people engaged in themselves. Nevertheless, it was probably common in encounters between Whites and Indians in this part of Brazil over the preceding sixty years. Who can say in what measure the term's usage in these epistemological encounters itself spawned the need for an appropriate response? Auto-designations seem often to serve the interests of outsiders more than those of insiders, of those observing the phenomena rather than those constituting the noumena, of the nation-state as opposed to the cultural enclave.

I note further that the term "Kaingang" has a cognate in the P. I. Ibirama community — the word *kò̃ŋàg*, as indicated earlier. There can be no doubt that the latter refers to "man" in opposition to "woman." It is also used as an age-graded term — "man" as contrasted with "boy." Possibly, the term "Kaingang," as a group-designator, had its origins in a word indicating "man" in the unmarked sense of "human being," if not in opposition to "woman" or "boy." We may never know for sure. The question of self-appellation even for these groups remains cloaked in mystery.

"Kaingang," whatever its status in these neighboring communities, was never, and is not now, an autodesignation within the P. I. Ibirama community. Nor was its local cognate *kòŋàg*. Nevertheless, like "Shokleng," it employs the morphology and phonology of an indigenous language. It thus appears more genuine than other, spurious-sounding, Portuguese-derived terms. It is part of the quest for an authentic name.

For Jules Henry, "Kaingang" served an additional function. It grouped the P. I. Ibirama people with those already so designated. The relationship had long been recognized, but it was first systematically explored in the 1940s in the work of the linguist R. F. M. Guérios (1944, 1945). Henry's usage reflected his own scientific predilections. If the P. I. Ibirama community were assigned the label "Kaingang," its classification would be apparent every time the group was mentioned.

Alas, the term turned out to be, for this very reason, unsatisfactory. The people assembled ethnologically under the name "Shokleng" were simply different from those already called "Kaingang"; consequently the latter never caught on as a unique descriptor. There was the added problem that, in the P. I. Ibirama community, the term "Kaingang" was already in circulation, albeit not as an autodesignation. It referred rather to the same people already designated by that term.

Taking us further along the continuum of points established by these terms is "Aweikoma," which, however, has had only limited currency, with almost no circulation in Brazil. It was used principally in North American and European publications. Its origins lie in a word list published by Dr. Hugo Gensch (1908: 752), where we find the entry "Indianer — *awei-koma*." The hyphenated designation *Aweikoma-Caingang* appears in the ethnologically important *Handbook of South American Indians*, Vol. 1, in an article by the renowned French-Brazilian ethnologist Alfred Métraux, who remarks that "Nimuendajú calls them *Aweikoma*, a word of their language meaning Indians" (1946: 449). Curiously, however, in Vol. 6 of the *Handbook*, J. Alden Mason (1950), in his comparative linguistic map, uses the term "Shocleng." In any case, "Aweikoma" was then taken up and used by the British anthropologist, David Hicks (1966a, 1966b, 1971a, 1971b), although Hicks based his knowledge of the community exclusively on secondary sources.

Through the term "Aweikoma" we gain further insights into the personal struggles within Western science that influence name choice. Hicks (1966a:

841) mentions that "the term 'Aweikoma' . . . has been adopted increasingly by anthropologists since it was first employed in published form by Nimuendajú in 1908." Here he appeals to Nimuendajú's ethnographic authority, the latter having been widely recognized for his years of field research, particularly among Jê-speaking peoples, including the Kaingang. Regrettably, Hicks did not include in his bibliography the 1908 publication by Nimuendajú he mentions here. Perhaps he meant the 1908 article by Hugo Gensch, in which the term first appeared. Hicks cites only the 1948 letters between Nimuendajú and Guérios, where, however, Nimuendajú observed: "I myself provisionally prefer this name [Botocudos]." He went on to say: "In 1908 I proposed to H. von Ihering the name Aweikóma (i.e., 'Indian' in Dr. Gensch's vocabulary) which he used at the Congress of Americanists in Buenos Aires, and that has since appeared in the literature . . . I myself have never seen even a single Botocudo" (Nimuendajú and Guérios 1948: 215).

Hicks's choice of names mirrors the academic power struggle in which he was locked; the term sets him in explicit opposition to Henry, who lumped these people with the Kaingang. Hicks (1966a: 839) opened his essay by saying:

> It has been maintained by some south Americanists, prominent among them JULES HENRY (1964, p. xxi, *et passim*) and ALFRED METRAUX (1946, p. 448, *et passim*) that Aweikoma society is merely a smaller unit within the larger entity that is Kaingang society. The purpose of this essay is to demonstrate that this confoundation is erroneous and that, contrarily, the two societies are more aptly conceived of as separate cultural conglomerations.

What is the discursive reality beneath this politics of representation? The word "Aweikoma" was elicited by the German-speaking Gensch from a captured girl — this was before the first amicable meeting between Eduardo and Wòmle, and in 1975 I would learn from Wãñpõ that the captured girl's name was Kòziklã. In any case, if we imagine the word "Aweikoma" pronounced in accord with German orthography, with stress on the final syllable, it was probably an attempt to transcribe the native word, still in use in the 1970s and 1980s, *wãñkòmãg*.[7] The latter refers to the seclusion a widow or widower undergoes after the death of a spouse. It is also a term I elicited in 1975 for an ancient social grouping, perhaps an analogue to one of the Kaingang exogamous patrilineal moieties, although we cannot be certain of this. It was definitely not an autodesignation of the P. I. Ibirama community.

So the historical rise of this term in the North American and European literature in the recent period confirms the quest pattern we have documented. Whereas the term "Shokleng" is probably a native term among the neighboring Kaingang peoples, with possible cognates in the language of the P. I. Ibirama community, the term *wãñkòmãg*, in its tangible phonetic shape as well as its meaningful segmentation, is genuinely from that community. It is like a shell, picked up from the seashore, which can remind us of its origins, of the salty air and sunny days or of the gray mists and seagulls and cold air that reddens the cheeks. It is a reminder that the sensible world is out there, and that we can retrieve experiences from it and inspect them under the light of the intellect.

The historical movement in naming is thus from an external description based on effects ("Bugre") to an external description based on intrinsic characteristics ("Botocudo"), to an external description from a neighboring and related people ("Shokleng"), to a word arising from within the community that is still in circulation there today. Unfortunately, the term *wãñkòmãg* is used only to refer to the seclusion ceremony. Few, if any, living speakers would recognize it as group-denoting. Were the ancient usage still current, we would still not have found an autodenomination but a label for a constituent subgroup. While the object was plucked from the native community, our pundits have misled us. It was not a seashell at all but a coquille, a shell-like dish used to serve seafood. The object was from the right place, but it was not the object we thought it was.

The last proper name found in the literature, "Lakranó," today is not widely known in the community, though I myself did record it. I was told the name by Wãñẽkï, who had been kidnapped as a child from the so-called *glòkòzï-tõ-plèy* subgroup by members of the P. I. Ibirama community. I suspect that the name was not an autodesignation, but an external descriptor, used by the people called *glòkòzï-tõ-plèy* to refer to the people at P. I. Ibirama.

Scholars have only recently employed the term "Lakranó." The name appeared in Germany in two articles authored by Heinz Kühne (1979, 1980), evidently based on library research. The name is also mentioned by the linguist Ursula Wiesemann (1978), who, however, preferred the term "Xokleng." "Lakranó" is perhaps as close as outsiders have gotten to an autodenomination of the P. I. Ibirama subgrouping. However, the term does not circulate widely in the community. Moreover, since it apparently originated in another subgrouping, it is not properly an autodesignation. Finally, it does not refer to the group consisting of three communities that ethnologists sought to encompass under the terms "Bugre," "Botocudo," "Shokleng," and "Aweikoma."

We are therefore left with a puzzle — none of the names proffered is a proper autodesignation. None is analogous to the terms United States or Americans, which are a regular feature of our own publicly accessible discourse. Who has not tuned into a presidential address only to hear "my fellow Americans," or "we Americans," or "the United States?" In contemporary American discursive practices, there seems to be an easy acceptance of collective self-identity. Is there some counterpart to this in the publicly circulating discourse in the P. I. Ibirama community itself?

One possible answer is that collective identity, if not encoded in a third person noun, might be expressed in the first person plural pronoun "we." Surely, "we" ought to encode a subjective sense of belonging, of membership in a larger entity. Hence, it might possibly lead us to an intellectually recoverable collective essence or object — what I am here calling a noumenal object — that corresponds to the phenomenal object named by the nouns just reviewed. The latter do not permit us to reconstruct a noumenal object because they circulate in Brazil, Europe, and North America but not in the community in question. The nouns, in short, do not reflect the way the discourse in this community constitutes its own intelligible sense of itself.

Entering the realm of discourse is like going into hyperspace in *Star Wars*, a rush of acceleration as the universe shoots by, followed by an eerie serenity as we break through to a new dimension. And the world that awaits us is different and unexpected. Who knows what lurks out there? Perhaps the phenomenal object itself does not look the same from this vantage point — recall Boas's notion of the "seeing eye as organ of tradition." In asking people what they called themselves, we assumed the existence of the object to be named. But what if the object itself is not similarly intelligible from the other side? Ethnography's claim has been to magically transport us into other worldviews. We see now, however, that the method of questioning fails in this regard. In presupposing its object, it stops short of its own goal. The exploration of naturally occurring discourse, in contrast, opens up a new frontier of experience.

A key feature of "we" is its malleability; it takes on different meanings in the different instances in which it occurs. Nuanced and colored and locally inflected, it must be studied in its specific contexts. I am not denying our ability to attribute to the first person plural pronoun an abstract meaning, for example, "speaker plus others." But I am suggesting that the cultural interest of "we" lies not in this abstract and naked "we," but in the concrete costumes it dons. Interpreters must ask themselves in each instance: What does this "we" mean? What others does it include?

No doubt you will object that, from this point of view, "we" has too many meanings, infinitely many, in fact. An instance bears the traces of its origins in a specific context, and contexts are infinitely differentiable. Ergo, the meanings of "we" are infinitely differentiable. If settling for the abstract meaning "speaker plus others" has been the Scylla of linguistic research on "we," throwing up our hands at its infinite richness has been the Charybdis. I propose to show that there is a middle passage. We can find broad regularities in the use of "we" within particular cultures. The contextual shape of "we" crystallizes around certain meanings. Additionally, some meanings may be more prominent in certain genres than in others.

Because the meaning of "we" is determined by ambient discourse, its usage is always in some measure subject to individual manipulation. In turn, manipulations can result in changes to the patterns or regularities in "we" usage. Consequently, the existence of patterns needs to be assessed against the backdrop of agency — especially, in the P. I. Ibirama community, against the interethnic strife that has characterized so much of its modern history. At the same time, it is important to appreciate that we are dealing with patterns, regularities across multiple instances, not only with momentaneous effects.

How does one go about discovering the meaning of "we" in a specific instance? The main method is by inspecting an instance within its context, and asking two questions. First, is "we" co-referential with a noun that has come before it? If so, then the noun defines the scope of the "we." Consider the following pair of clauses: "now it is women who have breasts; it's for this reason that we are now like that."[8] One would assume that "we" in the second clause is co-referential with "women" in the first, and that the meaning of this instance of "we" is therefore "women." The second question is, Does "we" contrast with any other nouns within its vicinity? If so, those nouns tell us what "we" is not, what falls outside its purview. Given a sentence such as "We had never seen the Whiteman," the reader/hearer would judge "we" to be exclusive of "Whiteman." Correspondingly, the sense of subjective belonging here is to an internal collectivity defined in part, at least, as "not Whiteman."

The questions for us in this chapter are: What meanings does "we" assume within the naturally occurring discourse of the P. I. Ibirama community? Are there "we's" corresponding to the phenomenal object proposed by anthropologists — the so-called Bugres or Botocudos or Shokleng as a cultural grouping? And how prominent are the various kinds of "we's" within the broader scheme of discourse? To be sure, we must also ask ourselves who the purveyors are of the discourse in which a "we" occurs. Do different segments of the population operate with different kinds of "we's"?

Let us take an example from a story dealing with the origin of death. Throughout most of this story, there are no "we's" — the pronouns for "we" being *ãg* (used for all except nominative case) and *nã* (used for nominative case), which I have underlined in the transcript below. The story proceeds in the third person. Then, abruptly, at the very end of Wãñẽki's 1975 narration, the following philosophical musing appears:

| | |
|---|---|
| 164. ãg tèl gèke tògtẽ yè | 164. It is for this reason that <u>we</u> die. |
| 165. ãg tèl kũ wèg tũ tẽ gèke tògtẽ yè | 165. It is for this reason that, when <u>we</u> die, (<u>we</u>) are not seen again. |

| | |
|---|---|
| 166. ti tèl hā wā | 166. It was this death. |
| 167. ñāglò ti tō un | 167. However, had he done it well, |
| 168. ti tō zāg | 168. had he put (the bones) away, |
| 169. lò wū āg tèl tògtē wū | 169. then, although <u>we</u> would die |
| 170. tà katē gèke tē gèke wā | 170. (<u>we</u>) would always come back from there. |
| 171. ñāglò ti hā wū u tū tē | 171. However, because he did not do it well, |
| 172. hākū āg tï gèke tògtē | 172. therefore when <u>we</u> die, |
| 173. tà katē wañ kū tē | 173. (<u>we</u>) never come back again. |

Who is the "we" in "It is for this reason that we die?" One cannot rest here simply on knowledge of the language. Nor can one discover the meaning by looking at the isolated sentence — although the reader might suspect that it means "people," an interpretation that proves partially correct. For our purposes, the instance must be understood by taking it within the broader discourse environment in which it lives.

In the present instance, the answer is subtle. "We" refers to people who came after the mythical ancestors who form the subject matter of this narrative. It does not include those ancestors. The narrative is about them, but they came before "us." The story actually describes an event that precipitated the first irreversible deaths, although we discover this only at the end. The story is of a man who seeks to retrieve the bones of his brother. The latter — with a premonition of his own death — had instructed the man to retrieve the bones and to bury them on a mountainside far away from the people. Dutifully, the man retrieves the bones, but he buries them too close to the village. When people happen upon the burial site — on top of which a miniature man (the dead brother) has magically appeared — the latter dies again, this time never to return. Tragically, irreversible death is introduced into the world.

"We" appears without warning in this narrative, and its appearance marks a temporal divide. The great chasm between "we" and non-"we" is the chasm of time. "We" refers to those proximal in time to the narrator, not-"we" to those distal — that is, to the early ancestors. So one question is: Does "we" regularly serve as a temporal marker? Is it bound up with a more fundamental identity contrast having to do with time — present as opposed to past? In fact, in many instances — or so I will argue — it is. The "we" is a "we" of the present as opposed to the past. It is a "we" of the here and now that typically includes only others who share the empirical experience of the speaker.

In formulating this typical meaning of "we," you should note what "we" is not in this context. Importantly, in light of the historical conflicts with the Whiteman — which have subsided only somewhat in the present century — "we" is not here an ethnic or group boundary marker within the present. It does not differentiate the phenomenal group, as conceptualized by the anthropologist, from other contemporaneous groups, including that of which the anthropologist is a part.

Of course, one can readily imagine sections of the narrative in which group-designating "we's" might have been strategically placed. At the beginning, for instance, the speaker might have thrown in a clarifying clause: "Whereas the Whiteman has always died, there was a time when we did not die." In fact, however, nothing of the sort is to be found in the entire narrative. The narrative is not *ethnicized* in this sense; indeed, none of the mythical narratives I recorded in the P. I. Ibirama community appears to be so ethnicized. This is a point to which I shall return, as it bears upon the problematic of agency and change. "We" is linked to ethnicity formation within the nation-state context, and the ethnicizing of a culture has to do, in part, with the colonization of some genres (for example, myth narration) by other genres (political oratory about the Other).

Is the instance of "we" usage discussed above anomalous? While there are but few occurrences of "we" in myth narrations, they exhibit an intriguing uniformity — they highlight the present/past temporal divide, but are ethnically nonspecific. The pattern is confirmed by a study of absences: Where it seems most logically that "we" should occur, it frequently does not. Instead, a distanced third person form is found. This is especially striking when it comes to historical narratives about the period leading up to the Eduardo-Wòmle encounter of 1914. Here are the opening lines from one such narrative:

| | |
|---|---|
| 1. ũ nõ wèn mũ | 1. Those who were there first, |
| 2. òg zug tẽ òg we wañ kũ tẽ | 2. they had never seen the Whiteman, |
| 3. wãcà tẽ ka | 3. a long time ago. |
| 4. kèke kũ kapil wũ aklèg tẽ mũ | 4. And so it was until Kapil went hunting. |

In this instance, ethnicization would involve a simple pronominal switch, for which the discourse context seems tailor-made. The speaker need only have substituted "we" for "they" (*òg*). This would have contrasted the subjectively defined community ("we") with the Whiteman (*zug*):

| | |
|---|---|
| 2. nã zug tẽ òg we wañ kũ tẽ | 2. we had never seen the Whiteman, |

Had this kind of clause occurred, we could truly imagine a community stretching back in time, with speaker and hearers — excluding the anthropologist — identified with a collectivity that was there before they were and that would be there after they were gone. Re-reading Durkheim's *The Ele-*

*mentary Forms of the Religious Life*, one must be struck by the sense — the feel — of something larger than the individual, a controlling force that takes charge over the lives of those in the present. If the discourse at P. I. Ibirama in fact operated in this way, one could believe that those members, too, would feel the controlling force. One could then reasonably assert that the phenomenal community, described externally by travelers, settlers, missionaries, and anthropologists, was also the noumenal community, intelligible to its members.

Alas, the discourse does not configure in this way. Instead, we find speaker and listener alike equally distanced from those in the past. The speaker identifies with a present generation, with those who came along after the historical figures, after the ancestors. His is not an identity set in opposition to the anthropologist or to White people. The noumenal community appears in these discourse instances as temporally bounded — the boundary is between "those who came before us" and "us." The temporal bounding is suggested by actual instances of "we" usage. It is also suggested by the occurrence of third person forms where one would expect "we's," that is, precisely when the subject of White people comes up. But the community is not ethnically bounded; instead, it encompasses potentially all human beings.

Now you will object that the problem is with the discourse I have chosen. Had I looked at other genres, such as political oratory, the ethnicized "we" opposed to White people or other indigenous peoples would emerge. You are partially correct. The point I am making here, however, is somewhat different: It is that the ethnicized "we" does not colonize or dominate those genres that are the core of culture, that is, the mythological and historical narratives shared throughout the community and passed down across the generations. The ethnic "we" does not seem to invade this territory.

What to make of this? One interpretation is that the culture itself is broken down, a mere remnant. Henry (1964 [1941]: 175) subscribed to this view, and there is an element of truth in it. Traditional culture is treated discursively as experience-distant in "we" usage. Indeed, this experience-distant sense permeates conversations with members of the P. I. Ibirama community. The "they" of historical narratives is a "they" of the distant past that seemingly has little or nothing to do with the "we" of the present.

Paradoxically, however, the stories continue to be passed down, in many cases in word-for-word fashion. Certainly, there is evidence of continuity over the past forty years, but the unbroken transmission process apparently has been going on much longer. The empirical facts contradict the sense that the community is acculturated or out of touch with its past. The form of discourse suggests a detachment from the past, but the very cultural elements from which the speaker and hearers are subjectively detached are the ones that circulate most widely; they are the ones that get passed down across the generations.

An interpretation of this apparent paradox suggests that the so-called distancing of the cultural forms is part of the mechanism that enables them to be circulated and passed down across the generations in the first place. The less the forms in question are understood as bound up with individuals in the present, the less likely they are to be the subject of political bickering; the more likely they are to be seen as politically neutral; and hence the more readily will they circulate. This is of contemporary political relevance, since not all P. I. Ibirama speakers agree with an ethnicized "we" set up in contrast with the Whiteman. Some members of the community even seem to want to melt into the White population. For this reason, the insertion of ethnicized "we's" into narratives jeopardizes the survival of those narratives, and hence the survival of an ethnicity defined in terms of them. What we see here is a schism between the consciousness of culture and its embodiment. The two are at cross purposes, at odds. Consciousness of shared culture, through the pronoun "we," makes it more difficult, in this case, for the culture to be embodied.

Further, striking evidence can be found that the pronominal acculturation hypothesis is incorrect. In telling the origin myth, something occurs that is quite strange to North American ears: Now and again, the narrator slips into a trance-like state and substitutes a first person "I" for a third person "he" or a proper name, thereby assuming the role of a kind of I-witness to the events described. Compare, for example, a line from two different narrations of the origin myth by Nil, the foremost cultural authority of his time in the community. In the 1981 version, which is didactically oriented, teaching me the story, Nil uses a third person ("he")[9]:

wãgyò  tõ   zàgpope tõ   patè  ø no       katèle
relative erg. name    erg. name ø̱ in front of arrive descending
"Relative Zàgpope Pate arrived in front of him."

But in his 1975 narration, Nil, in a self-absorbed state, uses the first person, "I" (*ẽñ*):

wãgyò  tõ   zàgpope tõ   patè  ẽñ no       katèle
relative erg. name    erg. name I̱  in front of arrive descending
"Relative Zàgpope Patè arrived in front of me."

If we think of the absence of first person plural ("we") identification with the ancestors as distancing, a rejection of the past culture, this kind of first person singular ("I") identification is the opposite. Here we find a thoroughgoing involvement of the speaker with his narrative; the speaker inhabits the discourse he reports. Where "we" distances the present company from a past "they," "I" provides for a connection across time, the present speaker assuming the "I" of some distant ancestor. Where "we" makes the question of transtemporal connection conscious, "I" makes the transtemporal experience a felt one. In pronominal usages at P. I. Ibirama, therefore, sensibility and intelligibility clash. The felt experience of culture — the experience of continuity — runs counter to its reflective awareness — the awareness of disjuncture. If "we" usage suggests acculturation, "I" usage suggests continuity.

Another disproof of the pronominal acculturation hypothesis occurs in one of Wãñẽki's narratives: the story of a great conflagration that consumed the araucaria forests. In this narrative, people build subterranean earth lodges to escape the raging fires, throwing water on the mud from the inside. When they come out, the landscape is scorched. Near starvation, they wander about dazed, until a scouting party stumbles on a wondrously verdant forest. The party sends word to those who remained behind. As in other narratives, references to these ancestors are all in the third person. Then, suddenly, at the very end, we find:

| | |
|---|---|
| 1.  ãg tõ mẽ nõ tòg tẽ yè | 1.  In order for us to be here, |
| 2.  òg òg mõ kamèn | 2.  they told them, |
| 3.  kũ òg to kamũ | 3.  and they came, |
| 4.  kũ ũ òg kamũ ñã | 4.  and where some of them had come, |
| 5.  amẽ òg ñãgyò kàgyel | 5.  along the path they suffered hunger. |
| 6.  hãñãglò ñãgyò kèke ñã | 6.  And they continued until |
| 7.  òg kute tẽ ka ge | 7.  they entered the forest. |
| 8.  kũ ãg tõ mẽ nõ wã hã wũ ki nõne | 8.  And it's for this reason we are here. |
| 9.  ñãglò tũ tẽ lò | 9.  However, had they not done this, |
| 10. nã kàgtãn kan | 10. we would have died. |
| 11. ãg kàgyel ãg kàglãn tẽ | 11. Our hunger would have killed us. |
| 12. kũ nãlòñ katèle ñã hã wã | 12. And the great conflagration really came, |
| 13. zàg tògtẽ | 13. wherever there were araucaria pines, |
| 14. zàg tõ ũ mẽ tẽ tògtẽ | 14. wherever there were even a few araucaria pines, |
| 15. le to tògtẽ | 15. where the savanna is. |

In the first line, "us" evidently refers to present-day, actually existing people. If the speaker were trying to distance himself from the elements of culture in question, this line, with its first person form, should have been excluded. While contrasting the living "us" with deceased ancestors, the pronoun here also establishes a link between the two. "We" are here because of "them" who were there. The narrative asserts continuity between past and present, but the subjectively identified collective "we" is a "we" of the living present.

The actual connection is established in lines 7 and 8: "they entered the forest; and it's for this reason we are here." The actions are of a "they," but the effects are felt by a "we." The same relationship exists between lines 9 and 10: "had they not done this, we would have died." In both instances, the "we" refers to the living, and, particularly, to the subjective experiences of the actual speaker. It is as if "we" can only be used if the actions or states attributed to the "we" are actually applicable to the speaker of the discourse in question.

However, the very next sentence violates this principle; "we" is extended to include experiences the speaker cannot possibly have had: "Our hunger would have killed us." The speaker could not have been subjected to the hunger felt by the characters in his narrative, who lived long before his own parents were born. There is, therefore, a transcendence of the limits placed on "we" by its normal usage. This "we" manages to unite the speaker with others whom the speaker does not know personally, others whose experiences he did not directly share.

Such a "we" is rare in the narrative discourse of the P. I. Ibirama community, but it is a "we" that is essential to the imagination of a broader community, a community in which speakers identify their subjective experiences with those of others who could not have shared them, or, correspondingly, who identify themselves with the experiences of others they could not have known, a "we" like the one that probably grounds Benedict Anderson's (1983) imagined community. Such a "we" is fundamental, for example, to the conceptualization of "we Americans." The presupposition of the latter is that utterers of the phrase identify with others they do not directly know. American discourse patterns make this kind of "we" unexceptional, taken for granted. How else to explain the Texan in California who, spotting another Texas license plate, waves and gives the rebel call? In the P. I. Ibirama case, however, such usages are atypical, something that stretches the limits of discourse, and with it, the limits of imagination.

It appears, then, that the phenomenal community described by anthropologists and others does not correspond to the subjective experiences of that community's putative members; it does not correspond to the intelligible sense of themselves that is encoded referentially in their discourse. The phenomenal community, in short, is not a noumenal community; it is not a community that is understandable as such to its members through words. Western assumptions that the externally defined grouping corresponds to how its members subjectively experience themselves is not borne out in this case.

You will note that I am not denying the possibility of change in the discursive patterns. Indeed, I want to return shortly to some evidence that ethnicization may be under way, if only haltingly. What I do wish to assert here is that anthropologists cannot presuppose the kind of fit to which they have grown accustomed. They cannot presuppose that the phenomenal grouping, externally defined by objective behaviors — the wearing of lip-plugs, for instance — corresponds with the internally defined understanding of groupness.

However, they can investigate the constitution of noumenal objects, such as the collectivity, in discourse. First and third person pronominal usage patterns, indeed, may be of broad importance for understanding ethnicity and the ethnicization of culture, an importance entirely out of proportion to their tiny physical appearance. For without a "we" that encompasses the externally defined ethnic grouping,[10] how could political mobilization occur? The latter consists in self-conscious action by members of a group on behalf of the group. Since self-consciousness occurs through the referential aspect of discourse, to fathom the conditions under which an ethnic "we" might emerge is to understand the conditions for political mobilization.

What about the political arena in the P. I. Ibirama community? Surely there one can find a group "we." Unfortunately, I was unable to record but a few political discussions, owing to the sensitivity of issues pertaining to deforestation at the time. You will recall that the Indians were selling off lumber from the reserve, contrary to FUNAI policy. I was at the time under investigation by the secret police. They wanted to know whether I was a political agitator, responsible for the lumber problems. These were the same police — scar-faced, gun-toting thugs passing themselves off as "agronomists" — who were implicated in so many political disappearances in the 1970s. I was advised not to record political meetings, and I heeded the advice, though I did attend.

Some indirect insights into political discourse, however, can be culled from a study of reported speech in narratives. One of the best examples of a political discussion occurs in a narrative regarding an owl spirit who threatens the community with extermination. The collective deliberations are represented as follows:

| | | | |
|---|---|---|---|
| 1. | kũ yi òg | 1. | And, it is said, they [said]: |
| 2. | hãlike kũ nã yè yòñ tẽ ñãnka kàklen yè | 2. | "How are we going to escape the mouth of the spirit?" |
| 3. | kũ òg ke | 3. | they said. |
| 4. | kũ nã yazïl ñã | 4. | "We're going to climb up. |

5.  zàg tòg to kuzĕn

6.  kū nā̱ lò yazïl
7.  kū nā̱ kò kle
8.  kū nā̱ ti pāndu tĕ mĕmā tõ pazĕn
9.  kū nā̱ gò yè wāzï

10. kū nā̱ ki yazïn
11. kū ki win
12. kū nā̱ kagñān
13. kū klĕ nõ
14. kū tà tĕ òg yè wāzï
15. kū òg yazïn ñā ke mū

5.  [We're] going to tie vines to these araucaria pine trees,

6.  and we're going to climb up,
7.  and we're going to cut up wood,
8.  and we're going to tie up the branches,
9.  and we're going to make baskets for dirt,

10. and we're going to ascend with it,
11. and put it in,
12. and we're going to throw it down,
13. and stay up there,
14. and make baskets for the women,
15. and raise them up," (one man) said.

In this narrative, "we" is defined in opposition to "it," the *yòñ* (owl spirit), an opposition that is established in line 2. The "we" has no overtly temporal reference to a past "they." Instead, it encompasses the internally defined group that is immediately threatened by the owl spirit. This is a grouping based on shared experiences and task orientation. Evidently, it does not represent an imaginary extension to other individuals or groups not so threatened.

A striking feature of the present instance of discourse, however, is that the "we" is also gendered. This emerges through an analysis of lines 9–15. The overt form of the first person plural pronoun does not appear in line 14, where the third person noun "women" (*tà tĕ òg*, "woman plus definite article plus plural marker") first appears. However, it reads as if the "we" were there: "and [we're going to] make baskets for the women." The process at work is known as anaphoric deletion, and it is made possible by the occurrence of "we" in previous lines, with the grammatical parallelism carrying the "we" into the present line. Indeed, line 14 is directly parallel to line 9:

9.  kū nā̱ gò yè wāzï

14. kū tà tĕ òg yè wāzï

9.  and we're going to make baskets for dirt,

14. and make baskets for the women,

Just as baskets are to be made in order that men may carry dirt up into the tree tops, so they are being made so that men may carry women up. The subjectively defined "we" is thus implicitly gendered as male.

It is interesting, however, that the "we" is only implicitly so gendered. A survey of the broader discourse shows that male speakers are generally reluctant to create a "we" that is explicitly male, even when one seems mandatory. This is so even in the traditional narrative that explains why women have breasts and men do not. I have recorded several tellings, and none uses "we" to include the speaker within the category of males as opposed to females. In the instance transcribed below, this is so despite the fact that there were no women in the audience on this occasion:

1. òg nõ tẽ ka yi wũ

1. During the time of those who were [first] there, it is said,

2. òg nõ tẽ ka yi

2. during the time of those who were [first] there, it is said,

3. tà tẽ klã gèke
4. kũ yi òg mèn tõ kòñgàg hã yi wũ nũgñe mũ
5. kũ yi òg ẽ klã tẽ pèzam gèke mũ

3. women would bear the children,
4. and, it is said, their husbands, who were men, had breasts,
5. and, it is said, they would breast-feed the children.

6. ñãglò tà tẽ yi ñẽl tẽ pèzam wañ kũ tẽ gèke mũ
7. kèke ñã yi wũ kòñgàg ũ yi ti plũ yi lègle ñãgnẽ
8. kũ ti nũgñe tòg tẽ yi wũ tà nũgñe tòg hãlike
9. kòñgàg nũgñe tẽ tẽg
10. tẽkũ tã hãliken kũ ñã

6. Meanwhile, it is said, women did not breast-feed the children.
7. So it continued, it is said, until one man had two wives,
8. and his breasts, it is said, were like a woman's breast,
9. the man's breasts were such,
10. and so he did like that [i.e., breast-fed the children].

11. kũ zàg to mũ mũ

11. And [they] went to the araucaria pines.

12. zàg càn
13. kũ yi òg zàg to mũ

12. The pine nuts were ripe,
13. and, it is said, they went to the pines.

14. kũ yi tã ẽ plũ tẽ òg mlè tẽ

14. And, it is said, he went with his wives.

15. ẽ plũ tẽ òg mlè tẽ
16. kũ yi tã to taplï mũ
17. to kuzen
18. kũ yi tã to taplï mũ
19. kũ yi ti nũgñe tẽ ti yi wèl wèl wèl ke
20. kũ yi ti plũ tẽ òg yi nïg mũ

15. When he went with his wives,
16. it is said, he ascended.
17. With a belt woven for that purpose,
18. it is said, he ascended.
19. And, it is said, his breasts, it is said, flapped and flapped and flapped.
20. And, it is said, his wives, it is said, laughed.

21. òg tõ nïg tẽ kũ
22. kũ yi tà tẽ òg nũgñe nẽ ke tòg tẽ yè

21. When they laughed,
22. in order for the women to get breasts like that,

| | |
|---|---|
| 23. yi tã pumke òg klē mū | 23. it is said, he squirted (breast milk) on them, |
| 24. tà tē òg klē | 24. on the women. |
| 25. kū tà tē òg nūgñe nõ kèke wã | 25. And it's for this reason women's breasts are like that. |
| 26. nãglò tū tē lò yè | 26. However, had (they) not done that, |
| 27. wū tà tē òg tõ nïg tū tē lò | 27. had the women not laughed, |
| 28. wū kòñgàg hã yè wū ñēl pèzam gèke ke wã | 28. men would have continued to breast-feed the children. |
| 29. hãñãglò tà tē òg tõ nï | 29. However, because the women laughed, |
| 30. hākū kòñgàg nūgñe tē tõ òg klē po tē | 30. therefore the man squirted on them with his breast, |
| 31. kū tà hã nūgñe mū kèke wã | 31. and now it is the woman who has breasts. |
| 32. hã wū tà tē hãlò ñõne kèke mū | 32. It's for this reason that women are now like that. |

In only one obvious place might a male-gendered "we" have been substituted for "men." That is in line 28, which could have read: "we would have continued to breast-feed the children." However, other clauses containing a male-gendered "we" might have been added. For example, after line 31 there might have been a clause such as: "and we do not [have breasts]." The important point, however, is that such clauses are nowhere to be found. Moreover, even in the version narrated by a woman, the female-gendered "we" does not occur. There is no representation of a collective female identification in opposition to men.

Two somewhat separable factors may be at work here. On the one hand, there is a positive desire to use third person forms. I have tried to account for this desire in terms of the likelihood that a given discourse instance will circulate in a community and be replicated over time. The more distant from any specific individuals the discourse instance seems, the more likely is it to be replicated. Hence, third persons function better than first persons to make discourse circulate, and to make it, therefore, part of traditional culture.

On the other hand, there is also a reluctance to use "we." It is not simply that first person plural pronouns are not as good as their third person counterparts. It is that there are strong motivations for avoiding them. I suggest that this has to do with their implicit association with factionalism and opposition, a tendency not well understood in the broader literature on pronouns.[11] "We" usage lends itself to fragmentation. "We" typically implies a not-"we," an exclusion of some as against others. In a community such as the one here considered, where politics is consensual rather than democratic, there is a positive desire to avoid discourse that even implicitly fragments. One could understand why, in such a community, "we" might be avoided.

As the previous discussion indicates, however, the P. I. Ibirama group does not avoid "we." Rather, it channels "we" usage in a certain direction — namely, differentiating present from past. In those instances where it occurs, "we" is used to indicate an alliance with those alive presently, as opposed to those who came before. And it tends to be encompassing with respect to the present, including the anthropologist in addition to others defined by external observers as members of the community. The predominant "we" is that of a present, living, breathing, flourishing population as opposed to the ancestors. The tendency, therefore, is to displace any possible factionalism of the present — whether based on political subgroupings among men or gender opposition — onto a contrast between present and past. "We" usage thereby functions to neutralize the schisms of the present, at least insofar as these schisms are represented to consciousness. I emphasize consciousness here: The issue pertains to more- and less-conscious forms of representation of unity and disunity.

To return to the owl spirit narrative for a moment, the "we" used there is consistently of a single type, but it is not a "we" of the present. It is an in-group "we," opposed to an "it." What is crucial about this "we," as well as about the broader discourse in the P. I. Ibirama community, is that it is a shared experience and collective-task-oriented "we," what might be called an empirically restricted "we." So, for example, in narratives of the momentous events of 1914, "we" is used only when the narrator was actually part of the events described. Everything is done in meticulous empirical fashion. The actual personages involved are described; generalization to a "we" that could not have included the narrator in the empirical experiences in question is avoided. Here is an excerpt from Wãñpõ's January 1975 account:

7. There were tents,
8. one closer to the river,
9. filled with things, knives, axes.
10. Wòmle and Kowi came
11. and took everything.
12. They knew these were presents,
13. and they knew Eduardo was watching.
14. Next day Eduardo was farming
15. on the other side of the river.
16. Wãñěkï, Wòmle, Paci, everyone came.
17. Kowi wanted to kill Eduardo,
18. so he shot,
19. but his arrow missed the mark.

20. The Whites quickly crossed back over the river,

21. screaming in their canoe.

22. Then Eduardo was showing them clothes and things,

23. saying:

24. "My relative, I want to give you these red clothes,[12]

25. these white clothes, too."

26. So Wòmle said:

27. "Bring the clothes here."

28. These he put in a sack

29. and carried away.

30. He said:

31. "My relative, leave the shotgun over there."

32. So he gave the gun to someone else.

33. I did not see this,

34. because <u>we</u> were up in Papanduva.

35. But everyone told me about it later.

Although Wãñpõ was a young man in 1914, and he was part of the community that later settled at P. I. Ibirama, he avoids "we." As he explains in lines 32–34, he was with a small group that was not present on that day. His only use of "we" — in line 34 — is in reference to the small group.

This restricted or empirical "we," I would venture, may be most basic across cultures, and should prove important to the general theorization of "we" in social processes. Its focus is specific events or tasks or experiences to which each of the individuals under its purview is oriented. If the events have already transpired, the narrator reports them to hearers who canonically are not part of the experiential "we" group. If the events are part of a projected future, then the narrator is proposing them to hearers who have not yet thought of them. The condition in which the hearers occupy a different status than the speakers is crucial. There is an implicit opposition between them. Speakers are communicating something to the hearers that the hearers have not (or have not yet) experienced directly. Because the "we" presupposes an opposition between speaker and addressees, it is potentially dangerous in consensual political processes if used beyond the limited scope of reporting.

How might it be used beyond that limited scope? Suppose, for example, that the "we" is used not just to describe an event or experience, but to assert a commonality in attitude on the part of speaker and others from which the addressees are excluded. It then becomes potentially divisive and confrontational: "We [exclusive] do not like what you are doing." The shift is subtle, but it is one that takes "we" beyond its empirical or experiential limits and moves it in the direction of political factionalism. The "we" usage involved is akin to that of reporting an event, but the report is instead of an attitude or inner state that assumes the appearance of timelessness, of essential difference. It is such discursive movements that consensual formations need to avoid if they are to remain consensual. The crucial feature is the essentializing character of the "we" usage.

What if the restricted "we" is used to describe an experience or event that the addressees themselves have also experienced? In that case, the "we" might be termed historical or celebratory, involving a recounting of group activities to the group. Such a "we" again crosses the boundary into essentialization. Even if the events recounted were of an empirical nature, the recounting fixes them for the group. The function here goes beyond the reporting of experiential information or the projection of a possible future. The historical or celebratory "we" asserts a general understanding of the past that is, ironically, timeless, in other words, that makes no room for present differences in interpretation. Rather than leaving the conscious formulation of past experience to the consciousness of individuals, the celebratory or historical "we" fixes the experience, fixes the consciousness of it for the group as a whole.

The "we" of the owl spirit narrative discussed earlier is of a future, task-oriented variety, but it is still restricted in the present sense. Each instance of use refers to a future action in which the interlocutors are to take part: "We're going to climb up"; "and we're going to cut up wood"; "and we're going to tie up the branches"; and so forth. The empirical experiences are ones that the addressees themselves have not yet had. Consequently, there is no attempt to impose shared meanings on the group, to define what the group is or has been in a timeless way. The attempt is rather to suggest what the collection of individuals might do, not who they are.

The limitation of "we" usage to restricted varieties is one reason that the noumenal community does not match the phenomenal community described by outsiders. For the future task-oriented "we" to extend out to the phenomenal grouping known as "Shokleng" or "Botocudo" or "Aweikoma" in the literature, it would have to encompass individuals who are not in regular communication with one another. Since the phenomenal grouping Shokleng includes two subgroupings that were on hostile terms prior to 1914, and that have no relations with one another today, it is presently impossible to create a consciousness of the broader grouping through use of this restricted, task-oriented future "we."

Political mobilization thus seems to involve, as a sine qua non, communication. This enables the restricted or task-oriented "we" to circulate. If the present analysis is correct, however, political mobilization must also involve essentialization — the movement from a restricted empirical focus on events, whether past or future, to an assertion of timeless characteristics or conditions that are shared. The essentialized "we" makes that sharing conscious. Interestingly, the consciousness of shared traits or conditions is one way in which anthropologists have understood culture, although it is not the understanding developed in this work, whose focus is publicly occurring discourse. The study of discourse reveals how the consciousness of shared culture may be culturally (that is, discursively) constructed. It also reveals, however, how and why culture may sometimes proceed without the consciousness of shared culture, or with different refractions of what the culture is that is shared, although in the latter case it proceeds without the possibility of self-aware political mobilization.

I say different refractions because it is probably not the case that any culture can avoid essentializing "we" altogether. It is just too linguistically easy to move from the restricted-empirical to the generalized-essential. Even in the discourse here investigated, there is an essentialized "we"; however, the essentialization takes the form of "we the living or present" set in opposition to a "they" who have come before "us." There can be no question that this is an essentialization. However, it is an essentialization that avoids the imputation of features to ethnic groupings. It is a "we" more in the sense of "human beings." At the same time, it is specifically oppositional, contrasting living humans with dead ones. There is a notion of shared culture or shared condition built up through this "we," but it is not a notion of culture that is ethnicized or restricted to a specific population. It is thus not the notion that has been in vogue recently in anthropology and the humanities, where culture and ethnicity are closely related, if not coterminous.

Why, in the P. I. Ibirama case, does the notion of "we" not take the form of an ethnic group? I have already suggested an answer to this. It is that essentialization of "we" entails a risk, a threat to consensual politics. It is potentially divisive because it involves the representation to consciousness of a fixed grouping, which denies to the individuals in question their autonomy. To maintain the appearance of autonomy, and to enable a consensual politics, it is necessary to avoid potentially divisive essentializations. If the patterns of "we" use at P. I. Ibirama accomplish this, then they do provide the conditions for their own circulation, as well as for the circulation of other discourse. They are part of the glue holding this community together.

It is for this reason that the present/past split appears to be such an appropriate tool for essentialization. If "they" are the ancestors, then, while they may control "us," the living, by virtue of participation in a common culture, the control is not by any one living person over another, or by any one subgroup over another. Paradoxically, by representing to consciousness a disjuncture between present and past, those in the present can be culturally unified without experiencing themselves as subject to the control of other living individuals.

What does it mean to be culturally unified without representing the unity to consciousness? It means that a social group, a phenomenal entity as externally defined, is characterizable in terms of socially transmitted practices, beliefs, and values that are distinctive with respect to other social groups, without that distinctiveness being talked about. If the "we" were to segment the present population, asserting to consciousness an oppositional unity within the present, without an appeal to a "they" of the past, it could be explicitly denied. If the unity is only implicit, defined by phenomenal characteristics but not explicitly formulated, except in the opposition between living and dead, then it becomes harder to explicitly deny it. Who could dispute the proposition "we are not the dead ones who have come before us?" So a present/past or living/dead essentialization effectively undercuts the divisiveness of ethnic and other forms of group essentialization, but it simultaneously allows implicit unity and permits a high degree of individual autonomy in the conscious formulations.

I would not wish to advocate this form of "we" usage as a means to political unification. The internal strife in the history of the P. I. Ibirama community, and the tendency for individuals and subgroups to hive off and go their own way, are testimony to the difficulties with this type of discourse process. Indeed, the specific political processes undergone in this area of Amerindian Brazil may be in part a function of the way in which unity has been represented (or not) to consciousness through "we" usage. On the positive side, this pattern allows people to experience themselves as autonomous, as distinct individuals, without making this distinctiveness manifest through conflict over the proper forms of culture. Individuals can de facto be culturally unified without experiencing themselves as directly controlled.

Ethnic essentialization differs from that formulated in the "we the living"/"they the dead" contrast. In discerning ethnicity, the explicit representation to consciousness is of a cultural grouping which may or may not be coterminous with a phenomenal grouping. One can imagine ethnicities wherein "we" is asserted without a corresponding set of empirically describable practices, beliefs, and values. But where there is such a phenomenal grouping, the assertion of an ethnic "we" is potentially divisive. In addition, it can involve a giving up of autonomy with respect to underlying cultural practices. In the present case, if the "we" were asserted in opposition to the Whiteman, a potential dispute could erupt around issues of acculturation, and, as I have noted, some members of the P. I. Ibirama community would vociferously deny an opposition between themselves and other Brazilians.

At the same time, there is some evidence that an ethnic "we" — and, correspondingly, an actual noun designating the ethnicity — may be emerging. The discourse I have been considering thus far is primarily that of the eldest stratum in the community during the 1970s and early 1980s. These individuals had all been raised prior to the fateful exchange of words between Wòmle and Eduardo. I collected and analyzed their discourse because it was the publicly circulating discourse of that period. I anticipate that changes may develop as that stratum disappears. At the time, these elders were the bearers of traditional culture, and younger members of the community did not have the confidence or public position to tell the narratives that these elder men did. The issue is one of discourse circulation, and the elders in the 1970s and early 1980s controlled the circulation of discourse that formed part of traditional culture.

Even at that time, however, two terms were beginning to emerge among the younger speakers that may contribute to long-term ethnicization, with or without persistence of the present/past opposition. Both nouns make use of the first person plural pronoun, "we." One of these terms, seemingly, represents a direct reading off the living/dead pronominal contrast, already made salient for younger speakers through the dominant public discourse of the elders. It is *ãg lēl* (lit., "we live" or "we the living"). The term rarely occurred in the narratives of elders at the time of my research, except in the sense of "human being." Its principal locus of circulation was informal conversations among younger individuals.

The other term is *ãg kòñka òg* (lit., "our relatives"). An example of its use can be culled from a text collected by the missionary Paul Mullen[13] from a somewhat younger speaker. The narration was probably elicited, not part of a public display, but it may indicate the kind of public discourse that is emerging with the changing of the guard. In any case, it is startlingly distinct from the narratives I collected in its ethnic marking, although it is in other ways similar to, and in some instances word-for-word identical with, the discourse of the elders I collected:

| | |
|---|---|
| wãñcï-tẽ ka | A long time ago, |
| ãg kòñka òg nõ kèke tẽ ka | in the time of <u>our relatives</u>, |
| òg yòpõ tẽ tẽ kèke mū | they would go to the (corn) gardens. |

What is striking is the use of a nominalized form to effect a cultural essentialization. Moreover, the nominalization involves a first person plural "our" that violates the living/dead contrast. It is intriguing to compare this mythical narrative—in fact, it is a version of the owl spirit narrative discussed above—with the historical narrative of early encounters with the Whiteman. The opening line in the latter, you will recall, was "they had never seen the Whiteman." It is hard to imagine one of the elders with whom I lived and worked using "we," or the nominalization of which it is part, in this way, and especially not in the opening to a traditional narrative.

The opening lines of the younger speaker's version are part of a verbal formula used by elders as well. But, whereas in the elders' version a third person form ("they") is invariably used, in the younger speaker's version "our relatives" is substituted. Here are some examples of opening formulas in elders' speech:

Example 1:

| | |
|---|---|
| òg nõ tĕ ka yi | They were here, it is said. |
| òg nõ wèn tĕ ka yi | They were first here, it is said. |

Example 2:

| | |
|---|---|
| òg nõ tĕ ka yi wũ | During the time of those who were [first] there, it is said, |
| òg nõ tĕ ka yi | during the time of those who were [first] there, it is said, |

Example 3:

| | |
|---|---|
| ũ nõ wèn mũ | Those who where there first, |

Whereas elders distance the speaker and hearers from the events described, portraying to consciousness a disjunction with respect to the present, the younger speakers create an alliance across the generations, and assert what can only be characterized as an ethnic boundary. The change may be minor as regards linguistic detail, but from the point of view of consciousness it is major.

In the case of *ãg lĕl* (we the living), the term concisely captures the regularities of the narrative use of "we," fixing the living/dead distinction in a nominalized form. What could be more appropriate and accurate? Could one do better if one were trying to invent a name for the phenomenal grouping that would, simultaneously, capture the noumenal reconstruction of community woven into the fabric of discourse? It is as if the discourse community were itself continuing the quest for a true name that could accurately refer to the community, the same quest in which external observers have been engaged for a century. But, ironically, that noumenal contrast was carefully crafted to avoid the kind of ethnicization the term effects. The new term undercuts its practical effect and plays into the discourse of the nation-state, where it is important to have properly named ethnicities.

Essentialization is a remarkable process; it objectifies a culture, turns it into a thing. It molds a group out of a collection of individuals, giving speaker and audience alike a consciousness of something enduring and far-reaching — part of the immutable stuff of the universe. At the same time, from a discourse-centered perspective, the consciousness is really the product of something small and fleeting and insubstantial: a few words that waft through the air. How firmly fixed and structural the "we"/"they": living/ dead proportion seems to be in elders' speech. It is the way things are. Yet that contrast proves subtle and delicate, susceptible to change across the generations. Here is discourse magic. Through it, what is presented to the senses can be made intelligible; in being made intelligible it becomes real, more fundamental than the sensations. Yet the life of that discourse itself is fleeting, its substance mercurial.

However, we should not underestimate the magnetic effect of discourse. Patterns are formed by the way in which one discourse fragment mimics others, one use of "we the living" as opposed to "they the dead" confirms other uses. The alignments radiate outward, as I hope to show in subsequent chapters. The discursively constituted oppositions of living/dead and present/past pull into their fields of attraction other areas of discourse; they form the ground of intelligibility for ritual practices. Manifested in microsnippets of discourse is a broader culture structured around the living/dead polarity.

Let me return to the problematic of social organization, conceived as the social conditions for discourse circulation and, simultaneously, the product of circulating discourse. "We" plays a role within this problematic. If two individuals can use the term "we" in its inclusive sense in talking to one another, they can create the conditions for regularized social interactions in which discourse flows. But is the actual use of that pronoun necessary? For further circulation to occur, must "we" have been uttered first? Insofar as P. I. Ibirama is concerned, my answer is no. "We" is not primordial with respect to social interaction.

How regrettable it is that no tape recorder whirred in the background when Wòmle and Eduardo exchanged their first words in 1914. We will never know for certain whether they used the pronoun "we." However, the 1975 accounts suggest that they did not. There was no "we" that encompassed both Wòmle and Eduardo. The discursive interactions between the two occurred without the conscious formulation of a social grouping that included them both. Yet discourse flowed between them, and, with that flow, an inchoate social relationship assumed intelligible form. Prior to 1914, a forest of unsociability stretched across the frontier of Santa Catarina; no linguistic communication was possible through it. Once words passed between Eduardo and Wòmle, however, a metaphorical road was laid down that would only years later become a real road. The metaphorical road enabled the flow of words. But what originary words had the power to effect that kind of transformation, to cut a communicative path through the forest?

Recall that, according to his 1975 narrative, Eduardo's first words to Wòmle were: "*My relative*, I want to give you these red clothes, these white clothes too." And the second line Wòmle uttered to Eduardo was: "*My relative*, leave the shotgun over there." I can compare these with similar encounters I had in 1974, in which individuals used "my relative" (*ēñ kòñka* or *ēñ kake*) to establish new relations with me, and vice versa. There is a pattern of path making here. To build social relationships, you must constitute them through kinship. The magical words were kinship terms.

An older generation of anthropologists coined the phrase "kinship-based societies." The problem comes into focus here from a different angle, but I think it is the same problem. Kinship-based here means that kinship terms supply the machetes that cut the communicative paths. The initial encounter between Wòmle and Eduardo depended upon the mutual interpretation of a fleeting social interaction as kinship-like — "my relative" — or at least so it has been remembered in narrative. With this phrase, an enduring social bond came into existence. Here is discourse creating its own conditions for circulation, laying down its own road surfaces, making possible the ghost-like movement of culture through the world of things.

So where does this leave us as regards the significance of the pronoun "we?" Probably you will not doubt its role in political mobilization. For a group to act self-consciously as a single entity, it is necessary that there be a shared sense of the relevant acting collectivity. This can only be achieved by a circulating "we" or something like it — a proper name designating the collectivity for its members, for instance. The pronoun or noun allows the group to occupy the position of propositional agent:

| | | | |
|---|---|---|---|
| 6. | kũ nā lò yazïl | 6. | and we're going to climb up, |
| 7. | kũ nā kò kle | 7. | and we're going to cut up wood, |
| 8. | kũ nā ti pāndu tē mēmā tō pazēn | 8. | and we're going to tie up the branches, |
| 9. | kũ nā gò yè wāzï | 9. | and we're going to make baskets for dirt, |
| 10. | kũ nā ki yazïn | 10. | and we're going to ascend with it. |

The task-oriented group is a projection off discourse. It is a creation of discourse. And it can facilitate the flow of further discourse. But it is not a precondition for the circulation of discourse in the first place. Hence, it is not a precondition for culture in the broad sense of social transmission.

However, it is probably a precondition of culture in the narrower, epistemological sense — the sense in which we speak of different cultures. Understanding the noumenal world as consisting of societies or cultures or ethnicities is so firmly embedded in Western discourse practices that it is difficult to comprehend the secondary character of the group-bounding, ethnic "we." Not every discourse tradition produces a consciousness of itself as a "culture." One wants to believe with Durkheim that the collectivity is an agent prior to its discourse encoding, that it has explanatory value independent of the words through which it is represented. But we now see that the collectivity has efficacy precisely because of its representation.

This is a curious proposition: Representation affects and even effects the phenomena it purports to represent. Yet, though it is curious, I believe that it is the key to social organization. Unlike the Serra Geral mountain range or jaguars or araucaria pines, the organization of society is not a thing that is out there, waiting to be understood. The organization must be created, and it is something elusive, intangible that does the creating. It is culture — here understood as circulating discourse. Moreover, it is not the sensible side of culture; it is its intelligible side, the side of meanings. It took physicists so many generations to conceptualize the interconvertability of matter and energy. Similarly, it has been difficult for anthropologists to imagine the interconvertability of the material world and the meanings through which it is made intelligible. It is for this reason that we have so often sealed off the study of meaning, imagining it to require a separate discipline in its own right. Yet this interconvertability — noumena into phenomena, so to speak — is at the heart of social life. An ideal society, a society such as Augustine describes in *The City of God*, the "heavenly city," subsists in a realm independent of the real one, the "earthly city." Yet between the two there is commerce. The heavenly city struggles to give birth to an earthly one. Just so does the meaningful side of discourse become the organization of society — the word turned flesh — creating the observable patterns of social coordination.

# *Chapter 3.* The Hole in the Sky

Physical space — the medium through which culture travels. This was the idea of the diffusionists, who, like Clark Wissler in *The American Indian*, traced the geographical dispersion of pottery styles, basketry weaves, and myth themes. On maps, these dispersions resembled concentric waves, radiating out from a center, as if one had dropped a pebble into a pool of still water. The center was the point of origin or invention of the culture trait. The rings closest to it showed the trait in greatest abundance; those further out exhibited a more meager presence, until, at the periphery, the trait vanished altogether.

From a discourse perspective, we can agree with the diffusionists that culture moves or flows or circulates in physical space. This happens when discourse is rendered publicly accessible through acts of speaking or writing or signing. Culture passes from one person to another, from one mind into the next.

But is physical space only an objective medium, only the locus of discourse circulation? Generations of culturalists have taught us otherwise. Viewing culture as schemata in the mind, they saw any experience of the world as organized by it. Physical space was no exception. Ethnographers were instructed to look for a people's view of space — the cosmos, including the microcosmos of daily life. And where did they look? Certainly not to their own experiences or perceptions. On the contrary, they were interested in what lay inside the minds of the natives themselves. To gain access to those minds, ethnographers were forced to go through discourse, albeit usually discourse of the interview variety. While we now recognize the distortions and superimpositions inherent in that approach,[1] preferring, in this book at least, the naturally circulating variety, this line of research brought into focus another side of space. Space was not only sensible, it was also intelligible. It was construed by peoples within their own discourse traditions, as well as by outsiders eager to measure the physical movement of culture through the world.

Over the years, the two sides of space — the sensible and the intelligible —

have become detached from one another. Ethnographers paid attention to how this or that tribe talked about their cosmos; but they lost interest in how that talk, that culture, itself circulated within space. The one problem seemed irrelevant to the other. Yet I think that the two, far from independent, are intimately bound up with one another. We cannot adequately assess the significance of meaningful cosmological ideas without also looking into how those ideas themselves make their way through space. I do not mean only the space of Wissler's culture areas, but I do mean a space that can be described by an outsider. Such a space is orthogonal, so to speak, to the intelligible construals present in ethnographically circulating discourse. I mean the space of domestic groups, villages, and regions.

Theoretical reasons compel us to consider these two spaces interrelated. If discourse provides the conditions for its own circulation, it might well do so by how it makes the social dimensions of space intelligible. The intelligible side of discourse could provide maps, or even build roadways, along which it itself travels. Since circulation requires interaction among individuals, and since interactions are facilitated by propinquity in space, the basic idea would be to structure the relations of people in space in such a way that circulation is enhanced. Such would be the discourse, for example, of city planners in the United States, or of the "pivot of the four quarters" for the ancient Chinese city (Wheatley 1971).

Discourse in many cultures undoubtedly operates in just this way, mapping social interactions onto physical space, symbolizing and making meaningful the perceptible space of immediate social interactions. As I hope to show, however, the situation at P. I. Ibirama is less straightforward, and, perhaps for that reason, ultimately more interesting. There, the discourse itself implicitly distinguishes between sensible and intelligible space, between immediately perceptible and only inferentially knowable space. In so doing, it does, finally, facilitate its own circulation, and it does so in keeping with some of the general patterns we have already encountered. However, paradoxically, it leaves perceptible space unintelligible, and intelligible space imperceptible. In other words, it creates a disjuncture between consciousness and other forms of spatial experience.

Gerardo Reichel-Dolmatoff's *Amazonian Cosmos* and Napoleon Chagnon's *Yanomamö* were among the stacks of ethnographies I read before departing for Brazil in 1974. At the time, I recalled vividly the diagrams of the cosmos contained in each. Reichel-Dolmatoff (1971: 44) showed a universe resembling a side image of a bowl sitting on top of a saucer, enveloped in a misty circle with a sun on top. The earth sat like a dense layer of breakfast cereal on milk within the bowl. This was the Desana cosmos. Chagnon (1968: 27), in turn, showed four layers or worlds, one stacked atop the other, each resembling an Almond Joy candy bar, with tiny palm trees stick-

*Plate 6.* Wãñpõ's house in 1974, when anthropologist (*right*) was still treated like
a Brazilian — seated on a chair rather than on the ground. If you look
carefully, you can see Wãñpõ's wife peeking over his left shoulder. At left is
Mu (Wãñpõ's daughter) holding Kàmlẽn (Wãñpõ's son), who was named
after Wãñpõ's father (see Plate 5).

ing up. This was the Yanomamö cosmos. How intriguing these diagrams
seemed at the time. How interestingly different, yet each summed up a
universe I thought to be staggeringly vast with something on a human
scale, something possessing a childlike magical quality.

I was inspired by the diagrams, and by the discourse surrounding them,
to search for the cosmological image of the people at P. I. Ibirama. Of
course, looking back on it today, I recognize the influence on me of the
circulating discourse within my own little community, the community of
ethnographers working on native South America. But at the time I imagined that the diagrams corresponded to how each of these peoples saw the
universe, to the images they must have had inside their heads. I wanted to
discover the analogous image at P. I. Ibirama.

To that end, on July 4, 1975, I set out to question my neighbor and friend
Wãñpõ (see Plate 6). He was the son of the great shaman Kàmlẽn, pictured
in Plate 5. I was sure that, through interviews, I would be able to reconstruct his image of the cosmos. I asked him point-blank whether there was

a world above this one, thinking in my own mind of the Almond Joy shapes of Chagnon's diagram. Unhesitatingly, he responded that there was, and he briefly described it. In the middle of the sky, there is a hole. If you go through that hole, on the other side you will find a land like this one. However, there the ground looks like ladders spread about. After this, he added something else, which, at the time, meant nothing to me, but which I dutifully recorded: "It was Klañmàg who told of what it is like in [the world above this one]."[2]

Only a decade later did I ponder this statement. What to make of it? Evidently, Wãñpõ was at pains to deny any firsthand knowledge of that extraterrestrial world. Unlike our immediate physical ambience at the time, that upper world was not an object of perception for him, not accessible through his senses. He made a point of attributing the knowledge to someone else, one Klañmàg. I wondered at the time who that was, but let it pass. Probably no different from other ethnographers, I felt confident I had secured Wãñpõ's image of the cosmos, or a piece thereof. I thought of it as a little diagram, perhaps, that he held in his head.

Now you might ask yourself: Why did Wãñpõ report that "it was Klañmàg who told of what it was like?" Was he distancing himself from the knowledge? Perhaps he no longer believed in the upper world. Such a hypothesis would be consonant with the radical changes taking place in the community, as encounters with Brazilians, including missionaries and school teachers, increased. Or perhaps Wãñpõ wished to bolster the authority of his knowledge by someone's firsthand experience, albeit not his own.[3]

When the problem finally began to intrigue me, I searched my field notes as well as those of my wife for other, similar, instances. To my surprise, I found that the discursive practice of reporting the experiential source of discourse was widespread. In a separate context seven months earlier, Wãñpõ briefly described the land of the dead — honey tastes like water there, ants look like jaguars, and humans nourish themselves on dirt. He noted, further, that it was because of one woman, nicknamed Lẽl Tẽ (Goes Living), "that we know things about that land" (field notes, January 1, 1975). In yet another context, in which my wife talked with another of our neighbors, the ever philosophical Wãñẽkï, she asked him about the land of the dead. He came up with much the same information that Wãñpõ had given. No doubt, this was evidence of shared culture. At the end, however, echoing Wãñẽkï's words, my wife recorded, "this information was given to the Indians by Lẽl Tẽ, the woman who went with her dead husband to visit the land of the dead; she came back from there and told this to her mother before she died" (field notes from September 16, 1975).

Who was Lẽl Tẽ? And who was Klañmàg that his authority should be cited in connection with the land above the sky? At the time I evidently ignored the problem. But in re-reading my notes, I could not help but be struck by it. Klañmàg was a mythical figure. He was the main character in the origin-of-death narrative discussed in the previous chapter, which I had published in its entirety earlier (Urban 1991: 60–66). Here is the fragment that solves the mystery:

| | |
|---|---|
| 1. kuyankàg tē wū ē nūgñēn tē mõ tā | 1. Kuyankàg said to his brother: |
| 2. yugug tõ | 2. "When the falcon, |
| 3. kòñgàg tē òg wun kū òg ko gèke ñã | 3. who has been carrying off men and eating them, |
| 4. li ēñ cõ ken | 4. does this to me, |
| 5. kū mã ēñ kukò tē tu yè tapã | 5. you go up there to get my bones." |
| 6. ke tã ē nūgñēn tõ klañmàg tē mõ | 6. So he said to his brother Klañmàg. |

This is the only Klañmàg of whom I have ever heard; no one in any of my genealogies, living or dead, shares that name.

The story goes on to describe Klañmàg's journey to the land above the sky. Donning falcon feathers that he had carefully stored away, Klañmàg flew upward, ascending, ascending:

| | |
|---|---|
| 38. zàg tug klē ñã mū | 38. Above the dry araucaria pines |
| 39. klē ñãñã tã taplï | 39. above them he ascended. |
| 40.kòñka low tē lòlam mū | 40.He entered the hole in the sky. |
| 41. kòñka low tē lòla | 41. (He) went through the sky's hole, |
| 42.kū tã lò *escada* tòge tã tē | 42. and there (the ground) was like ladders. |

The passage is revealing. From it we can extract a cosmological image, its central feature the existence of another land above the *hic et nunc* phenomenological earth of the narration. The entrance to that land is through a hole in the sky vault, which must be directly overhead, as we can infer from the winged brother's vertical ascent — "and he ascended; he was ascending; above the dry araucaria pines, above them he ascended; he entered the hole in the sky." This portion of the narrative is even accompanied by a rising pitch in the speaker's voice, synesthetically suggesting verticality, and the kinesthetic image is confirmed by a spatial gesture in which the speaker raises his gaze gradually skyward, a gesture that in this case was accompanied by a vertically pointed index finger spiraling upward in accord with the glance. Everything about the bodily performance of the narrative reveals to the audience the location of this upper world: It is directly overhead.

The reader will recognize from this description the *axis mundi*, the axis of the world, recently described for native South America by Lawrence Sullivan (1988), building on the work of Mircea Eliade (1963): "The image of the *axis mundi* symbolizes communications between spatial planes. . . . The experiences of ascent and descent that characterize the center entail a concept of verticality" (Sullivan 1988: 131–132). To be sure, our hero returns to earth after his quest. Furthermore, we will see a concept of the spatial center emerge subsequently in connection with village arrangement. This will confirm the idea of an *axis mundi* through which the upper world makes contact with earth. In the history-of-religions literature, it is through this axis that sacred power diffuses into the world. The key point for us presently, however, is the relationship of spatial imagery in discourse to embodied experience.

You must appreciate that when a member of the audience for this narrative looks skyward, as I did that day, the hole in the sky is not visible. No phenomenal experience of the extradiscursive world confirms what the narrative makes intelligible. This is a crucial point. The narrative tells the audience what they do not know through their senses, what they cannot see, taste, touch, feel, or smell. It is not about sensible experience. It is about the construction of space, of a world, beyond the senses. This is a general characteristic of the narratives in this community. They do not tell the audience what they already know by virtue of phenomenal contact.

At the same time, the actual discourse, as a physical substance, and the other material signs accompanying the narrative—facial gestures, bodily orientations, movements of the hand—are phenomenal experiences. They situate the audience within a here-and-now space. The rising intonation contour that accompanies the man's ascent into space has a synesthetic effect on the audience. The listener's whole body is made to feel the verticality. Discourse, in this sense, is a kind of fulcrum, a bridge between the senses and the intellect, between perception and knowledge, between the phenomenal and what we have been calling the noumenal. It is the point at which what Victor Turner (1967: 28) called the "ideological" and "sensory" poles come into contact, exchanging their charges. The world of the mind is brought into contact with that of the body. It is the diaphane through which reality can be glimpsed. Who knows if it itself is not also a kind of *axis mundi*, through which sacred power diffuses into a secular world?

The diaphanous quality of discourse—intelligibility showing faintly through sensibility—should not mislead us into imagining that experience is unified. In the case of Wāñpō and Wāñĕkï, there is a discursively formulated awareness of the nonequivalence of sensibility and intelligibility. Recall that it was these two men, who, in independently recorded interactions—in the one case, with me, and in the other, with my wife—insisted upon the discursive source of their extrasensory knowledge: "It was Klañ-màg who told of what it is like"; "this information was given to the Indians by Lĕl Tĕ." While as scribes we dutifully recorded these statements, as ethnographers we ignored them. We read through them to the meanings that lay beneath or behind them.

The cosmological image we had been reconstructing was not a sensory image of the world at all, whether of the cereal bowl or candy bar variety. I am pretty sure at this point that it was not even directly experienced as a separate image — whether discursive or extradiscursive — by members of the P. I. Ibirama community. Nowhere in the publicly circulating discourse within this community do we find the cosmos as a topic of conversation. Nowhere, that is, except in conversations initiated by the anthropologist. The cosmological image is dependent upon a special kind of ethnographic retrieval process. Our anthropologist asks questions about space, but he is befuddled. The answers he receives are not about space; they are about discourse.

We can imagine a child asking an adult about the sky: Daddy, what is it made of? What is it like up there? Or we can imagine a group of adults seated around the campfire animatedly discussing space, flickering shadows dancing in the background. But I have never observed this kind of interaction. Moreover, the evidence suggests that if questions regarding space do arise, they are answered by reference to narratives such as I have been describing. The canonical reference point for any inquiry into space beyond perception is mythological narrative.

Narrative, not talk about space per se, is also the cultural unit most salient to consciousness. What we hear around the campfire is not "what is it like up there?" but *ēñ ñō wāmèn* — "tell me a story." If we want to investigate the diaphanous quality of discursive experience, where intelligibility shows through the surface of perception, the proper objects of scrutiny are stories, or, minimally, episodes of stories. Stories are the reproducible units of discourse circulation, the stuff of which, at P. I. Ibirama, culture is made. Until it is encoded in discourse and socially shared, the experience of phenomena languishes in the subjective realm. Once it circulates in discourse, it becomes objective, part of the storehouse of wisdom about the universe and how to live in it. There may be locally shared discourses, of a momentaneous sort, in which phenomena are organized without the aid of narrative. However, the discourse at P. I. Ibirama that is fully cultural — in the sense of widely circulated, as well as of passed down across the generations — is narrative.

Then, is the study of space as a category a ridiculous waste of time? I don't think so. First of all, although the category is orthogonal to discourse practices in the community, although it is extractable only by means of the artificial interview process, it is still extractable. People can and do answer questions about space, and they answer them consistently.

The little segment of myth is particularly compelling; it sticks in the mind — a man dons falcon feathers and flies skyward, like Icarus. Unlike his

Greek counterpart, however, the man here succeeds. He reaches a strange land above the sky, a land no one had visited before, a land no one has seen since. What trips our imagination is not only the flight but also its success. Two spatial planes come into contact. We follow Wãñpõ's finger as it spirals skyward; it seems that we can almost touch the sky, touch what is untouchable, see what is invisible. It is as if the intelligible were here made perceptible, the noumenal made phenomenal. And, as when the limp hand of Michelangelo's Adam approaches the outstretched finger of God, a charge seems to pass between the two. Something within this culture focuses our attention, however fleetingly, on space. And it is a part of culture that is circulated throughout the community and passed down across the generations.

In the second place, however, and regardless of the poetic salience of this discourse image, regardless of any consistency in interview responses, space is central to the ethnographer. Spatial relations among people are describable; the space in which culture moves is immediately knowable. Hence, an outside observer can feel entitled to use the category of space, if only as a base for the exploration of the relationships between what is observable and what is knowable only through discourse.

Let us return to our earlier, and still unanswered, question: Why did Wãñpõ and Wãñëkï insist upon the sources of their knowledge? We are now in a position to answer the question. I believe that their utterances resisted the interview format. Without rejecting outright our questions, both men tried to reframe them. They interpreted them as questions not about the world they could see, but about the discourse they had heard. "Is there a world above this one?" became "Do traditional narratives describe a world above the present world?" If their culture was to flow toward me, they had to resist the pressure of my culture — the interview format — flowing toward them.

Our anthropological questions presuppose an organization of circulating discourse like that of our schoolbook subjects and academic disciplines — they assume that physical science, including cosmology, is distinct from social studies. We can keep questions about the universe separate from those about society. But at P. I. Ibirama, discourse does not circulate in the same way, or at least it did not then. If you wanted to understand the intelligibility of the world through discourse, you had to forget the Western academic disciplines — which bear too eerie a similarity to the Aristotelian categories anyway. You had to look to narratives.

How odd that anthropology should ever have regarded space as a unified category, amenable to direct ethnographic investigation. After all, historically, space has been problematic within Western traditions of thought.[4] One need only recall the Greek thinkers Parmenides and Melisus, who first reasoned that, unlike the things that filled it up, space itself must be nothing. But they concluded that space could *not* be nothing, since they were capable of asserting, and indeed needed to assert, its existence. Since you could not assert the existence of nothing, space had to be a thing. We see subsequent generations of thinkers stumbling over this problem. Is space a thing? And, if it is, is it then phenomenal, directly apprehensible by the senses? Alternatively, is space an assemblage of relationships among things? And if it is, is it then only intelligible, inferable from other sensory facts, but not itself directly apprehensible?

Sir Isaac Newton's treatment of space in the *Principia* is intriguing in this regard. He deals with the problem in a scholium to the opening definitions, remarking, "I do not define time, space, place, and motion, as being well known to all" (1934 [1686]: 6). While space is "well known to all," however, he goes on to observe that "common people conceive those quantities under no other notions but from the relation they bear to sensible objects," and he notes that "thence arise certain prejudices, for the removing of which it will be convenient to distinguish them into absolute and relative, true and apparent, mathematical and common" (1934 [1686]: 6).

We recall Wãñpõ's image — a hole in the sky directly overhead, as indicated by gestures. We recall a land on the other side where the "ground was like ladders." Is this a part of what Newton, from his perspective, would have termed *apparent* space? No, the hole was obviously not something Wãñpõ saw with his own eyes; the ladderlike quality of the ground was not something he directly perceived. We are forced to conclude that Wãñpõ's account is not of apparent but of *true* space, of a space hidden beneath the surface of appearance, of a space that cannot be directly apprehended. Where the senses leave off, discourse takes over; it produces truth. And in this context, how eminently cultural truth seems — Einstein rejecting Newton's space. Truth is a part of intelligibility; it depends upon discourse.

But wait, discourse is not only intelligible; it itself is also sensible. It circulates within perceptible or apparent space. Consequently, ethnography that takes discourse as its object has an inherently twofold purpose; it cannot be reduced to a single undertaking. On the one side, it seeks to discover truths that are built up about the world, how perceptual reality is construed, what native speakers imagine lies on the other side of the diaphane — for example, a universe, once the size of a grapefruit, that then exploded, producing a vast expanse of space-creating matter, as in the modern big bang theory. On the other side, however, ethnography also studies the sensible. It looks at discourse as perceptible, as circulating within a sensorily confirmable ambience.

Figure 1 is redrawn from my field notes. It diagrams spatial relations between individuals and things within my perceptual reach on May 2, 1982, at around 4:00 P.M. I am represented by the letter F. Next to me runs a tape

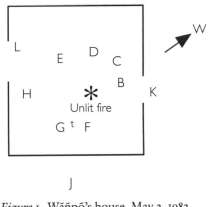

*Figure 1.* Wáñpõ's house, May 2, 1982,
circa 4:00 P.M.

recorder (t), continuously, unobtrusively. The room is dark with late afternoon shadows, the dirt floor cleanly swept and free of debris. Objects hang
from the ceiling or are stuffed into the rafters. Charred remains of a fire that
has gone out form the central point of spatial orientation for those gathered
round. Is this a kind of *axis mundi*? Around the unlit fire sit mainly elderly
individuals, some eighty years of age or more. Several children play outside
with a woman (J) ; we would guess her to be their mother. A boy next to
me (G) is perhaps in his early teens. B and C are an elder man and woman,
respectively, as are E and D. H is another elder man, seated off to one side
and apart from the rest. Standing in one doorway is a somewhat younger
man (K), and, in the other doorway, a still younger man (L), who arrived
sometime after 4:00 P.M. B is the principal speaker; others break in at various points.

Sensibility provides us access to more: the small holes, now largely closed
up, in the lower lips of the men B, E, H, and K through which lip-plugs or
labrets once protruded; seating postures, women on their haunches, their
legs beneath them or on either side; men, their feet in front of them, knees
raised, elbows typically on the knees (no "Indian-style" crossed legs here);
the rugged feet, their splayed toes put to good use to secure an arrow or a
piece of cord. We have to grant that many of these embodied characteristics
are cultural;[5] they are socially acquired and transmitted. This is true even of
the seating arrangements, men next to women. How different this is from
the larger political gatherings where men are all seated together in a group;
the women, if they are present, occupy the periphery with their children.

Sensibility, however, fails to exhaust cultural significance. This local space
is made intelligible by discourse, albeit not only the discourse that was circulating locally at the time. Discourse has the remarkable property of tran-

scending local contexts. In fact, the discourse that unfolded between 4:00 P.M. and 6:00 P.M. on that afternoon of May 2, 1982, transported its audience far beyond the immediately perceptible space surrounding them. It took them back to events that occurred long before Wòmle accepted Eduardo's gifts. Intellectually, we are hurried through an amazing space-time journey, though our perceptions show us to be seated in the same phenomenal space.

At the same time, that phenomenal space was itself illuminated by the intellect, made intelligible by other discourse that circulated in space-time contexts removed from the present one. Like everyone else, I knew the names of all of the individuals there, with the possible exception of the children of J. The names were as follows:

> B = Kañã'ï Nãnmla
> C = Nãg
> D = Yu'o
> E = Wãñpõ
> G = Kàmlẽn
> H = Wãñpõ Patè
> J = Wanda and her children
> K = Kuzug Nuzi
> L = Zeca Olímpio

A careful observer might have been able to infer some of these names in the course of those two hours. But everyone present, myself included, had no need to do so. The names were known to us through our prior experience with discourse. As a result, we were able to imbue this context with a significance it might not otherwise have had.

Names are crucial to culture at P. I. Ibirama. They tie living individuals to those from the past, and they thereby embody the continuity of culture. Basked in the light of names, mundane local contexts of individuals and events come alive with history. The here and now makes contact with remote times and places. This is part of the remarkable property of time travel made possible by the referential aspect of discourse — we are able to talk about and summon persons and events that are far away and long gone.

Proper names are part of the discourse magic whereby perceptions are imbued with meanings and meanings seem to be perceptible. Names tap into the world, allowing us to retrieve something from it. In many cases, they are contiguous with that to which they refer. How many times did I hear them shouted out, as someone was summoned from a distance: "Wãñpõ, Wãñpõ, come here!" By virtue of space-time co-occurrence, a connection can be discerned between the name, as both sound and phonological form, and the flesh-and-blood individual to whom it is linked.

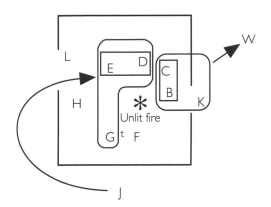

*Figure 2.* Wãñpõ's house, May 2, 1982 circa 4:00 P.M.:
Intelligible relations made sensible

Names are a kind of conduit or bridge between intelligible discourse and the sensible world.

But names are not the only such trick in our magician's kit. Similarly used, and perhaps as important, are kinship terms. Indeed, their special virtue at P. I. Ibirama is in making linkages, not just between present and past, as in the case of names, but also within the present itself. They establish an order or principle to what is seen and experienced, much the way Newton's laws made intelligible the motion of ordinarily perceptible objects—pendulums swinging back and forth or projectiles arching through the air. While the pendulums and projectiles could be seen by anyone, they were not necessarily understood. The discourse of physics renders their spatial translocations explicable.

Around the unlit fire that May afternoon in 1982, I understood principles of grouping—of spatial location and movement—that I could not see. From prior discourse, I knew, as did everyone else, that B and C were related as husband and wife, as were E and D. Moreover, I knew that G was considered the child of E and D, as was J, and K was a son-in-law of B and C. Aside from the anthropologist, the two other individuals present were more distantly related, less firmly attached to the physical space. L arrived after 4 : 00 P.M., and both L and H left before 6 : 00 P.M.

This knowledge may seem modest, but it rendered the spatial arrangements understandable; it revealed the tendency of family members to sit together. Figure 2 makes those intelligible relationships palpable. I have drawn rectangles around husbands and wives. Curved lines enclose broader family groupings, including children and children-in-law. By means of an arrow, I have indicated J's subsequent dislocation in space; sometime prior to 6 : 00 P.M., she and her children took up a position next to her father (E).

By 6 : oo P.M., when I redrew the diagram, H and L had departed. K had moved into the anthropologist's former position, the latter having relocated near H's former position. At this time, there were thus two family groupings present. Each was spatially clustered, one to the north and the other to the south of the fire.

You are probably wondering about the relations between the two families. And you may also be thinking about the relationship of H and L to them. One thing that you would know immediately, if you were a member of the community, is that there is a relationship. Everyone in the community is, axiomatically, related to everyone else. It is only a question of learning, through discourse, precisely what the relationship is. The emerging group designator, *āgkònka òg*, in fact, crystallizes the axiom. It means, literally, "our relatives."[6] If someone is a member of the community, then you can trace a kinship relationship to them. The term *āgkònka òg* is thus metadiscursive; it characterizes community in terms of the ability to make kinship relationships intelligible through discourse.

At the same time, you might be unsure about some of the relationships, and this would lead you to ask questions about them, to strike up a conversation. Indeed, I was unsure about some at the time, or, at least, I am unsure now as I think back on them. I must take up these old genealogies — the sheets carefully taped together, the tape now yellowed and dried and cracked. Inspecting them, I see that Kañā'ï (B) is related to Wāñpō (E), but only distantly. He is the son of Wāñpō's mother's sister's husband's (by a second wife) son. That seems a ridiculously complex relationship, but it is one that was known to both Kañā'ï and Wāñpō. Evidently the relationship between the two principal families is based on friendship.

My genealogies are a residue of past conversations, prior discourses. Studying them today, I see that Kañā'ï's wife Nāg (C) is also Wāñpō's father's sister's daughter's daughter. Something I think I did not recall at the time, moreover, is that Nāg (C) had once been married to Wāñpō Patè (H). I wonder whether the situation was uncomfortable for them — evidently not sufficiently to drive either immediately away. I go on tracing connections in different ways, and I find it interesting to do so, as did the elders gathered there on that day in May.

What about the presence of L? As I look back now, I am sure that he was there for the *wāmèn* (telling session), there to learn *nèn ci* (old things), though I did not realize as much at the time. For, interestingly enough, L was the somewhat younger man I mentioned in the previous chapter. He had helped the missionary Paul Mullen in his linguistic work. That connection makes sense of his narrative. You will remember, from the earlier discussion, that, with exception of his reference to the community as *āgkònka òg*, L's narrative was remarkably similar to that of the elders. No doubt, this very storytelling session was one of the occasions on which he tapped into the circulating discourse of the elders, solidifying his knowledge of the traditions. This enabled him — the stories fresh in his mind — to give the Summer Institute of Linguistics (SIL) linguist a nearly word-for-word copy of what he had heard. Wãñpõ's house was a workshop of cultural replication in more ways than he knew.

In any case, from this welter of detail, let me bring into focus two general points. First, kinship is not sensible; the connections I described earlier could not have been fathomed from the situation perceptible to me on May 2, 1982; through no amount of careful observation could I have figured these out without the aid of discourse. Second, however, any of the adults present that day could have articulated the connections. There is a kind of shared cultural construction of space at work, although it is grounded in access to publicly occurring discourse.

The connections were intelligible even if they were not perceptually accessible. At least, they were potentially intelligible. I have no idea whether any of those present thought about them that afternoon, as they busily whittled away on arrows, sewed, and prepared food, all the while tuning in and out of the collective conversation. However, because of prior discourse, they could have thought about them. The connections could have been intellectually recovered, even if that recovery did not take place in their minds that day.

I have been going on at length about kinship, but it is time to make a crucial observation: The discourse of kinship is *not* a discourse of space. We make inferences about the relationship between kinship and space. We note, for example, that those who sit next to one another are members of the same family. But the circulating discourse in the community is about kinship connections; it is not about the relationship between kinship and space.

Ethnographers would try in vain, in this community, to find publicly circulating statements about the fit between kinship and space. There is a surfeit of discourse about kinship. However, the relationship between kinship and space is passed over, untheorized; it is something that must be inferred by members of the community as well by the anthropologist.

In this, the present community probably differs from some others. There is no explicitly formulated postmarital residency rule here. One can detect an empirical tendency toward matrilocal or uxorilocal extension. Men were more likely to be spatially near their wives' fathers than their own fathers. Figure 2 suggests this tendency. K is B's daughter's husband; it is not coincidental that the two happened to be in Wãñpõ's house, near one another, at the same time. Similarly, although J's husband was not present, she was there near her parents; she was not with her husband's parents. Despite these patterns, whenever I inquired about postmarital residence, I would get the response, "You can live anywhere." No circulating discourse codified what I was able to infer.

From the point of view of discourse laying down the roadways for its own circulation, you can see why residence rules might be codified. Such rules, along with those governing marriage and exogamy, would guide the flow of discourse by guiding the spatial propinquities among individuals. Discourse would be telling individuals how to array themselves in space so as to foster its own circulation. Alas, such a discourse does not occur at P. I. Ibirama.

What is happening here? The tentative generalization I wish to propose is that publicly circulating discourse in this community shuns the perceptible.[7] Perceptions are implicitly treated as knowable in themselves; they require no explication. How different this is from Newton's way of thinking. How different from much of Western philosophy. In the latter, perceptions are often a source of illusion. One needs discourse to bring out truth, a truth that lies hidden behind the surface of appearances, on the other side of the diaphane. A youthful James Joyce wrote an essay entitled "Trust Not in Appearances," which began, "There is nothing so deceptive and for all that so alluring as a good surface" (Joyce 1989 [1896?]: 15). For the P. I. Ibirama community, however, the title might be reversed: "Trust in Appearances, Things Are as They Seem." Perception provides an anchor to phenomena; it need not be encoded in talk. The latter can be used as easily to cloud as to illuminate. In any case, culturally standardized talk seems to be reserved, in this community, for that which is not immediately perceptible, not directly phenomenal.

Let us go back to the hole in the sky. It is apparent that the hole is known only because it is talked about. One cannot simply point to it and say, "See, there!" When the narrator gestures skyward, we cannot follow the gesture to the perceptible object. The gesture picks out location, but discourse is needed to fill in what cannot be seen. The sky's hole is too remote to be seen from the ground. It requires words to make its existence known. What is regularly rendered intelligible is that which is not normally perceptible.

The philosophical principle at work here is continuous with that detected in the previous chapter. There, you will recall, the ethnographically describable community was nameless; the closest we could come to a naturally occurring designator was the pronoun "we." However, the latter was a special kind of "we," a "we the living" as opposed to a "they the dead." Death marks a key epistemological divide; we can appreciate that it is the divide between intelligibility and perceptibility. To conflate the dead with the living would be to mix epistemological categories. The dead are known through discourse, not through perception, although the issue is complicated by dreams and shamanic visions, as I will show subsequently (Chapter 7). In any case, patterning in accord with a living/dead opposition, "we"/"they" usage confirms the epistemological principle apparently ordering discourse about space. Publicly standardized discourse is reserved for that which cannot be directly perceived.

Kinship connections are a focus of public discourse precisely because they are not immediately accessible to the senses. In this sense, kinship is to be "heard" and not seen. It is true that kinship terms are used to build relations, as when Eduardo and Wòmle called one another "my relative." They were trying to bring a relationship into existence. They were not simply pointing to something that was already there. We do not find discourse directing our attention to the perceptible. Insofar as perceptible regularities in kinship relations can be found, as in the case of space, they must be found through private inference and reasoning. They are left unspoken.

How different the P. I. Ibirama house is from those Eastern Indonesian Sumba houses, built of four pillars, each named according to a principle — "godliness," "marriage," "prosperity," and "life and death" (Keane 1995: 6; cf. Cunningham 1964, Kana 1980). Indeed, Webb Keane (1995: 5) mentions that he was originally "skeptical at the apparent ease" with which ethnographers came up with such house discourses, until he "quickly found [himself] the involuntary recipient of similar accounts." You will appreciate how Sumbanese house discourse lays down the roadways for its own circulation. It is discourse about apparent space, but it is a discourse that is so intriguing, so catchy in its own right, that it itself is being transmitted even as the apparent space and social processes surrounding it are changing!

This is not true at P. I. Ibirama, where there is no house discourse to be passed on. The house is untheorized, uncosmologized. But what if we move further out? Is there some point at which space does become the topic of conversation, the way the Sumbanese house is? The problem can be thought of in terms of spatial (and also temporal) distance from a here-and-now center — Wãñpõ's house on May 2, 1982, at 4:00 P.M. The house is left unspoken, unilluminated by standardized public discourse. But what about more remote space?

Long before I arrived in my dilapidated Jeep at P. I. Ibirama in 1974, I was fascinated by central Brazilian Indian villages. David Maybury-Lewis (1967: 326, Fig. 2; 329, Fig. 4; 330, Fig. 5) had sketched the horseshoe-shaped arrangements of Xavante settlements, which could also be detected from aerial photographs. The fully circular shapes of Eastern Timbira and Apinayé communities had been long known through the work of Curt Nimuendajú (1946: 38; 1967 [1939]: 16). Claude Lévi-Strauss (1967 [1952]) created quite a stir with his interpretation of the encrypted meaning of Bororo village arrangements. The matrilineal exogamous moieties were located on

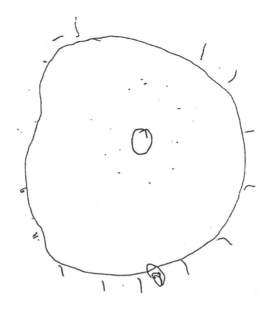

*Figure 3.* Wãñēkï's sketch of the village (1975)

opposite halves of the village circle; the clan groups occupied specific houses. All of this suggested a typical egalitarian social system. However, a peculiar upper-middle-lower division of house groups seemed to provide an alternative organization. Lévi-Strauss suggested that, despite the egalitarian symbology, Bororo village space in fact reflected a class structure.

Imagine my disappointment when I arrived at P. I. Ibirama in 1974 — the houses were built along the sides of a fourteen-kilometer road that followed the winding course of the Itajaí River. What was worse, far from being the "involuntary recipient" of village discourse, I could persuade no one to discuss the significance of the spatial arrangement of the present-day community. I should not have been surprised by this, of course. Henry (1964 [1941]: 11) had already observed that their "camp sites are any shape at all. Level ground is rare and what there is is so irregular that the Indians have to distribute themselves about it in the most economical way possible." But this reluctance to talk about spatial layout did seem to suggest that perhaps the traditional order had broken down.

I was, therefore, surprised when I asked Wãñēkï and Nil to draw the traditional pre-1914 village. Each separately drew a circle, with something in the middle, in the one case a small circle and in the other a squiggly line. The original drawings took up nearly the whole of a legal-size sheet of paper. I have scaled them down in Figures 3 and 4. With these drawings of village arrangements, Wãñěkï and Nil gradually warmed to the idea of talking about them. They said that villages were only temporary dwelling areas, used for those few months out of the year when the entire community assembled for ceremonial purposes. During the remainder of each year, the group disbanded into subgroups, what Maybury-Lewis described for the Xavante as "trekking groups." These in turn might disperse into even smaller units, consisting of perhaps a single extended family. The shape of village space was probably significant for only a small fraction of each year.

This explains in part why the P. I. Ibirama community I found in 1974 was not a nucleated settlement. A conversation with Eduardo de Lima e Silva Hoerhan, furthermore, revealed that it never had been. As soon the group had begun to spend more time around the attraction post, in the years following 1914, the houses were disbursed. There was never a tightly nucleated year-round settlement, as there had not been prior to 1914.

A further surprise awaited me. In August of 1975, the community held a ceremony — the *ãgyïn* ceremony for reintegrating a widow or widower into the community. Not far from the left bank of the Itajaí River, in a forest clearing, the men made a dance plaza. Around this circular plaza, household groupings spontaneously arrayed themselves in a semicircle, with an opening pointing to the west. While I was unable to photograph the spatial arrangement — it would have required aerial photography — I did photograph the palm fronds arrayed around the center of the dance plaza (Plate 7). For the most part, households effected this arrangement without instruction from the elders. The exception was the opening of the semicircle. The elders insisted on this, and they insisted that it be in the west. The souls of those sleeping in the west might be attracted to the land of the

*Figure 4.* Nil's sketch of the
village (1975)

*Plate 7.* Center of dance plaza, August 1975. Notice that palm fronds are arranged
in a semicircle around the central fire.

dead, a place from which they would not return. I was also told, in this
connection, that a corpse was traditionally placed on its funeral pyre—
nowadays burial takes place without cremation—with its head to the west.

Witnessing this spontaneous arrangement of the community, I realized
the semicircle spatial array had been going on all along. Henry himself, who
had referred to the campsites as "any shape at all" (1964 [1941]: 11), alluded
in passing to a "camp circle" (1964 [1941]: 195), formed at one of the ceremonies he witnessed. He was not contradicting himself. Both of his asser-
tions were true. The circular or semicircular arrangement pertained, as late
as 1975, to ceremonial space. Except for those occasions, there probably was
prior to 1914 no specific village shape, just as the array of households in the
period from 1974 to 1982 violated expectations stemming from the typical
central Brazilian plan.

What is going on here from the perspective of sensibility and intelligibility? The spatial arrangement of households in this community, at least
as regards ceremonial space, is evidently phenomenologically accessible.
Community space is what Newton called "apparent" as opposed to "true."
In being phenomenological, it is also for the most part not intelligible, that

is, not the focus of conscious reflection through the referential content of publicly circulating discourse.

We do find such discourse in connection with the semicircular opening. Intriguingly, the discourse concerns death. I think this is not coincidental. We have seen the prominent discursive role of the "we the living" versus "they the dead" contrast. Death is the thin membrane or diaphane separating sensibility from intelligibility. We know what lies on the other side through imaginings and through words, not through direct sensation. Fittingly, therefore, sensible space becomes intelligible around the area of the diaphane — the membrane between "apparent" and "true" space — the passageway between the here and now and the antiworld of the dead.

Aside from this publicly standardized narrativization, space is something in which people maneuver and negotiate; they do not symbolize it or make it meaningful in publicly circulating or ritualized speech. I am not suggesting that the construction of space is not cultural. It is. But this is a kind of embodied culture that one knows by living it without necessarily reflecting upon it. It is part of a habitus, in Bourdieu's (1984 [1975]) sense, which is also the sense employed in medicine — the patients' bodily appearance, as opposed to their verbal description of symptoms. In the P. I. Ibirama community, the habitus, like perceptual space, is left untheorized. An episte mological principle seems to separate it from public discourse. It reflects a different kind of knowing.

This kind of knowing is based on perceptible similarities and contiguities, which, because they are left unspoken, take on an added aura of mystery, as I will argue later in connection with ceremonies (Chapter 6). Think back to the diagrams of Wãñpõ's house in Figures 1 and 2. You will recall the circular distribution of people around an unlit fire. An obvious homology links this spatial configuration to that of the ceremonial village. Indeed, leafing through my field notebook, I see that on March 29, 1982, I made another sketch of Wãñpõ's house. It had been raining, and this time the fire was lighted. In addition, however, grass or palm fronds were strewn about the fire. Moreover, as in the ceremonial village (Plate 7), they formed a semicircular array, with the opening to the west. Although no circulating discourse recorded this homology — indeed, it would probably be denied — the ceremonial village was palpably a macrocosm of household space, or conversely, Wãñpõ's house was a tiny replica of the broader social landscape.

I proposed earlier that the household fire was the physical locus of the *axis mundi*. It was the common point of spatial orientation for those around it. And the discourse across it, the physical sound, was also the point of contact between two realms: a here and now of the senses and a world beyond contained in meaning. Meaning diffuses into the world like a bolt of lightning from the heavens, illuminating the surroundings, allowing us to peer into an otherwise inscrutable darkness. The same is true of the ceremonial dance plaza, albeit on a communal scale. The discourse that takes place there, indeed, is of an even more highly standardized, historically transmitted form. The dance plaza is the locus of recitation of the origin myth.

Curiously, the homologies and contiguities of lived space are not themselves the subject of public reflection. It is as if there were two kinds of culture: the kind contained in publicly circulating discourse meanings, and the kind embodied in sensible practices and habits. Why is this sensible space unreflected upon? Why also are discourse meanings directed at parts of space that are not immediately perceptible?

We can think of the problem in terms of the very nature of pure reference. What is most distinctive about language is its ability to allow us to talk about what is not in our immediate context. The latter can be brought into perceptual focus by signs operating through similarities and contiguities. It does not require reference. Therefore, the P. I. Ibirama pattern reflects a universal division of labor between pure reference and other forms of contextual signaling.

But my argument here is not that people at P. I. Ibirama always avoid words when interacting with their immediate surroundings. Obviously, they do use words. Without such use, task-oriented collaboration in immediately perceptible space would be impossible. My observation is instead that their culturally standardized, publicly circulated discourse does not take apparent space as its object. This is a distinct problem. It reminds us of the basic division of labor between pure reference and other forms of contextual signaling. But why is the distinction codified at the level of publicly circulating discourse at P. I. Ibirama?

I suggest that the pattern is ethnographically specific. We have the discourse of Newtonian physics as a counterexample. And I pointed earlier to Sumba house discourse, where immediate space is reflected upon, where it is explicitly linked to sociocosmological principles. Perhaps we did not need to go so far afield. Christine Hugh-Jones (1979: 236 ff.) reports an elaborate spatial symbology among the Northwest Amazonian Barasana people, much closer to home. She details a system of homologies between the *maloca* (longhouse), the human body, and the womb; and she links these homologies to broader physical space — the river territory and even the entire universe. Just how much of this symbology is inferred, how much consciously articulated in circulating Barasana discourse, is difficult to say. She does note, however, that her starting point is "statements made by Indians," among them the statement that "the house is the universe" (1979: 235). We are thus possibly dealing here with a standardized public discourse that reflects upon immediately perceptible space, much as in the Eastern Indonesian case. Both contrast with P. I. Ibirama.

At P. I. Ibirama, sensible homologies between domestic and communal space go unnoticed by discourse. No one would think to talk about them, let alone to link them to the land above the sky, or to the *axis mundi* that connects it to earth. Why should discourse shun perceptible space in this way? Why should it miss the possibility of bridging embodied practices and explicit ideology?

The answer I give throughout this book is a simple one: To keep discourse circulating at P. I. Ibirama, you must avoid disputable referential content. If something is the focus of immediate perception, it is disputable. To get a bit of discourse to circulate broadly, you must make sure that it cannot be contradicted by immediate experience. What lies beyond perception is, therefore, the proper stuff of tradition, of circulating culture. We can see how Sumba house discourse lays down the roadways for its own circulation; it is harder to see that for P. I. Ibirama. Yet I believe that the discourse of space there is constructing its own arena of circulation. However, it is doing so, so to speak, in a negative fashion. Rather than laying down a roadway, cutting a path through the forest, P. I. Ibirama discourse circumscribes a clearing. Inside the clearing, inside perceptible space, it is free to circulate. But it must be careful not to take as its object the clearing itself; it must focus its attention on the mysterious forest beyond.

Steven Feld (n.d.: 9), describing the Kaluli of Papua New Guinea, notes that: "In everyday talk there are a great variety of naming practices. . . . Every naming practice, whether talk of home, of the world within reach, of a journey, of travel . . . involves path-making through constant co-referencing of specific placenames." Motivated by this observation from the other side of the world, I looked into place-names within the discourse at P. I. Ibirama. After all, although I used the metaphor of a circumscribed clearing to describe the arena of discourse circulation, there is also the reality. The community was, even at the time of my stay, surrounded by forest. Perhaps parts of that forest, to which individuals could journey, had become the focus of discourse.

Place-names are not entirely absent from P. I. Ibirama discourse. But neither are they common. Indeed, you would be struck by their infrequency in historical narratives and myths. How different this is from the narrative discourse of native central Australia, as reported in the classic ethnography by Spencer and Gillen. There mythical events occurred in immediately perceptible space, of which Spencer and Gillen have kindly provided us photographs! — the "rocks at Quiurnpa which arose to mark the spot where the Illpongwurra were burnt during the Engwura" (1968 [1899]: 391, Fig. 91), or the block of stone at Emily Gap or Unthurqua (1968 [1899]: 427, Fig. 94), which is "the *Nanja* rock of Intwailiuka, the leader of the Witchetty grubs." Visible to us now, pieces of the landscape are connected by discourse to a mythical time and to mythical events. They embody the intelligible history of the world. Discourse illuminates what can be plainly seen, enchanting perceptible space, making it more real than it is to the senses.[8]

No analogy can be found in the narratives at P. I. Ibirama. In the extended origin myth, indeed, we find only one prominent place-name — "Hawk Mountain." It functions there as part of a poetic refrain:

| | |
|---|---|
| klẽ yugug yòklãm kòñgàg wagzul tẽ to | Beneath Hawk Mountain where many men had gathered, |
| yi òg kulõ to mẽ glè le | it is said, [to that place] to the savanna they descended dancing. |
| klẽ yugug yòklãm kòñgàg wagzul tẽ ki yunke | Beneath Hawk Mountain where many men had gathered, (he) appeared; |
| cuwañ nã nõ yi yug tõ cuwañ wañcõ mã yè katèle | Cuwañ, it is said, "Father Cuwañ, come hither [lit., "descend in this direction"]. |
| hul nẽ klẽ yugug yòklãm kòñgàg wagzul tẽ mẽ nẽ tà tẽ mlè wãñõ kàkòl tẽ | Now, beneath Hawk Mountain where many men were gathering all about [they] finished getting together with the women [i.e., they married all the women]. |
| hul nẽ klẽ yugug yòklãm kòñgàg wagzul tẽ mẽ nẽ kuñõ mlè wãñõ kàkòl tẽ | Now, beneath Hawk Mountain where many men were gathering all about [they] finished getting together with the eligible females [i.e., they married all the eligible females]." |

Hawk Mountain is discursively associated with "many men" gathering. Indeed, it becomes a trope for this event and for the fighting that occurred as a result of it. The discourse of place fails to illuminate perceptible physical space here, unlike the "rocks at Quiurnpa" or the "*Nanja* rock of Intwailiuka." Indeed, I cannot be certain that any living individual actually knows where Hawk Mountain is; certainly, I myself have never seen it. Hawk Mountain instead functions as a discourse device; it evokes an event that is remote in time far beyond the memory of any living individual. Insofar as contemporary discourse is concerned, it has little or no relation to an actual physical place.

Remarkably, many historical narratives occur without any reference to definite spatial locations whatsoever. One such example is given by Henry (1964 [1941]: 134–141). The narrative includes references to going "along the trail," and swimming across "the river," but which trail and what river? These remain undisclosed in the discourse. There is a darkness and lack of specificity regarding spatial location — the narrative seems free-floating, suspended in some spaceless realm, a memory of some earlier time unanchored in a here-and-now world. Past events occur in a spatial void, as if to preserve the dichotomy between sensibility and intelligibility. They appear disconnected from the present, sensible surroundings.

Despite this lack of spatial anchoring, the journey becomes the basis for talking about what lies beyond the sensible, empirical world. It is a trope of knowledge, acquisition of which requires travel, dislocation, displacement in space. A returning traveler is in a position to report back on what he or she has seen or heard or tasted or touched or smelled. No idle speculators, P. I. Ibirama thinkers would probably consider themselves hardheaded empiricists, grounding their knowledge, ultimately, in sensory experience. Recall Wãñpõ's insistence that "it was Klañmàg who told of what it is like" in the land above the sky.

Contrary to the discourse of Newtonian physics, we find no inferences from the here and now to the beyond. Information must be based on witnessing, or on the report of what someone else has witnessed firsthand. I hope to show later (Chapter 7) that dreaming is a form of witnessing. For the present, I am concerned with reports that purport to be of waking experience.

Knowledge of a world on the other side of the diaphane — a noumenal world — involves, from this point of view, a tripartite narrative structure. An opening situates travelers in a here and now, and provides a motivation for their journey to the other realm. We then have the journey itself, and the experiences that occur along the way. Finally, we have the return and re-establishment of connections with the narrative here and now. In the case of Klañmàg, we find him first on the receiving end of instructions from his brother:

| | |
|---|---|
| 1. kuyankàg tẽ wũ ẽ nũgñẽn tẽ mõ tã | 1. Kuyankàg said to his brother: |
| 2. yugug tõ | 2. "When the falcon, |
| 3. kòñgàg tẽ òg wun kũ òg ko gèke ñã | 3. who has been carrying off men and eating them, |
| 4. li ẽñ cõ ken | 4. does this to me, |
| 5. kũ mã ẽñ kukò tẽ tu yè tapã | 5. you go up there to get my bones." |

Klañmàg then experiments with flight. Finally, he ascends:

| | |
|---|---|
| 38. zàg tug klē ñã mū | 38. Above the dry araucaria pines, |
| 39. klē ñãñã tã taplï | 39. above them he ascended. |
| 40.kòñka low tē lòlam mū | 40.He entered the hole in the sky. |
| 41. kòñka low tē lòla | 41. (He) went through the sky's hole, |
| 42. kū tã lò escada tòge tã tē | 42. and there (the ground) was like ladders. |

After the narration of his adventures in the land above the sky, he again dons falcon feathers:

| | |
|---|---|
| 142. kū tã ē nūgñēn kukò tē tē katèle | 142. And he descended with the bones of his brother. |
| 143. tu | 143. Carrying (them) on his back, |
| 144. kū yi tã nañ katèle gèke ñã | 144. it is said, he was spiraling downward, |
| 145. apla tawig | 145. until he reached the ground. |

Verticality poses special experiential problems within this community. Traditionally, it had been impossible to journey upward above the earth to directly encounter the sky firsthand. One evening in 1982, I joked with a group of women about airplanes. At that time, to my knowledge, no one at P. I. Ibirama had ever flown in one, although, from time to time, airplanes passed overhead, like children's toys in the distance. I recall one woman saying to me:

> "You came here in an airplane?"
> "Yes, I did," I replied.
> "But you are so big,
> and the airplane is so small!"

Because of the dearth of firsthand experience, the sky is ripe for a narrativization.

Horizontal space posed fewer problems. To know what lay beyond the perceptible here and now, it was necessary only to go there. Correspondingly, there is far less narrativization of information about the land beyond in horizontal space, unlike what we find in many other societies. Since horizontal space can be experienced directly, there is no need to narrativize it. Since vertical space could not be experienced, it had to be narrativized to become intelligible.

For Western science, death is not a spatial transformation. When people die, they do not go someplace; they change states. Still, the conceptualization of death as spatial is a powerful one in Western imagination, as in so many cultures around the planet. "Abandon all hope ye who enter here" — words chiseled in stone above hell's gate in Dante Alighieri's fourteenth-century poetic excursion through the land of the dead, the source of so many Western images. The older Orpheus theme supplied a precedent for round-trip journeys to that land, and, while popular Christian notions of a spatialized heaven and hell come with only one-way tickets, reports of near-death and out-of-body experiences, from which protagonists return, continue to energize our tabloids. The mind struggles to bridge the sensible and the intelligible through reported experience.

In P. I. Ibirama discourse, the land of the dead is directly analogous to the land above the sky. Both lie beyond the reach of waking sensibility. Both are narrativized as round-trip journeys — forays into a palpable world from which knowledge is retrieved, which can then enter into discourse circulation. Indeed, the narrative of the land of the dead provided the basis for Wãñpõ's January 1, 1975, descriptions of afterlife, of which he insisted that it was because of one woman, Lẽl Tẽ (Goes Living), "that we know things about that land." Nine days later, I was able to record his narration of the story, which I have transcribed below:

| | | | |
|---|---|---|---|
| 1. | lẽl tẽ zi mèn tẽ tï mũ | 1. | Goes Living's husband died. |
| 2. | ti tèl tẽkũ | 2. | When he died, |
| 3. | zi yi wãñkòmã gèke ñã | 3. | she went into seclusion for a long time, it is said; |
| 4. | zi kakutãdẽn kũ nẽ | 4. | until she came out. |
| 5. | kakutãdẽn kũ | 5. | When [she] came out, |
| 6. | òg zi glèn òg mũ | 6. | they danced [for] her. |
| 7. | zi glèn ñã | 7. | [After they] danced [for] her, |
| 8. | òg mũ mũ | 8. | they went. |
| 9. | kute tẽ mẽ òg aklèg mũ mũ | 9. | Throughout the forest they went hunting. |
| 10. | yòklèg gèke ñã | 10. | They were continuously hunting. |
| 11. | ñãglò zi pil ẽ nõ zi mlè zi nẽ kèke mũ | 11. | Meanwhile, she was alone with her mother. |
| 12. | ẽ nõ zi mlè zi ẽ wãle ka nẽ kèke ñã | 12. | She was always with her mother in the camp. |
| 13. | zi mèn tẽ zi to tawig mũ ti kuplẽg tẽ | 13. | [Until] her husband came to her, his ghost. |
| 14. | zi to tawi | 14. | [He] came to her, |
| 15. | kũ tã zi mõ tã | 15. | and he [said] to her |

| | |
|---|---|
| 16. ẽ tõ zi to tawig | 16. when he came to her, |
| 17. kũ ti kuplẽg tẽ tawi | 17. when his ghost came, |
| 18. kũ tã | 18. he [said]: |
| 19. akle mũ ñã | 19. "Let's go hunting," |
| 20. ge mũ | 20. he said. |
| 21. kũ zi ti mlè akle tẽ mũ | 21. And she went hunting with him. |
| 22. ẽ nõ zi mõ zi nõ | 22. To her mother, her mother [she said]: |
| 23. ẽñ ñõ mã òg tolẽl | 23. "Take care of them [the children] for me; |
| 24. yè nũ nèn nã tõ ẽñ cõ ẽ ki aklèg ñã | 24. the one I have been thinking about |
| 25. ẽñ co tawig | 25. [he] has come to me, |
| 26. kũ ti tõ ẽñ mõ | 26. and he [has said] to me: |
| 27. akle mũ ñã | 27. 'Let's go hunting,' |
| 28. kũ ẽñ cõ ti mlè tẽ | 28. and I'm going with him," |
| 29. ke wã | 29. [she] said. |
| 30. kũ ti mlè tẽ mũ | 30. And [she] went with him. |
| 31. ti mlè tẽ | 31. [She] went with him, |
| 32. kũ zi tà tã zi mõ mõg pètï mũ | 32. and there he pierced a beehive [to get honey] for her; |
| 33. mõg pèzïn | 33. when he pierced [it], |
| 34. kũ yi tã to zi mlè ñã | 34. it is said he was with her |
| 35. mõg tẽ kagmẽg mũ | 35. and he took out the honey; |
| 36. zi tõ mõg tẽ ñã | 36. she was eating the honey. |
| 37. mũñãglò zi la zãnduñ mẽ nènmlu gèñ | 37. Meanwhile, he was beside her on the ground, gathering up dust. |
| 38. kũ ko ke | 38. And [he] was about to eat [it]. |
| 39. kũ zi ne ti tõ ko pi wè | 39. And she thought: "What is it that he's eating?" |
| 40. mõg tẽ ñã mã ka | 40. [He] did not eat the honey there. |
| 41. ẽ pil mõ zi mõg tẽ ñã mũ | 41. By herself she ate the honey. |
| 42. ti mlè zi mẽ katẽ man | 42. She came about with him again. |
| 43. lò mõg ũ nẽ man | 43. There was honey again, |
| 44. kũ tã pèzïn man mũ | 44. and he pierced it again, |
| 45. kũ tã kagmẽg man mũ | 45. and he took it out again, |
| 46. kũ tã li ke man | 46. and he did like that again. |
| 47. mõg tẽ ñã tũ | 47. [He] did not eat the honey. |
| 48. zãñnuñ mẽ yi tã nèn mlu gèñ | 48. He went about on the ground, it is said, gathering up dust, |
| 49. kũ ko ke | 49. and [he] was about to eat [it]. |
| 50. ẽ mõ | 50. [She thought] to herself: |

| | |
|---|---|
| 51. tòg ñãglò ti tõ ẽ ñàn hà ko hã wã | 51. "This, however, must be the food he eats!" |
| 52. kũ zi | 52. And she thought: |
| 53. ne ti tõ ko wã | 53. "What does he eat? |
| 54. hã ne nũ wã | 54. Oh, what is it?" |
| 55. kũ yi tã zi mõ yi tã | 55. And, it is said, he said to her, it is said: |
| 56. a blè kũ ẽñ cõ ẽñ klàgnẽ mẽ ko wã | 56. "Like you I am eating my meat [i.e., food]," |
| 57. ge mũ | 57. [he] said. |
| 58. ti mlè tawig mũ | 58. [She] came with him. |
| 59. tawig mũ | 59. [She] came. |
| 60. ñãglò zi mõg kãy nẽ tag kũ tẽ tawig mũ | 60. Meanwhile, she came with her basket full of honey. |
| 61. ẽ nõ tẽ zi mõ tẽ katẽ zãg mũ | 61. [She] came and gave it to her mother. |
| 62. zi mlè ñã mũ | 62. [She] ate it with her. |
| 63. ñãglò tã zi mlè katã nẽ | 63. Meanwhile, he had come with her. |
| 64. ñãglò zi ti wèg tũ tẽ | 64. However, she could not see him. |
| 65. ti tõ gàyun tẽ | 65. Because he was a spirit, |
| 66. wèg tũ tẽ | 66. [she] could not see [him]. |

I have been arguing that an epistemological principle is at work at P. I. Ibirama. The immediately sensible is *not* the focus of public discourse. Perception taps into a kind of implicit truth about the world, or, in any case, it provides access to a world that is already public. Any individual can experience the sensible realm directly; it need not be made the focus of discourse. You do not have to learn about that world through discourse. Correspondingly, whatever lies beyond the realm of the senses—the land above the sky or the land of the dead—can only be known through discourse. As a consequence, the most widely circulated public discourse is about what is not ordinarily sensible. To ensure that a bit of discourse circulates, you must make sure that you construct it around the problem of intelligibility.

This characterization, however, is inaccurate in one important respect. It makes it seem as if there were no commerce between sensibility and intelligibility, no possibility of interchange or interconversion. But this narrative, like the narrative of the land above the sky, asserts that interchange is possible. Not only is it possible, it is the only basis for understanding the world. The discourse is not only about what lies beyond the senses; it is about getting from the immediate sensory world to the world beyond. It is about having a firsthand look at that other world and coming back to tell about it. The spatial discourse that circulates is thus about bridging the sensible and the intelligible, moving back and forth between perception and knowledge.

Let us take a closer look at the microarchitecture of the "Goes Living" story. Lines 1–12 portray an immediate world. While perhaps exotic to you, it is a world that is well known to the audience. It is the familiar world in which they live. A woman's (Goes Living's) husband dies. She goes into seclusion, a practice that will be discussed subsequently (Chapter 6). She comes out. A ceremony is held to reintegrate her into the community. After this, the others go hunting. She is left alone with her mother.

Nothing about these events would strike a member of the P. I. Ibirama community as unusual. In line 13, however, the unusual begins — "her husband came to her, his ghost." Here we have movement across the diaphane, across Cocteau's mirror. So begins the narrative of displacement to the land of the dead. Lines 13 through 31 are dominated by a verbal parallelism involving "coming" and "going." The former verb occurs five times, and the latter six. In fact, the only other verb in this section is "to say." What we have here is a description of movement, of displacement. Our heroine has left the familiar world for a strange and rather discomforting one.

Lines 32 through 57 allow us a glimpse of what life is like in that strange land. This narration actually contains only one episode. In other tellings, we encounter other episodes. Like this one, however, each is dominated by a single activity. Here the activity is eating honey, with the verb "to eat," in the form of *ñã* (to eat or suck honey) or *ko* (to eat [other foods than honey]), occurring ten times, dominating all other verbs in this section.

However, though a familiar activity in the everyday world of the audience, eating is here made strange. The dead husband nourishes himself on dust from the ground. While honey is highly prized by members of the P. I. Ibirama community, and while the wife happily consumes the honey that has been given to her, the husband shuns it. In the land of the dead, eating is perverse — not at all what it is in our sensible, here-and-now world. Such a familiar activity made strange makes the world of the dead seem strange, something the audience recognizes as nonordinary reality.

In a different telling, the wife samples some honey wine (*mõg*) — a ceremonial mead prepared in everyday life and well known to the audience. It tastes to her like water, not at all what she had expected. The episode emphasizes the faculty of taste. In the land of the dead, things taste different, strange. In still another episode, what appears to the wife like an ant looks to her dead husband like a jaguar. Here the faculty of sight is singled out. The visible world and the objects in it are themselves transformed. The land of the dead appears as a crazy, inverted, disquieting world. Insignificant insects become terrifying creatures; highly valued foods become tasteless; and worthless, nonfood items become the staples of daily life.

If you were to ask them, anyone conversant with the Goes Living narrative could rattle off for you the salient features of life in the land of the dead, as if they had been there themselves and were describing it to you. I put the question to Wãñpõ on January 1, 1975, before I had heard the story of Goes Living. He responded, unhesitatingly:

> *gàyun* [spirits of the dead] eat the head of the *xaxim*,
> which for the living is inedible.
> They eat squash,
> but it is not squash
> because it is without taste.
> For the *gàyun* the ant is a jaguar.

Wãñpõ's comments suggest a consciousness of the world, a direct knowledge of what is out there. But that knowledge is the product of reflection on publicly circulating discourse. It is metadiscursive knowledge. No wonder Wãñpõ, like Wãñẽkï, felt compelled to report his sources of information. He did not experience the information as an image of the world, like the Almond Joy bar or cereal bowl cosmos; he experienced it as second- or thirdhand information about the world, recovered from publicly circulating discourse. It was only the anthropologist who tried to turn it into a worldview.

In lines 58–63, Goes Living returns to the present world. These lines are again dominated by verbs of movement—"to come" occurs five times. The section is a mirror image of the earlier travel section (lines 13–31); it reverses the direction of spatial displacement back to the here and now. However, as if to confirm the opposition between the activities in the land of the dead and those in the land of the living, the section also contains a final instance of eating—the wife gives honey to her mother, and the mother eats it appreciatively, as any normal human being would. We know we are safe, back in a familiar world. Our journey is over. But we know as well that that strange world is out there, even though we cannot see it.

The final three lines (64–66) bring this point home, articulating the problematic of sensibility and intelligibility. They concern "seeing"—the experience of a here-and-now reality through visual sensation. The dead husband has returned with Goes Living, but she can no longer see him:

| | |
|---|---|
| 65. ti tõ gàyun tẽ | 65. Because he was a spirit, |
| 66. wèg tũ tẽ | 66. [she] could not see [him]. |

There is something behind the surface of appearance, but, like Goes Living, we cannot directly see it. Nor can we touch it or smell it or taste it. Yet we know it is there.

I have argued that P. I. Ibirama discourse reveals an implicit epistemological principle. If discourse is to circulate broadly, it must be about what cannot be readily perceived. Correspondingly, the immediate surroundings — what Newton called "apparent" space — are left unspoken, untheorized. But our analysis of the Goes Living narrative has added another level to the ethnographic problem. The discourse that circulates is not only about a world that is imperceptible; it is also about the interchange between that imperceptible world and this one, between the strange and the familiar, between the knowable and the sensible. The stories report a commerce between the two. A man flies above the sky. A woman travels with her dead husband to the antiworld of the dead.

The discourse concerning what Newton called "true" space also accounts for the sources of information about that true space. It anchors them in perceptions. But the perceptions are not ordinary ones. If they were, then everyone would have ready access to them. And if everyone had ready access to them, they would pertain to the phenomenal and not to the noumenal, to the sensible and not to the intelligible. Consequently, there would be no need to circulate discourse about them. This would violate the basic epistemological principle, which is also a principle of discourse circulation — the interest that individuals have in discourse is inversely proportional to their ability to directly experience the phenomena described.

A fine line exists here. If the phenomena are accessible to the senses, then there is no need to talk about them. But if they are beyond the senses, then there is no way to know about them. To be of public interest, something must be phenomenally accessible, but only under extraordinary circumstances. Space is of interest when it is beyond apparent space, beyond what we can ordinarily see with our own eyes. But it is only of interest if someone else did manage to see it, triumphing over adversity — a winged flight into the heavens, a perilous journey into a frightening unknown.

If the stories themselves describe a commerce between sensibility and intelligibility, between this world and a world beyond, do we find commerce manifested as well in our own sensible world? Is there an interchange whereby what is intelligible through discourse is actually experienced by the senses?

During my first few months at P. I. Ibirama, an event occurred that Wãñpõ later recounted to me. The event concerned his sister Ãglò, whose husband Wãñẽkï (not the Wãñẽkï mentioned above) had died five years earlier. Here are my notes from our January 1, 1975 conversation:

> His [the dead husband's] *gàyun* [spirit] came back to call her.
> He told her there were many tapir
> and much honey in his land.
> She conversed with him,

but nobody else saw him.
She appeared to be crazy,
but it was really only that she was being called by her husband Wãñēkï.
They had made a little *rancho* [thatched hut] for her
next to Wãñpõ's house.
One night she came in with a torch
looking for Wãñēkï.
She said she followed him in there,
and she began to search with the torch in all of the corners.
Yu'o [Wãñpõ's wife] got angry
and told her that Wãñēkï had in fact not come in.
Eventually Āglò became sick.
She said that she had gone with Wãñēkï to visit his land,
to a "good place."
Ten hours later she died.

Wãñpõ experienced this event firsthand; it was part of an immediate, sensible world, not something he had heard. Here was his flesh-and-blood sister, in the middle of the night, with a torch, nightmarishly searching his house (the house shown in Plate 6, incidentally). Phenomenally real and immediate, this experience was remarkable enough to merit conversion into discourse, unusual enough that the discourse into which it was converted would be of interest to a broader community. Discourse about this kind of experience might enjoy wider circulation.

At the same time, Āglò behaved as if she were enacting a variant of the Goes Living story. We are reminded of a play, whose script originated in an oral narrative. We drop the quotation marks around reported speech; we strip away background narrative and replace it with a here-and-now setting; a real person (Āglò) speaks the reported speech and acts out the described behavior. The event is one in which the referential content of publicly circulating words is replaced by an icon of what those words stand for. Sensible objects in the physical world substitute for intelligible objects formulated in language.

This is a matter of enactment, of the intelligible made sensible. But there is a flip side: the sensible made intelligible. Not only did Āglò enact a traditional story, casting herself in the heroine's role, but Wãñpõ reported her behavior in terms of that story. The situation was strange, perhaps frightening, and certainly something in need of explanation. Wãñpõ had an explanation at hand. It was available to him through the circulating discourse in which he had been immersed all his life. Her strange conduct could be construed in terms of the heroic journey of Goes Living. Wãñpõ's task was therefore to construct a new discourse analogous to a preexisting one, to report his experience the way Goes Living's mother reported hers. Conversion of the intelligible into the sensible thus requires, simultaneously, conversion of the sensible into the intelligible — it requires a new bit of discourse, a new story, modeled on an old one. We know that experience reflects discourse meanings made tangible because that is the way the experience is reported. We know it, in other words, because of the similarity between two pieces of discourse.

Public discourse, widely accessible to members of the community, becomes a private event, accessible to only a few. But the event is once again given life in words, circulated throughout the community. These words may not circulate as widely as the original ones; fewer than twenty years have passed, and the story of Ãglò may have been forgotten, even if its happenstantial capture by an anthropologist ultimately bequeaths it a longer life. But the new discourse is of interest — and hence is circulated — because it is simultaneously novel and familiar, because it crosses and recrosses the fine line between sensibility and intelligibility.

In Eastern Indonesia, as in aboriginal Australia, discourse circulates in a physical space that it simultaneously illuminates; it enchants local space, thereby attaching or anchoring itself to it. By this means, it ensures its own circulation, staking out a claim to a piece of the perceptible world that it can call its own. It keeps people interested in it by keeping them interested in the physical milieu to which it is attached. What a seemingly natural method for discourse to ensure its own survival.

At P. I. Ibirama, however, it does no such thing. Instead, it establishes a clearing — the sensible surroundings — inside of which it circulates. But it does not illuminate that clearing, except negatively. Its interest is in what lies beyond and in the possibilities of experiencing the beyond, even though that is not within the normal perceptual reach of people in the everyday waking world. Though negatively, however, this spatial discourse, like that of Eastern Indonesia and aboriginal Australia, fosters its own circulation. It keeps people interested in it because it illuminates that which they cannot normally see, like lightning showing us shapes and forms on a dark night. It is the *axis mundi* through which sacredness diffuses into a secular world, through which noumenal objects come into contact with phenomenal ones. But it simultaneously makes meaningful the unusual conduct that people do see. It interprets that conduct as extraordinary encounters with a world beyond this one, as journeys beyond the security of the senses.

# *Chapter 4.* A Lock of Hair
# in a Ball of Wax

"As far back as the year 1846," Lewis Henry Morgan (1871: 3) wrote in *Systems of Consanguinity and Affinity of the Human Family,* "I found among [the Iroquois], in daily use, a system of relationship for the designation and classification of kindred, both unique and extraordinary in its character, and wholly unlike any with which we are familiar." Morgan dubbed the system "classificatory," opposing it to the more familiar "descriptive" type, and in so doing he initiated a more than century-long fascination with kinship, which was to be, until recently, the defining core of anthropology as a discipline.

But what did Morgan mean in saying that he "found . . . a system of relationship?" How did he find it? You might conjure an image of someone espying an unusual rock—a fossil, perhaps—while out for a walk in the woods. Or maybe it is a geologist, chiseling away in some quarry. It is almost as if Morgan stumbled into an Iroquois village, and there it was, something that could be seen, a visible object, like a monolith.

The question may seem frivolous, especially since it has been ignored by generations of kinship specialists. They were concerned not with how it was found, but with its explanation. Kinship was a prototypical anthropological object, and the classificatory system was its most intriguing exemplar. Yet, as I hope to show, the question of finding is a fascinating one. It stirs things up, rekindles interest in the nature of kinship as a cultural object. And it is closely bound up with the question of circulation. How was the classificatory system passed down across the generations? How did it move through communities and between communities? Did Morgan tap its public life? If not, can we be sure that the system he found was not really of his own manufacture, a product of the observer's paradox—something whose existence depends on the presence and methods of the ethnographer?

While students today no longer study the classificatory system, its contemplation was de rigueur for earlier generations. Everyone knew that the system distinguished two kinds of "cousin." One kind—a child of the father's brother or of the mother's sister, a so-called parallel cousin — was classified with one's own siblings. Parallel cousins were differentiated, terminologically, from cross-cousins, that is, children of the mother's brother or of the father's sister. This was quintessential culture. The Iroquois had something fascinatingly different from anything within the reach of the European imagination. The question was not how Morgan found it, but how to explain it, how to account for this instance of cultural difference.

Before I come back to the question of how it was found, let me briefly leaf through the history of anthropological attempts to explain the classificatory system. The history discloses a kind of institutionalized split personality, where the two personalities have been unable to fully communicate. I think that, in the discourse-centered approach, we may have a kind of therapy, a way of getting the two sides talking with each other.

On one side were the social anthropologists, who traced their lineage to E. B. Tylor (1889) and W. H. R. Rivers (1968 [1914]). They viewed kinship terms generally, and the classificatory system in particular, as the product of something out there in the world, social conditions or properties that the terms named. Tylor, in particular, linked the classificatory terminology to exogamous unilineal moieties — the division of society into two halves, with individuals of one half required to marry someone from the other half, and with their children joining the father's side (in the case of patrilineal moieties) or the mother's side (in the case of matrilineal moieties). Tylor made the discovery that cross-cousins would always be members of the opposite half or "moiety," and that parallel cousins, like siblings, would always be members of one's own half. This was a remarkable discovery and a defining moment in the history of anthropology as science.

Alfred Kroeber (1909) later observed that the classificatory system could be found in the absence of exogamous unilineal moieties. Conceding that Kroeber's empirical observation was correct, W. H. R. Rivers (1968 [1914]) rejoined that where the classificatory system occurred, you could be certain that exogamous moieties had once been there, even if they were not there today. In the latter event, the classificatory system was a survivor or vestige of an older system.

Despite Rivers's rejoinder, Kroeber became the ancestor of the other major lineage (or personality?) — the culturalists, who saw the classificatory system, like all kinship terminologies, as part of language. Each term was a piece of a jigsaw puzzle. It meant nothing by itself, but if you put it together with the other pieces, a pattern emerged. Kinship terminology was, in this sense, language internal. Its explanation depended on the fit of the linguistic pieces with respect to one another.

The methods for the linguistic analysis of kinship terminologies grew considerably more powerful with the development of componential analysis and formal semantics — associated especially with Ward Goodenough

(1956) and Floyd Lounsbury (1964). In a flash of brilliance, articulated in his characteristically modest and unassuming way—in a footnote, actually—Lounsbury attacked the very foundations of the social position. He restudied the Iroquoian system originally described by Lewis Henry Morgan. He showed that the social analysis failed even there, where unilineal exogamous moieties were present. More distant cousins were not classified in the way that moiety membership would predict! Yet the classification could be explained by some simple linguistic rules.

When I arrived at P. I. Ibirama in July of 1974, I expected to find something relevant to this problem. In one suitcase, I had a stack of photocopies, and among them was Herbert Baldus's (1952) brief article "Terminologia de parentesco Kaingang" (The Kinship Terminology of the Kaingang). You will recall that the Kaingang are a neighboring and closely related people. The language of the P. I. Ibirama community, indeed, is sometimes regarded as a mere dialectal variant of Kaingang.

What was interesting about this article was that it described a terminological system that conformed to the unilineal exogamous moiety model proposed by Tylor (1889) so many years ago. Some terms applied to members of the same moiety; some terms applied to members of the opposite moiety; some applied irrespective of moiety. Among the moiety terms, the cousins were distinguished into two groups, just as Morgan had described and as Tylor's model predicted. Below are the moiety-linked terms given by Baldus, although I have reorganized them and altered Baldus's orthography to conform to that employed in this book:

*Same Moiety*

*yog* — father, father's brother, father's father, men of the father's generation.

*mï* — father's sister, father's mother, mother-in-law, women of the mother-in-law's generation.

*règre* — brother, father's brother's son, mother's sister's son, males of the same generation as the brother.

*we* — sister, father's brother's daughter, mother's sister's daughter, females of the same generation as the sister.

*Opposite Moiety*

*kakre* — mother's brother, mother's father, father-in-law, men of the father-in-law's generation.

*nï* — mother, mother's sister, mother's mother, women of the mother's generation.

*yamré* — mother's brother's child, father's sister's child, brother-in-law, sister-in-law, individuals of the same generation as the brother-in-law or sister-in-law.

*prü* — wife

*mèn* — husband

What was so interesting was the contrast between these data and those for P. I. Ibirama, as reported by J. Henry (1964 [1941]: 177–179). The terms were cognate, but they had deliciously different meanings. Let us take a closer look. The Kaingang term for "father," as reported by Baldus, was *yog*, almost identical in phonological form to the P. I. Ibirama term *yug*, which also meant "father." Both terms, moreover, included the "father's brother." So far, so good. But at P. I. Ibirama, *yug* included as well the "mother's brother," who, among the Kaingang, was singled out by a distinct term — *kakre*.

You will recall Tylor's reasoning. In a patrilineal moiety system, one's father and father's brother belong to the same moiety or half of society as oneself. But since one's father must, by the principle of exogamy, marry someone from the other half, one's mother, together with her brothers and sisters, would be from that other half. This means that one's mother's brother is also from the other half. Hence, the contrast between the terms *yog* and *kakre*. The former applied to same half, the latter to opposite half.

Now at P. I. Ibirama, the analogous term *yug* applied to relatives of both halves, irrespective of moiety. It was used for the father and his brother, but also for the mother's brother. Here the moiety principle failed! And for good reason. P. I. Ibirama, according to Henry, had no patrilineal moieties. I therefore arrived in the field with data already in hand that cast light on one of the great controversies of twentieth-century anthropology. If I could substantiate the contrast, this would show that, *pace* Lounsbury, at least in the Kaingang case, social groups — the patrilineal moieties — were responsible for some of the terminological contrasts. Their disappearance at P. I. Ibirama would account for the absence of the contrast there.

Now you may be curious as to whether there is a term at P. I. Ibirama that is cognate with the Kaingang term *kakre* (mother's brother). Indeed there is. The cognate is *kòkla*. However, the latter is not a kinship term. It is used instead for one's ceremonial father — a man your parents choose to pierce your lip, if you are a male child, or to tattoo your thigh, if you are female. In some cases, the man will be your mother's brother, since women like to have their brothers play this role. But it is not always the mother's brother. Moreover, should the mother have more than one brother, only that brother who has actually pierced your lip or tattooed your thigh will you call *ēñ kòkla* (my ceremonial father). The others are *yug*. The form *kòkla* — the phonological word — survived, as historical linguists say, but it acquired a new meaning.

I will not examine all of the contrasts here. You can work these out for yourself. That between *nī* (mother; mother's sister) and *mï* (father's sister) followed the pattern of *yog* and *kakre*. The cognate term *nō* at P. I. Ibirama applied to "mother," "mother's sister," and "father's sister." The term *mï* acquired the nonkinship meaning of "ceremonial mother."

Among the cousins, the change took a different but related course. Kaingang distinguished "brother" (*règre*) from "sister" (*we*). As Tylor predicted, these terms were used as well for some of the cousins — namely, those cousins who belonged to one's own moiety, the so-called parallel cousins (children of the father's brother or mother's sister). But the terms were not used for those cousins who belonged to the opposite moiety. The latter, so-called cross-cousins — children of the mother's brother or father's sister — were called *yamré*.

What became of this contrast at P. I. Ibirama? In fact, none of the Kaingang terms survived as a term for cousin or even for sibling, for that matter. The ancestors of the P. I. Ibirama came up with a new term — *nũgñẽn*. The latter applied to all of one's siblings, irrespective of gender, and to all of one's cousins, irrespective of moiety. There was no distinction between cross- and parallel cousins.

As in the case of *kakre* and *mï*, some of the cousin terms survived, but took on different meanings. The term *yamré* has a cognate at P. I. Ibirama in the term *yòmlé*. The latter means "in-law," including "brother-in-law," "sister-in-law," "father-in-law," and "mother-in-law." In fact, the Kaingang term *yamré* was used for "brother-in-law" and "sister-in-law," as well as for cross-cousins. However, in Kaingang the term for "father-in-law" was *kakre*, and the term for "mother-in-law" was *mï*. So the P. I. Ibirama term *yòmlé* retained some of its meanings, lost some of them, and acquired some new ones. It was reconfigured in the absence of the moiety contrast.

Of the other two cousin terms, *règre* survived as well in the P. I. Ibirama term *lègle*. The latter, however, had taken on a new meaning. It was used for a co-husband in a polyandrous marriage. In fact, Wãñpõ's father, Kàmlẽn, who is pictured in Plate 5, had two wives whom he shared with another man — one Mõgñã, whose name set Wãñpõ bestowed upon me in 1975. Kàmlẽn referred to Mõgñã as *ẽñ lègle*. As regards the Kaingang term *we* (sister), however, there seemed to be no Kaingang counterpart.

As I bided my time at the FUNAI post in July of 1975, waiting for the rains to subside and battling wild rats for food, kinship terminology was on my mind; it was the problem I wanted most eagerly to investigate. You will be surprised to learn that, when I left Brazil in 1976, I felt that I had pretty much confirmed these earlier results. Henry's data seemed unassailable, and, while I quibbled with some of Baldus's results, based on my three months of research at P. I. Manoel Ribas in central Paraná, I could not help but be aware of the sharp contrast between P. I. Ibirama and P. I. Manoel Ribas usages. In the latter case, moiety membership seemed to determine kin terminological usage; in the former, it was irrelevant.

The results did not confirm the claim by W. H. R. Rivers. Remember that he believed that moiety-like kin contrasts persisted, even once the moieties themselves had disappeared. It was in this way that he hoped to account for the widespread occurrence of Iroquoian terminologies in the absence of moieties. But the comparative historical linguistic evidence in the P. I. Ibirama and P. I. Manoel Ribas cases did seem to contradict Lounsbury's findings for the Iroquois. Here we had a substantiated case in which the presence versus absence of social groups went along with a difference in kinship terminology. I believe that anyone who investigates the problem as I have will come to the same conclusion. In this case, moieties make a difference.

Yet back in Chicago I had doubts, and these would only grow over the years. The basic contrast seemed certain, but there was something troubling about it. Many years later I would realize what I was concerned about was the problem of "finding." Had I "found" the contrasts between P. I. Ibirama and P. I. Manoel Ribas? In what measure had I created them through the finding process?

What strikes me most in thinking back on it is the difficulty I had in investigating the kinship terminology at P. I. Ibirama, and even at P. I. Manoel Ribas. I was using a procedure similar to that employed by Morgan and those who collected data for him. I was, in effect, filling out "schedules," which asked for the term used for a particular relative — What is the term for "mother's brother?" What is the term for "mother's brother's son?"[1]

One quickly recognizes the difficulty of doing this kind of work in the native language. There is no word for "word," no effective way to gloss terms. Even using Portuguese with bilingual speakers, I was stymied. People like Wãñpõ, Wãñẽkï, and Nil had no experience with definition giving. The very idea of talking about meanings or even usages — so common in the Western academy — had no counterpart in this remote region of Amerindian Brazil. One had to train speakers to give the kind of responses one wished to elicit. But what did this mean? Could one assume that the responses corresponded to a reality that lay behind them?

Let me be clear that in the Western academy glossing is a naturally occurring process. Our dictionaries are filled with this sort of thing. What we do is define one term with respect to others. Kinship terms seem to us to be closely related to one another — pieces of a jigsaw puzzle — because we, in fact, treat them that way in our discourse practices. Consider the definition of "uncle" found in *Webster's Third International Dictionary*: "the brother of one's father or mother," "the husband of one's aunt." And if we look up "aunt" we find: "the sister of one's father or mother," "the wife of one's uncle."

Our assumption is that in every culture kinship terms are similarly related. It is just a question of asking the natives about them. But what if there is no underlying jigsaw puzzle? What if the puzzle is in fact the product of metadiscursive practice — of glossing one term by means of others?

I realize that in posing this question I am committing a sort of heresy. I am casting doubt on linguistic assumptions that extend back nearly a century — to the work of the great Swiss linguist Ferdinand de Saussure. Saussure had said that language is a system in which everything hangs together, and in which the parts are related by difference. In the lexicon, this was understood in terms of domains, such as kinship. Assuming all the terms to be related, the question was what features differentiated them.

Here I am suggesting something quite different. I am proposing that the sense of total relatedness comes from an ethnographically specific discourse process — the practice of glossing. By means of it, we are in fact bringing terms into relation with one another, systematizing them; and the relationship is one that may not have existed as such prior to our questioning. By bringing two terms into contact, we force our interlocutors to find or fabricate a connection between them. The connection may not have otherwise existed. Does the questioning process therefore result in the creation of a "system" *ex nihilo*? Is the system a figment of the ethnographer's fancy, a projection off the ethnographer's talk about it?

I do not think so, at least not entirely. True, we can influence responses to our questioning. This is particularly easy when there is no naturally occurring practice of talking about meaning. In English, because of native practices of talking about meaning, we can say definitively that a father's sister is an "aunt," a child of the father's sister, a "cousin." But at P. I. Ibirama, a father's sister might be in one instance *nõ* (if she is sufficiently older than you ), in another instance *nũgñẽn* (if she is more or less the same age or younger), and in still another *mï* (if she happens to have been involved in piercing your lip or tattooing your thigh). Relative age appears to be more important than genealogical connection. Yet sometimes you can convince your interlocutors that "father's sister" is called *nõ*. You juxtapose a complex term with a simple one — something that is not normally done; no naturally occurring discourse practice, analogous to dictionary making, does this. By means of the juxtaposition, however, you are able to induce your interlocutor to accept it. Perhaps he or she recognizes the grain of truth in it.

At the same time, however, you cannot get people to say just anything. Their responses are, partially, at least, independent of your will. At P. I. Ibirama, I at one point believed I could discover a set of terminological usages analogous to those Baldus had reported for the Kaingang — I believed I could show that the P. I. Ibirama community conformed to the broader Kaingang pattern. One day I actually convinced Wãñpõ that *mï* really meant "father's sister," and *kòkla* meant "mother's brother." However, when I later sought to confirm this with Wãñĕkĭ and Nil and Kañã'ĭ, I was unable to do so. Even checking out my earlier result with Wãñpõ at a later date failed to confirm my "finding." The terms *kòkla* and *mi* could not be made to mean "uncle" and "aunt," no matter how hard I tried. They meant something like "ceremonial father and mother," respectively. No amount of influence on my part could change that. Native responses resisted my attempts to impose patterns where no foundation for them existed.

But if there was no socially standardized talk about meanings in this community, where did the resistance come from? What was the basis for native responses? The lineage stemming from A. L. Kroeber believed the basis to be an abstract system. I am now convinced that something else was at work. The responses were read off naturally occurring discourse, especially narratives, that circulated in the community. In the course of these narratives, kinship terms were used, and from their use, similarities and contrasts could be inferred. When people are pressed to come up with answers to unnatural questions, they turn to what they naturally know. At P. I. Ibirama, that means reflecting upon the role of kin terms in discourse. Discourse is the holding environment for grammar.

Narratives and other segments of naturally occurring discourse are elements of material culture, like ceramic pots or bows and arrows. They can be circulated throughout a community and replicated across the generations. But that is not all that they are. They are also repositories of relationships among linguistic elements; and kinship terms, from the point of view of the Kroeberians, were primarily linguistic elements. We see them as related, however, not only to one another, but to other linguistic elements as well. In these relationships are to be found the bases for native responses to abstract ethnographic questions. Not talk about meaning — our dictionary making — but reflection on discourse is the source of resistance.

Let me illustrate a few of the kin term interrelationships discoverable in actually occurring discourse. One of these relations is co-reference. That is, kin terms refer to something that is also referred to by means of a pronoun or name or noun. The kin term is co-referential with that pronoun or name or noun. Consider the following example:

| ti | yi | tõ | kaklozàl | zi | u | ñã |
|------|-------|------|-------------|------|-----------|-------------|
| his | child | erg. | proper name | fem. | beautiful | stand-cont. |

"His daughter [or female child] Kaklozàl was beautiful."

What discourse function does the kin term *yi* (child) serve here? Together with the possessive pronoun "his," it introduces a new discourse participant or actor. Inspection of the prior discourse discloses that the possessive pronoun "his" refers back to the topic of the earlier discourse — "he." The "he" in turn leads us back to a proper name — Nẽwo — the initial topic of the narrative from which the above clause was plucked.

The kin term *yi* appears, at this moment, as a device for introducing a new discourse participant, one that will later become the discourse topic. The new participant is indicated both by possessive pronoun coupled with kin term ("his child") and by proper name (Kaklozàl). When the new participant (Kaklozàl) becomes established as the discourse topic, and the old participant (Nẽwo) is later reintroduced, this is again accomplished by means of a possessive pronoun coupled with kin term:

| ñãglò | zi | yug | tẽ | tawig | mũ |
|---|---|---|---|---|---|
| meanwhile | her | father | def. | arrive | active |

"Meanwhile, her father arrived."

The "her" refers to Kaklozàl, the entire expression "her father" leading us back by a circuitous route to Nẽwo. Kin terms thus serve as discourse devices for tracking participants, for introducing new ones and for reintroducing old ones.

These examples make clear that *yi* and *yug* are not only linked to other pronouns, names, and nouns. They are also linked to one another. They form a system or subsystem. The one introduces a new discourse participant — *ti yi* (his child). When that participant has become the presupposed topic, the other reintroduces the original participant — *zi yug* (her father). As a general rule, if there are two discourse actors or participants, B and C, and C is B's *yug*, then B is C's *yi*. The expression "B's *yug*" refers to C, and "C's *yi*" refers to B. The terms *yug* and *yi* are thus reciprocals of one another.

The system, extracted from a single, contiguous stretch of discourse, can be extended further. There is another reciprocal of the term *yi*. This is the term *nõ*. It occurs in the phrase *zi nõ* (her mother), at a point in the discourse when Kaklozàl has assumed the position of discourse topic. Like the earlier instances, this one introduces another participant:

| kũ | zi | nõ | tẽ | zi | wũ | zi | mõ |
|---|---|---|---|---|---|---|---|
| and | her | mother | def. | she | nom. | she | to |

"And her mother [said] to her."

Like *yug*, therefore, actually occurring discourse discloses a connection between *nõ* and *yi* — the two are reciprocals of one another.

The term *yi* thus has two reciprocals, both of which track relations among participants. What is the connection between them? Discourse again provides an answer. Examining the broader stretch in which these sample clauses are embedded, one notices that the terms *yug* and *nõ* are never both used for the same discourse participant. They track different actors. Moreover, they contrast as regards gender co-referencing. Third person pronouns here are distinguished by gender, as in English. There is a "he" (*ti* or *tā*) and a "she" (*zi*). Where *yug* occurs, it refers only to a discourse participant that takes the masculine pronoun *ti* (or *tā*), as in the following example:

| kū  | zi  | yug    | tẽ   | zi  | yògzẽ       | hãlike  | kū  | tā | lõ    |
|-----|-----|--------|------|-----|-------------|---------|-----|----|-------|
| and | her | father | def. | her | deeds/state | similar | and | he | fever |

"And <u>her father</u> was like her, and <u>he</u> had a fever."

Similarly, *nõ* is used only for a discourse participant that is also referred to by *zi* (she). In other words, the terms *yug* and *nõ* are gender differentiated; for this we have discourse evidence. The same cannot be said for *yi*, which takes either masculine or feminine pronouns, depending on the participant.

These three terms thus form a system, recoverable from actually occurring discourse, not imposed through the interview process. The terms *yug* and *nõ* are reciprocals of the term *yi*, and *yug* and *nõ* are distinguished by gender, *yug* being masculine and *nõ* feminine. One phase of a discourse-centered ethnography must be to examine actual discourse evidence of linkages among kinship terms. Do some terms interact more with one another than with other terms? Do some terms interact not at all? What kinds of cleavages do we find?

You will appreciate the difference between this method and that deriving from the Kroeberian "psychological" view. The latter makes use of questioning about language—a distinctive form of discourse interaction with no counterpart in the P. I. Ibirama community. The method creates a *de facto* system. Terms are brought into discourse interrelationship by the questioner. But how does this induced system compare with the interrelationships as manifested in actually occurring discourse, especially that for which we have evidence of widespread public circulation?

Naturally occurring discourse is a reservoir or holding environment for systematic contrasts. It is the physical locus in which float the contrasts that inform native intuitions and responses to ethnographic questions. From its depths, however, emerges as well something of quite a different order. If we refer back to an earlier example—"his daughter [or female child] Kaklozàl was beautiful"—we can appreciate that kinship terms introduce new discourse participants. But why introduce a participant in this way? Why not use, for example, only the proper name? The answer is that kinship terms not only introduce new participants. They set up expectations about relations between new and old participants, about the kind of discourse that will unfold. It is such expectations, I propose, that are the locus of what social theorists call roles.

Here you can see coming together the two sides of the debate with which this chapter began. I have focused on one side — the side that regarded kinship terms as part of language, as components of an abstract system. The other side, you will recall, regarded kinship terms as reflections of underlying social categories, which lay outside of language. Kinship terms were seen as labels for role relations, understood as rights and duties and expectations. And roles were part of a distinct social level.

The role concept took shape in Sir Henry Maine's (1965 [1861]: 105) notion of the *universitas juris*, which he described as "a university (or bundle) of rights and duties." As a legal scholar, Maine's model was laws that were actually codified in discourse. However, in the P. I. Ibirama community, as in many others around the globe, there were no legal rules codified in discourse. In the absence of such rules, the tendency in twentieth-century thought has been to see roles — made up of rights and duties — as inhering in behavior or riding along with it. Robert Merton (1968: 41), for example, referred to roles as "the behavior of status-occupants that is oriented toward the patterned expectations of others (who accord the rights and exact the obligations)." And Talcott Parsons (1951: 25) defined the role as "what the actor does in his relations with others seen in the context of its functional significance for the social system."

What I wish to propose is the existence of a missing level, a *tertium quid*. On the one side, we have rights and duties as rules codified in circulating discourse — "fathers must provide for the material well being of their children," for example, or "honor thy father and thy mother," from the Book of Exodus in the Bible. On the other, we have rights and duties as expressed in "behavior" or "what the actor does." But between these two levels is a third — the use of socially charged terms in momentaneously unfolding discourse. Discourse is the vehicle for expression or representation of behavior. Can we not, therefore, entertain the thought that our expectations about behavior are in some measure expectations about how it is described, about the words, assembled in specific ways, by means of which it is transmitted or circulated?

Indeed, when we think about it, it seems astonishing that this level — the inner workings of discourse expectations — has been neglected. After all, behavior is but a fleeting thing. Every instance of it can be given life only by its descriptive encoding in discourse. How else could those who did not experience the behavior firsthand pass judgment on its appropriateness or inappropriateness? How else could the opinion of a broader community be brought to bear on that evanescent thing? The behavior can be "oriented to the patterned expectations of others," in Merton's words, only because the discourse in which it is descriptively encoded circulates in a broader community.

What proof can we marshall that role expectations reside in discourse, rather than the behavior described by the discourse? Important evidence comes from myths. These are stories that are told and retold, circulating throughout the community, and filtering across the generations. Yet they have no counterpart in sensible behavior. No one at P. I. Ibirama witnessed the events recounted in the story of Nẽwo, from which our earlier examples were extracted. The events described — like Berkeley's tree — have no phenomenal basis for anyone alive today. Despite this, from the narratively deployed kinship terms arise powerful expectations, without which, indeed, the story would not work. Let us examine it more closely:

| | | | |
|---|---|---|---|
| 1. | nẽwo tẽ tõ põn we kũ | 1. | Nẽwo had seen the snake[spirit]. |
| 2. | kũ ti ẽ tõ põn tẽ wèg gèke kũ | 2. | And during the time when he would always see the snake [spirit], |
| 3. | ti y̲i tõ kaklozàl zi u ñã | 3. | his <u>daughter</u> Kaklozàl was beautiful. |
| 4. | kũ kòñgàg òg ẽ tõ zi mlè wẽ cul gèke | 4. | And men would want to speak with her. |
| 5. | kũ òg ti to mũ | 5. | And they would go to him, |
| 6. | kũ òg ti mõ | 6. | and they would say to him: |
| 7. | y̲ug ẽñ ñõ wãmèn | 7. | "Father, tell me stories." |
| 8. | gèke | 8. | So it was repeatedly. |
| 9. | kũ tã òg mõ wãmèn nẽñã | 9. | And he would tell them stories |
| 10. | utã kutïg gèke | 10. | until it became dark always. |
| 11. | kũ tã hã | 11. | And then it was the man [who would say]: |
| 12. | y̲ug hãlò nũ nõ yè | 12. | "Father, where will I sleep?" |
| 13. | kèke mũ | 13. | So [he said] repeatedly. |
| 14. | ãtã lò zi mlè nõ | 14. | "Over there, sleep with her." |
| 15. | kũ kòñgàg tẽ zi mlè nõ gèke mũ | 15. | And the man would sleep with her. |
| 16. | kũ tã to mã nõ ñã | 16. | And he [the father] listened |
| 17. | tã ti nũl | 17. | for him to be asleep. |
| 18. | kũ tã to klẽkàki tẽ tã nèñ tõ toglẽn | 18. | And he would glue his hair together with beeswax, |
| 19. | kũ tã tõ kïmke | 19. | and he would cut [it]. |
| 20. | kũ tã ẽ tõ põn wèg gèke mũ | 20. | And he would always see the snake [spirit], |

| | | | |
|---|---|---|---|
| 21. | kū tā ti to mò tē kèke mū | 21. | and he would always bring it to him. |
| 22. | ti mò tē kèke mū | 22. | When he brought it, |
| 23. | kū tā ti ñān ki zun mū | 23. | he would throw it in his mouth. |
| 24. | kū kòñgàg tē tï kèke mū | 24. | And the man would always die. |
| 25. | kòñgàg tē tï kèke kū | 25. | When the man would die, |
| 26. | òg ē tō we yè cul gèke | 26. | they would always want to see [why]. |
| 27. | kū ū wū ti to tē kèke mū | 27. | And one would go to him. |
| 28. | yug ēñ ñō wāmèn | 28. | "Father, tell me stories," |
| 29. | gèke | 29. | [he would say] repeatedly. |
| 30. | kū tā òg mō wāmèn gèke ñā | 30. | And he would habitually tell them stories |
| 31. | tā kutïg gèke | 31. | until it became dark always. |
| 32. | kū tā | 32. | And then he [would say]: |
| 33. | yug hālò nū nō yè | 33. | "Father, where will I sleep?" |
| 34. | gèke | 34. | So [he said] repeatedly. |
| 35. | kū tā | 35. | And he [said]: |
| 36. | ātā lò zi mlè nō | 36. | "Over there, sleep with her." |
| 37. | gèke | 37. | So it continued, |
| 38. | kū tā zi mlè nō kèke mū | 38. | and he slept with her. |
| 39. | kū tā ti nūl to mā gèke ñā | 39. | And he always listened to him sleep. |
| 40. | ti nūl gèke | 40. | When he would sleep, |
| 41. | kū tā wèg tē | 41. | he would see [this]. |
| 42. | ti klē kàki tē tā nèy tòg to pèmke | 42. | He would glue his hair with beeswax, |
| 43. | kū tā kïm gèke mū. | 43. | and he would cut it. |
| 44. | kïm | 44. | When [he] cut [it], |
| 45. | kū tā pèyu | 45. | he would hide it, |
| 46. | kū nēm | 46. | and leave [it], |
| 47. | kū tā kulag gèke | 47. | and when the next day would dawn, |
| 48. | kū tā mò tē gèke mū | 48. | he would take it. |
| 49. | mò tē | 49. | [He] would take [it], |
| 50. | kū tā pōn tē ñān ki zun gèke mū | 50. | and he would always throw it in the snake's mouth. |
| 51. | kū kòñgàg tē tï kèke mū | 51. | And the man would always die. |
| 52. | kèke | 52. | So it was. |
| 53. | kū òg we yè cul kèke mū | 53. | And they always wanted to see [why]. |
| 54. | hālike kū nēwo tē yògzē pi wè | 54. | "How was Nēwo doing this?" |

| | | | |
|---|---|---|---|
| 55. | kèke ñā | 55. | So it continued. |
| 56. | u wũ wel ti to katẽ man mũ | 56. | Another really came to him again. |
| 57. | kòñgàg lègle tã kàglãn mũ | 57. | Two men he killed. |
| 58. | kũ ũ wũ | 58. | And one [said]: |
| 59. | yè nũ pi tòg wèg nĩ | 59. | "If I could see [what he did]," |
| 60. | ke mũ | 60. | he said. |
| 61. | ne kũ ti yògzẽ pi wè | 61. | "What could he be doing?" |
| 62. | kũ tã ti to katẽ | 62. | And he came to him. |
| 63. | kũ tã | 63. | And he [said]: |
| 64. | yug ẽñ ñõ wãmèn | 64. | "Father, tell me stories," |
| 65. | ge | 65. | [he] said. |
| 66. | kũ tã ti mõ wãmèn gèke ñẽ | 66. | And he continued telling him stories |
| 67. | ñā tã kutïg tẽ | 67. | until it became dark. |
| 68. | kũ tã | 68. | And then he [said]: |
| 69. | yug hãlò nũ yè nõ yè | 69. | "Father, where will I sleep?" |
| 70. | kũ tã | 70. | And he [said]: |
| 71. | ãtã lò zi mlè nõ | 71. | "Over there, sleep with her," |
| 72. | ke mũ | 72. | he said. |
| 73. | kũ tã zi mlè nõ | 73. | And he slept with her. |
| 74. | kũ tã ti nũl to mãg gèke ñā | 74. | And he listened to him sleep. |
| 75. | tã ti nũl | 75. | When he slept, |
| 76. | ti klẽ kàki tẽ tã nèy tòg to tõpèmke | 76. | he glued his hair with beeswax, |
| 77. | kũ tã tõ kïmke mũ. | 77. | and he cut it, |
| 78. | kũ tã gïñ mõ nẽm | 78. | and he placed it above [in the thatch], |
| 79. | kũ tã punke | 79. | and he did it slowly. |
| 80. | kũ tã ti wèg nõ | 80. | And he [the other man] was looking. |
| 81. | to ti tõlẽl yògcal | 81. | He took care to pretend |
| 82. | tã nũl nõ | 82. | that he was sleeping. |
| 83. | ñãglò tã ti klẽ kàki tẽ kïm | 83. | However, when he cut his hair, |
| 84. | tẽkũ tã ti li kèn | 84. | he did the same as him. |
| 85. | tã ti to mãg ñā | 85. | He listened to him. |
| 86. | tã ti nũl | 86. | When he slept, |
| 87. | tẽkũ tã ti tõ ẽ klẽ kàki kïm tẽ mag tã mú | 87. | he fetched the hair that he had cut. |
| 88. | man | 88. | [He] fetched [it], |
| 89. | kũ tã nèy mẽ ẽ klẽ kàki tẽ tõ mẽ tolen hòn | 89. | and removed all of his hair that was [stuck] all over the beeswax. |
| 90. | kũ tã ti <u>yi zi</u> klẽ kïki hã to tã nẽm | 90. | And it was his [Newo's] <u>daughter's</u> hair he got, |

91. to tõ pègké
92. kũ tã kïm mũ
93. kũ tã ẽ tõ kïm
94. tẽ kũ tã ti tõ nẽm ya tẽ ka nẽm mũ
95. kũ tã nõ mũ
96. kũ tã to ti tõlẽl gèke ñã
97. ñãglò tã kulag
98. tẽkũ tã man
99. kũ tã tẽ mũ
100. kũ tã ti nu tẽ mũ

101. ti nu tã ti pawañ tẽ kèke ñã

102. põn tẽ wũ zàg tug zake ka nẽ

103. kũ tã põn tẽ ẽ tõ ti mã
104. tẽ kũ tã ti to katèle mũ
105. ñãglò tã wañmèyu

106. kũ tã ti wèg ñã
107. tã ti mõ nẽm mũ

108. ti ñãn ki zun tẽ

109. tã tẽ mũ
110. kũ tã ti yògnẽgàñ tà tã wèg ñã

111. hã tõ pi kũ togli kèke

112. kòñgàg tẽ tèn gèke mũ
113. ge
114. wèg tẽ
115. tã an mõ tẽ mũ
116. an mõ tẽ
117. kũ tã pẽ hòn mũ
118. pẽ hòn
119. kũ tã mò katẽ
120. wàg tug tẽ tã mẽ tugzen
121. kũ zigzig ge ñã
122. kàpũn
123. kũ zàgtug tẽ yake tẽ ka nẽm mũ

91. [and he] stuck it [on the beeswax],
92. and he cut [it].
93. And when he had cut [it],
94. he put it in the same place as he [Nẽwo] had.
95. And he lay down,
96. but he remained on the alert.
97. Then, when morning came,
98. he [Nẽwo] took [it],
99. and he went.
100. And he [the other man] went after him.

101. He went after him always espying [him].

102. The snake was in a hole in a dry araucaria pine.

103. And when the snake heard him,
104. he descended [the tree] to him.
105. Meanwhile, he [the other man] was concealed,

106. and he was watching.
107. He [Nẽwo] gave it to him [the snake].

108. When [he] threw it in his [the snake's] mouth,

109. he left.
110. And from behind him he was watching.

111. "So that's how he has been doing it,

112. repeatedly killing the men,"
113. [he] said [or thought].
114. [He] watched,
115. then he went to a distant place.
116. He went to a distant place,
117. and he made fire.
118. [He] made fire,
119. and he brought [it] back.
120. He put dried bamboo over it,
121. and left [it]
122. [until it] burned.
123. And [he] put [it] in the hole in the dry araucaria pine.

124. kũ põn tẽ ẽ pũl tẽ
125. kũ tã juuuu ke
126. kũ tã ẽ tẽ ya tẽ tà

127. mãg mũ
128. kũ tã mã
129. kũ to katẽ mũ
130. ñãglò tã pũl kan mũ

131. kũ ti yi tõ kaklozàl tẽ zi kògò mũ
132. ẽ kògò
133. tẽkũ zi pènke mũ

134. ẽ lõ
135. kũ zi plãl kaklozàl tẽ zi
136. kũ zi nõ tẽ zi wũ zi mõ
137. kaklozàl wãñkàpey tẽ
138. ñãglò zi yògzẽ hã wã

139. ẽ tõ kuyà tẽ
140. kũ zi yògzẽ hã wã

141. wãñkàpey tẽ
142. yè a hà tẽ
143. ge mũ
144. kũ zi mã
145. kũ ẽ mõ wãñkàpèg mũ
146. ñãglò kakò mõ
147. ñãglò zi yug tẽ tawig mũ
148. kũ zi yug tẽ zi yògzẽ hãlike
149. kũ tã lõ
150. kũ kucug
151. kũ tã ẽ tawi
152. kũ tã plãl
153. zõ tã mũ
154. hã wũ ti plãl togtẽ
155. kũ tã
156. hã tõ ẽñ yi zi
157. hã tõ wãñkàgnãg mũ
158. ke
159. kũ zi yi tẽ zi ti mũ
160. zi tel

124. And the snake, when it burned,
125. it went "juuuu."
126. And from where he [Nẽwo] had gone,
127. [he] heard [it].
128. And when he heard [it],
129. [he] came back there.
130. However, it [the snake] had [already] burned up.
131. And his daughter Kaklozàl became ill.
132. When she became sick,
133. spots [or wounds] appeared [on her body].
134. She had a fever,
135. and she cried, Kaklozàl [did].
136. And her mother [said] to her:
137. "Kaklozàl, go to wash yourself!"
138. since this was her way of doing things.
139. She was a shaman,
140. and this was her way of doing things.
141. "Go to wash yourself!
142. You will feel better,"
143. [she] said.
144. And she listened [to her mother],
145. and she washed herself,
146. but it didn't help.
147. Meanwhile, her father arrived.
148. And her father was like her,
149. and he had a fever,
150. and was red
151. and, when he arrived,
152. he cried.
153. He ritually wailed [for the dead],
154. that is what his crying was.
155. And he [said]:
156. "For sure, my daughter,
157. for sure [I] have erred,"
158. [he] said.
159. And his daughter died.
160. When she died,

| | |
|---|---|
| 161. tèkù tǎ tel kàgnǎg gèke n̄à | 161. he almost died [lit., "he repeatedly erred at dying"]. |
| 162. tǎ lḗl mū | 162. [But] he lived. |
| 163. nēwo tē ti lēl | 163. Nēwo lived, |
| 164. tèkū̃ tǎ nē̃ kèke mū | 164. and remained there. |
| 165. n̄ǎglò ti yi tē zi tï mū | 165. However, his daughter died. |
| 166. kū ̀og tõ nēwo tē tõ kòñgàg põn mõ ̀og klē̃ kàki mag gèke tē we hǎ wǎ | 166. And they saw that Nēwo gave men to the snake, habitually taking their hair. |
| 167. hǎ wū̃ ti pūn mū | 167. It is for this reason they burned it [the snake]. |

A kinship term is used here first in line 3. If the narrator simply wanted to refer to Kaklozàl, he could have used her name without the kinship term. But how little discursive sense this would make! Indeed, if we did not know that Kaklozàl was Nēwo's daughter, there would be no story at all. That she is defined as his "daughter" (lit., "female child") sets up narrative expectations; these, in turn, make the story click. Why would men, desirous of talking with this beautiful woman, come to talk to Nēwo? It is because Nēwo is the beautiful woman's father. The relationship of father and daughter establishes discursive expectations and understandings, and channels feelings. In particular, we understand that the father controls sexual access to his daughter. Moreover, we understand that he cares for her — that his is a caring relationship with respect to her. He would be deeply pained, should any adversity befall her. You will note that we are not talking here about something in the real world apart from discourse. We are talking about expectations regarding the unfolding of discourse.

Already in line 90, a sense of tragedy is aroused. Here the kinship term *yi* (child) crops up a second time. Our anonymous hero has cut a lock of hair — Nēwo's daughter's hair. By remarking the kinship connection between Nēwo and Kaklozàl, the narrator (who, incidentally, was my neighbor Wāñēkï) signals the impact this action will have on Nēwo. The hero substitutes Nēwo's daughter's hair for his own. The lock of hair in the ball of wax becomes a trope of kinship. It matters to Nēwo whose hair is stuck to the wax. If it is the young man's hair, Nēwo can rub his hands together in evil anticipation. If it is the young woman's hair, however — his "daughter's" hair — then we know that misfortune awaits.

The kinship term alerts us, the audience, that whatever hurts the daughter will also hurt her father. Though he had been seemingly unaffected by the deaths of the young men, her death would strike him deeply. The men were nothing to him; they were nonrelatives. However, she was his daughter. Though he had been wicked, consorting with the snake spirit, we feel for him. It is the kinship term that channels our emotion. We feel for him because we can imagine how we would feel ourselves, were it our own daughter.

The theme of parental caring is brought home by the sequence of events in lines 131 through 161. In line 131, note, it is not just Kaklozàl who becomes sick; it is Nēwo's daughter. As an audience, we know that her sickness will matter to Nēwo. The sequence from 136 through 146, indeed, forms a microcosm of the broader tragedy. A new character is introduced here — Kaklozàl's mother. Like the relationship between father and daughter, that between mother and daughter evokes expectations of caring. As if to confirm these expectations, the mother sends her daughter to wash herself — listeners at P. I. Ibirama recognize this as a method for curing fever — and the daughter obeys, as is discursively expectable in this relationship, but the cure fails.

We do not yet learn that Kaklozàl is to die. For this to happen, and to bring closure to our story, we must await Nēwo's return. It was his nefarious deeds that led to this tragic situation, and, sure enough, in line 147 he returns. But he returns now not as Nēwo but as Kaklozàl's father. As if to make sure we heard it the first time, the usage is repeated in line 148.

Lines 149 and 150, as well as 160 through 162, remind us that Kaklozàl's sickness and death affect Nēwo as well. The evil shaman himself becomes sick and nearly dies. Here, indeed, is the crucial moment of the tragedy. Nēwo recognizes his *hamartia*, his own fatal flaw. While weeping over his daughter, he laments, "for sure, my daughter, for sure [I] have erred." We can almost hear him mourn, "I should not have consorted with the snake spirit; I should not have appeased the snake spirit; I should not have led those men to their death. As a result of my deeds, I must lose my daughter." This is tragedy. Nēwo's pain is all the harder to bear because he does not die. He must live with his memories, with the certain knowledge that he caused his daughter's death.

So the kinship terms *yug* (father), *nõ* (mother), and *yi* ("child," which can be inflected with the feminine marker *zi* to yield "daughter") are not just linguistic devices for achieving stability of reference. They do not only maintain discourse cohesion. Because of their discourse presuppositions and entailments, they create narrative expectations. They charge the narrative with poignancy, and, by doing so, they make it work. Without kinship — and, discursively, without kinship terms — Kaklozàl's death might have been insignificant. It might have meant nothing more than the deaths of the first two young men. However, because she is Nēwo's daughter, because he cares for her, and because we, as an audience, appreciate all this (through the kinship terms), therefore her death is tragic. The story leaves us with complex feelings toward its main character — an evil shaman, but a loving father.

What about the young men? From a discourse perspective, their reported usage of kinship terms is a most intriguing feature. Each of the three youths calls Nēwo *yug* (father). The kinship terms, indeed, form the poetic backbone of the first half of this narrative. Through line 80, the narrative consists in three repeated episodes. In each, the young man arrives, converses with Nēwo, and asks where he should sleep. We find a word-for-word repetition, especially of those lines reporting the young man's speech. I have excerpted the relevant segments below:

| | | | |
|---|---|---|---|
| 7. | yug ēñ ñō wāmèn | 7. | "Father, tell me stories." |
| 12. | yug hālò nū nō yè | 12. | "Father, where will I sleep?" |
| 28. | yug ēñ ñō wāmèn | 28. | "Father, tell me stories," |
| 33. | yug hālò nū nō yè | 33. | "Father, where will I sleep?" |
| 64. | yug ēñ ñō wāmèn | 64. | "Father, tell me stories," |
| 69. | yug hālò nū yè nō yè | 69. | "Father, where will I sleep?" |

What is so striking is that the young man calls Nēwo "father." The narrator cajoles us into recognizing this by his persistent repetition. He drums the word *yug* into our heads, rhythmically pounding it out in line after line. And he thereby sets up a contrast with his later use of the word in lines 147 and 148.

What is the nature of that contrast? In the earlier lines, "father" is used as a term of address. It contributes nothing to the propositional content of the reported expression. In each case, it is a device for attracting the elder man's attention — like the exclamation "father!" But it is not only that; it also does something else. It establishes, or rather, attempts to establish, a social bond. In the language of the previous chapter, it lays down a roadway along which discourse and culture more generally can circulate. We are reminded of the contact narrative — Wòmle and Eduardo reportedly calling each other *ēñ kake* (my relative). Indeed, in the myth, discourse circulation is explicitly described. The young man says in each case, "tell me stories." And the older man tells him stories.

Alas, the young men's strategy here fails, at least in the first two cases. The young men call the older man "father," expecting thereby to create a caring relationship. Superficially, they succeed. The old man tells them stories. Then they ask the old man where they should sleep, and, as if he could read their innermost desires, their secret wishes, he tells them to sleep next to the beautiful woman. Surely, he must have their best interests at heart. But the old man betrays them. At night, he cuts a lock of their hair, affixes it to beeswax, and feeds it to the snake spirit. The young men die. No "father" would do this to his son.

From a linguistic point of view, the contrast is between this vocative use of "father" and the referential use found in lines 147 and 148:

| | |
|---|---|
| 147. ñãglò zi yug tẽ tawig mũ | 147. Meanwhile, her <u>father</u> arrived. |
| 148. kũ zi yug tẽ zi yògzẽ hãlike | 148. And her <u>father</u> was like her, |

Here the term *yug* contributes to our understanding of the referential meaning of the utterance. In line 147, it is part of a phrase that is the subject of the verb "arrive" — who arrived? It was her father. In line 148, it is part of a noun phrase in a comparative construction — who was like her? It was her father who was like her.

A key here is that in lines 148 and 149 the narrator himself uses the term "father." And he uses it matter-of-factly, as if he were merely describing something in the world — "her father." The social relationship is solid, real, extradiscursive. It is simply out there, in the world, like a phenomenally accessible object that is linguistically described. The feeling of solidity is enhanced by the contrast between these usages and those in the earlier portion of the narrative. There the young men were trying to create a social relationship where it did not already exist. Here the relationship existed prior to its linguistic constitution by the protagonists in their reported speech. The contrast intensifies our feeling that the latter kind of social relationship is a thing, an entity prior to its linguistic constitution.

But, of course, both kinds of usage — vocative/road-building and referential/descriptive — are here only part of discourse. The only sensible object is the sound of the words or their visible shapes on paper. Yet the narrative furnishes us with an understanding of the objects lying behind the surface of appearance — the noumena. There are real roles, real fathers that are such not only in name but also in deed. And the narrative itself circulates in perceptible space, ensuring the circulation of the noumenal understandings. Ironically, perhaps, the narrative circulates in the same kind of social setting as that it describes — young men sitting with the fathers of their wives or potential wives, listening to stories. Recall that day in May of 1982, when Kañã'ï was the principal storyteller. Among his audience was Kuzug, his daughter's husband.

Through the watery surface of discourse, we glimpse the *universitas juris* — the "bundle of rights and duties" we call a role. We infer it from the discourse articulations of terms, in this case, kin terms. Thus, *yug* (father) proves to be not just the reciprocal of *yi* (child), nor only the masculine complement of *nõ* (mother). The term also engages a set of discourse expectations. We infer the "father's" right to control over sexual access to his female child. We infer that it is his duty to care for that child. Were we to study all of the discourse interrelationships into which *yug* enters, superimposing them like transparencies laid atop one another on an overhead projector, we would have our fullest possible image of the role of "father" at P. I. Ibirama.

Our key methodological technique in each instance is to ask: Why use the kinship term here rather than a pronoun or proper or common noun? What does the term add to the narrative? What discourse relationships do we infer from it? What kinds of expectations do we have as a result of its use?

In the "Land above the Sky" narrative, discussed in Chapter 3, the term *nūgñēn* ("sibling," used with a male proper name to yield "brother") occurs in the very first line. Why is it there? Why not, in this mythical story, simply designate the two men by proper names? This is certainly linguistically possible. If we examine the first six lines, however, we see that the term *nūgñēn* occurs not just once, but actually twice. A listener or reader cannot miss it:

| | |
|---|---|
| 1. kuyankàg tĕ wū ĕ <u>nūgñēn</u> tĕ mõ tã | 1. Kuyankàg said to his <u>brother</u>: |
| 2. yugug tõ | 2. "When the falcon, |
| 3. kòñgàg tĕ òg wun kū òg ko gèke ñã | 3. who has been carrying off men and eating them, |
| 4. li ĕñ cõ ken | 4. does this to me, |
| 5. kū mã ĕñ kukò tĕ tu yè tapã | 5. you go up there to get my bones." |
| 6. ke tã ĕ <u>nūgñēn</u> tõ klañmàg tĕ mõ | 6. So he said to his <u>brother</u> Klañmàg |

At the same time, we appreciate that from a linguistic point of view only an elementary change would be needed to eliminate the kinship terms. Line 1 might read:

kuyankàg tĕ wū ĕ <u>nūgñēn</u> tĕ mõ tã    →    kuyankàg tĕ wū <u>klañmàg</u> tĕ mõ tã
"Kuyankàg said to <u>his brother</u>"    →    "Kuyankàg said to <u>Klañmàg</u>"

And line 6 might become:

ke tã ĕ <u>nūgñēn</u> tõ klañmàg tĕ mõ    →    ke tã <u>klañmàg</u> tĕ mõ
"So he said to <u>his brother Klañmàg</u>"    →    "So he said to <u>Klañmàg</u>"

So here is the puzzle: Why use the kinship term?

The answer is intuitively obvious. The term *nūgñēn* (brother) fills us with expectations. We imagine that Klañmàg will try to do what "his brother" has asked him to do. Were the two men above unrelated, were the kinship term omitted, we would be forced to await the subsequent discourse to make inferences about the relationship between them. Because it is used, however, we already have a sense about the discourse participants. They are brothers, and brothers owe it to one another to do as the other asks. In the language of roles, brothers have a right to expect loyalty from one another; they have a duty to do as the other requests.

If we were not already familiar with these expectations, we might infer them from this narrative. Such an inference would in turn inform our future interpretations. Of course, from the point of view of ethnography, as well as of learnability of culture, this is crucial. Expectations can be inferred from use, just as use kindles expectations. Discourse is the stuff from which roles can be ethnographically recovered, as well as the locus of circulation of those roles themselves.

Note that expectations associated with the term *nūgñēn* are distinct from those associated with *yug, nō*, and *yi*. The latter are characterized by caring of an asymmetrical variety. The difference may be best captured in the arena of commands. In the case of siblings, a command obeyed represents a favor to the commander. The sibling who follows the command is doing something for the sibling who issued it. When Kuyankàg tells his brother to go fetch his (Kuyankàg's) bones, it is in order to help Kuyankàg, to bring him back to life. The command benefits the issuer.

Parents, however, issue commands because, if the child obeys, it will be good for the child. In the story of Nēwo, this is true of the mother of Kaklozàl:

| | |
|---|---|
| 136. kū zi nō̲ tē zi wū zi mō̲ | 136. And her <u>mother</u> [said] to her: |
| 137. kaklozàl wãñkàpey tē | 137. "Kaklozàl, <u>go to wash yourself!</u>" |

Why does she issue this command? There is no direct benefit to her. It is rather because the mother wants to help out, to take care of her daughter. The command is for the daughter's benefit. The command benefits the one commanded. Whereas each of a pair of siblings knows what is good for himself or herself, in the parent-child relationship it is the parent who knows better. Whereas the sibling issues a command out of self-interest, counting on the obligation of the other to comply, a parent issues a command altruistically, knowing that it is in the best interest of the child. So the expectations surrounding *nūgñēn* and *yug* are distinct. The former suggests loyalty and obligation, the latter caring.

In the case of siblings and parents and children, the discursively constituted role relations are familiar to Westerners. We might dispute the right of a father to control sexual access to his daughter, but that is not so foreign to our narrativizations. Certainly, the caring relationship of parent to child, and the loyalty among siblings, sound a familiar chord. Husband and wife relations, however, are differently narrativized. A key discursive expectation in this case is a surprisingly formal respect, which goes along with the more familiar loyalty and companionship. You will search in vain for a discursive encoding of romantic love or even verbal intimacy — no sharing of knowledge and secrets.

This peculiarity of husband-wife relations illuminates the story of how women got breasts (Chapter 2), which perhaps seemed quirky or whimsical. Here is the original framing:

| | |
|---|---|
| 3. tà tẽ klã gèke | 3. women would bear the children, |
| 4. kũ yi òg mèn tõ kòñgàg hã yi wũ nũgñe mũ | 4. and, it is said, <u>their husbands</u>, who were men, had breasts, |
| 5. kũ yi òg ẽ klã tẽ pèzam gèke mũ | 5. and, it is said, they would breast-feed the children. |

As in previous examples, the kinship term functions here to introduce a discourse participant. Note, however, that the introduction could have been accomplished by using only the common noun "men" — "and, it is said, the men had breasts . . ." Why use the kinship term here? Evidently, it is because the term sets up expectations. The narrator signals the centrality of kinship by using the reciprocal term "wives" in line 7 and, later, in lines 14 and 15:

| | |
|---|---|
| 7. kèke ñã yi wũ kòñgàg ũ yi ti <u>plũ</u> yi lègle ñãgnẽ | 7. So it continued, it is said, until one man had two <u>wives</u>, |
| 14. kũ yi tã ẽ <u>plũ</u> tẽ òg mlè tẽ | 14. And, it is said, he went with his wives. |
| 15. ẽ <u>plũ</u> tẽ òg mlè tẽ | 15. When he went with <u>his wives</u>. |

Here, however, Western expectations fail us; they are out of sync with those in the P. I. Ibirama community. Hence, the story seems so odd, quirky, whimsical. The man ascends an araucaria pine. His breasts, full of milk, flap up and down. No doubt an amusing scene, but it would be disrespectful for a wife to laugh at her husband. Narrative tension is built around this problem: a funny situation, but one in which a wife is expected to control herself. To laugh at her husband would be to disrespect him. A P. I. Ibirama listener hangs on the words and wants to know: Can the wives control themselves? And the answer is no. The women succumb. They violate role expectations, which are, of course, simultaneously discourse expectations surrounding the kinship terms "husband" (*mèn*) and "wife" (*plũ*). Indeed, at the crucial moment, the narrator drives the point home by using the kinship term:

| | |
|---|---|
| 20. kũ yi ti <u>plũ</u> tẽ òg yi nïg mũ | 20. And, it is said, <u>his wives</u>, it is said, laughed. |

Note, it is not the "women" who laughed; it is the "wives." The violated expectations here pertain to relations between husbands and wives, not men and women.

We learn something ethnographically significant, but we learn it the hard way, by studying kinship terms and making inferences about the discourse expectations surrounding them. Western intuition is inadequate in this case. Consequently, we either dismiss the story as odd, or try to fathom what other expectations might be at work. Ours is an empirical encounter with an ethnographic object, but the object is not actual behavior — laughing in a real-world context. It is discourse. It is a narrativization of behavior, which, in this case, was not witnessed by any of those presently circulating the discourse. Nevertheless, because the discourse is sensible as well as intelligible, because it externally constrains interpretation, it forces us, as ethnographers, to rethink our presuppositions, to formulate cultural differences, attributing them to roles.

Where do the expectations regarding kinship roles reside? I have insisted that they reside in the relationships among linguistic elements within unfolding discourse. The expectations are discursive suppositions about the lexical items we call kinship terms. If a term is used, we expect discourse to unfold in a particular way; we anticipate dramatic effects.

Kinship expectations are crucial to the stories we have been discussing. At the same time, these stories — these myths — are only discourse. There is no real Nēwo — at least none with whom any living member of the P. I. Ibirama community has had firsthand contact. Nēwo subsists only in the mind, nourished by words. The role expectations surrounding him are nothing more (or less) than expectations surrounding the unfolding of discourse. Our ethnographic method is this: In any particular instance, ask why a kinship term, rather than some other linguistic designator, has been used. The very method suggests that kinship roles reside in discourse.

So we may ask: If role relations involve discourse expectations, is a role anything more than discourse? Does it inhere in extradiscursive reality, as well as in discourse? Role expectations concern narrativization, how stories are told, events recounted, possible futures contemplated. In this sense, they are not inferences from empirically observed behaviors, at least not direct inferences. They are rather inferences from narrativizations of behaviors, some of which have never taken place.

Kinship roles, in a given culture, are read off the surface of discourse. They are metadiscursive, that is, discursive characterizations of other discourse, namely, stories and narrations of events. But they are only potentially so — the pragmatic expectations of storytellers and listeners. Whether they are publicly circulated, in the form of rules, for example, is an empirical question. In fact, at P. I. Ibirama we find no such explicitly coded norms. Nevertheless, discourse is constructed in accord with empirically recoverable expectations, and these expectations are implicit counterparts of explicitly formulated roles.

Mythical narratives are not the only kinds of stories told in this community. True, they are the most widely known stories. They are most likely to be transmitted across the generations. In this sense, they are the *materia prima* of what anthropologists traditionally called culture, with its presupposition of sharedness and transmissibility. However, there are other local, fleeting narratives of everyday life, some mere one-time recountings of a day's events, of little incidents soon to be forgotten. Not carriers of archetypal culture, these narratives nevertheless reflect archetypal culture. They are built on the model of enduring narratives, and kinship term use within them conforms to broader discourse expectations. So narrativization of everyday life is brought into the orbit of circulating discourse.

What about the everyday life that is narrativized? Is it possible that individuals orient their sensible behavior so as to conform to intelligible narratives? Do they act out roles because of the way they want their lives narrativized, or, alternatively, because of how they have previously narrativized a future? If so, we can think of domestic morality as a kind of localized categorical imperative à la Kant — act such that your behavior can be narrativized in accord with the discourse expectations operative in your community.

To be sure, any behavior can be narrativized. The question is whether narrativization displays your behavior flatteringly, as according with discourse expectations. Or, like the laughing wives, will you be portrayed in violation of them? Perhaps behavior that violates expectations is more regularly narrativized than behavior that conforms to it. In that case, the command may be to act so as to minimize the possibility that your behavior will be narrativized in the first place, and so that, if it is narrativized, your behavior conforms to discourse expectations. Safer to remain unspoken than to be spoken of badly.

In either case, narratives of behavior and behavior that is narrativized come into contact. Words become flesh, just as flesh transmogrifies in the alembic of words. Either conduct directly imitates art — think of Ãglò's acting out of the "Goes Living" story in Chapter 3 — or it silently conforms to the expectations that art, as a means to an effect, so dramatically violates. If roles are discourse expectations, some discourse is, nevertheless, about extradiscursive behavior. While it may be impossible to directly infer roles from the observation of extradiscursive behavior, that behavior is shaped by discourse. It is pulled into the force field of discourse — like a comet whose trajectory is deflected by gravity, acting mysteriously at a distance.

From Lewis Henry Morgan's perspective, it may seem that something is lost in the discourse approach to kinship. After all, Morgan's point was that the "classificatory system" found among the Iroquois (and others) was a *system*. That is, its parts hung together. This notion of kinship as systematic carried over into subsequent approaches, whether that of kinship terms as part of an abstract system of language, as advocated by Kroeber, and later by Lounsbury, Goodenough, and the ethnosemanticists; or kinship terms as labels for a system of social roles, as in the original analysis by Tylor and W. H. R. Rivers, who insisted upon the priority of social groupings — in this case, unilineal exogamous moieties.

But I must confess to holding something back, something that sheds light on this question of systematicity. Before telling you what it is, however, let me review and extend the critique of systematicity, which is simultaneously a critique of Saussure's concept of *langue*, or language as system. I have suggested that, in the absence of glossing, or dictionary-like defining, as a discourse practice within a community, we cannot presume that kinship terms form a contrastive set; that is, we cannot assume that they are definable with respect to one another. The interview method introduces glossing as a type of interaction. Think of the question "By what term do you call the brother of your mother?" The very question juxtaposes terms that might otherwise never enter into contact. In so doing, it creates what it purports to observe — kinship terms as an isolable system. It thereby risks distortion: If we employ the questioning method, how can we know whether the system we discover is in the heads of our informants, or is merely a residue of our externally imposed discourse strategy?

You must look to publicly occurring discourse to find systematicity. There you will find linkages among the terms *yug* (father), *nō* (mother), and *yi* (child), such as I have already described. And you will infer the connections between *mèn* (husband) and *plū* (wife). You will even discover discourse contexts in which these two sets of terms enter into contact. In the "Goes Living" story, for example, you will find the terms *mèn* and *nō* co-occurring in the same stretch of discourse, and you can gauge the nature and degree of interrelation between them.

You will discover, however, that some terms seem never to interact. Where terms occupy distinct niches, distinct discourse spaces, you may question the reality of the "system." At P. I. Ibirama, the term *yòmlè* (in-law) furnishes evidence of fragmentation. In no discourse context with which I am familiar does it occur with other supposed kinship terms. Many years after returning from my sojourn in Brazil, after concluding that I had confirmed Henry's and Baldus's earlier results, I began to wonder, Is it the same kind of term at all? In fact, in actual discourse it functions primarily as a verb: *yòmlèn* or *yòmlan* (pl. *yàgmlan*). Here is an instance:

| | |
|---|---|
| 1. kũ òg wãñõ kàkzèg nõñã | 1. And they were content. |
| 2. wãcõ nã yè tòge | 2. "Now it is done, |
| 3. kũ nã ãg tõ wãñõ <u>yàgmlan</u> | 3. and we have become <u>in-laws</u>." |

And it never occurs in close propinquity to other kinship terms.

Interestingly, it occurs in none of the household myths I have studied, being confined, instead, to the origin myth. An intriguing aspect of that myth is that it has a distinct sociospatial locus. It is told in the central dance plaza, principally at ceremonies for the dead. I should not exaggerate this contrast. It is also told, albeit in less formal style, in the household. However, the household myths are never told in the dance plaza. So the supposed kinship term *yòmlè* (in-law) occupies not only a distinct discourse space, but also a distinct sociophysical space.

Why is this significant? The contrast is not just anti-systematic evidence. It is evidence as well of a positive desire to keep kinship and affinity distinct, to create a two-level community. On one level, there is the household; it is built around terms like *yug* (father), *nõ* (mother), *yi* (child), *mèn* (husband), and *plũ* (wife). On the other level, there is the community; it is built around *yòmlè* (in-laws), as well as terms of more distant relationship, such as *kòñka* (relative). Isolating relational terms in this way simultaneously opposes family and broader society, and it is around this opposition that social life, at P. I. Ibirama, has intellectually unfolded.

Strikingly, only one nuclear family kinship term can be found in the more than hour-long origin myth narrative; this is the term for "father" (*yug*), which occurs principally in one small segment. There is no linguistic interaction between this term and the others. The entire segment containing the term *yug* is given below:

| | |
|---|---|
| 1. kũ yi òg ti mõ | 1. And, it is said, they [said] to him: |
| 2. pazi ne yè mã zõ mũ | 2. "Pazi, why are you ritually wailing [for the dead]?" |
| 3. ke mũ | 3. [they] said. |
| 4. pazi tẽ òg ñãn kugmã mũ hà we | 4. Pazi said nothing indeed to them. |
| 5. kũ tã ti mõ ẽ kòñka hà tõ wãñẽkï mõ tã | 5. And he [said] to him, to Wãñẽkï, |
| 6. wãñẽkï ne to mã kòñgàg tï mũ | 6. "Wãñẽkï, why did the man die? |
| 7. nã mã ñã | 7. We [want to] know. |
| 8. akle wagzun | 8. Gather together game. |
| 9. akle tõ penkãn | 9. Make *penkãn*[2] with the game." |
| 10. wãñẽkï tõ akle wagzun mũ | 10. Wãñẽkï gathered together game. |
| 11. ñãglò gòy màg zïl ki òg ẽ no yè lũlũ kàgzan nõñã | 11. Meanwhile, on the banks of the big river they put feathers on their arrows. |
| 12. ẽ no yè ẽ tõ lũlũ kàgzan kan | 12. They finished putting feathers on their arrows. |
| 13. kũ gòy màg zïl to tã ñã | 13. And they descended to the banks of the big river, |
| 14. kũ kaklo yè kïl mũ | 14. and they called the fish. |

| | |
|---|---|
| 15. lò wòlà hã yï òg klãm tul ko mū | 15. Meanwhile, the *traira*[3] fish [came] below them, eating *piava*. |
| 16. kū òg hãki ū tõ humke mū | 16. And they finished off some of them right there. |
| 17. kū mò kakutãnĕ | 17. And [they] came out with [the fish], |
| 18. kū wãñĕkï tõ akle wagzun tĕ ka zig tĕ | 18. and put it together with the game Wãñĕkï had assembled. |
| 19. òg ĕ yògwañ tõ pazi tõ ãma we to | 19. [Where] their chief Pazi saw the savanna, |
| 20. ĕ yò gò kule mĕ | 20. where he cleared their ground all about, |
| 21. òg glè nõ | 21. they were dancing. |
| 22. huli yi pazi ĕ ñã hà to | 22. Really, it is said, Pazi who always ate very much, |
| 23. ĕ ñãn kuleg | 23. whose mouth was bad, |
| 24. kū ĕ yug tï mū | 24. and whose <u>father</u> [therefore] died, |
| 25. lò òg yòkle tõ wòlà kòto ko kan mū | 25. was the first to finish eating their *traira* fish. |
| 26. pazi ne to wū a <u>yug</u> tĕ tï mū | 26. "Pazi, why did your <u>father</u> die?" |
| 27. iwo <u>yug</u> wū amĕn zaklĕ kòyuñ klè we mū za nĕ tã to | 27. "Well, above the path where <u>father</u> saw the parrot's nest, where [he always] was, in that direction, |
| 28. tã wū mlul tòl tõ kuzĕn | 28. he tied up a strong vine, |
| 29. kū kukam taplï mū | 29. and there in front climbed up. |
| 30. ti tõ ĕ lò kamlanke | 30. It broke (while) he was along there, |
| 31. kū ĕ kutã | 31. and he fell, |
| 32. kū tã kutï mū | 32. and he died." |
| 33. ĕ mõ yi òg nïg nõña | 33. They continued poking fun at him, it is said. |

What is this story all about? On its surface, it is about a man and his father—how the man was always demanding food; how the father, in his caring role, endeavored to satisfy his son; how the result was disaster. One day the father climbed up a vine to reach a parrot's nest, presumably to obtain eggs for his son. The vine broke. The father fell to the ground and died. The story is in part about the excesses of the son, possibly suggesting a role expectation—that sons should exhibit restraint in expressing desire to their fathers.

Reading the episode in this way, we see parallels with the "bird-nester" theme common among central Brazilian Amerindians. Lévi-Strauss's *The Raw and the Cooked*, indeed, began with that theme. A boy sets out in search of macaws with one of his relatives. In the Bororo story, the relative is the boy's father, who is furious at his son because he suspects the son has raped his own mother. In Lévi-Strauss's (1969b [1964]: 36) version:

". . . the father invited his son to come with him to capture the macaws, which were nesting in the face of a cliff. The grandmother did not know how to ward off this fresh danger, but gave her grandson a magic wand to which he could cling if he happened to fall. The two men arrived at the foot of the rock; the father erected a long pole and ordered his son to climb it. The latter had hardly reached the nests when the father knocked the pole down; the boy only just had time to thrust the wand into a crevice. He remained suspended in the void, crying for help, while the father went off."

Here it is the son rather than the father who climbs up. Moreover, in contrast to the P. I. Ibirama case, despite the attempt by his father to murder him, the climber survives. We can see the snippet of discourse from the P. I. Ibirama community as a structural transformation of the bird-nester theme.

At the same time, closer inspection of the P. I. Ibirama discourse reveals something strikingly different. The father-son story is embedded within a broader narrative. It occurs as reported speech, with Pazi telling about his father to other men. What significance should we attribute to this? On the one hand, the story is like the domestic morality tales—the Newo story, for example. Here we learn of the potential excesses of the father-son caring relationship. The son is too demanding, the father too compliant.

On the other hand, this segment is also about how the story, as told by Pazi, plays among the adult men. The reported episode is narrated in the context of an encompassing story in which men go about their business as men—they prepare arrows, hunt, and fish. And the response of the men to the great tragedy of Pazi's father's death is to laugh! They summarily dismiss it.

The story of Pazi's father—discursively embedded within a broader story about relations among adult men—is simultaneously subordinated to that broader story. Similarly, domestic kinship relations are subordinated to a broader field of relations among men. In the overall narrative, that field is constituted by intergroup encounters. A constant refrain is the arrival (and departure) of men:

| | |
|---|---|
| 1. wãgyò tõ zàgpope tõ patè no katèle | 1. relative Zàgpope Patè arrived in front |
| 2. kũ yi tã wũ | 2. and it is said he (said) |
| 3. ne to agèlmĕg wũ mũ ke mũ | 3. "what is all of this noise about" (he) said |

or, again:

| | |
|---|---|
| 1. wāgyò tō kïy òg nu katèle | 1. relative Kïy arrived behind them, |
| 2. tā òg glè yò ki kala mū | 2. he arrived in their dance plaza. |
| 3. ū tō kòñgàg nū ki ñā | 3. "What kind of man is this?" |
| 4. ke mū | 4. (they) said. |

The mind-bogglingly complex origin narrative seems, from this vantage, an endless stream of arrivals, of get-togethers among men who often do not know one another. The narrative describes the arena of extranuclear family contact.

Simultaneously, the origin myth's tone differs from that of the stories that portray domestic morality. This myth is told in a high style, appropriate to its role as a narrative by adults, for adults, and about adults. Even the myth's language contains numerous lexical items absent from everyday domestic speech. This is in part what distinguishes the style of the myth. Among the lexical items is the relational term *wāgyò* (relative), which appears in the two fragments given above. The term alternates with *kòñka* (relative), its everyday equivalent. We know this from a comparison of versions of the same fragment told by different speakers. The first of the two arrival passages above was narrated by Nil in 1981. The analogous passage from a narration by Wāñēkï Patè in 1982 is as follows:

| | |
|---|---|
| 1. ti kōñka hà tō zàgpope ti no katèle | 1. his kinsman Zàgpope arrived in front of him |
| 2. ti glè yò ki kala | 2. (he) arrived in his dance plaza |
| 3. ne to agèlmĕg wū mū ke mū yi tā | 3. "what is all of this noise about?" he said, it is said. |

Note that *kòñka* occurs in this 1982 version in the analogous position to *wāgyò* in the 1981 version.

What we have here is a discourse logic of kinship — a complementary narrative distribution between nuclear family terms, on the one side, and terms pertaining to affinity and more far-flung kinship, on the other. Nuclear terms occur in narratives concerned with intragroup relations, affinal terms in those with intergroup relations. The former are associated with the domestic sphere and everyday speech, the latter with communal space (the ceremonial dance plaza) and ritual speech. In the narratives of intergroup encounters, domestic relations appear in reported speech, subordinated to the broader narrative of adult activity.

Saussure argued for a distinction between *langue*, or language as a system, and *parole*, or speech. A key component of the *langue* concept was the paradigm, consisting of relations *in absentia*, that is, in contrasts between terms that could alternate with one another in the same paradigmatic slots, even though they were not juxtaposed within the same syntagmatic chain. Ethnosemanticists presumed that kinship terms could be treated as such a paradigmatically contrastive set, built up from relations *in absentia*. However, it should now be patent that the interview method employed by ethnosemanticists creates relations *in praesentia*. By asking questions about terms, it draws them together in a stream of unfolding discourse. It artificially induces a system by artificially creating a new discourse interactional type. Who else but ethnographers would think to physically juxtapose all kin terms in the contiguous flow of a single dialogic interaction?

Far better to look to the juxtapositions in actually occurring discourse. There, we find systematic interconnection — the relations among *yug* (father), *nõ* (mother), and *yi* (child), for example. But we also find disjuncture — the relationship between those terms and *yòmlè* (in-laws), for example. Disjuncture is significant not only as evidence indicting system, as ethnosemantically conceived. It is also evidence for a more complex kind of discourse logic. That discourse logic is nothing other than the social organization of the community.

I said that I have been holding something back. Let me now tell you what it is. I have been tracing two historically distinct lines of thought about kinship — one grounded in language as system and one based on social role. I have shown you how both grow out of discourse. Systematicity (or the lack thereof) is carried in the actual interconnections among kinship terms as deployed in publicly occurring discourse; and roles are only the expectations surrounding the use of those terms. What I have held back is that these two are not just related by virtue of a common origin; they are actually the same phenomenon. Interconnection among terms involves expectations associated with the deployment of a given kinship term. The expectations have to do with how those other terms will be used. But they are still expectations; they can be violated for dramatic effect.

Let me offer one small example of this kind of violation. We have systematic discourse evidence for the use of the terms *mèn* (husband) and *plū* (wife). The terms are reciprocals, and, in addition, *mèn* is typically co-referential with a masculine pronoun — *ti* or *tã* (he) — and *plū* is typically co-referential with a feminine pronoun — *zi* (she). Our expectations derive from inferences based on concrete usages, but we apply those expectations to new usages.

You will find a curious episode, however, in the story of the land above the sky. While the man searches for his brother's bones, he comes across an old woman. She informs him of the location of the bones. However, then — strange to say — she commands him to kill her, to take her place, and to prepare soup for her husband. The man literally assumes her discourse role, and the result is linguistically odd. Instead of the phrase "her husband," the seemingly oxymoronic "his husband" occurs:

| kū | tā | ẽ | mèn | mõ | zi | nẽm | ge | nẽ |
|----|-----|---------|---------|------|---------|------|-----|-------|
| and | he | co-ref. | husband | to | she (it) | give | do | cont. |

"And he gave it (was giving it) to his husband."

As I sit here, I wonder about the translation. Could I have gotten it wrong? Perhaps, but I see that the translation is actually Nānmla's — a young member of the P. I. Ibirama community who was bilingual. Moreover, I observe other obvious instances of gender inversion with respect to these kin terms in adjacent clauses. No wonder the narrator remarked, "I don't know what this means"! Our expectations about the grammar of the term *mèn* (husband) are violated.

If systematic interconnections among terms are just a form of expectation, then what influences expectations potentially influences systematic interconnections. Of course, one influence on expectations is dictionary-like definition, in those cases where a native glossing tradition operates. *Webster's Third International Dictionary* defines "husband" as "a man who on the basis of his tribal or societal institutions is considered to be married." Think of this together with its definition of "marriage" — "the state of being united to a person of the opposite sex as husband or wife." From these definitions, we would be surprised to encounter the phrase "his husband." The definitions establish expectations, but discourse violates them.

Glossing, or definition giving, however, is only one means of establishing expectations. An explicitly formulated marriage rule is another. In fact, at P. I. Ibirama I heard people utter such a rule on numerous occasions — "you must marry (sit with) someone with different paint designs (than your own)." The rule is a free-floating fragment of discourse, one that can be summoned in various situations. It is not part and parcel of a longer narrative context.

However, the rule establishes expectations about other discourse — it is a bit of metadiscourse, like a dictionary definition, even though it does not define one term by means of others, does not, in fact, invoke kinship terms at all. Because a contextual association exists between marriage and the terms *plū* (wife) and *mèn* (husband), you can make inferences about subsequent discourse from an instance of use of these terms. In particular, in a contiguous stretch of discourse, if you learned that a woman painted with certain designs, you would anticipate that *zi mèn* (her husband) painted with different ones. You would be surprised if it turned out otherwise.

The free-floating metadiscourse at P. I. Ibirama is what an older generation of social anthropologists called a rule of exogamy. However, that generation attributed little significance to the distinction between exogamy as a descriptive rule, formulated by ethnographers, and exogamy as a part of ethnographically describable discourse within a community. What I am trying to bring home to you is that the distinction is important. At P. I. Ibirama, the rule is a naturally occurring stretch of discourse. It circulates like other discourse. However, it is also about that other discourse — it is meta-discourse. And it establishes expectations about that discourse. Its ethnographically describable circulation is a key to understanding broader discourse patterns within a community.

Why does someone paint with one design rather than another? Is there an explicitly formulated rule about that as well? Indeed there is. I will come to it in the next chapter. However, I first want to tell you what the rule is not. It is not like the one I heard at P. I. Manoel Ribas, among the people called Kaingang. There the rule is formulated in terms of the father-child relationship. Its analog at P. I. Ibirama would be, "children must paint with the same designs as their father." I am simplifying, since the Kaingang rule makes no reference to paint designs. They do have designs, and the designs are transmitted in the same way as at P. I. Ibirama, that is, together with proper names. At P. I. Manoel Ribas, however, the exogamy rule actually pertains to groups — what social anthropologists call "moieties." But let me follow through with the simplification.

If a rule such as that I have described did circulate at P. I. Ibirama, a further set of expectations would develop. These are the expectations that E. B. Tylor deduced. However, now we can see them for what they are — discourse expectations rather than natural laws. Having learned that someone painted with given marks, we expect to learn that that person's father — together with his brothers and sisters — also painted with those marks. Further, we expect that the same person's mother — together with her brothers and sisters — painted with different marks. If, as discourse unfolded, we were to learn otherwise, our expectations would be violated. We would be surprised.

Now what does this have to do with kinship terminology? Insofar as the expectations concern designs, not terms, seemingly nothing. Yet there are associational effects. These depend on the expectations already present in publicly occurring discourse. And we can imagine alternative possibilities. Nevertheless, the possibilities are deducible from the rules. At P. I. Ibirama, the descent rule would be formulated in terms of *yug* (father) and *yi* (child). You would therefore expect that all those called *yug* — i.e., all elder male kinsmen — would paint with the same designs as oneself. If your mother's brother were included under the term *yug*, this would create a contradiction in expectations. Your mother's brother must paint with different paint designs. Since a *yug* is one who paints with the same designs, your mother's brother cannot be a *yug*. How to resolve this contradiction?

One way is to introduce a distinct term for "mother's brother" — *kòkla*, for instance. Calling your mother's brother *kòkla* allows you to maintain an association between the term *yug* and people painting with the same marks as you. From an ethnographic perspective, the result is a contrast analogous to that between *yog* and *kakre* among the Kaingang. This is the simplest solution.

An alternative, however, is for you to distinguish different senses of the term *yug*. Your descent rule might invoke only the narrow sense — the *yug* who actually raised you. Such a possibility would weaken the influence of the rules on kinship terms. You might still call a mother's brother *yug*, even though he painted with different designs. The solution would require you to delicately formulate the rules, but it is a possible solution. Its result is a kinship terminology — not unlike that envisioned by A. L. Kroeber — that is relatively independent of exogamy and descent rules.

Even without a separately circulating descent rule, numerous expectations haunt unfolding discourse, like so many ghosts. Among them are role-like suppositions, as well as suppositions about interconnections among terms. The rules, as pieces of metadiscourse — circulating independently of other discourse — create some new expectations about that other discourse. But there is a cornucopia of expectations even without them.

A further question concerns the forcefulness or power of the metadiscursive rules, even where they are found. You do not have to look hard to discover discrepancies — some of them blatant contradictions — between the rule and the actual workings of other discourse. No doubt, some discrepancies occur wherever we encounter rules as metadiscourse. However, the discrepancies are pronounced at P. I. Ibirama.

Perhaps this is due to the absence of an actually circulating rule of patrilineal descent, analogous to that among the Kaingang. Without a descent rule, the exogamy rule makes less sense, is taken less seriously. Put the two rules together, however, and members of the community, like ethnographers, are able to deduce from them expectations. The result is something resembling an axiomatic system — the rules being axioms, the expectations deductions. The application of reason to the axioms yields an impressive array of deduced expectations. Lewis Henry Morgan would be proud. With just one rule, however, deducibility is limited, expectations paltry. No wonder people are less concerned about discrepancies. The rule itself has a diminished intellectual force.

With due respect to Kroeber and Lounsbury, metadiscursive differences between P. I. Ibirama and P. I. Manoel Ribas explain the astonishing contrasts as regards kinship terminology. Where the extra rule actively circulates (P. I. Manoel Ribas), the distribution of kin terms accords with the expectations deducible from the rules. Correspondingly, the rules themselves are taken more seriously. At the same time, you can understand the

P. I. Ibirama terminology, in considerable measure, by asking yourself what the P. I. Manoel Ribas terminology would be like stripped of that extra rule.

You will note that I have not talked about social groupings — such as E. B. Tylor's moieties. I plan to do so in the next chapter. My concern here is entirely with discourse. I am convinced that, from the perspective of circulating discourse, we are able to reformulate the problematic of kinship terms as part of an abstract system of language. We are also able to encompass the problematic of kinship terms as emblems for social roles. Both language-like interconnectedness and social roles are read off of the surface of discourse.

Perhaps the most startling discovery, however, is that the rules of descent and exogamy, so long taken to be about the world of things, can be so profitably understood as about discourse. Before all else, they create expectations about discourse. Moreover, they create expectations not just about this or that bit of discourse, but about all discourse that includes kin terms — and, at P. I. Ibirama, that is almost all discourse. They are thus powerful metadiscursive devices, fragments of discourse that exercise regulatory effects over other discourse. They are a means of controlling and ordering speech and even thought. Because they are luminous to consciousness, moreover, they allow people to take conscious, intellectual control over the organization of their own representations of reality.

That the rules themselves should ever have been thought up, and injected into the circulating discourse within a community, is a source of wonder. The rules are encapsulated in compact, replicable stretches of discourse, a clause or two in length. Yet they exert an influence vastly greater than their physical size suggests. What a marvel that they should ever have developed. Because they themselves are salient to consciousness, they induce a consciousness of discourse. In so doing, they create expectations about it, and they result in the modification of it, as it is replicated over time.

A co-evolution is at work here. The rules as discourse (or metadiscourse) evolve historically within communities, undergoing development and change. The rest of the discourse also evolves. But the two evolutions are linked. The rules draw upon patterns already present in discourse, but they also influence and change those patterns. Their magic lies in their intellectual force, their power to control and direct the mind — they generate a "system." I am referring here not to a Parsonian social system independent of discourse. I am referring not even to a system cullable from distributional relations within actually occurring discourse. I am referring instead to a system *sensu stricto*, a deductive apparatus built up from the application of reason to axioms. The rules are significant in the evolution of discourse because they enable deductive thought about discourse, thought that simultaneously explains and regulates the discourse it is about.

# *Chapter 5.* The Jaguar's Spots

*The first logical categories were social categories; the first classes of things were classes of men, into which these things were integrated.*

— Emile Durkheim and Marcel Mauss (1963 [1903]: 82)

How dull, how lackluster the problematic of social integration now seems — *sans* intellectual cache. From our Gramscian, Derridean, Foucaultian, Bakhtinian heights, the mid-twentieth century debates about descent versus alliance appear two-dimensional, flatland. Descent theory, typified in Meyer Fortes's (1953) essay "The Structure of Unilineal Descent Groups," viewed society as emerging from its internal organization into groups — lineages, in the African case. These groups loosely cohered into a society. Alliance theory, typified by Lévi-Strauss's (1969a [1949]) *The Elementary Structures of Kinship*, in contrast, viewed exchange, and especially marriage, as of paramount importance in society building; social groupings crystallized out of the exchange process. Societies were like molecules formed through the physical sharing across space of actual individuals — one's siblings or children — resulting in bonds between the "atoms of kinship," or elementary families. Yawn.

How poorly some of the notions have worn! I admit, perhaps by way of defense, to a certain trepidation in broaching them with you again today, in the 1990s. At least I can report that they were considerably more in vogue in 1974, the year I arrived at P. I. Ibirama. Foucault was actually lecturing at the University of São Paulo around that time, but he languished under the shadow of the Parisian *maître* Lévi-Strauss, who, after all, together with Roger Bastide, reputedly helped to found the university. And then there was the ill-fated Pierre Clastres, dressed in motorcycle leather, also lecturing in São Paulo, whom I met at a soirée one night. His *Society Against the State* would foreshadow later postcolonial, postmodern themes, but he would die pitifully young. In any case, at the time he was still largely undiscovered.

You would be wrong to think, however, that it was only the times that caused anthropologists to fantasize the importance of descent groups and alliance, to project their own images willy-nilly onto the tabula rasa of indigenous communities. That they did, but my experience suggests that people at P. I. Ibirama talked more like Fortes and Lévi-Strauss than like Gramsci or Bakhtin. They were interested in similar issues — Who painted with which designs? By what pathways of descent were those designs acquired? Something would be lost were we to focus just on hegemony and resistance or double-voicing and hybridization.

Perhaps, however, I have found in these speech similarities — between anthropologist and native — a way of resuscitating the older discourse. The question of social integration is this: What kind of glue holds society together? The answer given by descent theory is the organization of society into social groupings. But is it the organization of society into groups or *talk about* the organization of society into groups? Is it alliance or *talk about* alliance?

You can already tell that I want to look at talk and, especially, talk about social organization, rather than at social organization per se. I will be examining evidence from embodiment — the application to bodies of paint designs, made from crushed charcoal agglutinated with sap, as in Plate 8. However, I want to suggest from the beginning the centrality of talk about community building; it is a key part of the community-building process. Indeed, it may be *the* key part. Social organization — not existing independently — owes its phenomenal palpability to a literalization of discourse, that is, to noumenal understanding, to publicly circulating conceptions of what the social world is all about.

The problem of social organization thus becomes an epistemological one. You must inquire into not only what social groupings are present in society — as if their existence were unproblematic. You must also inquire into how they are known. This means looking at their representation in signs, notably discourse. You will find that a gap opens between the social grouping and its representation; that gap causes you to question the epistemological status of the group.

Another way to think of the problem is in terms of a methodological error: reasoning from the representation of a social grouping or alliance to that social grouping or alliance in reality. Perhaps you can compare it to the error of literalizing a metaphor, although it is not precisely the same. Take the phrase "Richard, the lion-hearted." If you took it literally, you might conclude that Richard had in his body the physical heart of a lion. You would obviously be mistaken, and this is a limiting-case example. My question is, however: Are we making the same sort of mistake in assuming the existence of descent groups or alliance, just because people talk about them?

Now, there is a difference. A metaphor is not designed to trick you. If

*Plate 8.* Kúñépá paints with designs, October 1974. Notice the dots on her forehead and circles on her cheeks. Later she would paint circles on her chest as well.

you grew up in Anglo-American culture, you know that Richard did not have the physical heart of a lion. You would never be that naïve. You know that the metaphor draws a comparison. In some respects—courage, bravery, dominance—Richard is like a lion. The whole point is that you do not mistake the comparison for absolute equivalence.

In talk by natives about social organization, however, you are meant to do just that. You are supposed to buy into the reality of what is represented. The talk is not just metaphorical — although I hope to show that anthropologists sometimes take the talk too seriously. They (I suppose I should say we) tend to be literalists. I want to make the case, however, that social organizational talk, and, in some cases, even practice, is not always about what it appears to be about. The talk is designed to produce interconversion — to turn noumenal understanding into phenomenal experience, to manufacture groups from words. But the creation or labeling of groups is not necessarily the ultimate purpose of the talk. It may be that sharing of the talk — its replication and circulation throughout a community — is more important than what the talk is about per se.

You can think of descent theory as a literalization. It takes (or mistakes) talk about the community in terms of descent group classification as evidence that descent groups are responsible for community, for social integration. In one sense, this is correct. If people are interested in groups, if groups motivate talk, and if the circulation of talk fashions community, then the groups are, in some sense, indirectly responsible for community, for social integration. But to ignore the intervening steps is to hopelessly distort the process, leaving us befuddled about the mechanisms of community building. In the alternative proposed here, it is the circulation of discourse, not the existence of groups, that makes community possible.

If this is true of descent and alliance — metaphors of community derived from the family — might it not also be true of other metaphors of community? Might not the significance of the market place lie in talk about markets, rather than in the facts of exchange? Might the role of the public sphere reside in talk about public-sphere processes, rather than in the mechanics of debate? More generally, is talk about community building the social glue through which communities are built?

I have snuck in an old topic under a new guise, but I will probably not get away with it. My postmodern friends are too vigilant for that. Let me therefore give social integration or cohesion a different spin, because I am aware of the postcolonial critique of the integrationist perspective — namely, that it goes hand in glove with eufunctionalist perspectives that themselves help to suppress dissent, and, consequently, that bolster hegemony.

Here is the alternative spin: Community building is not a matter of social integration *per se*. The latter is only a means to something else, namely, to the circulation of discourse. Community building is significant from a discourse-centered perspective because it is a means for establishing and maintaining the circulation of discourse. This is why the discourse of social organization is so significant. Before talk about ethnic boundaries or about

*Plate 9.* Men dancing at *ãgyïn* ceremony, August 1975. *From left:* Nil, Kuzug,
Kuzug, and Kañã'ï. Nil adopted the disk designs for their "beauty,"
though he should have painted with lines. Notice the circular designs on
the cheek of Kuzug (*second from the left*) despite the lines on his forehead.

physical space, the discourse that most obviously lays down the conditions
for its own circulation is discourse about social organization. If the discourse works, a broader community is fashioned. Not necessarily an ethnically bounded one, the community is nevertheless one in which discourse
flourishes, in which it flows from person to person, house to house, laying
down roadways, keeping the paths of communication clear, staving off the
encroaching jungle that threatens to isolate us one from another. It creates,
thereby, the conditions for circulation of all other discourse, and, consequently, for the transmission of culture.

What about descent groups — lineages, clans, moieties? Are they not phenomenal entities in the world? Is not discourse something that merely
names what is already there? The P. I. Ibirama case tantalizes ethnographers
in this regard. You can detect embodied descent groups, or, at least, you
can detect what have been described as groups. To convince yourself that
something is going on, you need only glance at Plates 8–10, made from
photographs shot in 1974 and 1975. You see different body paint designs,
and these supply evidence — just what kind of evidence remains unclear —
about social differentiation within the community. Not everyone paints
with the same designs.

By this point, you may be too leery to rush to conclusions, however. Maybe you do not automatically assume that the paint designs correspond to social groups. Others before you were not so cautious. J. Henry (1964 [1941]: 175), for example, referred to "five groups," adding that to each "belongs a distinct body paint design and a series of names." His remark lends credence to some of the accusations leveled against anthropologists. How easy to project a theoretical discourse where it just does not fit. To Henry's lasting credit, however, he sensed the lack of fit. He attributed it to the fact that P. I. Ibirama "theoretical social structure . . . has been largely so much cultural flotsam for at least two hundred years and probably much longer" (1964 [1941]: 175). But why has the "theoretical social structure" lasted so long? Why did it continue even into the 1970s and 1980s?

*Plate 10.* Kàyèta dancing at *āgyïn,* followed by unidentified woman, August 1975. Notice the disks on his cheek and chest, despite the lines on his forehead.

The discourse of descent theory is a discourse of groups. If you believe that society consists in groups, then you have to find them ethnographically. Whether Henry believed in groups is moot; however, the dominant discourse of his time posited groups as bedrock social institutions. Consequently, he had to find them. When things were not as they should be, he attributed the problem to the people he studied. Naturally, he could not trace its cause back to his own metadiscourse of description.

Descent theory made some dubious assumptions, however innocuous they may have been. First, it supposed that descent groups were sets — in the sense of set theory, prior to the advent of fuzzy sets. The sets consisted of individuals. And the sets exhaustively parceled up a society, so that no one was left unclassified. Second, it assumed that the sets were mutually exclusive. If someone was a member of one, they could not be a member of another. Third, it construed the sets as corporations — that is, as collective actors — as Fortes (1953), following Sir Henry Maine (1965 [1861]), proposed. The groups had to do something other than have members. They had to act collectively.[1]

Such assumptions cloud our vision in the P. I. Ibirama case, which, however, perhaps because of its extreme nature, has something important to tell us about more middle-of-the-road cases. Do paint designs at P. I. Ibirama have something to do with groups in the descent theoretic sense? In trying to answer the question, you will find yourself asking another one: Do the putative groups have names? Well, the paint designs do. Alas, the names appear to be descriptive of the designs. However, Henry (1964 [1941]: 175) does report the existence of "group names." Here is his rendition of the system:

| Design | Name of Design | Translation | Name of Group |
|---|---|---|---|
| ● | mêvidn | scattered all over | Wanyekí kôika hë |
| \| | kalébm | coming down | Klendó kôika hë |
| ○ | kuikên | in a ring | Kainlé kôika hë |
| ⊓⊓⊓⊓ | kaktêng kũ kalébm | horizontal and coming down | None |
| ⬤ | kanêm | placed there | None |

*Figure 5.* Jules Henry's representation of communal level differences

I confess to chuckling at the representation. In my years at P. I. Ibirama, I have only seen paint designs on bodies, never abstracted in Henry's way. As I look at the representation, I appreciate how easy it is — our consciousness steered by a metadiscourse of descent groups — to imagine a group for each isolated design. Perhaps I can steer our consciousness in another direction, however. Without abandoning the problematic of group, can I ask you to consider the aesthetic dimension? What if paint designs are a matter of "beauty"?

You might want to think about aesthetic choices. One kind of choice you make is for your children, before they can decide on their own. This kind of choice rings a bell for ethnographers — they hear "descent." But let us listen more closely to what people at P. I. Ibirama have to say. Something like descent is at work, but the talk about it is specific. It differs from Fortesian talk in important ways.

You will find that paint designs and proper names tend to travel together across the generations. Parents choose names for their children. The names come from a deceased relative. When you give names to your child, the child should paint with the designs of the deceased relative. What is the principle for choosing names? My neighbor Wãñpõ was blunt about this. In August of 1974, he insisted that you choose the name that is "most beautiful."

Now this is not as simple as it might seem. Your sense of beauty relates to the person whose names you wish to pass on. You do not pass on just any names. You pass on names of those you consider morally worthy, those you admired, those who were "beautiful" in your eyes. This is a kind of descent, but aesthetic discourse here dominates over a discourse of mechanical principles, such as you find in descent theory. If a community consists in individuals, and each individual wishes to preserve the memory of ancestors who were good or beautiful in their eyes, then you have a type of descent that selects for qualities the community esteems best. One of those qualities is the intrinsic beauty of paint designs.

You often do not make the aesthetic judgment yourself, however. Others convey their wishes to you, making the aesthetic decision itself a process of building social relations, and hence of building community. Sometimes there are conflicting suggestions. Fortunately, because names come in sets — of from two to eight names — you can pass on names from distinct individuals. For example, you might pass on to your daughter the names of both your mother and your sister, if they are deceased. In this way, new name sets are born, the community repertoire continuously rejuvenated.

You make another kind of choice in regard to paint designs. Not only do you select your children's names, and their associated designs, but you, as an adult, can modify your own designs. A case was reported to me soon after I arrived at P. I. Ibirama in 1974. Kàyèta mentioned a conversation he had with Nil—the old culture vulture himself, who, in 1981–1982, would become my constant companion. Nil told him that people (like himself) who painted with lines (*mēkalem*) should use no other mark, but that "sometimes they find the *mētōpam* [disk design][2] beautiful and so they take it for their own." In fact, a year later—August 26, 1975, to be precise—I photographed Nil at a ceremony (see Plate 8). Shunning lines, he had painted only with disks.

Let me zoom out and give you a broader picture. You have, as evidence of groupness, embodied phenomena—in this case, body paint designs, as illustrated in Plates 8–10. Here is something visible, phenomenally accessible, the aspect of groups that suggests in-the-world existence. They are simply waiting to be named. But you also have circulating talk about names. At P. I. Ibirama, this focuses on aesthetic choices pertaining to transmission and usage. There are other aspects to that discourse, in particular, magical ones—the designs ward off ghosts, and, in the origin myth, help to bring animals to life. But what you do not find is a circulating rule of unilineal descent, as in classical descent theory.

I propose that the same two levels—embodiment and discourse about embodiment—are at work in the African cases most familiar to Fortes. However, in those cases (such as the Ashanti and Tallensi) the descent talk is not predominantly aesthetic. Rather, there we find a circulating discourse of descent rules, which, as we have seen, are really a metadiscourse of kinship. The very circulation of the rules is a binding force. Community is produced by a discourse agreement.[3] The agreement is to allow difference, which then is concretized in the form of descent groups. This construal conflicts with the notion of loose cohesion emerging from groups that have some prior existence. But you can see why Fortes and others would come up with their view. It corresponds to how community is talked about in those cases with which they are familiar.

Descent theory, as a universally applicable approach, consists of applying this culture-specific view to other cases, where it may or may not accord with the locally circulating discourse. At P. I. Ibirama, it does not accord. But that does not deter those deluded by their own discourse preconceptions—Henry and I among them. So when I discovered that paint designs passed with names, I wanted to determine whether there was a unilineal principle buried in there somewhere. I was disappointed to find that names passed from both the father's and mother's side. I could not hear the discourse of "beauty" woven throughout talk about paint designs and names.

You see what we have here, however. The aesthetic discourse, like talk about unilineal rules, is a circulating discourse. Insofar as it flows from one person to the next, gets replicated over the generations, it is community building. It is a force of integration, laying down the pathways for other discourse, regardless of what it happens to be about. But I am not so naïve as to think its content unimportant. People are interested in this kind of talk because of how it conceptualizes community. Not all conceptualizations are equal. Talk of unilineal rules, in particular, seems to have a powerful persuasive appeal, probably much greater than that of the aesthetic discourse at P. I. Ibirama. But the latter case allows us to see unilineal descent for what it is. It is talk.

Let us return to our earlier question: Are there descent groups at P. I. Ibirama? In interviews, I had no trouble confirming four out of Henry's five paint designs — the dot, line, circle, and disk. These not only could be elicited; they were sprinkled throughout publicly occurring discourse, especially that of the origin myth. Here is a sample:

| | |
|---|---|
| wãgyò tõ zẽzẽ wũ ti ẽ tõ ẽñ mãg | Relative Zẽzẽ, who feared my creation |
| kòmãg hãke mũ ñã | [the jaguar], stood far away from it. |
| kũ ti làn hà tõ ti tey ka kuñkẽn[4] kũ | And he painted [it] well on its back |
| win mũ | [with] circles and dots. |
| zẽzẽ wãñlàl hã wũ kuñkẽn kũ | Zẽzẽ's paint designs were always circles |
| mẽwin gèke mũ | and dots. |
| ti tõ ẽ wãñlàl tẽ tan hã wã | He was telling about his paint designs. |

I also photographed each of the four.

The comb-like design, however, proved refractory to elicitation. I never detected it in public discourse, and only grudgingly did I prod someone into acknowledging it. The name itself looks ad hoc and ungainly, a linguistic contraption fabricated on the spur of the moment. Yet I do not doubt that Henry elicited it, and, moreover, that the design was in use during his time, or shortly before.

Why do I not doubt it? Because I detected other designs as well. One was called *mẽ tõ nïm* — two stripes on the upper arms. Eduardo de Lima e Silva Hoerhan, the colorful frontiersman and government Indian agent, reported another design, called *zo'o zi* — two horizontal lines with a row of dots in between. The existence of these alternatives only confirms the aesthetic interpretation. The designs were meant to render their users "beautiful," in addition to frightening away ghosts. You could modify them, in some measure, to enhance your beauty.

Not all designs are equally aesthetically appealing; not all have the same longevity. You may dote on the effects of your innovation, but others may not. If your design proves uninteresting, it will languish in the rubble heap of the present, uncopied and not passed on. The aesthetic descent principle is a sieve. You put in the present, with its debris of innovation, and out comes tradition, pure and orderly. What has come out at P. I. Ibirama are four designs — dot, line, circle, and disk.

Do the designs correspond to groups? In the case of three — dot, line, and circle — the answer is "yes," or, at least, "maybe." Henry furnishes us with "group names" for each, and I had no difficulty corroborating them. Closer inspection, however, turns up a reason for the "maybe." The reason is that the putative group names are designators of individuals by way of kin relationship.

Someone painting with dots — see Kūñēpã's forehead in Plate 8 — can be called *Wāñēkï kòñka hà*. This is from the proper masculine name Wāñēkï, common at P. I. Ibirama during my time there. You will recall that it was the name of my neighbor in 1974–1975. Attached to it is the word for "relative," *kòñka*, together with a particle meaning "good" or "whole," *hà*. In the origin myth, *kòñka hà* is used simply to mean "relative." Hence, the expression would mean "Wāñēkï's relative." Similarly, someone using stripes would be *Kleno kòñka hà*, "Kleno's relative" — see Kuzug's forehead in Plate 9. And someone painting with circles would be *Kāñle kòñka hà*, "Kāñle's relative" — see Kūñēpã's cheek in Plate 8, also the cheek, chest, and forehead of the unidentified man in Plate 11.

Grammatically, it is easy to turn these individual-designating phrases into collective nouns. You can induce someone familiar with the circulating discourse at P. I. Ibirama to give you this kind of phrase. Your interlocutor need merely supplement the phrase with the particles *òg* (plural marker, "they") and *nāli* (all); hence, *Wāñēkï kòñka hà òg nāli*, "all of Wāñēkï's relatives," or "the group of Wāñēkï's relatives."

A question still haunts us, however. Are the group designators employed in publicly occurring discourse? Do we find mention of the groups qua groups? Surprisingly, we do not. The group descriptors are grammatically possible. You can readily elicit them. However, they do not occur in narratives. Nor have I ever encountered them in spontaneous discourse. Indeed, the actors in P. I. Ibirama discourse are almost invariably individuals. Grammatically, actors are pronouns or singular proper names, with or without relational terms linking them to other actors.

How important this is from the perspective of a discourse-centered interpretation of descent! Fortes (1953: 164) regarded the African lineage as "a single legal personality — 'one person' as the Ashanti put it." Ashanti discourse, apparently, makes reference to the corporate character of descent groups, to the existence of collective actors. I would guess that lineages function as grammatical actors in their publicly circulating discourse. The lineages probably appear as the subjects or objects of verbs, capable of acting and being acted upon.

*Plate 11.* Studio portrait of an unidentified man (possibly
Kowi), circa 1920. Notice
the circles on his cheeks, and,
if you can make them out,
on his forehead and chest.
Photo courtesy of Eduardo
de Lima e Silva Hoerhan.

This is not true at P. I. Ibirama, however. Not only do we not find the group designators as discourse actors, we do not find them at all. What we find instead are individuals. Even the relational terms associated with the paint designs are derived from proper names.

A discourse-centered perspective adds a dimension to this otherwise flat concept of the descent theoretic "group." It shows groupness to be a matter of degree. The discourse encoding of the group as actor — as subject or object — is the crucial feature of groupness. But just how frequently does groupness appear? Are groups regular topics of narratives? In what measure is the individual eclipsed as an agent?

What we find, I conjecture, is a continuum. At one end — P. I. Ibirama is a case in point — groups are only nascent, fledgling. The group is grammatically possible and capable of being elicited, but does not occur in the public discourse within the community. At the other end — the Ashanti may be a case in point — the group is not only elicitable but actually occurring and frequent in public discourse, and, moreover, luminous to consciousness as articulated in metadiscourse — the lineage as "one person."

There is another continuum as well. Groupness is not only more or less nascent or fully formed in discourse; it is also more or less phenomenally accessible. Does the group exhibit observable and describable characteristics, such as body painting or geographical localization or collectively coordinated action? I will venture a risky proposition, but one, nevertheless, in keeping with the principles of interconversion. It is that the more a group is represented in discourse, and the more it assumes the role of a "single legal personality," in Fortes's words, the more it will be actualized as a phenomenal group. Correspondingly, the less a group is implemented discursively, the less likely will it be to have any practical social significance.

An enigma presents itself. At P. I. Ibirama, groupness is at best nascent in community discourse. Why then have different paint designs? An answer might shed light on the Ashanti lineage and other seemingly luminous cases, where the very obviousness of descent groups diverts our attention from what is actually going on. At P. I. Ibirama, the groups are sufficiently puzzling that they seem unnatural, artificial. Something is not right. They cry out for explanation.

I stated earlier that one preconception of descent theoretic groupness is that group membership is mutually exclusive. If one is a member of one group, one cannot be a member of another. However, at P. I. Ibirama, this assumption is violated. Through examination of photographs taken in 1974 and 1975, you can see that many, though by no means all, people painted with more than one design.

Plate 8 shows Kūñēpā using the typical dot design on her forehead. The design usually consists in two rows of dots, with four or five dots per row.

The design is drawn on the forehead, and, sometimes as well, on the chest. By this visible assessment, Kūñēpā is *Wāñēkï kòñkà hà*, that is "Wāñēkï's relative." However, you will notice that Kūñēpā has also painted with circles on her cheeks. This design makes her *Kāñle kòñka hà*, "Kāñle's relative." That is, if groups were reflected in embodied behavior, Kūñēpā is a member of two distinct groups.

Plate 9 shows Kuzug painted with stripes on his forehead. Normally, these consist in four or five vertical lines. However, if you look closely, you will see that Kuzug, like Kūñēpā, has painted with circles on his cheeks as well.

In still another photograph, Plate 10, Kàyèta has painted with stripes on his forehead, and with disks on his cheeks. Other combinations are possible as well.

Of the four principal designs, the only combination I have not seen — as if the wearers were thumbing their noses at group exclusivity — is dots with stripes. This may be due to a practical unfeasibility; both designs are painted on the forehead. However, you could think of creative solutions. For example, you might paint stripes on your forehead and dots on your chest.

An analogous problem occurs with circles and disks. These ought to be mutually exclusive — both are painted on the cheeks. However, another photograph, unfortunately unsuitable for reproduction, reveals that Kuzug has painted with circles on his cheeks, but also with disks on his chest and shoulders. From such evidence, I would not be surprised to find dots and stripes co-occurring. However, I suspect that they do not. The designs function in some measure dualistically. The aesthetic sieve winnows out a moiety system — two dominant paint designs (stripes and dots), supplemented by two others (circles and disks), with sundry innovations here and there.

So what is happening in the P. I. Ibirama case? I propose that we are dealing not with groups, as traditionally conceived, but with representations of groupness, representations of difference. Embodied practice, like discourse, stands for something else. It is a sign vehicle from which meaning is culled, in addition to being a phenomenon in perceptual reality. Embodied groups are about the social world even as they are part of it.

Social processes are intrinsically murky, unclear, mysterious. People encountering other people outside of the warmth and security of their families is dangerous, unpredictable. Communal reality is mercurial and shifting; alliances and loyalties unstable; individuals whimsical and unfathomable. From the point of view of a circulating discourse, counting on social relations for its survival, communal reality is a nightmare.

What is discourse to do? It must try to bring about some semblance of orderliness, and it does so by creating images of community. The paint design groups at P. I. Ibirama—themselves a product of descent discourse—are one such image. They are a sign through which community can be fathomed.

Factions as "groups" cannot be readily delineated, as descent theory would like. Interestingly, in the P. I. Ibirama case, no attempt is made to name factions, let alone to formulate them in discourse as the basis for social integration. Instead, what we find is a community grappling to come to consciousness of itself, to achieve self-understanding, but settling on something less than full disclosure. "Wãñēki's relative," "Kleno's relative," "Kãñle's relative"—the names suggest interest groups led by powerful figures. Yet the groups are anything but that. They stand in no practical relationship to factions. Rather, they suggest how a smoothly functioning community might be built.

Why not name presently existing factions rather than use a nonanchored image of groupness? Here we run smack up against the problem of permanence, so central to the culture concept. Because factions are shifting and impermanent, people would face the problem of continuously redesigning their image. They would have to redesign it each time they actually came together—a deplorable situation little better than no image at all. A workable image should be sufficiently durable that it can be recycled, used over and over again.

Community building therefore presupposes some culture, as narrowly conceived, that is, as passed down over time. The culture that it presupposes is a blueprint of community. Startlingly, therefore, Durkheim and Mauss may have been literally correct: "The first logical categories were social categories; the first classes of things . . . classes of men" (1963 [1903]: 82). Theirs is another way of saying that culture lays down the roadways for its own circulation. The road-cutting portion of culture is the discourse of community.

You can only have community if you have a specific form of culture, namely, a blueprint of community, a social organization. Correspondingly, however, community becomes the holding environment for culture more generally—conceived primarily in terms of discourse. Therefore, to have culture more generally, you have to have already established some form of community. Since the mechanism for establishing community is the creation of an image of groupness, as descent theory contends, the "first classes of things were classes of men."

The basic problem of social integration—and hence of culture conceived as circulating discourse—is that people disagree about community. This is why we have factionalism in the first place. Consequently, any image of community must be distinct from the immediate reality. People agree on abstract blueprints more readily than on the immediate realities. Hence, the image must not too closely resemble its object.

Fortes took the African lineage at face value. But could it be that the same disjuncture between sign and object is at work? Are lineages only a discourse-generated image of sociability, rather than the independently existing basis of sociability? I am proposing precisely that. However, I need to qualify my claim: There may be differing degrees of dissimilitude between sign and object, differing doses of self-delusion. In images that seem more reality-like — because they more thoroughly translate into practical activity — it may be harder for you as a native or as an ethnographer to see that they are images.

If my reading of Fortes is correct, the Ashanti and Tallensi naturalize the lineage concept to a high degree. They live it in their daily lives. If this is so, discourse as well as embodiment ought to reflect a heightened prominence of the lineage. But I hope you will not be deceived by this. Social processes among the Ashanti and Tallensi may be more in line with the discourse blueprint of community than at P. I. Ibirama. But you should never expect them to be identical. And, if they are never identical, then the fundamental proposition of descent theory must be inverted. It is not the case that there simply are groups which the ethnographer discovers. It is that there are representations of groupness, naturalized in greater or lesser measure.

Having made the point that images of community are just that — images — I do not want you to think that I have fallen prey to total relativism. Some images are better than others. The widespread usage of kinship metaphors as a basis for talking about community points to their natural appropriateness. The public sphere, however, is an alternative image of social integration, one that is not grounded in kinship, at least, not in the same way. In Habermas's view (1989 [1962]; see also Calhoun 1992), the public arena is defined in opposition to the private domestic or family sphere, rather than in terms of it. Nevertheless, you can construe it as an appealing image of community in an increasingly globalized world. And it is an image with universal aspirations.

Seeming fixity with respect to a reality in flux is one characteristic that an image of community must possess. If people cannot agree *prima facie* about community, the solution is for discourse to develop an image upon which they can agree. The image itself must also seem to be fixed or permanent as opposed to shifting. Present agreement must seem to be constrained by prior agreements. You use the weight of the past to help you with the present.

The problem of permanence and the problem of culture as narrowly defined — that is, as passed down across the generations — are linked. To say that an image of community is fixed or permanent is to say that the publicly occurring discourse in which it is carried is fixed. You can encode the image in rules — exogamy and unilineal descent rules, for example. Since you can reason from the rules to their consequences, permanence depends only upon replicating the rules. The rest follows.

Research on the Jê-speaking relatives of the P. I. Ibirama people (see Da Matta 1976: 108–118; Lave 1979; Lopes da Silva 1986; T. Turner 1979; Seeger 1981; Vidal 1977: 107–112) provides objective evidence about permanence. In these societies, as at P. I. Ibirama, group membership is often determined by names. You belong to the group to which the person belonged whose names you have now received. Because these societies probably diverged from a common ancestor several thousand years ago, we know that there is something durable, something long-lived, about the image of community grounded in bilateral, name-based descent.

However, it is one thing to scientifically detect replication, quite another to appreciate it practically — as a participant. To accomplish the latter task, you must slip fixity or permanence into the image itself. In public sphere and market place conceptions of community, for example, you sneak in presuppositions about human nature and reason. These create a sense of timelessness. You are saying, in effect, "our image of community is as old as human beings; it will persist as long as they do. Community is an outgrowth of human nature. Human nature is permanent — always was, always will be."

However, you can also represent permanence by transhistorical linkage. This is where the trope of descent comes in. Descent demonstrates — or seems to demonstrate, by a sleight of hand — the prior historical existence of the group to which you presently belong. You know that the group was there before you; people now dead, but with a traceable relationship to you, were members of it. The group appears ancient, long-lived.

What gives it this appearance? Obviously, it is talk. At P. I. Ibirama, as you grow up, you learn history through talk. You learn about the people who came before you. One thing you learn especially well concerns your names — Who had them before you? What were they like? People you meet will recall those whose names you now carry. The anecdotes make you feel connected. There is something about you in them. You are tied by an invisible thread to a distant past.

For many years, what was considered important about descent was the unilineal principle. You belonged to a group because your father before you (patrilineal descent) or your mother (matrilineal descent) belonged to that group. The structuring properties of unilineal principles fired the anthropological imagination. But you can now see that bilateral, name-based recruitment to groups accomplishes the same communicative function. It sets up the image of community as something already existing, already agreed upon. It fires native imagination.

The various types of descent have one thing in common: They all represent community groupings as long-lived — like the pyramids, mysteriously ancient, yet obviously human products. In each case, group membership is calibrated with respect to the past. The calibration points to the venerable age of the group; it existed before you did. Today, the community is negotiated afresh. But the discursively transmitted social organization is taken as a given. It is a backdrop to present relations, one itself seemingly beyond negotiation, prior to it.

At the same time, since community images are carried along in publicly occurring discourse, as well as embodied practices, they are in fact mutable, like other discourse. Each instance of image-encoding talk, each embodied practice, represents a negotiation. Even though you presuppose descent groups, you may dispute the exact wording of the descent rule.

How wrong it would be, however, to conclude from this that the circulating image of social organization is fleeting and insubstantial, a momentaneous thing. In the first place, the discourse and practices may be, indeed, relatively fixed. Only empirical investigation can determine this. At P. I. Ibirama, where the publicly performed origin myth is an important vehicle for transmitting the community image, evidence suggests remarkable stability. Microchanges can be detected here and there, but you also find nearly verbatim repetition, over a period of fifty years from the 1930s to the 1980s.

In the second place, insofar as people buy into the circulating image of community, they may produce it in the phenomenal world. At P. I. Ibirama, I witnessed with my own eyes the paint designs I had previously only heard about through discourse. Similarly, any member of the community could confirm the image circulated in discourse. The discourse image takes on an independent life in practical activities. A community is, indeed, formed in the way discourse tells you it is. The senses, in short, confirm the intellect.

However, there is a bit of chicanery here. The image seems to emerge from the world, as if the world were the locus of continuity and permanence. If my argument is correct, however, it emerges from discourse about the world, rather than the world itself. There is a part of the world that confirms the image, but that part grew out of the image, through the process of interconversion. The part itself is not identical with underlying social processes. It is a kind of embodied trope of obscurely amorphous, inscrutably elusive sensibility.

You might say that discourse has hit upon a mechanism for ensuring its own perpetuation, its own survival. Since with discourse circulates a consciousness or awareness of the world, a discourse of permanence—as in descent rules—produces a consciousness of permanence. That consciousness is what guides embodied behavior, causes it to organize itself in spite of the chaotic, unpredictable quality of social encounters. That in turn is what allows some semblance of social integration, and it is social integration that ensures the survival of the original discourse. Here is to be found the boot-strapping core of culture, where roadways are laid down. Culture as discourse creates the very presuppositions it needs to survive.

We again stalk that mysterious terrain — the relationship between intelligibility and sensibility, discourse and perception, reference and experience. Discourse is two things simultaneously: It is an image of reality, and it is itself part of reality. It is both a sign standing for something else and an object that can be perceived. In its latter capacity, it is part of the chaotic, swirling cauldron of social encounter where regular contact gives way to primal passion. Its magic, however, is its ability to render that cauldron intelligible, like some soothsayer reading into the swirling surface a distinct image of the future. It does so by forging an image of social reality in consciousness, and circulating that image through the process of replication. What our discourse represents reality to be our consciousness understands it to be. And if our consciousness construes reality as orderly, then we struggle to see orderliness in the cauldron of social interaction, perhaps to enact it in our own lives. Insofar as discourse is successful, it tames and organizes social interaction in such a way that the continued circulation of the discourse itself is ensured. The discourse survives.

The reader cannot help but notice that my position is diametrically opposed to descent theory in one key respect. The latter espouses what is really the native's point of view, some natives' point of view, at least. Descent in descent theory is a means of constituting groups. In contrast, in discourse theory it is a means of constituting representations of group permanence. It functions communicatively, telling people that groups are ancient; they were there before the present generation; they will still be there when the present generation has gone. Why else should people accept them as givens? Why else should they attribute to them pyramid-like solidity?

Since my last visit to P. I. Ibirama, more than a decade has elapsed. Sitting here today, I contemplate the threads that still bind me to people there, to the "community." No longer phenomenally accessible — save through photographs or memorabilia — the people live on in my mind. They are noumenally real.

As I think back on it, I appreciate that my engagement with the community has never been uninterrupted. There was rather always a kind of *pas de deux* between mind and sense, intellect and perception. My wife and I would spend three or four months at P. I. Ibirama — in face-to-face, perceptual involvement — then a month in Rio or São Paulo — in distanced contemplation; another round of three or four months at P. I. Ibirama, then a month in Rio or São Paulo, and so forth. Like a seasonal cycle, the alternation of phenomenal and noumenal attachment repeated itself for two years between 1974 and 1976. With our return to Chicago, perceptual contact ceased. However, in 1981 I again journeyed to P. I. Ibirama, and the cycle of comings and goings started afresh.

There was a rhythm to the encounter — immediate perceptual involvement alternating with distanced contemplation. I now recognize the rhythm as singularly appropriate. It was isomorphic with the rhythm of attachments at P. I. Ibirama that people themselves maintained with one another, at least outside their families. Because the community was dispersed, people were forced to visit often at great distances, renewing and refreshing their ties. You may recall Wãñpõ's house on May 2, in 1982, as described in Chapter 3. On that day, more than half of those present were visitors.

No wonder key institutions have sprung up around coming and going. One sunny day in 1975, I would experience this firsthand. We had returned from a field break in Rio. Rattling back in our cantankerous but faithful Jeep — it broke down incessantly, but always in town — we happened on a small group of elderly women. They spontaneously broke into mournful wails, intermingled with sobs, stroking my arms and chest. I had no idea what was going on. Only much later would I put two and two together, recognizing in this the celebrated "welcome of tears," described with incredulity by travelers to coastal Brazil in the sixteenth century. A number of us have more recently studied the phenomenon in some detail (Briggs 1993; Graham 1984, 1986; Urban 1988, 1991: 148–171). Ritualized lamentation marks a return after a prolonged absence. A person who has been, for some time, only noumenally real — through memory — is made once again phenomenally accessible. Perceptual contact triggers the lament.

Now what does this have to do with the problem of social integration? I am sketching for you here a type of communal or extrafamilial attachment. It is distinct from the attachment to bounded groups, whether ethnicities or communities. In the group idea, there is a set; you are either in or out. In the periodic attachment idea, you experience a cycle of alternation. The other is now phenomenal — a flesh-and-blood being with whom you interact; now noumenal — a memory trace, recoverable only through thought. Attachments are matters of degree.

You will object that this is what all of our attachments are like all the time. I could not agree more. However, the periodicity varies. The cycles of communal attachment at P. I. Ibirama obey a distinctive rhythm. But, more than this, there is a startling fact: Comings and goings form the poetic architecture or backbone of their origin myth. The periodicity of real-world comings and goings is mirrored in discourse rhythms of reported comings and goings. Without explicitly talking about community, the discourse embodies it in its poetic form.

The hauntingly recurrent image in the myth is that of arrival and departure. The image lulls you, soothes you, works its way into your discourse unconscious, creates for you expectations which you yourself can later build into your own narratives. Each episode is demarcated by movement toward or away. Here is the opening to the first of the four more or less discrete narratives making up the origin myth:

| | |
|---|---|
| 1. kòñgàg yazïn yò tē ki òg nō ñā | 1. They were there in man's rising place. |
| 2. kòñgàg yazïn yò tē yè nèn tū nō ñā | 2. They felt the absence of the men who had already gone up. |
| 3. ū yè kòñgàg ū yè kòñgàg yazïn ya tògtē we yè kakutā | 3. "Which of you men will go out to see man's rising place?" |
| 4. yògwañ tō pligyug tē to kakutānĕg ñā | 4. The chief Pligyug came out, |
| 5. kū tā | 5. and he [said]: |
| 6. hālò kòñgàg tē yaplï ñā | 6. "Where did the men ascend?" |
| 7. iwo tòg hālò wū kòñgàg tē yaplï ñā | 7. "It's over there that the men ascended." |
| 8. ĕ yògwañ tō pligyug mō kòñgàg yazïn yò ki nĕyu ñā | 8. He showed his chief Pligyug where the men had ascended, |
| 9. lò taplï mū | 9. [and] there he ascended. |

In this episode, Pligyug goes on to experience the outer world—the world we see around us today. He is a stranger in what is for him a strange land, and we tag along, knowing, however, that this land is the phenomenal world. Although nowhere noted in the narrative, metacommentary—by Nil and Wāñĕkï separately, in this case—clues us into the fact that mankind emerged, in the beginning, from a hole in the ground. Here Pligyug espies the first savanna, plucks some of its grass, and brings it home for the others to see.

How curious that the initial speaker goes unnamed. We—members of the audience—learn the name of the person who leaves. However, we take the point of view of the nameless ones; this point of view becomes our narrative home base. We depart discursively with Pligyug, but we return to nameless others. Subsequently, we will depart with other characters, but we will always come back to these nameless ones. They are the community— a loose aggregation of adult relationships built around departures and arrivals.

The arrivals/departures are what hold the narrative together, just as comings and goings hold the community together. The words from this opening episode are repeated nearly verbatim in succeeding ones. In the linear unfolding of the narrative, Pligyug returns from his adventures—the home crowd praising him for his leadership. Then, abruptly, the earlier formula is revisited:

1. ū yè kòñgàg ū yè yògwañ tō nè wèg tē tògtē we yè kakutā
2. mūlò wāgyò pazi tē to kakutānēg ña
3. kū
4. hālò wū kòñgàg tē yaplï ñā
5. ke mū
6. iwo tòg hālò wū kòñgàg tē yaplï ñā
7. ke mū
8. pazi tē ē mō kòñgàg yazïn yò ki nēyu ñā
9. tā lò taplï mū

1. "Which of you men will go out to see what the chief has seen?"
2. At that time, relative Pazi came out,
3. and [he said]:
4. "Where did the men ascend?"
5. [he] said.
6. "It's over there that the men ascended,"
7. [he] said.
8. He showed Pazi where the men had ascended,
9. [and] there he ascended.

And the same formula is repeated, *mutatis mutandis*, with a third figure.

From the problematic of community building, these sequences of departure and return create an image of community as presence periodically alternating with absence. Time and again, departures threaten community, but arrivals rebuild it. The community-building dimension of arrival is made especially salient in a series of episodes involving, curiously, the paint designs.

If you study the discourse, you will find a series of four arrivals. These occur in connection with the creation of two animals: the jaguar and the tapir. As in earlier episodes, a formula is repeated *mutatis mutandis*. The formula consists in the arrival of an unknown person. The main character asks the person his name, and the person replies. Here is the opening to the first of these four:

1. wāgyò tō zàgpope tō patè ēñ yo katèle
2. glè yò ki kala
3. kū ne to agèlmēg wū mū ke mū
4. iwo ēñ cō kòñgàg kale yògï mā
5. kū ēñ cō ēñ māg yè
6. kàplug kèg
7. mūlō ti kï tū
8. ēñ cō wèg mū

1. Relative Zàgpope Patè arrived in front of me,
2. (he) arrived in the dance plaza,
3. and he said: "What is all of this noise about?"
4. "I hear the sound of many men coming
5. and so for my creation
6. (I) fashioned *kàplug* wood.
7. However, he did not call out,
8. I have seen,

| | |
|---|---|
| 9. kū ēñ cō ēñ mãg yè | 9. and so for my creation |
| 10. zàg tèy kèn | 10. (I) fashioned araucaria pine wood |
| 11. kū ēñ cō ti làn ke | 11. and I painted it |
| 12. kū kàgnãg | 12. and (I) erred |
| 13. kū tō gèlmẽg nẽ wā | 13. and that is what all the noise is about |
| 14. kū ã yïyï tẽ hãlike tẽ ke mū | 14. and what would your name be?" he said. |
| 15. iwo ēñ yïyï hã wũ zàgpope ke tẽ | 15. "My name would be Zàgpope, |
| 16. ēñ yïyï hã wũ patè ke tẽ | 16. my name would be Patè." |
| 17. ũ ke mò yè ēñ ñõ ēñ mãg làn yè kala ke mū | 17. "Well then come help me to paint my creation," he said. |

I will not give the other occurrences of this formula here, as these have been scrutinized in some detail elsewhere.[5] What I wish to observe, however, is the usage of paint designs and their relationship to community building. The principal speaker endeavors to fashion an animal—one that has not existed before. In this case, the animal is a tapir. To make it, the man fashions araucaria pine wood. He attempts to paint it with designs. However, he fails. The animal does not come to life.

To complete the task, the man requires the assistance of different men who arrive on the scene. From the point of view of community, it is interesting that the men who arrive are represented as being unknown to the speaker. The speaker asks them who they are, and they respond by giving their names. Perhaps most interestingly, what the new arrivals contribute is different paint designs. They help to complete the animal. Here is a purpose for community. It allows individuals to complete work that they cannot finish by themselves. The narrative provides a rationale for community, for commerce outside the family. It provides a rationale as well for the cohesion of people with different paint designs. Rather than being taken literally, the narrative can be taken as a metaphor of community. It consists in cooperation among those who paint with different designs.

The designs are not only something that humans use. They are also part of the natural world. As Durkheim and Mauss proposed in *Primitive Classification*, the natural world is created in the image of the human world. The marks on a tapir's body (Plate 2), the spots on a jaguar (Plate 12), resemble designs used to decorate human bodies. The designs are not only similar, this narrative informs us. Their origin in nature is causally linked to their presence in culture.

The scenario in the origin myth, however, is distinct from what Durkheim and Mauss propose. For them the issue is "logical categories," "the first classes of things [being] classes of men." Nature is divided into species

*Plate 12.* Photograph of jaguar (*Panthera onca*). Notice designs — circles (*mēkuñkēn*), dots (*mēwin*), and disks (*mētōpam*) — said to have been painted by the ancestors on the first jaguar at the time of its creation. Photo by Gary A. Fink.

the way society is divided into descent groups. In the P. I. Ibirama narrative, however, there is no suggestion of parallels between natural and social classifications. It is, rather, cooperation among human classes that results in the creation of a single animal species.

A single paint design is insufficient. To produce a tapir, you need cooperation. To produce a jaguar, you need cooperation between those who paint with different designs. Cooperation — in the form of multiple designs — breathes life into an inanimate log. When the tapir and jaguar have been properly painted with human markings, they finally "call out," i.e., come to life.

Paint designs are linked to the animacy of nature. They kindle the life force. No wonder they are used at ceremonies for reintegrating a widow or widower into the community. Through the multiplicity of designs, inanimate objects come to life. The wooden inertness of the world — of death — is overcome. In the process, community is born.

Not all of the natural world requires such cooperation among humans. In a brief episode from the third origin myth, men make the first *jaguar-*

*terica*, a smaller feline. They also make the first snake. In these cases, the creation is less arduous. The main speaker fashions them from beeswax, then paints them himself. He requires no assistance from others. The paint designs are still what bring the animals to life. But you see no need for different designs. Elaborate cooperation is necessary only in the case of truly great animals.

Creation of the animal world is a metaphor for the creation of community, but not all animal creation requires community, that is, cooperation outside the family. Only truly great animals require full cooperation; only great social tasks call for full community. It is too easy for us (ethnographers) to suppose that natives subordinate all social values to community. In fact, community, as imagined and metaphorically represented, is not an absolute value. It falls within a hierarchy of values. Its scope of operation is limited.

Perhaps you can see how the limited-scope notion corresponds to the idea of community as periodic attachment. You need not be always together. You can go about your business inside the family. But for some purposes, on some occasions, you need something the family cannot provide. Consequently, you must, on those occasions, refresh your ties. You must rebuild community. To do that, you must already have a noumenal attachment, one that can be made phenomenal. Still, the community plays a limited role. You need refresh it, phenomenally, only periodically, only now and again.

"Out of sight, out of mind" — the adage bespeaks the half-life of attachment unnourished by physical co-presence. Noumenal understanding perpetuates ties, perpetuates involvements — but only for so long. If unrenewed, the attachment fades, and with it fades community. After a decade of absence, my own attachments have worn thin. The noumena have become translucent, less real.

By this time, you may be baffled. After all, I have argued two seemingly contradictory positions. One is that talk about descent groups is metaphorical — distinct from the unpredictable, murky stuff of social encounter. The other is that social encounter obeys a phenomenal regularity; the periodicity of interhousehold visitations at P. I. Ibirama resembles the rhythms of arrival and departure in the origin myth. Not distinct from phenomena, or a metaphor of them, origin myth discourse grows directly out of them. Can I have it both ways?

Well, I think so, if you grant that I have been talking about two distinct kinds of discourse, each with its unique circulatory patterns, its characteristic social properties; each replicable in its own way. One is the abstract discourse of descent. This discourse is generalized, decontextualized. You find it in statements such as, "you should give to your children the names of those [among your kinsmen] who have died," and "you paint with the designs of the one whose names you received." This is boot-strapping discourse — people accept it because of its presupposition of transhistoricity, because it seems detached from specifics. At the same time, by accepting it, by circulating it, people create commercial pathways along which other discourses can circulate as well.

The origin myth is another thing altogether. It is a narrative or a set of narratives. It purports to tell of events unfolding in time. Its statements are concrete, specific, temporally bounded: "Zẽzẽ's paint designs were always circles and dots. He was telling about his paint designs." The discourse is circulable, but its circulability derives from its subject matter. It refers to people and events so ludicrously old as to seem irrelevant, except perhaps as metaphor. Why squabble over it? If the narrative were concerned with current affairs, there would be reason to contest it. People would find something to squabble over. As a result, it would be, ultimately, less circulable.

Let me give you an example. In late 1974, the government post ran out of medical supplies. To do something about this, my wife and I set out in our Jeep — whose maximum velocity on the open highway, incidentally, was about twenty-five miles per hour — inching our way to the state capital at Florianópolis. After days of mindless haggling, we secured a load of medicines, which we dutifully brought back to P. I. Ibirama and turned over to the FUNAI agent. Within hours, a story circulated among the faction opposed to FUNAI that the medicines "had the name on them" of someone in that faction. I had presumably stolen them. When the story reached me, I protested vigorously. That did finally dampen the story's circulation, though, given its absurdity, it had a remarkable half-life. I heard about it for weeks to come.

In any case, like such contemporary narratives, the origin myth's statements pertain to specific individuals. They are not a master plan for community the way descent discourse is. The statement "you paint with the designs of the one whose names you received" refers not just to a specific person, but to everyone. It applies to infinitely many individuals and situations. In this sense, its position within the inferable sequence or order of discourse processes is distinctive. I have called this kind of statement "metadiscursive" because it sets up expectations about other, concrete statements, such as those in narrative. You reason from metadiscursive statements to conclusions about discourse.

Here is a specific example. Given what you know about Zẽzẽ — his "paint designs were always circles and dots" — the descent discourse sets up for you expectations about what is to follow. You might learn nothing further about Zẽzẽ, which would not surprise you. But if you thought about it, you would assume that Zẽzẽ's children, or, if not them, then some other of his relatives, would pass on his name to their own children. You would also anticipate that those receiving the names would paint with circles and dots. If the narrative reported something different, you would be surprised. It would violate your expectations.

When I claim that the discourse of descent is at odds with the realities of social encounter, I mean something like this. If you narrativize social encounters, the narratives violate the discourse expectations set up by the descent rules. You would be surprised, possibly startled, by outcomes. But you would still accept them. You would conclude that the world fails to match up with your expectations, but you would not necessarily, therefore, reject the metadiscourse.

Descent discourse is metadiscursive because it is closer to (or at) the beginning in an inferable sequence or chain of discourse processes. It instills in you expectations about other discourse. It leads you to anticipate how narratives will unfold. The reverse is not true. Narratives do not instill in you expectations about descent discourse. The statement "you paint with the designs of the one whose names you received" remains placidly unaffected by your interpretation of "Zẽzẽ's paint designs were always circles and dots." True, the narrative juxtaposition of concrete statements might violate your expectations, but the individual statements would not lead you to expect anything about the metadiscourse. Descent discourse and narrative are asymmetrically related. They occupy distinct positions within a sequence or chain of discourse processes.

If I am correct, the problem of social organization is not only practical. It is also epistemological. It is a profoundly intellectual problem. It forces you to confront the fit between knowledge and experience, intellect and sense. But I hope it is now obvious that the relationship is not a dyadic one. It is mediated by intervening discourse processes. How does decontextualized knowledge (descent discourse) align with contextualized knowledge (narratives)? How in turn do narratives match up with sensibility? The chain can be accordioned out.

The axiomaticity of descent discourse — the derivability of conclusions about other discourse from it — is what makes it so intriguing, so appealing in the first place. Furthermore, it makes it intriguing not just to anthropologists, but also to natives. Axiomaticity catches us in its snare of inference. Because it does so, it also perpetuates the discourse in memory. People remember a descent principle because it is good to reason with, good to think with. Axiomaticity, therefore, facilitates circulation.

At the same time, being of a distinct order, or occupying a distinct position in a chain, descent discourse derives its credibility from its relationship to narratives. It appears immanent in them, transparently true when the narrative unfolds according to its predictions. Correspondingly, it appears honored in the breach when the narrative violates them. Its veracity as "discursive knowledge," in the philosophical sense, depends upon its sweeping applicability to other discourses. It fails only when it is hopelessly out of sync with other narratives. In that case, it can be jettisoned, revised, or taken lightly, with a certain whimsy, as at P. I. Ibirama.

Please do not think, from what I have said, that there are two and only two levels of discourse — axiom-like, general statements and concrete, specific ones. The origin myth itself is, in some sense, metadiscursive. It comes earlier than some other narratives in the sequence or chain of discourse processes. Because of its stability — it is replicated precisely, in syllable-for-syllable fashion — it forms a fixed point of reference. Other more fleeting, less stable discourses can be fashioned after its image. Some historical narratives, indeed, obey origin myth-like rhythms of coming and going in almost slavish fashion. Where I expect resolution, the narrative sends the protagonists away, postponing it. When the resolution occurs — through a fight, for instance — it may be hardly noticeable, mentioned only in passing.

The sequence or chain of discourse processes I have been sketching parallels degrees of consciousness of the world. Axiom-like descent discourse is maximally luminous to consciousness. People have a sense that its statements are directly about reality, that it reflects the world, the way things are. But such statements are really only the first step in a chain of discourse processes leading back into the world. Narratives that are of a fleeting nature, that circulate but little, fail to fix the world in consciousness the way descent discourse does, the way even highly replicable narratives — such as the origin myth — do. They maintain contact with experience. But the brevity of their lives permits them little opportunity to influence the broader structures of community consciousness, as assembled in circulating discourse.

At the same time, the less consciously coded in discourse a phenomenal pattern from the world is, the more readily may it be circulated without contestation. The periodicity of comings and goings is a case in point. It is not coded in such a way as to be immediately accessible to consciousness. If you are familiar with the myth, you would never say that it is about comings and goings. You would say that it concerns the discovery of the world, the making of animals, the exchanging of things. But you would never say that it is about arrival and departure.

True, if you focus on specific utterances, the fact of arriving or departing is obvious:

| | |
|---|---|
| 1. ẽñ ẽn màg ka | 1. [From] inside my big house, |
| 2. ẽñ klẽ yun | 2. I stuck out my head, |
| 3. kũ ẽ yè awañ nõ | 3. and I waited for him. |
| 4. yògnẽgàñ tà katèle ñã | 4. [He] was descending from behind. |

| 5. ū yè kòñgàg ū yè | 5. "Who among you men, who [will come to see] |
| 6. cõ dè wèg tẽ | 6. this thing I have seen; |
| 7. we yè kakutā | 7. [who] will come to see [it]?" [he said]. |

You know that the above sequence is about arrival, in this case, Pligyug's. But this is only one part of a longer episode — Pligyug's exploration of the outer world. The latter is what seems salient.

Periodicity is not explicitly remarked. Rather, it is something that is sensed or felt. It is culled from sensory contact with the physical substance of linearly unfolding discourse, as well as from referential content. Snippets like the one above are sprinkled throughout at regular intervals. The pattern is not brought to consciousness — except when I remark it to you here — but neither is it wholly inaccessible. It lies beneath the surface of awareness, but not so far as to be out of reach. It can be replicated intuitively, subliminally, as when you hum music, unaware that someone around you hummed it first, that yours is a copy.

"It is exchange, always exchange, that emerges as the fundamental and common basis of all modalities of the institution of marriage," remarked Claude Lévi-Strauss (1969a [1949]: 479), and it is marriage that binds community. From such a starting point, what an easy step it is to agree with economists that the exchange of goods and services likewise produces community, that the binding force is localized in the physical act of transacting. But is it exchange, or is it the idea of exchange, that binds? Must commerce take place, or is it sufficient to believe in the idea of commerce?

Where actual exchange occurs, where goods and services are traded, phenomena confirm noumena. People act out the processes; they make things move around, change hands. But do the ideas merely reflect the practices? Or are the practices designed to confirm the idea, so that the idea itself may survive? If my argument is correct, the noumenal construal of community — its representation in consciousness through discourse — is aimed at ensuring the longevity of the construal itself. What is of prime importance is that people circulate the idea. They must think that they need each other. In circulating the idea, in the actual process of talking to one another — "you have something I want, and I'm willing to give you this for it" — they are ensuring the survival of that discourse, and, in so doing, they make possible as well the circulation of other discourse. The idea of mutual need creates the conditions for discourse circulation.

A chicken-and-egg matter? If people actually do exchange, how can you know which came first, the idea or the practice? P. I. Ibirama is fascinating in this regard. Virtually devoid of the practice — either of arranged marriage or of the exchange of goods — the community nevertheless supports and circulates the idea. In terms of the inferred order or chain of discourse, exchange is near the beginning, at the higher levels of consciousness, but it vanishes as we move toward the side of practice or embodiment. Here is my evidence, from the origin myth. You will see that "exchange" is what these episodes are about. In this sense, exchange differs from the arrival/departure pattern, which is present here, but not salient to consciousness:

| | | | | |
|---|---|---|---|---|
| 1. | wãgyò tõ kïy òg nu katèle | 1. | Relative Kïy arrived descending behind them. |
| 2. | tã òg glè yò ki kala mū | 2. | He arrived in their dance plaza. |
| 3. | ū tõ kòñgàg nū ki ñã | 3. | "What manner of man is this?" |
| 4. | ke mū | 4. | [someone] said. |
| 5. | iwo ēñ yïyï hā wū kïy ke tē | 5. | "My name would be Kïy," |
| 6. | ke | 6. | [he] said. |
| 7. | kū mā ēñ mlè glè yè kala | 7. | "Then come and dance with me," |
| 8. | ke | 8. | [he] said. |
| 9. | kū òg tõ ti mlè glè | 9. | And they danced with him. |
| 10. | ē zuwàgzàl tõ ē yògtà pègzē | 10. | His sisters were clothed in his loincloths. |
| 11. | òg mlè glè hà we | 11. | He really danced with them. |
| 12. | kū ē yògtà pègzēn | 12. | And his sisters were clothed. |
| 13. | kū ē tõ zuwàgzàl tõ ē yògtà pègzē | 13. | And though he had clothed his sisters [only] in loincloths, |
| 14. | kū tã ti mlè glè hà we | 14. | he really danced with him. |
| 15. | kū ti ñēglam | 15. | And [I] observed him, |
| 16. | lò ti kuce tū | 16. | and he had no raiment. |
| 17. | ē tõ zuwàgzàl tõ ē yògtà pègzē | 17. | He had clothed his sisters [only] in loincloths, |
| 18. | kū ti mlè glè | 18. | and [I] danced with him. |
| 19. | ē yàko tõ gal gluce nē | 19. | His dance ornament made of maize was there, |
| 20. | kū tã to tã | 20. | and he went to it. |
| 21. | tã ti to ban katã | 21. | He came back with it. |
| 22. | tã ti pã to cò | 22. | He tied it to his ankle. |
| 23. | tõge kū mā ēñ yàko tõ nēgè | 23. | "Now you are decorated with my dance ornament, |
| 24. | kū mā ēñ mlè glè | 24. | and you dance with me. |
| 25. | ne yè mā ēñ cõ wãgyan tū we | 25. | Why are you not related to me? |
| 26. | a kuce tū | 26. | You have no raiment, |
| 27. | hãñãglò ēñ mlè glè mū | 27. | but you dance with me." |
| 28. | wãgyò tõ kïy tõ yàko tõ nēcèg | 28. | Relative Kïy danced with the dance ornament,[6] |

29. kū tā ti mlè glè tèle

29. And he descended dancing with him.

30. glè yò ū ki òg glè nõ

30. In the place where they had danced once, they remained dancing.

31. kòñgàg kale yògï mā

31. [I] heard many men descending in this direction,

32. kū òg kòñgàg yòglè nõ

32. and they waited for them.

33. wãgyò tõ kïy òg nu katèle

33. Relative Kïy[7] descended behind them.

34. glè yò ki kala

34. [He] arrived in [the] dance plaza.

35. kū ū tõ kòñgàg nū wā

35. "What manner of man is this?"

36. ke mū

36. [he] said.

37. iwo ẽñ cõ wãgyò hā wū ki ñā

37. "It is a relative that I am,"

38. ke

38. [he] said.

39. kū a yïyï tẽ hālike tẽ

39. "And what would your name be?"

40. ke mū

40. [he] said.

41. ẽñ yïyï hā wū kïy ke tẽ

41. "My name would be Kïy;

42. ẽñ yïyï hā wū nūklèg ke tẽ

42. my name would be Nūklèg,"

43. ke mū

43. [he] said.

44. hà we

44. "Very well,"

45. kū nū ke mū

45. and I said,

46. mò ya ẽñ mlè glè ya kala

46. "come here and dance with me."

47. kū tā ti mlè glè hà we

47. And he danced very well with him.

48. kū ti tõ ti ñẽglam

48. And he observed him,

49. lò ẽ kuce tū

49. and he had no raiment.

50. ẽ tõ zuwàgzàl tõ ẽ yògtà pẽgzẽ

50. Though he had clothed his sisters [only] in loincloths,

51. kū ti mlè glè hà we

51. he really danced with him,

52. kū tā ẽ kul co tõ tā ti klẽ len

52. and he threw clothing[8] on top of him,

53. kū tā

53. and he [said]:

54. tòge

54. "Enough,

55. kū mā ẽñ kul tõ kul co tõ mā a yògtà pègzen

55. you will clothe your women with my clothes,

56. kū ẽñ mlè glè

56. and you will dance with me.

57. ne yè mā ẽñ cõ wãgyan tū we

57. Why does it seem that you are not related to me,

58. kū mā a kuce tū

58. and you have no raiment,

59. hāñaglò ẽñ mlè glè mū

59. but even so you dance with me?"

60. ke mū

60. [he] said.

61. wāgyò tõ nūklèg tõ kïy tõ òg kul tõ kul co tõ tā ē yògtàpègzē
62. kū òg mlè glè hà
63. mūñāglò hul wāgyò tõ wāgyò tõ klēno nā nõ òg nu katèle
64. glè yò tē ki kala mū
65. ū tõ kòñgàg nū ki ñā
66. ke òg ti mõ mū
67. iwo ēñ cõ wāgyò hā wū ki ñā
68. ke mū
69. kū a yïyï tē hālike
70. ēñ yïyï hā wū klēno ke tē
71. ēñ yïyï hā wū zughà ke tē
72. ke mū
73. mò yè ēñ mlè glè yè kala

74. ke mū
75. kū tā ti mlè glè hà we
76. kū òg tõ ti ñēglam
77. lò ē kuce tū
78. kū zuwàg zàl tõ ē yògtà pēgzē
79. òg mlè glè mū
80. hā ne yè mā ēñ cõ wāgyan tū we
81. kū mā a kuce tū
82. hāñāglò ēñ mlè glè mū
83. ē kul tõ kul kucug nā tõ ti klē len mū
84. tòge
85. kū mā ēñ kul tõ kul kucug tõ a yògtà pègzē
86. kū mā ēñ mlè glè
87. ne yè mā ēñ cõ wāgyan tū we

88. kū mā a kuce tū
89. hāñāglò ēñ mlè glè mū
90. òg kul tõ kul kucug tõ wāgyò tõ klēno yògtà pēgzē
91. kū ti mlè glè mū
92. mūñāglò hul ti yògtà ka ū mlè nõ kàgkòl

61. Relative Nūklèg Kïy clothed his sisters in the clothing,
62. and he really danced with them.
63. Meanwhile, relative, relative Klēno descended behind them.
64. [He] arrived in the dance plaza.
65. "What manner of man is this,"
66. they said to him.
67. "It is a relative that I am,"
68. [he] said.
69. "And what would your name be?"
70. "My name would be Klēno,
71. my name would be Zughà."
72. [he] said.
73. "Then come and dance with me,"

74. [he] said,
75. and he really danced with him,
76. and they observed him,
77. and he had no raiment,
78. and although his sisters were clothed [only] with loincloths,
79. he danced with them.
80. "Why indeed does it seem that you are not related to me,
81. and you have no clothes,
82. and yet [you] dance with me?"
83. His red clothing he threw on top of him.
84. "Enough,
85. and you dress your sisters with my red clothing,
86. and you dance with me.
87. Why does it seem that you are not related to me,
88. and you have no raiment,
89. but even so you dance with me?"
90. With their red clothing relative Klēno's sisters were clothed,
91. and [they] danced with him.
92. Meanwhile, his sisters had all married [them], it seems.

93. wãñõ kàgzèg nõñã

93. [They] were happy with one another.

94. tòge kũ nã yè ãg tõ wãñõ yàgmlan

94. "Now we are in-laws,

95. kũ wãñõ yï nõ hòn

95. and let [us] lie together,

96. kũ wãñõ yï pẽ lï yig le ñã

96. and [let us] put our fires in front of one another,"

97. ke

97. [they] said,

98. kũ òg wãñõ kàgzèg nõñã

98. and they were happy with one another.

99. ti mlè glè tèle

99. [They] descended dancing with him.

100. glè yò ũ mẽ glè

100. Where [they] danced once, they danced all about,

101. mũ lò hul wãgyò tõ zàgpope tõ patè òg nu katèle

101. and then at once relative Zàgpope Patè descended behind them.

102. òg glè yò tẽ ki kala mũ

102. [He] arrived in their dance plaza.

103. ũ tõ kòñgàg nũ ki ñã

103. "What manner of man is this?"

104. ke mũ

104. [they] said.

105. iwo ẽñ cõ wãgyò hã wũ ki ñã

105. "It is a relative that I am,"

106. ke mũ

106. [he] said.

107. kũ a yïyï tẽ hãlike tẽ

107. "And what would your name be?"

108. ẽñ yïyï hã wũ zàgpope ke tẽ

108. "My name would be Zàgpope.

109. ẽñ yïyï hã wũ patè ke tẽ

109. My name would be Patè."

110. ke mũ mò ya ẽñ mlè glè yè kala

110. "Well then come and dance with me."

111. ke

111. [they] said.

112. tã ti mlè glè we

112. He danced with him, indeed,

113. kũ tã ti ñẽglam lò

113. and he observed him,

114. lò ẽ kuce tũ

114. and he had no raiment.

115. kũ tã ẽ tõ zuwàgzàl tõ ẽ yògtà pègzẽ

115. and even though he had dressed his sisters [only] with loincloths,

116. kũ òg mlè glè mũ

116. [he] danced with them,

117. kũ tã ẽ kul tõ kul kupli tõ tã ti klẽ len mũ

117. and his white clothing he threw on top of him.

118. tòge

118. "Enough,

119. kũ mã ẽñ kul tõ kul kupli tõ mã a yògtà pègzẽ

119. and you dress your sisters with my white clothing,

120. kũ ẽñ mlè glè

120. and dance with me.

121. ne yè mã ẽñ cõ wãgyan tũ we

121. Why does it seem that you are not related to me,

122. kũ mã a kuce tũ

122. and you have no raiment,

123. hãñãglò ẽñ mlè glè mũ

123. but even so you dance with me?"

124. òg kul tõ kul kupli tõ zàgpope
     tẽ ẽ tõ yògtà pẽgzẽ

124. With their white clothing
     Zàgpope clothed his sisters,

125. kũ òg mlè glè mũ

125. and [he] danced with them.

126. ñãglò hul nũ ti yògtà ka ũ mlè
     nõ kàgkòl kũ

126. Meanwhile, his sisters had all
     married [them], it seems,

127. kũ òg wãñõ kàgzèg nõñã

127. and they were happy with one
     another.

128. tòge nã yè tòge

128. "Now it is done,

129. kũ nã ãg tõ wãñõ yàgmlan

129. and we are in-laws,

130. kũ nã wãñõ yï nõ hòn

130. and let us lie together,

131. kũ wãñõ yï pẽ lï yig le ñã

131. and [let us] put our fires in front
     of one another,"

132. ke

132. [they] said,

133. kũ wãñõ kàgzèg nõñã

133. and [they] were happy with one
     another.

134. ẽ yògwañ tõ pazi tõ ẽ tõ ãma
     we to

134. Where the chief Pazi had seen the
     savannas,

135. ẽ yo gò kule tẽ

135. where [he] had cleared the ground
     before him,

136. mẽ glè le

136. [they] descended dancing all
     about.

Though obscured by archaic language, though fogged in by dense expression, the ideas of marriage alliance and exchange shine through. In each of the four subepisodes, a visitor comes to "dance" with those present. Those present in turn give the visitor "clothes," blankets painstakingly made from plant fiber. The last two visitors—and possibly also the first two, though we only infer this—marry off their sisters to those present. As if the message of community building were not already obvious, as if it were not painted in giant letters, we are elbowed into looking at it by such phrases as "they were happy with one another," as well as the reported speech, "let us lie together . . . let us put our fires in front of one another." Marriage and material exchange are explicitly conceptualized as bases of community.

If I am correct, however, the fact of exchange is less important than the idea. What is essential for the circulation of discourse is that people have some kind of social encounter, that they visit with one another. Moreover, because discourse has a half-life, it is important that they visit at regular intervals. There must be recurrent communication, renewed opportunities for discourse circulation. If the idea of exchange motivates such encounters, then the discourse that itself encodes that idea will circulate, laying down the roadways for further circulation.

You see how the idea of periodic visitation is coded in this segment of discourse. Not the conscious meaning of the discourse, it is implicit in the poetry of discourse, suggesting itself to you like a hummed tune that you unthinkingly mimic, even as your consciousness ponders weightier matters. Arrival sets off the subepisodes one from another, but arrival itself is discursively recurrent, as can be appreciated from the discourse snippets in which it is encoded:

| | | | |
|---|---|---|---|
| 2. | tã òg glè yò ki kala mũ | 2. | He arrived in their dance plaza. |
| 34. | glè yò ki kala | 34. | [He] arrived in [the] dance plaza. |
| 64. | glè yò tẽ ki kala mũ | 64. | [He] arrived in the dance plaza. |
| 102. | òg glè yò tẽ ki kala mũ | 102. | [He] arrived in their dance plaza. |

On a less conscious, more embodied plane, to paraphrase Lévi-Strauss, it is social encounter, always social encounter, that emerges as fundamental. Even as your consciousness preoccupies itself with exchange, the poetry of discourse works its way into your unconscious, insinuates itself into the processes whereby you narrativize the world.

You see the disparity between the referential content of publicly circulating discourse, which purports to be about the bases of circulation, about the ineffable experience of social encounter that makes circulation possible. The further you go toward the side of consciousness, of metadiscourse, the less in touch you are with elusive sensibility. At P. I. Ibirama, this out-of-touchness is expressed in the playfulness, rather than seriousness, with which the metadiscourse is employed.

An example of experience-distant metadiscourse is the circulating "rule" of exogamy at P. I. Ibirama. Henry (1964 [1941]: 176) noted that members of the community "say that people having the same marks cannot marry, but for two hundred years there has been absolutely no attempt to live up to the theory." Indeed, if people with the same design do marry, they simply change their designs — "no feeling of shame is connected with marrying a person of the same mark" (1964 [1941]: 176). This is not because the system is broken down. It is because the metadiscourse is taken for what it is, a metaphor of community rather than a literal truth. Anthropologists have been for too long literal-minded. They (and, again, I should say we) have wanted to see metadiscourse as a reflection of the really real, rather than as a community-building metaphor. But the metadiscourse is playful.

You can appreciate this playfulness by studying the special kinship terminology that is brought into play at P. I. Ibirama when paint designs are used. Metaphorical playfulness here contrasts with the matter-of-fact usage of the everyday kinship terms. The paint design "kinship" terminology is part of a special speech register, whose old-sounding words are drawn from the origin myth. Here is Henry's (1964 [1941]: 176–179) rendition of the terminology:

| Same Design | Different Design |
|---|---|
| *yògtà* = a woman with the same paint design (male speaking); [no counterpart in everyday usage] | *plū* = a woman with a different paint design (male speaking) [everyday usage = wife] |
| *kòñka hà* = a person with the same paint design [in everyday usage = relative (there, however, the term is *kòñka* without the *hà*)] | *mèn* = a man with a different paint design (female speaking) [everyday usage = husband] |
| | *wāmō hà* = a man with a different paint design (male speaker); woman with a different paint design (female speaking) [no counterpart in everyday usage] |

Two terms — *yògtà* and *wāmō hà* — are genuinely part of a special register. Evidently not vestiges of an earlier phase of language history — there are no apparent cognates in the closely related Kaingang language — they are never used in everyday speech. We seem to be dealing with a specially constructed, self consciously metaphorical set of terms. By using them — and their use was, during my visits, confined to elders and, even then, confined to ritual occasions — one is playing at kinship rather than living it. The terms are not construed as reflecting actual alliances or everyday social relations.

Why then employ such a terminology? I believe that its usage is in keeping with what we have seen of community more generally as it is reflected in discourse. The terms provide images for how to build community. You build it by marriage; you build it by thinking of it in terms of family. It just so happens that marriage alliance is not a matter of exogamy of the paint design group. It just so happens that all those people you call "husband" (*mèn*) or "wife" (*plū*) are not your conjugal partners. At the same time, even if you are only playing at community by using the terminology, even if you are only representing family-like cooperation within the community, the playing is itself a form of community building. You are aware of the artificiality of community, but, at the same time, you are actively living community.

For too long we have been victimized by a plodding seriousness on the part of descent and alliance theorists. They may have been the dupes, in turn, of peoples who took their own metadiscourse too seriously. P. I. Ibirama refreshes us in this regard. There it becomes obvious that the community, imagined as groups in alliance, is a metaphorical community. But the very obviousness of the case reveals to us what is hidden in the supposedly normal ones. Even in the latter we are dealing with forms of representation. The true nature of community slips away from us. It is ineffable. The discourse image of the phenomenon contradicts the phenomenon itself, which is not readily renderable in discourse. Yet, at the same time, the phenomenon depends on discourse.

How can this be? It can be if the practical effect of a discourse is distinct from its referential meaning. If the effect of talk about social organization is to motivate people to interact, and if the effect of interacting is to circulate discourse, then talk about social organization may be efficacious even if it is not veracious. It may produce the phenomenon it purports to describe — that is, community — even though its image of it is refracted and distorted.

The process I am describing depends upon a key aspect of discourse, namely, that it is both a representation of other things and a thing in its own right. Being a practitioner of a discourse — performing the origin myth, for example, or even talking about exogamy or descent — makes one a participant in the community. Discourse as embodied behavior is community building. But, at the same time, when you implement a discourse, you propagate what it purports to represent. You circulate what purports to be a truth. But it may be that the circulation is more important than the truthfulness; the actual content of the representation may be less significant than its movement through space and across time. In other words, it may not matter *what* image of community people subscribe to, as long as they subscribe to and circulate *an* image.

At the same time, it would be folly to imagine that the "what" of the representation makes no difference, that any old image of community will do. What allows a discourse to circulate is, in part, at least, the appeal of the idea, even if that appeal is enhanced by, or confused with, rhetorical or poetic persuasiveness. Principles of exogamy and descent circulate because they are about marriage and kinship. They represent the community in terms of the family, and it is the trope of family that makes them appealing, that facilitates their effectiveness.

However, you should not be misled by effectiveness. Because an idea holds sway over the mind, because it excites the intellect, does not mean that it corresponds to an *a priori* reality. You can be deceived especially in the case of discourses of community. If an idea is truly persuasive, it may be taken literally rather than metaphorically. And, if it is taken literally, people may actually produce a phenomenon that confirms their noumenal understanding. But the phenomenon, in this case, is itself a kind of sign. Like the lineage, it is a clarified representation of something murkier — social encounter in which discourse is created and circulated. Luckily, cases like that of P. I. Ibirama bring us back to our senses. They remind us that conscious representation and perceptible reality do not always correspond, that people can hold an idea of exchange without carrying out exchanges in practice, that they can form groups though those groups have no other practical purpose than embodying the idea.

The problem of social integration is, therefore, not at all lackluster, or, at least, it is one whose luster can be restored by burnishing. Beneath that dulled surface is a dazzling epistemological idea — thought about a phenomenon (community), when coded and publicly circulated in words, may bring the phenomenon into existence. Like the jaguar springing to life when painted with human designs, community comes to life when it is talked about. Simultaneously, what is important is not the phenomenon *per se*, but the process by which it came to be. People are interested in the phenomena about which they talk — lineages or exchange — but what is important is that they talk. In circulating discourse about community, they build community, and community makes all else possible.

# *Chapter 6.* This Is Your Making

In the game of "Telephone," one child whispers a message to another, who in turn whispers it to a third, and so on down the line. The fun is in seeing how the message changes, sometimes beyond recognition, by the end. From a discourse-centered perspective, the game is intriguing because it models one kind of circulatory process — linear and sequential. Discourse travels from person to person, family to family. Even if you conceptualize culture narrowly as tradition, the same kind of sequential, telephone-game-like interactions can suffice. Discourse — read "culture" — is replicated over time and across generations, as in the case of myth. You do not need to imagine that people assemble into groups, with everyone present at the same time, in the same place.

It is, therefore, a mystery that people do assemble into groups, that they do hold collective ceremonies. Assemblage is an empirical fact, but one not immediately derivable from the culture concept. In 1975, I witnessed and photographed a large-scale gathering at P. I. Ibirama, with several hundred people camped in a circle maybe seventy-five yards in diameter. The occasion was the celebration of one of two key community-wide ceremonies — this one the *ãgyïn*, for reintegrating a widow or widower after a two-to-four-week seclusion. In all likelihood, this was the last to be held, the elders mentioning that it was for the younger people "to see." In 1982, an *ãglan* was scheduled during my visit — and in my honor — but it was canceled at the last minute. This is the other community-wide ceremony, in which lip-plugs were given to young boys (approximately two to three years of age) and thigh tattoos to young girls (also two to three years of age). It also functioned as a community-wide party. More and more, nowadays, group assemblage centers around the Assembly of God church, which has taken hold, displacing the native forms.

What is the significance of these ceremonies? If they are not essential to culture, understood as circulating discourse, why do they occur? Why do people physically come together in large groupings, clustered in comparatively small spaces, in which they are immediately visible to one another, phenomenally accessible?

Durkheim (1969 [1912]: 246 ff.), contemplating the Australian aboriginal *corrobbori* ceremony, concluded that assemblage kindles respect for the collectivity, makes people feel its power over them. Implicitly, the group as assembled and culture as shared go hand in hand. Assemblage arouses sensations that attach people to their collective representations, to their culture. But you have seen that it is not necessary to imagine a group coming together in one place at one time in order to conceive of the circulation of culture. So what significance do those assemblages hold, what secret about culture do they conceal?

A second, and possibly related, question may shed some light on the first: How is the problem of assemblage conceptualized within the culture itself, that is, within its publicly circulating discourse? The P. I. Ibirama representation may strike you as curious. Group assemblage cuts a bad image in public discourse at P. I. Ibirama. It has a decidedly bad rep. Where it is talked about, the representation is negative: People fight, die; families burst apart; society is riven asunder. An entire myth focuses on these anticommunitarian themes, and the themes are central as well in the origin myth. You can find them also in numerous historical narratives. What are we to make of this?

From a Durkheimian perspective, there is a paradox here. Traditional discourse is one part of culture; it is passed down across the generations. Yet it values another part of culture — group assemblage — negatively. It represents assemblage as leading to fights, to permanent disaggregation. If, as Durkheim thought, assemblage demonstrates the dominance of groups over individuals, and, simultaneously, facilitates the transmission of culture, why should culture represent assemblage so negatively? Should it not celebrate it as community building? Here is an enigma.

A clue is that, in this culture, group assembly is a matter of embodiment. The ceremonies that go well are not the subject of discourse. There is no circulating discursive blueprint for how to do them. You can induce people to tell you about them, if you have not yourself seen them, but they are not a topic of discourse within the community — except for those ceremonies that resulted in violence and dispersal. Even in the latter case, the ceremonies do not come under scrutiny. They are the backdrop for violence, for antisocial behavior. The disjuncture between talking about and embodying ceremony parallels the split between intelligibility and sensibility you have already encountered in the case of space. Immediately perceptible physical space is not the subject of circulating discourse. Only space beyond the realm of the perceptible gets talked about. Talk is reserved for what cannot be directly seen or experienced.

The point of ceremonies, at P. I. Ibirama, is direct experience through the senses. In this community, ceremonies mean physical contact with others, seeing them, hearing them, smelling them, bumping up against them. No wonder emphasis is placed on decorating the body with paint, clothing, and ornaments. It seems important in this community, moreover, that the embodied aspects of culture not be the subject of elaborate discourse, that they not be talked about, interpreted. Better that you should see for yourself.

This is not to say that discourse is not an important component of ceremonies. Indeed, even the origin myth is performed primarily at the * āgyïn* ceremony, and a great deal of singing occurs there as well. However, this discourse is not *about* the ceremonies, at least not in a direct, referential way. I again distinguish two facets of discourse. On the one hand, discourse is a tool for reference. It encodes aspects of the world. It is about reality. On the other hand, discourse is a physical object, a set of embodied behaviors. It is a part of the world, publicly accessible. It is a sensible reality. While discourse as a physical object is part of ceremonies, ceremonies themselves are not the referential object of that discourse. Ceremonies elude the beacon of interpretive consciousness that the referential side of discourse casts about into the darkness. By preference, they operate in the shadows, on the periphery.

By way of contrast, the Ndembu of Zambia, as described by Victor Turner (1967), train the lens of reflective discourse on the phenomenal aspects of ceremonies, evidently believing that their meanings can and should be dissected. Exegesis of ritual as symbolic assumes a key role. You can get people to talk about objects such as the *mudyi* tree, and this kind of talk presumably circulates on its own. Local discourse interprets meaning. There is no reticence, no concealment. At P. I. Ibirama, ritual behaviors and objects are not "symbolic" in this sense; they are not consciously discussed and analyzed. Whatever meanings accrue to the behaviors stem from them directly. You are aware of a reticence around the issues, a reluctance to engage in interpretive discussions, as if either the behaviors were intrinsically meaningless, or, perhaps, they concealed some deep, awesome secret that had to be consciously denied. Your repeated questions about interpretation — "Why do you do this?" — are answered by the phrase "That is the custom." Even when you ask simple "what" questions, the response is often to show you rather than tell you about it.

I should be clear about this. The referential aspect of discourse is not absent from ceremonies. Indeed, it sometimes contributes crucially to the constitution of ritual meanings. In the *āglan*, for example, when young boys have their lips pierced, this is done by the ceremonial father (*kòkla*), who, together with the ceremonial mother (*mà*), plays a key role at various life-cyclic junctures, in the first instance disposing of the placenta by burial.

The ceremonial parents are selected by the parents, and are usually close relatives of the parents. What is significant, even though it is not talked about, is that the ceremonial parents represent the claims of a broader community over the child, and, in some ways, in opposition to the parents. At the *āglan* ceremony, toward the end, a game is played in which the ceremonial parents square off against the social parents. The two sides toss back and forth three basketry objects known as *kawig* — also the name of a kind of bird that you always see hovering back and forth overhead. What is interesting is that the *kawig* are given names. The two larger are called *yug* (father) and *nō* (mother), and the smaller one is called *yi* (child).

The referential aspect of discourse allows us — anthropologists and natives alike — to read deep significance into this game. We all imagine that the game has something to do with symbolizing the interplay between the differential claims of family and community over the child, that there is something here about "fathers" versus "ceremonial fathers," "mothers" versus "ceremonial mothers." The important point, however, is that these "symbolic" analyses are never put into words by members of the community themselves. It is not that they are incapable of doing so. It is that there is a reluctance to fix in discourse meanings that can be extracted by each individual directly from sensory experience, including the experience of discourse.

How much effort in anthropology has been directed at illuminating the "symbolic" meanings of behaviors that are not so illuminated by the people engaging in them! The bringing to consciousness by means of talk of otherwise unconscious meanings is the cornerstone of classical Freudian psychoanalysis. In our excitement about making meanings conscious, however, have we overlooked an important possibility, namely, that the point of some "symbolic" behaviors is that their meanings are not accessible to public consciousness? Rather than (or in addition to) understanding what meanings accrue to particular behaviors, we need to ask also why those meanings are not consciously formulated in discourse by the natives themselves.

The question may have to do with the experience of meanings and the affective significance attached to them. Referential discourse has a way of distancing individuals from immediate affective experience of, and involvement in, the world. It objectifies involvement. Rather than allow individuals to encounter the world with immediacy, discourse blinds experience with the light of consciousness.

There is an analogue here to the problem of expression of feeling. In cultures with a developed ritual wailing or lamentation tradition, as in many central Brazilian Amerindian societies, grief is expressed by means of formalized crying. Your stylized weeping tells others of your grief. Contrast this expressive style with one in which an individual says referentially — as is so often the case in American culture — "I'm feeling sad." You can, of course, express feelings by means of that referential utterance. For example, you can encode feelings in the actual sound, using lament-like intonations, creaky voice, or even cry breaks. But that is probably not the norm in middle-class American culture. More typically, you utter the words in a neutral voice. The referential meaning alone conveys the sentiment. Extreme cases occur when the affect contradicts the referential meaning of an utterance, as in psychoanalytic sessions when the patient barks, in a harsh, angry voice, "I am not angry!"

This discrepancy between reference and experience can be exploited by a culture. The advertising complex in America is largely built up around the discrepancy. The advertisement, understood as being *about* the object advertised, nevertheless has its own experiential dimension. Feelings and experiences built up by means of it can be transferred onto the object advertised, so that a confusion is created about the experience of the object. Are the feelings connected with the object a product of the experiences the individual has with the object? Or are those feelings a product of the experiences with the advertisement, which then make it impossible to have, relatively speaking, unmediated experiences of the object itself?

I am not suggesting that anyone anywhere ever has completely unmediated experiences of objects, but I am suggesting that this is a matter of degree. In the case of ceremonies at P. I. Ibirama, there is an implicit ban on explicit interpretation. We can understand this negatively, as an absence or lack of "native exegesis." Or we can understand it positively, as a way of encouraging experiences and meanings that are — again, relatively speaking — unguided by referential consciousness. A key to ceremonies at P. I. Ibirama is their implicitly positive valuation of experience without conscious scrutiny, of meaning without interpretation through discourse, of significance grasped through non-referential or only obscurely referential signs.

It may seem that we have drifted from the original questions: (1) why physically come together into groups and (2) why represent that assemblage negatively, as resulting in violence and dispersal? But it has been necessary to establish that the principal assemblages at P. I. Ibirama — the ceremonies — should remain outside the beacon of consciousness, that there is something positive here. Ceremonies should not be subject to scrutiny through the referential aspect of discourse, especially not discourse that circulates outside the context of the assemblage itself, for example, in the domestic arena.

In making these observations, however, we have already begun to lift the veil surrounding the problem of assemblage. In this culture, part of the attraction of ceremonies is their mystery. From the point of view of the domestic encounters, what goes on in ceremonies is unknown, or, rather, known only through the experience of it, not through the experience of something else—that is, the household discourse. Ceremony finds its attractive power, its seductive allure, in its inarticulateness; it is not talked about in everyday life. Far from the essence of culture, understood as replicable discourse, ceremony stands outside the reach of referential culture. Its essence is to be a kind of culture distinct from that associated with conscious meanings. For so many years, anthropologists studied only referentially accessible culture, using interview techniques, trying to get inside native minds, making articulate the unspoken meanings superimposed on the world by natives through their words. But if the very goal of P. I. Ibirama ceremonies is to remain unspoken, have we not missed something crucial—the positive valuation of inarticulateness?

Whereas the referential meanings encoded in discourse are decontextualized meanings, those surrounding ritual are contextualized. They are of the moment, enduring only as feeling traces subsequently. The meanings are not of the articulated kind that can be trotted out on any occasion and rescrutinized. To grasp the meaning, as the saying goes, "you had to have been there." If it is the case that the meanings cannot be rearticulated in a decontextualized fashion, if someone cannot simply tell you about the experience, then you must, if you want to know about it, go to the ceremony yourself. The very closed-mouthedness, in the everyday sphere, about ceremonial meanings is one way in which ceremonies acquire an attractive force. They are magnets that pull isolated individuals into their fields of attraction. Individuals want to know what the ceremony is all about, but to know it, they must go and see. Desire for an experience that is entirely contextualized is the mechanism by which group assemblage is perpetuated.

We seemingly cannot, from this one-time quality of ceremony, account for subsequent occurrences. Yet the quality may be precisely what engenders the most distinctive characteristic of ceremonies—their tendency to include prescribed behavior. To allow someone who was not there to experience the contextual meaning of an earlier assemblage, or to re-create that feeling oneself at a later date, one has to try to do precisely what was done on the earlier occasion. The attempt at precise replication is, of course, the hallmark of ceremony. Only by re-creating the forms—the behaviors, physical ambience, even the time of day or year—can one hold out any hope of re-creating the evanescent meanings.

This would seem to make group assemblage and inarticulable ceremony the birthplace of culture, and thus to confirm Durkheim's intuition, even if not his reasoning, about the ascendancy of the group over the individual. Indeed, an argument can be made that the ceremony is primeval with respect to culture. But it is culture of a particular sort: embodied, nonreferential, contextualized. It is not all of culture, a crucial component of which is the referential portion of discourse.

At the same time, you already appreciate that discourse itself has an embodied moment, in addition to being referential. It is a thing and hence also potentially ritualizable. You can and do find ritualized speech in ceremonial contexts. As a thing, discourse participates in embodied, non-referential, contextualized meaningfulness. Hence, when you consider the paradox of why discourse in this culture portrays group assemblage as leading to violent dispersal, you have to understand that the opposition between discourse and group assemblage is linked to a parallel opposition between the referential and nonreferential aspects of discourse. Group assemblage has something to do with nonreferential meanings.

To explore the opposition, I turn to one key discourse representation of ceremony and assemblage. This narrative circulates in the domestic arena and hence stands opposed to group assemblage itself. It does not depend upon the group coming together for its circulation or life. At the same time, it is part of culture. It is told and retold, undergoing changes but also exhibiting continuities, and it is passed down across the generations. Its circulation resembles that of the telephone game—linear, sequential, chainlike:

| | | | |
|---|---|---|---|
| 1. | kū wãtàñ tẽ wũ wãtàñ tẽ wũ mõg mũ | 1. | And Wãñtàñ, Wãñtàñ made mead. |
| 2. | mõg | 2. | [He] made mead, |
| 3. | kū tã ẽ tõ mõg tẽ ki tã akle wãñmõ tẽ tõ ki wagzun kan | 3. | and in the mead he assembled every kind of animal.[1] |
| 4. | akle tẽ tõ wãcïn tẽ ka tã tõ ãglẽl tẽ tõ wãcõ ãglẽl yè tẽ tõ ki win wã | 4. | The animals, a long time ago, humans, in order to make them into humans he put them in the mead, |
| 5. | kū tã ãglag mũ | 5. | and held an ãglan ceremony. |
| 6. | òg yòglag nõ | 6. | They were celebrating the ãglan. |
| 7. | mẽg wũ uyol to nẽ | 7. | The jaguar sat next to the tapir, |
| 8. | kū wũ hòw wũ kãme to nẽ | 8. | and the *jaguarterica* [Port.] sat next to the deer. |
| 9. | ẽ tõ ti tañ tẽ yè | 9. | He [the *jaguarterica*] wanted to kill him, |
| 10. | kū mẽg tẽ tõ uyol tẽ tañ yè ti to nẽ wã | 10. | and the jaguar was sitting next to the tapir in order to kill him. |
| 11. | kū wũ wel yugug màg wũ zuyin to nẽ | 11. | and, indeed, the eagle sat next to the porcupine, |
| 12. | kū tã zazan mõ wũ tã | 12. | and he said to the armadillo: |

13. ēñ kòkla ēñ ñõ mā ti mlè glè

14. a wòglu tē nē
15. ñãglò tē zàl tē tòl kò
16. kū zuyin lā tē wū ki yàn ke tū tē

17. tā ti mlè glè
18. ti mē hònhòn ke
18a. ñõ nïg
18b. ñõ mèn can
18c. ñõ ko yò nē wem
18d. mā yò ke nem
19. mūñãglò wū mēg tē wū uyol tē mē hun

19a. kagzal we
19b. kagzal we
19c. kò kònā hà we yò
19d. tà yò wā wè
19e. yò wā wè
19f. kï nug ke
19g. ñãgzò we
19h. ñãgzò we
20. ke tā kànātē

21. uyol tē ti yè hālike kànātē
21a. kagzal we
21b. kò kònā hà we yò
21c. to yò wā wè
21d. yò wā wè
21e. yò wā wè
22. ke tā kànātē

23. mēg tē ti mē hòn ke kànātē

23a. mēg yò wi wè
23b. mēg yò ko tū wā
23c. wãnò kòglē
23d. cà klā pe lè
24. mūñãglò mēg ū to òg tō how gèke mū tē
25. kāme tē mlè glè kànātē
25a. kāme tē

13. "My ceremonial father, dance with him for me.

14. You have a hard shell.
15. Because your hide is tough,
16. the porcupine's spines will not penetrate it."

17. He danced with him.
18. All about him he went: "*hònhòn*,
18a. mother, make fun of[2]
18b. mother, husband
18c. mother, eat, place
18d. listen."
19. Meanwhile, the jaguar went about the tapir going: "*hun*,

19a. like the *kagzal*,
19b. like the *kagzal*,
19c. tree, fruit, seen well
19d. toward, place, see
19e. place, see
19f. call out, belly, say
19g. feces see
19h. feces see,"
20. He went about saying this [i.e., singing].

21. The tapir went about like him:
21a. "like the *kagzal*
21b. tree, fruit, seen well
21c. toward, place, see
21d. place, see,
21e. place, see"
22. he went about saying [i.e., singing].

23. The jaguar went about him going: "*hòn*,

23a. jaguar, place, see
23b. jaguar, place, eat not
23c. [kind of tree] behind
23d. black, children."
24. Meanwhile, another jaguar, which they call the *jaguarterica*,
25. danced about with the deer:
25a. "the deer

| | |
|---|---|
| 25b. kǎme ñǎgzò yò | 25b. deer's defecating place |
| 25c. kòglẽ cǎ klǎ pe lò | 25c. [a kind of tree], children," |
| 26. ke mũ | 26. [he] said [i.e., sang]. |
| 27. ñǎglò how tẽ ti mlè wãñ | 27. Meanwhile, the *jaguarterica* [went] together with him, |
| 28. kũ tǎ | 28. and he [sang]: |
| 28a. mẽg yò wi wè | 28a. "jaguar, place, see |
| 28b. mẽg yò kò tũ | 28b. jaguar, place, tree, not |
| 28c. wãnò kò glẽ | 28c. [kind of tree] behind |
| 28d. kǎme | 28d. deer." |
| 29. ti yan gèke | 29. So his singing continued, |
| 30. kũ tǎ ti mõ | 30. and he [the jaguar] said to him [the deer]: |
| 31. kũ mǎ mǎ ẽñ cõ yan mũ | 31. "Are you singing [provocatively] at me?" |
| 32. kũ tǎ | 32. and he [the deer] [said]: |
| 33. i tõge kũ nũ | 33. "No, all I'm [singing] is: |
| 33a. kǎme ñǎgzò yò | 33a. 'deer's defecating place, |
| 33b. kò glẽ | 33b. behind tree,' |
| 34. gèke nũ mũ | 34. so I've been [singing]." |
| 35. ke tǎ kànãtẽ ñã | 35. He went about saying [this]. |
| 36. tǎ ti mlè glè kànãtẽ | 36. He went about dancing with him [until] |
| 37. mẽg tẽ kǎme tẽ ki pugke mũ | 37. the jaguar grabbed the deer, |
| 38. kũ tǎ ti mag mũ | 38. and he killed it. |
| 39. mũñǎglò uyol mẽg tẽ ti ki pugke | 39. Meanwhile, as for the tapir, the jaguar grabbed him. |
| 40. tǎ ti kugmẽ | 40. He was struggling with him. |
| 41. ti mlè wãcõ tǎ goy tòg tẽ tà goy tòg tẽ goy tẽ ki uyol tẽ kutǎ mũ | 41. The two of them together, the water — there was water there — the tapir fell into the water. |
| 42. tǎ mlòy tèle | 42. He floated down. |
| 43. tǎ ti klẽ plèn tèle | 43. He floated down ahead of him. |
| 44. tokè ti towañ mũ | 44. Now he let him go. |
| 45. mẽg tẽ uyol tẽ towañ mũ | 45. The jaguar let the tapir go. |
| 46. ñǎglò zuyin tẽ yugug tẽ ti ki punke mũ | 46. Meanwhile, as for the porcupine, the eagle jumped on him. |
| 47. ñǎglò wũ gòlõ wel zazan tẽ ki punke | 47. Meanwhile, the *gòlõ* [a wildcat] jumped on the armadillo, |
| 48. hãmõ tǎ gò tògtẽ tõ kumke | 48. but he dug a hole in the ground, |
| 49. kũ tǎ klǎm ge mũ | 49. and he went in below. |
| 50. klǎm tǎ ge mũ | 50. He entered below. |

51. *quatro* ke kũ òg nõne zazan tẽ

52. òg tẽ klãm tatà *vinte metro* ki tã tòg

53. ñãglò pò

54. kũ mũ mũ

55. ñãglò ti la yò tẽ lò amẽ

56. kũ tã

56a. mï tõ ñũ

56b. mï tõ ñũ

56c. mï tõ ñũ

57. ge ñẽñã

58. pèyẽn ti katẽ

59. lò ti pò ya tẽ nẽ

60. ñãglò wũ ũ tẽ òg wãcõ ũykòñkun

61. kũ mũ ke mũ

62. ug tẽ wũ wãcõ ug

63. kũ tẽ

64. ug tẽ wũ tõ ãglẽl tẽ

65. tokè wãcõ ug

66. kũ tẽ

67. mlal kè tã

68. ñãglò kòñãl tẽ ñugñug kò tẽ mẽ tẽ mũ

69. gug tẽ guggug kè taplï mũ

70. kũkũ tõ taka nẽ

71. ãtã ti tẽ mũ

72. ãmẽno zi wã

73. og zi wã

74. ti tẽ

75. kũ òg ti nu kï

76. kũ òg ti mõ

---

51. There were four of them, the armadillos.

52. They were under [burrowing] about twenty meters there,

53. but then [they] came out [the other end],

54. and went away.

55. Meanwhile, he [the wildcat] inserted his arm into the entrance [of the armadillo hole],

56. and he [sang]:

56a. "mad about the tail,

56b. mad about the tail,

56c. mad about the tail,"

57. [he] was saying.

58. Circling about he came,

59. and there was the place where he [the armadillo] had come out.

60. Meanwhile, some of those who had turned into humans [lit., "became related to us"],

61. went off [as animals].

62. The peccary became a peccary,

63. and went.

64. The peccary who had been human [lit., "we the living"]

65. now became a peccary,

66. and went.

67. He went: "*mlal.*"

68. Meanwhile, the monkey went through the trees going: "*ñugñug.*"

69. The howler monkey ascended going: "*guggug.*"

70. The *kũkũ* [a kind of plant] was there;

71. that one went away.

72. [Her name] was Ãmẽno.

73. [Her name] was Og.

74. It went away,

75. and they called after it,

76. and they [said] to it:

| | | | |
|---|---|---|---|
| 77. | og tẽ | 77. | "Og, |
| 78. | kũ mã kò pãno kòyake u we | 78. | you look for a good hole in a tree, |
| 79. | kũ mã lò amẽ | 79. | and you reach in, |
| 80. | kũ nẽ | 80. | and [you] remain there." |
| 81. | amẽno zi ũ ti mõ wel | 81. | To another Ãmẽno [they said], indeed: |
| 82. | amẽno a tẽ | 82. | "Ãmẽno, you go, |
| 83. | kũ mã pãnẽkẽ u we | 83. | and you find a clearing, |
| 84. | kũ mã ka mã wãcõ kumẽn | 84. | and you become a *kumẽn* [a kind of plant], |
| 85. | kũ ñãg we gẽke | 85. | and [you] remain [there] always," |
| 86. | kũ òg mũ kan mũ | 86. | and they all went away. |
| 87. | ce tẽ cègcèg kè taplï | 87. | The coatimundi ascended going: "*cègcèg.*" |
| 88. | òg tõ wãcõ *bicho* hã wã | 88. | They turned into animals. |

Perhaps you find this stretch of discourse hard to read; maybe you think it is confusing. The action is chaotic, skipping from one event to the next, and the songs are nonsensical, losing their pragmatic force when translated into pure referential words. Simultaneously, however, you would find the narrative easy and entertaining to listen to. It is filled with fascinating sounds — initially the songs, which the narrator for the most part actually sings, fading into a speaking voice. Toward the end there are also representations of sounds made by the different animals. Even this household discourse is greater than the referential meanings of its words. It is interesting sound; it plays on the ability of listeners to focus alternately on the meanings and on the sounds. More so than any other narrative from this community with which I am familiar, this one brings the sensible, perceptible qualities of discourse into awareness.

Why should it do so? What we have here is different from other domestic narratives. It is the only one that endeavors to represent a ceremony in words, though other narratives mention ceremonies in passing. One such mention occurs in a narrative we examined earlier — that of "Goes Living," the woman who followed her husband to the land of the dead and returned to tell of it:

| | | | |
|---|---|---|---|
| 1. | lẽl tẽ zi mèn tẽ tï mũ | 1. | Goes Living's husband died. |
| 2. | ti tèl tẽkũ | 2. | When he died, |
| 3. | zi yi wãñkòmã gẽke ñã | 3. | she went into seclusion for a long time, it is said; |
| 4. | zi kakutãdẽn kũ nẽ | 4. | until she came out. |
| 5. | kakutãdẽn kũ | 5. | When she came out, |

| | |
|---|---|
| 6. òg zi glèn òg mũ | 6. they danced [for] her. |
| 7. zi glèn ñã | 7. [After they] danced [for] her, |
| 8. òg mũ mũ | 8. they went. |

Here you have a breezy outline of some key elements of the ceremony connected with death. After her husband's death, a widow (Goes Living) goes into seclusion. Upon coming out of seclusion, the others "dance for her," then disperse, resuming their normal hunting-and-gathering lifestyle. The "dancing" is a reference to the *ãgyĩn* ceremony, but the ceremony itself is not described. In contrast, in the story of the animals' festival, you get a glimpse of what actually goes on at ceremonies. What goes on is in large measure singing. The narrative depicts the ceremony with faithfulness.

The attempt at faithful depiction, however, does not account for the songs and other sounds in the narrative. If the attempt were merely to talk about the ceremony, the narrator could have dispensed with the songs, or only mentioned their contents. If what mattered was the story, pure and simple, it would make no sense to sing the songs, which, indeed, make up a substantial portion of the narrative — 33 sung lines and 88 narrative lines, with four of the latter including representations of animal sounds. Indeed, if the narrator told us about the songs, rather than actually singing them, he would clarify matters for us. Our problem as listeners is that we do not know what the songs mean. The narrator could have helped us, by stating that the animals in question were provoking one another by their singing. Instead, we only infer this from the songs and the subsequent action.

A crucial point of clarification occurs in lines 30–33, where the jaguar asks the deer, "Are you singing at me?" and the deer replies, "No, all I'm [singing] is." If you are familiar with the literature on pragmatics, you will recognize in this a classic situation — someone denies the pragmatic meaning of an utterance by falling back on the referential meaning of the words. One might utter a sentence — "I read that book of yours" — with an insulting intonation. If the hearer called the speaker on the insult, saying, for example, "What, you didn't like the book," the speaker has the option of denying the insult by substituting a different intonation, perhaps an enthusiastic one, and saying, "No, all I said was, 'I read that book of yours.'" The deer is doing precisely this in the narrative, but it is hard for someone who is not a member of this community to pick up. In the written modality, one can only guess at such meanings.

The bit of mythic discourse suggests that the communication occurring during the animals' festival, and, for that matter, at *ãglan* ceremonies generally, takes place largely beneath the level of consciousness, in a murky realm not illuminated by referential discourse. I say "largely" because the myth also represents the animals as talking to one another, in fully referential form. For example, in the quoted speech lines 13–16, the eagle asks the armadillo to dance with the porcupine. You find fully referential speech again in lines 31 and 33, where the jaguar attempts to clarify the obscurely pragmatic message the deer is communicating, as discussed earlier. Lastly, in lines 77–80 and 82–85 the instructions given by some unidentified "they" to two plants are referential in character—though the instructions were presumably uttered long after the ceremony had ended. Nevertheless, no matter how you count the lines, nonreferential singing dominates the occasion, reported referential speech being far less prominent.

In representing communication within the ceremony as taking place largely beneath the level of consciousness, this narrative captures the opposition I have been positing—the world of ceremony is a world built out of contextual, nonreferential meanings. Such meanings I understand to be aligned more closely with the unconscious than with reflective consciousness. Ceremonies, in other words, borrowing again from the Freudian terminology, are a locus of primary process. They represent a modality of experience of the world that is distinct from reflective awareness.

Perhaps you had already guessed that I would find in the problematic of group assemblage an epistemological issue—in the way it is represented in discourse, group assemblage appears as a distinct kind of experience of reality, as a more direct bumping up against the perceptual world, as (relatively speaking) unmediated experience. Everyday life, in contrast, is portrayed as more closely bound up with the referential dimension of language, hence as more conscious, more experience-distant, further removed from the diaphane where the real and the apparent meet.

Foolish it would be, however, to go too far with the opposition: ceremonial is to everyday as unconscious is to conscious, as pragmatics is to semantics, and as experience-near is to experience-distant. After all, the animals' festival narrative itself circulates in the everyday, domestic sphere. It itself is not a part of ceremonial life. Yet, it makes use, in some measure, of the same modality as ceremonies themselves. It relies on nonpropositionally meaningful singing to communicate its own message. To be sure, the audience of the narrative recognizes that this is not "singing," but an icon of singing. All the same, the aesthetic value of the narrative lies in its music and acoustics. If you take them away, the story seems wooden, lifeless, if not actually boring. When these modalities are present, however, we have something that is brightly entertaining. The narrative transports a bit of the experience of group assemblage into everyday family life, to situations where, typically, fewer than a dozen people are gathered. By representing the nonreferential meaningfulness of ceremonies in nonreferential ways, the narrative breaks down the barrier between ceremonial and everyday, between group assemblage and dispersion.

Simultaneously, it points to an important fact: The opposition between ceremonial and everyday is grounded in an opposition that can be detected in each and every instance of discourse. This is the opposition between discourse as referentially meaningful, as a vehicle for significance, on the one side, and discourse as an object of sensory experience, as sound with iconic and contextual associations, on the other. The opposition lies dormant, our contact with talk presupposing the intermingling, or interpenetration, of the two. The aspects can be pried apart, and when they are, something like the opposition between the ceremonial and everyday takes shape. The ceremonial foregrounds discourse as sound, downplaying its referential aspect.

Alas, there is no necessary correlation between the ceremonial versus everyday opposition and group assembly versus dispersal. People do sing when they are on their own or in intimate family contexts. While there may be no necessary correlation, however, there is still an implied one: If discourse does split into ceremonialized versus everyday, and if that split is correlated with the assembled versus dispersed group, ceremonialization will occur on the side of group assemblage. I am arguing, in other words, that even if large-scale gathering is not requisite for discourse ceremonialization, the two tend to go together. This is not a matter of chance.

The reason is that group assemblage is one way of heightening nonreferential communication — the relatively more direct experience of social reality. It is one way of making nonreferential communication salient, and, simultaneously, of backgrounding the referential, of backgrounding language-based consciousness. The mechanism for doing this is the repetition of units, such as the line, which brings discourse as sound into prominence. Repetition is the basis for such phenomena as chanting and singing. It is the basis also of dance and dancelike kinesic forms. Repetition does not require group assemblage, but when the group does assemble, repetition tends to occur.

Group encounter results in the foregrounding of nonreferential signals. This is true especially if the group attempts to coordinate itself. Even at P. I. Ibirama, where coordination is usually minimal — collective singing tends, for example, toward cacophony — the sound dimension of discourse is heightened, made obvious. You are immersed in it, your own utterances intermingling with those of others. Signal transmission reaches such a feverish pitch that the very fact of transmission itself becomes obvious. You are overwhelmed by the quantity of nonreferential signals emitted by others. All of this distracts you from your otherwise referentially preoccupied consciousness; it opens you up to experiences other than those permitted by the overt meanings of words.

One lovely spring day in Chicago a few years ago, I was seated at an enormous wooden table, with about twenty other scholars, listening to the late great South Asianist poet and folklorist A. K. Ramanujan. In his softspoken manner, he was drawing a parallel between Wittgenstein on language and an Indian folktale. In the tale, the "water of life" is carefully guarded by lions, who thwart all attempts to gain access to it. Like everyone else around the table, I knew that the analogue to the "water of life" was direct, referentially unmediated experience of the world — something rendered supremely difficult, if not impossible, by the watch-lions of referential consciousness. Our hero, however, circumvents the lions. He throws meat to them, distracting them, giving him time to rush in and snatch the "water of life." I am suggesting that something like this happens in P. I. Ibirama ceremonies. The referential lions there are distracted by embodied signals that free people from the tyranny of consciousness, thereby opening them up to a different experience of the world, of reality. Indeed, that spring day, while Ramanujan talked ideas, his metaphors and poetry effected their magic. We encountered the immediate, sensible world around us, the images etched in sharp memory traces that linger to this day — smells of percolating coffee, light filtered through softly translucent, winter-grime-coated windows, the abrupt bellow of a fire truck horn punctuating engine snorts and siren wails.

Though my focus has been on the microarchitecture of signs, how their sensible characteristics interact with reference, my claim resonates with that articulated by Lawrence Sullivan, in his labyrinthine work *Icanchu's Drum*. At P. I. Ibirama, when the group assembles, it typically does so around a center, and "at the center," Sullivan (1988: 130) argues, "one obtains the most direct contact with the sacred." The sacred is awesome, sometimes terrifying. It is the emotional counterpart of the experience of divinity. Whether you think of group encounter as the experience of divinity, or as opening up the world in a different way, ceremony is doing something other than providing us with referential meanings.

You might well wonder, what is in it for culture? If the main task of culture is to ensure its own circulation, its own survival, why foreground nonreferential signs, embodied experience, immediate encounter with the world? The answer is that culture benefits from social encounter because social encounter is the medium for discourse circulation. Encounter enables talk to flow between individuals, across space, and over time. It enables replication. Nonreferential signals are devices used to seduce people into social encounters. By virtue of their mysterious, uninterpreted, yet meaning-laden quality, these signals exercise a magnetic effect, pulling people into their force fields. The very sense of mystery that draws public television audiences to so-called "primitive rites" attracts the participants themselves. Once lured into encounter, the groundwork is laid for the circulation of other discourse.

You may think that I have not explained the antagonism between embodiment and reference, sensibility and interpretation, in the P. I. Ibirama case. Why should referential discourse ignore ceremony and represent group encounter, when it does so very disapprovingly? Yet I think an explanation can be found here. Ceremony is the mysterious underbelly of culture, its flesh-and-blood side. Reference is culture's brain. The negative representation in referential talk — that group encounter is dangerous, unpredictable — is in part what makes ceremony intriguing. This is especially true of the *āglan*. The analogues in American culture are bars, nightclubs, and honky-tonks. Mothers warn their children about them. Bad things happen there! But the badness is part of the appeal, the allure. What is curious is that culture manages to have it both ways. By creating a space for the unspoken and for the disapproved of, culture simultaneously marshalls the rebellious, antisocial tendencies in us all to its own benefit. The encounters enable the circulation of the very discourse that disapproves of them.

I do not want to mislead you. I am not claiming that the splitting of referential from nonreferential signs occurs this way in every society. The Ndembu pattern may be more common. There the cerebral side of discourse interprets ceremonies, which the belly also feels. Interpretation adds layers of meaning to already meaning-laden signs. In doing so, it augments the attractive force of those signs. Simultaneously, the nonreferential signs also charge, or cathect the interpretations. Since interpretations are fragments of talk, their circulation is itself crucial to culture. Their cathexis adds to their circulability.

Even at P. I. Ibirama, discourse is made more compelling, more circulable by its involvement with ceremonies. I am thinking especially of the origin myth, which is told in acoustically stunning style at the *āgyïn*. Its sonic properties are foregrounded. But the very same referential material, the very same stories also circulate in the domestic arena, in telephone-game-like style, passed around from person to person, family to family. No doubt, part of the affective force propelling this domestic circulation is the allure of the performance style. Memory traces from past performances add to the discourse even when it is told in nonreferential fashion. People are eager to get inside its meanings, to learn its secrets, which are only obscured in performance. This discourse does not interpret ceremonial symbolism. But it does, similarly, acquire part of its propulsive force from ceremony's mystique.

Ceremony is, in certain respects, the flip side of social organization. If you think of social organization as a boot-strapping discourse, designed to secure its own circulation, the basis of its appeal is intellectual. It tries to make the obscure world of sociability intelligible, to give social integration a *raison d'être*. Social organization is a manifestation of cerebral culture, culture's reasonable, persuasive side. Ceremony, in contrast, is culture's belly. Its appeal is to emotion, to sensibility, to mystery. It constitutes an arena in which social encounters can take place; it clears a "dance plaza," making a space for assembly. As such, it is primeval with respect to culture, the source of culture's propulsive force.

If embodied ceremony is the belly of culture, whose brain is reference, we still need to know its appetite. What specific meanings are communicated by the nonreferential signals? What are they about? I will not keep you in suspense. My contention is that the messages contained in obscure ceremonial symbolism have to do with community. Ceremonies at P. I. Ibirama make community feel like family. You can say that the ceremonies construe community in terms of family because there is a cognitive component. The obscure symbolism of ritual behavior constructs an image of community as family writ large. The imagery is not blatant, but it is there. You can infer the message from the nonreferential signs. But more than just creating an image — which, after all, can be done better through the intellect, as we have seen in the case of social organization — ceremony plays upon feelings. It gives community the emotional tones of family.

Ceremonies are self-consciously meaningful, even if obscurely so. This is part of the mechanism by which they tap into emotions. Ceremonies lead you to believe that they contain cryptic representations of something else, even if you do not dissect the representational value. When you participate in a ritual, you do not think of yourself as simply enacting or living community, in some everyday sense. You think you are doing something meaningful, however obscurely. In doing it, however, you are also building community. Ceremony is the one and only opportunity for assembling the entire group. Apart from these occasions, the community disperses into smaller family units. So, while ceremonies are representations of community, they also *are* community. There is nothing else that one can call community apart from them, except for the cognitive and feeling traces that remain when you are back at home or off traveling.

The two major ceremonies at P. I. Ibirama — the *āglan* and the *āgyin* — draw for their communal imagery on different aspects of the family. The former picks up on the parent-child bond and the feelings associated with it. The latter picks up on the husband-wife bond and its associated emotions. However, both are built on the same spatial metaphor — the physical coming together of the group in space, with nuclear families, consisting of husband, wife, and unmarried children, forming the basic units. In the *āgyin* ceremony I attended in August of 1975, camps of individual families were arrayed around the central "dance plaza." Except when the dancing took place, this was the basic arrangement. The spatial organization is the same in the *āglan*, as demonstrated in the attempts to re-create the ceremony for me. The image of community reflected here is that of families coming together.

Because family groups were traditionally dispersed, aggregating only for ceremonial purposes, and because families today reside in dispersed households, the larger community typically does not impinge upon them. When ceremonies occur, however, the group makes its existence palpable. Durkheim was right. In ceremony, the group impresses itself sensibly on the individual. You see the assembled multitude, experience its phenomenal reality. Moreover, the actions of the group on these occasions are coordinated. The group behaves like a larger entity.

Significantly, as you have already seen, the experience of groupness is uninterpreted by referential discourse. Rather, the group is something that is apprehended in a more direct way, processed lower down on the brain stem. What you see are families, which, to be sure, you understand through discourse, through kinship terms. Nevertheless, you are able to see with your own eyes what you know through your intellect. There is a message embedded in the very act of assembling. You sense that the family of which you are a member is a part of something bigger. The question for you is: What is that bigger thing? How do you construe it? What do you feel about it?

Ceremonies create an image of community by shrinking the spatial distances between families, but they also transform the spatial relationships. They use propinquity itself as a sign, the foregrounded ceremonial contiguities causing you to think about everyday contiguities and vice versa. In the *āgyïn* ceremony, you begin with families clustered together, husbands next to wives, parents with children, as in the domestic arena. But, in the dancing, spatial relations are reconstituted. All the men assemble into a group, forming a column of dancers, and all the women, together with their young children, assemble as a group behind them. The men sing, shaking dance rattles, and proceed in circular fashion around the dance plaza. You can see a fragment of the dance groups in Plates 9 and 10. Community, in other words, is no longer an aggregation of distinct families. Now it consists of a group of men and a group of women plus children. The two groups come together, like a gigantic nuclear family.

You will recall that this ceremony is held in connection with a death. Henry (1964 [1941]: 181–194) discusses the procedures surrounding death, which I will not repeat here. I emphasize, however, that the *āgyïn* takes place after the widow's or widower's seclusion, which lasts two to four weeks. The seclusion camp is located deep in the forest, apart from the other families. The spouse is forbidden to see members of the community during this period. People say that spouses are "hiding" from their dead husbands or wives, who might return to seduce them, carrying them off to the land of the dead, as in the "Goes Living" narrative. The spouse is also, however, literally hiding from the community. The ceremony marks his or her re-entry.

As an aside, I note that the spatial segregation of men from women and children is perpetuated in the Assembly of God services I have attended. All of the men sit on the left side, all of the women and children on the right side of the church.

How suggestive that the spatial organization divides men from women! If you were trying to decode meanings, draw out hidden significance, you would conclude that the ceremony is about men and women, about husbands and wives. The spatial division into male and female creates an oversized, greater-than-life image of that fundamental relationship. The community becomes one huge husband-wife relationship, all of the men acting together as the "husband" and all of the women acting together as the "wife." The "husband" even leads the "wife" in dancing, just as husbands lead wives through the forest on trek. While no naturally circulating discourse interprets the spatial configuration in this way, you cannot help but feel that the ceremony is about the community as a large-scale marriage alliance. The reintegrated spouse resumes his or her position as a male or female, rather than as the spouse of some particular individual. In a tangible way, therefore, you can imagine the community as a family. Community-level relations are like relations between husbands and wives.

This is not the alliance model proffered by Lévi-Strauss, with distinct groups of men exchanging women with one another. Something more basic, more psychologically primitive, is operative here. The community is like a husband-and-wife bond. If you recall Wãñpõ's household on May 2, 1982, as discussed in Chapter 3 (and depicted in Figures 1 and 2), you appreciate that, in the domestic sphere, husbands and wives sit together, just as they travel together. The community is similarly a group of men bonded to a group of women who sit together and travel together. Your feelings for the community are like those you have for a spouse. If your spouse dies, you can find in the community the same companionship and support you found in your spouse.

In alliance theory, men are related to other men through women. Alliance theory views the community in terms of the processes by which families are created — marriage exchange. But in this ceremonial image, relations are not between men through women. They are between women and men. Your relationship to the community is like your relationship to your husband or wife, not like your relations to your in-laws. Community is fashioned in the image of family. It is like a husband-wife bond.

I do not wish to skirt the issue of emotions. As I have suggested, the significance of unarticulated symbolism — such as spatial arrangement — is that it taps into emotions, that it permits you to experience feelings without having to think about them, without engaging your referential consciousness. You have to sympathize with an old woman whose companion of more than fifty years has been snatched from her, never to be returned.

Who will lie there next to her when she wakes up in the morning? Who will watch out for her, making sure she has food to eat? Who will huddle next to her to keep her warm?

Yet as you empathize with her loss, you also appreciate that she is not alone. There is someone or something that can step in to take her husband's place. That something is the larger community. She is not just a wife to her now-deceased husband; she is also a woman amongst women, related to a whole group of men. They are her support; they are her companions. You feel reassured by this, and you have to have warm feelings for the community. The community is like a mate to you. It is there when you need it.

Though I did not witness it firsthand, except in reenactments, the *āglan* ceremony is distinct in both spatial imagery and emotional tone. Nevertheless, spatial relationships are meaning-laden here as well. As in the *āgyïn*, family groups cluster on the periphery of the dance plaza. However, in the *āglan*, men do not form a group in opposition to the group of women. This ceremony — held for the purpose of giving lip-plugs to young boys and thigh tattoos to young girls — instead opposes ceremonial parents (*kòkla* and *mà*) to social parents (*yug* and *nō*).

Space is significant in this way: Prior to the actual lip piercing or thigh tattooing, a father carries on his back the child that is to be initiated. He paces back and forth across the dance plaza, making sure that all can see him, that his connection to the child is publicly visible and prominently displayed. The connection is a phenomenal one, grounded in spatial contiguity, not only a matter of the intellect. Once the lip has been pierced, however, it is the ceremonial father (*kòkla*) who carries the child. Like the social father, he now paces publicly and visibly across the plaza, showing off his connection. The eyes of the community thus distinguish two types of relationship into which the child has entered: that with the social or biological father and that with the ceremonial father.

The contrast appears still more dramatically in the game of *kawig*, discussed earlier. The community arrays itself into opposing groups. On the one side are the parents of children to be initiated; on the other the ceremonial parents. Henry (1964 [1941]: 197), who witnessed an *āglan*, remarks that even those who are neither parents nor ceremonial parents join in. Spatial organization transmogrifies. No longer grounded in families seated next to one another, the community now appears as two opposed groups — ceremonial and social parents — squared off against each other.

The significance is amplified by the bag-tossing game already discussed. Recall that the bags are named "father," "mother," and "child." Reference here draws conscious attention to the problematic made visible when ceremonial fathers take over from social fathers. As the bags sail back and forth through the air, everyone shouts, "*ēñ māg kagmēg, ēñ māg kagmēg*" (catch mine, catch mine). Here is a tangible image of community. Communal relations are likened to those not between men and women, but instead now between social parents and ceremonial parents. The two sides toss the parent-child relationship back and forth.

In alliance theory, men are related to other men through women. In this ceremony, adults are related to other adults through children. The attachments of individuals to the community are likened to attachments of children to their parents. To be a member of the community is to be responsible for children born into it. As an adult, your relationship to any child born into the community is that of "parent." Correspondingly, other adults are to you like co-parents of a child. The entire community of adults assumes the role of "parent" to its collective "children."

One bit of publicly circulating discourse is critical here. When the ceremonial father pierces the lip or tattoos the thigh of a child, he picks the child up and shouts, "*a han*" ("you are made" or "this is your making"). The phrase is meant to be publicly heard. It is uttered to the child, but it is meant to be overheard. The community's attention is drawn to the child. What does the phrase mean? While unglossed by native exegesis, you now grasp its meaning: The child is socially recognized by the community. It has become a child not just of its nuclear family parents, but also of its communal parents, the assembled group of adults.

In "making" the child, however, people are also making the community. It is the bonds of co-parenthood that bind the community together. When you are a child, you learn to see other adults as parentlike in their relations to you. You extrapolate from your nuclear family to the community. When you are an adult, you learn to see other adults as co-parents to your children. The parent-child bond becomes the metaphor for community.

It has taken me a long time to grasp the significance of these two ceremonies. I had wanted to view the *āgyïn* and *āglan* as markers of death and birth. The ceremonies are these things, no doubt. But viewing them as life-cyclic markers fails to account for the specific forms the ceremonies take. Why focus attention on the similar attachments to children that parents and ceremonial parents maintain? Why have, first, the biological father carry his son back and forth across the dance plaza, then, the ceremonial father (*kòkla*)? Why have a game pitting parents against ceremonial parents? Why call the fiber bags that are tossed back and forth "father," "mother," and "child"? The answer is that the ceremony fashions an image of community after the parent-child bond. The ceremony makes it feel as if the child has not only its own nuclear family parents; it has the entire community of adults as parents. Similarly, the adults have not only their own children, but also those of every other adult in the community. Adults feel themselves to be related to one another as co-parents.

As an assembled group, people send messages to themselves, although they may be only subliminally aware of doing so. If one were to ask, "Why should I bother to get together with these other people?" the answer would come back, "Because these people are part of my bigger family." If one asks, "Will my death leave my spouse in permanent isolation?" the answer there is, "No, she (or he) is part of a much larger relationship, a bigger covenant." If one wonders, "Will my death leave my children uncared for?" the reply from the collectivity is, "No, other adults in the community can take care of them for me; we are co-parents."

Although you might not think so at first glance, the idea of imagining community in terms of family applies more generally to central Brazilian ceremonies. Among the Apinayé (Nimuendajú 1967: 37–72), Eastern Timbira (Crocker 1990: 272–275; Melatti 1978: 203–344; Nimuendajú 1946: 170–201), Kayapó (T. Turner 1979: 181–184; Vidal 1977: 125–139), Suyá (Seeger 1981: 156–167), and Xavante (Maybury-Lewis 1967: 115–137), ceremony focuses on the initiation of young men into adulthood. This is the transition when boys marry and change households, going to live with their wives. Why develop ceremonies around this transition?

My answer is that the ceremony projects an image of community off of the parent-child bond. Community is like the relations parents have to their children once the children have grown up, or as they are growing up. Relations among adult members of the community are fashioned after relations among parents to fully grown children. As a young child, you expected adults to care for you, to provide you with food and shelter, to protect you. Now you are no longer dependent. You are capable of doing these things on your own. But you still maintain contact with those who raised you. You still care for them and assume that they care for you. Your bond is a special one. Similarly, your bond to the community is like that of a child to a parent (or a parent to a child) in a similarly matured phase.

While the focus is distinct from that at P. I. Ibirama, you are similarly imagining community in terms of family, in terms of parents and children. There is an implicit idea here — relations beyond the elementary family are like family relations. Unlike P. I. Ibirama, however, they are not like the relations of a parent to a helpless infant. Rather, they are like the relations of parents to a child that has grown up and become independent.

In central Brazil, the entire community assembles to initiate its young boys. Initiation is the occasion for actualizing many of the communal relations. But initiation is nothing more than a representation of community in terms of the parent-child bond as it matures. Mature men assemble as a group, and they interact with boys and young men, also assembled as groups. By means of nonreferential representation or symbolization, therefore, the community comes together in order to represent the maturing parent-child bond. The representation of that maturing bond is the basis for community. Simultaneously, as community is symbolically represented, it is also practically enacted. People are actually building community.

Less evidence exists concerning the presence in central Brazil of a community image projected from the husband-wife bond, as at P. I. Ibirama. The innovative research of Manuela Carneiro da Cunha (1978: 51–53 *passim*; see also Melatti 1978: 106–124) suggests something similar among the Krahó. Especially intriguing is her observation regarding the ceremonial log races that conclude the period of mourning: "men run with the logs in the ceremony for the end of mourning of a woman and vice versa" (Cunha 1978: 68). You might detect in this an image of the community as a group of men (or women) acting like husband (or wife) with respect to a group of women (or men), one of whose members has suffered a loss. However, the connection to the P. I. Ibirama pattern remains unclarified.

No doubt you are still wondering: Why create a representation of community during the process of assembling the group? Why act out that representation, rather than simply putting it in words? Why not simply have a discourse that says, "the community is held together the way parent and child or husband and wife are?" This is a crucial problem and one not usually accounted for. If you circulated referential discourse, as in the case of social organization, you would also be building community. So why use embodiment rather than (or in addition to) the spoken word?

In his justly celebrated study of Ndembu ritual, Victor Turner (1967: 28–30, 54–55) distinguished two "poles" of meaning. Ndembu symbols had "ideological" or "normative" or cognitive meanings, on the one side, and "sensory" or "orectic" meanings, on the other. Turner suggested that, in the course of ceremonies, "an exchange of qualities may take place in the psyches of the participants . . . between orectic and normative poles" (Turner 1967: 54). Feelings, in other words, charge cognitive meanings with affective significance.

You will see a similarity to the argument here, but I think that I am adding something to it, or perhaps suggesting something slightly different. In the P. I. Ibirama case, there are normative or ideological meanings — that community is like a parent-child bond writ large, for example — as well as feelings that are called up. However, it is important that the normative meanings *not* be consciously articulated, that they *not* be encoded and circulated in referential discourse. The ceremony must operate outside the beacon of public consciousness. This is what makes the affective transfer possible in the first place. The entire sign process operates through similarities and contiguities, suggestions and inferences. While there are contributions from words — "this is your making," for example — ceremonies operate primarily in the sensible realm, so much so that you may wonder whether the normative meanings are correctly described as "ideological."

In P. I. Ibirama ceremonies, feelings are called up by nonreferential means. More even than this, however, reference can actually get in the way. Under its constant scrutiny, momentaneous feelings evaporate. Since reference offers you an acquaintance with a ceremony you may not have affectively experienced, it can actually make you, paradoxically, less likely to want to experience the ceremony firsthand. It confuses feelings about the ceremony with other feelings associated with the sensible discourse in which the referential meanings travel.

Lip piercing and thigh tattooing effect visible changes on people. You can see the plug in Kàmlĕn's lip in Plate 5. The changes are a publicly accessible display of belonging; they show to others that "you have been made." They thus serve a cognitive/perceptual function — clustering around Turner's "normative" pole — even if there is no group designator for those who "have been made," no circulating discourse that explicates the socially manufactured product.

However, you cannot help but appreciate that lip piercing and thigh tattooing also stir up powerful feelings. Adults inflict terrible pain on helpless children, and that pain is part of the ceremony. It is the "orectic" part. In the classical Durkheimian interpretation, you might say that the pain is a sign to the child. Through it, the child experiences the power of the group. However, these children — usually two or three years of age! — have no conscious memories of the process as they grow older. The pain that they suffer cannot be designed to make an impression on them, at least not a consciously rememberable impression.

You should not conclude, however, that the pain is not significant within the ceremony. On the contrary, it is highly significant. It makes a lasting, even indelible impression on the parents. They stand by and watch as someone inflicts excruciating pain on their unsuspecting child. Henry's (1964 [1941]: 196) description of an actual lip piercing[3] is vivid, and I quote it at length:

> "As the completely terrorized infant is held down by a number of people, while its mother and other women around it weep and the loud singing goes on, the *kôklá* thrusts his fingers into the child's mouth, distends the lip, and thrusts home with the knife. The child wriggles and screams, seizes the knife, and tries to pull it out as its mouth fills with blood and saliva. Now that the knife is extracted they try to insert the tiny lip plug until at last the plug breaks in an ugly splintery end. Evidently the hole is not properly made. Again the *kôklá* distends the little lip and thrusts again with knife. This time must be the last, so he twists and twists the knife until he is sure at last that the hole is big enough. When the

plug is successfully inserted it is bound around on the outside with a bit of fiber to prevent its slipping back. Then one of the men takes water in his mouth and squirts it over the wound.

What an impression the event made on Henry! You can imagine what his own feelings were at the time, how he empathized with "the completely terrorized child." Note his references to smallness: The *kòkla* "distends the *little* lip," attempts to insert the "*tiny* plug." Smallness appropriately captures the protective feelings of an adult for a helpless infant. You see also Henry's understanding of the emotional effect on the mother and other women, who "weep."

The pain is not meant to make an impression on the child. Its purpose is rather to impress the adults, especially the parents, but also all who empathize with the child and its parents. The ceremony, in other words, calls up in everyone the feelings of attachment that a parent has for its child; it transfers those feelings onto an image of relations within the community. Children are the responsibility of the community as a whole. All adults are co-parents of the community's children. The ceremony produces an emotional tone, bathes community relations in affect. Community is built on feelings of protectiveness and nurturance of elder for younger, of co-responsibility among adults.

How then, you may wonder, can a ceremonial father do this in the first place? If his feelings are of warmth and protectiveness, as if the child were his own, how can he inflict pain upon it? Evidently, he must look upon the pain as being in the child's best interests. This paradoxical sentiment must be shared by the parents and other members of the community, who would otherwise forcibly intervene on the child's behalf.

How is the pain in the child's best interests? I think you can only understand this if you regard it as something more than first order experience. It must itself be a sign and thus understood by participants — even if not consciously — as meta-affective, that is, as *about* affect in addition to being affect. The pain is about the feelings of protectiveness it kindles. It calls up positive social attachments, even if no circulating discourse rationalizes it to people in this way. The pain is therefore in the child's best interests because it causes the community of adults to bond with the child, while it simultaneously signals feelings of nurturance and attachment.

Why can't this sense of attachment be instilled by referential discourse? Why not have a publicly circulating discourse that implores, "take care of not only our own children, but also those of others," something, in other words, along the lines of a commandment? The answer is that the words alone are not enough. As referential meanings, they do not carry the necessary emotional force. They are lifeless, wooden. The force must come from nonreferential signs.

There is also a political problem with the commandment. Who is to utter it? A commandment explicitly stated can be explicitly rejected. However, implicit meanings, meanings inferred individually from nonreferential signs, are intuitively grasped. While the signs are out there for all to read — and they are public in this sense — no circulating referential discourse makes the reading explicit, gives it a place in public consciousness. The inference is a private, individual matter.

If unexplicated ceremonies help to establish community, they do so noncoercively. No one has decreed their intent. The very implicitness makes the agreement to establish community brittle and unstable, subject to revision or rejection. But it also makes the agreement noncoercive, not something decided by some individuals for others. Rather, the agreement is implicit, tacit, unspoken. The "meaning" of the ceremony that must not be revealed is that community is in people's best interests. That is what people are implicitly and subliminally telling one another.

You can now see why it is important that the meanings of ceremonies not be clear and plain, why they must be obscure and murky, mysterious. Participants sense that something important is going on, but they do not know precisely what it is. There is a clash between sensibility and intelligibility here. Sensible meanings are refractory to formulation in referential discourse. That in turn renders them more politically palatable.

P. I. Ibirama ceremonies are refractory to referential consciousness. They are, in this sense, not only unintelligible; they are anti-intelligible. You would be wrong to conclude, however, that they are therefore nondiscursive or extradiscursive. I have made this point so often that you may be drumming your fingers in impatience. Yet it is crucial to moving us beyond poststructural doldrums. Discourse is meaning — meaning's prototype being semantic reference — but it is also a sensible object in the world, whether sound, written designs, gestures, or something else. Sensibility makes discourse public, that is to say, intersubjectively accessible. It is the sine qua non of culture, whose distinguishing feature is its social transmissibility.

If the opposition were between discourse and nondiscourse, ceremonies would consist entirely in nonverbal behaviors. I cannot deny that nonverbal behavior forms a crucial component of P. I. Ibirama ceremonies — body painting and ornamentation, dancing, spatial arrangements, even the actual lip piercing itself. Yet how unthinkable it would be that the ceremonies should lack a language-like sound component — as in the scene from the film *Amadeus*, where the emperor forbids Mozart's musical accompaniment to the dancing, and the dancers prance about silently, the only sound their feet thudding against the floor.

Unlike the Amadeusian oddity, P. I. Ibirama ceremonies foreground music and song. The singing always involves sound that is recognizably language-like. It employs the same phonological apparatus as fully referential speech, and, while numerous sound combinations are meaningless vocables, as in scat singing, others are words from the native language. The songs elude referential interpretation, however, because the words are not arrayed according to proper syntax. You cannot extract from them full propositional meaning.

How many hours, days, weeks I spent recording and transcribing songs. I even trained an assistant — young Nānmla — to transcribe speech. He admirably transcribed and translated hours and hours of taped narrative and everyday speech, filling hundreds of pages. When I set him to the task of transcribing songs, he gave perfect phonological transcriptions, including word segmentations. However, he never transcribed more than a few words. I hope he will not imagine, if he reads this, that I am criticizing him. On the contrary, I intend these comments to show that the songs are not publicly intelligible, that they are not construable as propositional reference.

Some others were not as cautious as Nānmla. While they never attempted actual translations, they sometimes claimed to know what a song was about. My earlier statement that no domestically circulating discourse interprets ceremonial meanings must therefore be thrown out. Some people do give some songs some meanings. Interestingly, however, the meanings are not shared. In one song, you find the words *gòy* (water) and *cà* (black). The agreed-upon meaning is "black water." One individual opined that *gòy cà* refers to the Rio Negro (lit., "Black River") — a river marking the northernmost extension of the aboriginal hunting territory, and today far outside the reserve. Another believed it to be a person's name; indeed, you will encounter in the origin myth a character by the name of *gòy cà*. Still another person suggested that "black water" referred to "coffee." The person in question noted that, in the early postcontact days, one elder man used to sing the song while drinking coffee given to him by Eduardo de Lima e Silva Hoerhan. Like the meanings of the ceremonies themselves, the meanings of the songs must be individually inferred. They are not subject to public confirmation. No one interpretation is ratified by broader circulation.

If you study the story of the animals' festival, you see that the songs contain referential meanings. The mind struggles to put the meanings together, to assemble them into a bigger message. Alas, full propositionality is unobtainable. Look, for example, at the song in lines 18a–d. The song consists in four lines, which I have transcribed with interlinear and free translations. The free translations are entirely my own. I have used the same procedure the jaguar did, guessing at meanings. Nānmla transcribed the larger narrative and gave interlinear translations for some words. However, I could not coax him into giving a free translation:

18a. ñõ      nïg
     mother   make fun of, laugh
     "make fun of my mother"

18b. ñõ      mèn      can
     mother   husband
     "my mother, husband"

18c. ñõ      ko    yò        nẽ   wem
     mother   eat   place where   sit
     "place where my mother was eaten . . ."

18d. mã     yò        ke   nem
     listen   place where
     "listen . . ."

Line 18a comes closest to having semantic sense; both of its constituent words are interpretable. I translate it as "make fun of (or laugh at) my mother." However, you should know that the "sentence" is not grammatically complete. It lacks a sentential marker and a transitive subject. The form *ñõ*, furthermore, must be interpreted as a contraction of *ẽñ* (my) and *nõ* (mother). I feel on safe ground in translating it thusly here, since Nãnmla gave "mother" without the "my" as the interlinear. That clearly cannot be right, however, since the correct form is *nõ*. This can only be a contraction, if it is meaningful at all.

The remaining lines are senseless, and also grammatically incoherent. Line 18b juxtaposes "my mother" with "husband" in a grammatically perplexing way. It follows this with the nonsense syllable *can*. In 18c, the first three words seem to form a phrase — "place where my mother was eaten." One wonders whether it has a sexual referent — *ko* means "to eat" but also "to have sex with." The meaning is obscured by the subsequent form *nẽ*, translatable as "to sit," but here grammatically unfathomable. As if to confirm its nonsensicality, the line ends with *vem*, possibly construable as a variant of "to see," but here flagrantly violating syntactic rules. The last line contains the intelligible word *mã* (to listen). This is followed by *yò* (place where). Conceivably, the phrase means, "place where [something] was listened to." However, it is grammatically incomplete. Furthermore, it is followed by *ke*, which, in certain contexts, might be interpreted as the future marker; here it makes no sense. Finally, *nem* is, as far as I know, a nonsensical syllable.

Even if some elements are suggestive, therefore, the propositional or semantic meaning of the whole remains obscure. The mind cannot give a consistent linguistic interpretation to these lines. This is, to be sure, part of the allure of ceremonies. You do not find in them fully referential, propositional meanings. Such meanings are lacking from the crucial constituent signs. At the same time, you do find discourse. This song, while not an actual song from the *āglan*, to the best of my knowledge, is an example of discourse, rudimentarily constructed though it may be.

If the song is not referentially meaningful, why is it interesting? In fact, this little tune is a remarkable gem of complexity. When its poetic and sound structure is examined under the microscope, it sparkles. It is sung in a monotone, but its syllables are arrayed in a rhythmically fascinating way. In addition, there is an ear-catching modulation of volume or loudness. Let me show you a different graphic representation of the song, this one emphasizing temporal characteristics (beats) and syllable timing:

18a.   ñõ  ........          nïg
        ^           ^         ^              ^


18b.   ñõ  ........          mèn        can
        ^           ^         ^              ^


18c.   ñõ   ko   yò   nẽ   wem  .......
        ^           ^            ^              ^


18d.   mã    yò    ke    nem  .........
        |       |       |      ^              ^

You see a basic line structure consisting of four beats — represented by carats placed beneath the lines. The representation somewhat oversimplifies. Lines 18c and 18d are in a somewhat slower tempo, taking nearly four seconds each (or 1 second per beat), as compared to 18a and 18b, which take some 2.5 seconds each (or just over 0.6 seconds per beat). I am unsure how important this difference is to the overall aesthetic structure, but it is interesting.

The four lines come in pairs. The first two lines are similar by virtue of their initially elongated syllable *ñõ*, in each case held for just over a second. The last two are similar by virtue of their final elongated syllables, *vem* (phonetically [veb ᵐ]) and *nem* (phonetically [ ⁿdeb ᵐ]). One line has an initial, the other a final rhyme. This is what makes them mirror images of one another.

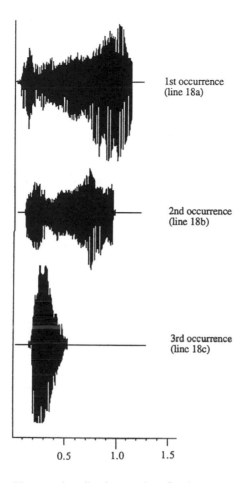

1st occurrence
(line 18a)

2nd occurrence
(line 18b)

3rd occurrence
(linc 18c)

0.5        1.0        1.5

*Figure 6.* Amplitude over time for three sung
occurrences of *ñõ*. Note similarities
between the first two and contrasts
with the third.

It is intriguing that the structure of similarities, in this short song, plays
sound against linguistic segmentation. The third line, like the first two, begins with the form *ñõ*. In other words, the linguistic segmentation is the
same. However, from the point of view of sound, the word is wholly distinct. The first two instances of *ñõ* are elongated, whereas the third is short
and staccato. The first two have nearly identical energy envelopes — the volume or loudness increases over time. You can see this by studying Figure 6.
Here you see amplitude or loudness (on the vertical axis) mapped against
time (on the horizontal) for the three *ñõ*'s. The first two are elongated, an

initial pulse followed by a gradually increasing volume, which peaks and then tapers off. The third is a single short pulse with one amplitude peak. You can see here how the song plays intelligibility against sensibility, linguistic segmentability against sound.

The intricacies of structure catch a listener's attention. The song is a sensible object, a gem for the ear. You discover the structure of sound similarities over time as you listen, and, especially, as you attempt to reproduce the song yourself. The similarity of the first two lines is obvious. You notice it immediately. The connection between them and the third, however, based on linguistic similarity, is downplayed. Instead, the third and fourth lines form a unit — staccato (or at least short) syllables characterize the first half in each case. Here again you notice a mirror effect — the last halves of the first two lines are similarly staccato.

From a sonic point of view, the elongated final syllables of the last two lines are also nearly identical. In each case, the sound starts loud, then tapers down in volume. It picks up again on the final beat. However, it never reaches the maximal amplitude displayed initially. In showing two amplitude peaks, it is similar to the elongated syllables of the first two lines. However, the final two elongated syllables show an overall downward amplitude, again creating a mirror image effect.

There is more to the structure. The first two lines have staccato syllables in their second halves. This contrasts with the last two. In 18c, you see a syncopated pattern. The syllables that occur on the beats are stressed, and the ones that follow them are unstressed. The syncopation is pronounced. There are two pairs of stressed syllables followed by unstressed syllables, confirming the structural dualism operative here and in so many of the *āglan* songs. However, in line 18d, the song switches to an unsyncopated staccato pattern; three syllables, each equally stressed, replace the two syncopated pairs. The tempo picks up on these three stressed beats as well. I have represented this by placing vertical lines, rather than carats, beneath them. The fascinating fact is that these three short stressed syllables take up exactly the same amount of time — two seconds — as the two syncopated syllables. These in turn take up the same amount of time as each of the two elongated syllables. The tempo here is 0.66 seconds per beat, nearly identical to that in the first two lines. Hence, the contrast in tempo between the first and last pairs of lines is repeated in the contrast between the first and second halves of the last line. Unbelievable complexity!

Even this little song, therefore, upon close inspection, offers up an intricate internal pattern. The pattern is sensed and reproduced by members of the community; it is socially circulated. The song is "catchy" once one figures it out. I confess to finding it difficult to pick up and reproduce. Having done so, however, it plays over and over again in my head. I marvel at its intricacies, as if this small fragment of culture were indeed a gem, beautiful to behold, with its numerous facets sparkling brightly, but truly remarkable when observed under the microscope, where the symmetries among the facets stand out. In the song, however, in addition to the symmetries there are crucial asymmetries; these carry the performer or listener through time.

The song is sensible without being fully intelligible. It is part of an alternative experience of reality, one that is more perceptually direct, less intellectually mediated, than that associated with the referential aspect of speech. It is based on perceptible similarities and contiguities within the discourse itself, understood simultaneously as sound and linguistically segmentable form. It is engaging and intriguing, fascinating because of its unarticulated saliency. Its very structure seems to reveal to the senses something about the nature of the world, to open up to us a part of the reality, without asking our referential consciousness to intervene.

The singing is discourse, even if it is not fully referential. Its very association with language, through meaningful words and phonologically correct syllables, suggests something significant, something designed to communicate. In this regard, it is distinct from nonverbal signals employed in ceremonies; participants more readily dismiss the latter as noncommunicative, as something merely "beautiful." The quasi linguistic nature of songs, however, leads listeners to believe that the singer is saying something. Songs are, therefore, part of the broader attractive force of ceremony. They help to make it a magnet for human beings, to pull them into its force field. Here you see in microscopic detail the forces behind group assemblage. At the same time, this song is but an imitation of actual singing    it transports into the domestic arena the affective allure of the ceremonies themselves.

If you turn your attention to the origin myth, performed prominently at the *āgyïn* ceremony I witnessed, you discover a similar magnetic effect, again produced at the sound level. While the origin myth is fully referential and propositional discourse — indeed, it embodies the most complex grammar of any piece of discourse — its most salient quality, during the ceremonial performance, is its acoustics. The performance involves two speakers, seated (or standing with hands on knees) facing one another. The first utters a single syllable and the second repeats it. The first then utters the second syllable, with the second repeating it, and so forth. The two continue in rapid-fire succession, rocking back and forth in time with the beats.

The acoustic property of the discourse assumes saliency here. Its content is backgrounded. In this way, the discourse becomes a form of embodiment, on the same plane as singing and dancing. It is sensorily accessible, making itself felt. Its referential content recedes in the face of dramatically foregrounded similarities and contiguities of sound. Sensibility here predominates — making the discourse phenomenally accessible. In the domestic sphere, however, where the myth is recounted in ordinary style, the semantic content, or story, resurfaces. The myth becomes intelligible as its sonic properties fade from consciousness, leaving only subliminally detectable traces.

From the point of view of culture, intelligibility and sensibility reinforce each other. People want to know the content, in part because of the ceremonial prominence of its sound. This desire propels the myth's circulation. Correspondingly, performance is saturated with meanings arising from mythic content. Content is carried along, replicated together with form, even if the content is relatively inaccessible during performance.

The interest in certain discourses can be traced to their poetic structuring, to their form, which, however, remains relatively inaccessible to consciousness. Formal patterning — manifested in the discourse as phenomenal object — provides an affective charge, cathects the discourse with feeling. The normal order of things in the domestic arena is for form to operate subliminally, for cathexis to take place on the periphery of the referentially illuminated circle of consciousness. In ceremony, however, discourse as physical object comes to the fore.

At P. I. Ibirama, ceremonies, and hence group assemblages, are associated with relatively unconscious processes. Rather than manifesting collective consciousness, ceremonies display a collective unconscious. They foster a relatively more direct encounter with perceptible reality. The encounter takes place through similarities and contiguities, icons and indices, rather than referential signs. At P. I. Ibirama, referential saliency is associated with dispersion, with family life, with telephone-game-like transmission of culture. Sonic saliency is associated with group assemblage, with ceremony, collective transmission of culture.

Group assemblage is the repository of mysterious unconscious symbols, functioning to kindle emotions, to imbue images of community with the warmth of family. It is, as Durkheim supposed, the birthplace of culture, which depends for its circulation, its reproduction, its life, on social encounter. How curious, therefore, that the conscious representation of group assemblage in public discourse is so negative. In the ceremonial dance plaza, animals in human form fight with one another, and the end result is permanent dispersal. They lose their ability to speak, becoming like the animals you see today, emitting only subhuman sounds: *mlal, ñugñug, guggug, cègcèg*.

If you study the matter closely, you see that the message is not simply remarked dispassionately in passing; it is drummed into you. You are made to feel it in your gut. In the origin myth, a sense of portentousness surrounds group assemblage, and that sense is built up throughout the narrative. It begins early on in connection with the making of the first jaguar and tapir. The main — but unnamed — character gives as his reason for wanting to make the jaguar "the sound of many men coming," a phrase assuming the tropological aura of "storm clouds on the horizon":

| | |
|---|---|
| 1. ne to āgèlmĕg wũ mũ | 1. "What is all of this noise about," |
| 2. ke mũ | 2. [he] said. |
| 3. iwo ĕñ cõ kòñgàg kale yògï mã | 3. (Speaker change) "I hear the sound of many men coming [lit., "descending in this direction"], |
| 4. kũ ĕñ cõ ĕñ mãg yè | 4. and so for my creation |
| 5. ĕñ cõ kàplug kèg | 5. I have fashioned *kàplug* wood . . ." |

"The sound of many men coming" refers to a large-scale gathering beneath "Hawk Mountain." The clause in which this is formulated — "beneath Hawk Mountain where many men had gathered" — is a poetic refrain, repeated over and over again. As a nonreferential narrative device, repetition focuses for you, the listener, what is referentially salient as well. The group assemblage is brought to your attention by the repetition of this sentence throughout the narrative. There can be no doubt that it is the central preoccupation of the latter portions of the first of the four origin myths. It occurs an astonishing nineteen times, mesmerizing you by its quantitative presence.[4]

The clause itself in the native language of P. I. Ibirama is rhythmically regular, and, for that reason, like the little tune analyzed earlier, interesting to listen to. After the initial stressed syllable, you find a series of disyllabic words, each stressed on its second syllable. You can easily tap out the rhythm while listening to it, and the rhythmical pattern is especially catchy, facilitating the replication of this bit of discourse over time, as well as within the narrative. I have attempted to capture some salient features of this line in the following transcription:

| | | | | |
|---|---|---|---|---|
| <u>krẽ</u> | yug<sup>ŋ</sup>ŋ<u>gug</u><sup>ŋ</sup> | y<u>ɔklãm</u> | kɔi<sup>ŋ</sup><u>gɔg</u><sup>ŋ</sup> | wak<u>ðulu</u>[5] |
| klẽ | yugug | yòklãm | kòñgàg | wãgzul |
| mountain | hawk | beneath | man | to gather many |

The first line depicts phonetic word forms, with stress indicated by underlining. The line below gives phonemicized forms, with their literal translations beneath. This is by no means the only poeticized line in this portion of the narrative. In fact, there is conspicuous rhythmic poeticization throughout. This line, however, is particularly striking. It is not coincidental that it is also the single most repeated line of the myth.

As the narrative proceeds, the sound of this sentence takes on a sense of ominousness, like the rumblings of war. As in earlier episodes, action here revolves around repeated arrivals and departures. However, the arrivals now take on dark overtones, each individual expressing his anger that all of the eligible women have been married off. The actual fighting is not described, but merely mentioned in passing. In the final portion, the narrator conveys a sense of loss; he does not know where his relatives have gone.

Here is the entire concluding portion of the narrative. You should read through the English translation for the feelings it builds up as a result of the repetitions, instead of (or in addition to) the content. You might try reading quickly, paying attention to whether a line (or a variant of it) has appeared before, taking less heed of semantic content.

| | | | |
|---|---|---|---|
| 1. | wãcuke hã mõ klẽ yugug yòklãm kòñgàg wãzul to | 1. | Alone, beneath Hawk Mountain where many had gathered, |
| 2. | nũ glè tèle | 2. | I descended dancing. |
| 3. | klẽ yugug yòklãm kòñgàg wãgzul ki | 3. | Beneath Hawk Mountain where many men had gathered, |
| 4. | yunke | 4. | [they] arrived [lit., "came out"]. |
| 5. | klẽ yugug yòklãm kòñgàg wãgzul ki | 5. | Beneath Hawk Mountain where many men had gathered, |
| 6. | yunke | 6. | [they] arrived [lit., "came out"]. |
| 7. | mũ lò cuwañ cuwañ tẽ mõ cuwañ yug tõ cuwañ wãcõ mã yè katèle | 7. | Meanwhile, Cuwañ, [I said] to Cuwañ, "Cuwañ, father Cuwañ, come hither [lit., "descend in this direction"]." |
| 8. | huli nẽ klẽ yugug yòklãm kòñgàg wãgzul tẽ mẽ nẽ | 8. | "Surely, beneath Hawk Mountain where many men have gathered all about, |
| 9. | tà tẽ mlè wãñõ kàkòl tẽ | 9. | [they] finished getting together with the women [i.e., they married all the women]." |
| 10. | yug tõ cuwañ tẽ ẽ tõ tà yè yũ | 10. | Father Cuwañ was angry because of the women, |
| 11. | kũ wãñcikatẽ yè cul nẽñã | 11. | and he wanted to return. |
| 12. | wãcikatẽ | 12. | [He] returned. |
| 13. | ẽ tõ wãcikatẽ | 13. | When he returned, |
| 14. | kũ | 14. | [he said]: |
| 15. | wãhãl nũ kè lò a tõ gò tòg tẽ mẽ wãcõ kòñgàg kugmã | 15. | "Now, when you become men all about this land, |
| 16. | kũ nũ a nu a nẽwi kukèg yè katèle hò | 16. | I will descend behind you and destroy your lives. |
| 17. | wãhãl nũ kè lò a tõ gò tòg tẽ mẽ wãcõ kòñgàg kugmã | 17. | Now, when you become men all about this land, |
| 18. | kũ a pipil we tẽ yè katèle hò | 18. | I will reduce your numbers [lit., "turn you into few"]," |

| | | | |
|---|---|---|---|
| 19. | ke ñã | 19. | [so he] was saying. |
| 20. | wãcikatē hà we | 20. | He really returned. |
| 21. | klē yugug yòklām kòñgàg wãgzul to | 21. | Beneath Hawk Mountain where many men had gathered, |
| 22. | ka nũ glè nē | 22. | there I was dancing. |
| 23. | gòy cà tō yahà ēñ nu katèle tã | 23. | Black Water descended behind me. |
| 24. | klē yugug yòklām kòñgàg wãgzul ki | 24. | Beneath Hawk Mountain where many men had gathered, |
| 25. | yunke | 25. | [he] arrived [lit., "came out"]. |
| 26. | gòy cà tō yahà wãcō mã yè katèle | 26. | "Black Water, come hither [lit., "descend in this direction"]. |
| 27. | huli nē klē yugug yòklām kòñgàg wãgzul tē mē | 27. | Now, beneath Hawk Mountain where many men had gathered, |
| 28. | tà tē mlè wãñō kàkòl tē | 28. | [they] finished getting together with the women [i.e., they married all the women]. |
| 29. | huli nē kuñō blè wãñō kàkòl tē | 29. | Now, [they] finished getting together with the eligible females [i.e., they married all the eligible females]." |
| 30. | gòy cà tē lō tà yè yū | 30. | Black Water was angry because of the women, |
| 31. | kū wãcikatē yè cul nē ñã | 31. | and [he] wanted to return. |
| 32. | wãcikatē | 32. | [He] returned. |
| 33. | wãhãl nũ kè lò a tō gò tòg tē mē wãcō kòñgàg kugmã | 33. | "Now, when you become men all about this land, |
| 34. | kū a nu a pipil we tē yè katèle hò | 34. | I will descend behind you in order to reduce your numbers [lit., "turn you into few"]." |
| 35. | gòy cà tō wãcika tà yè yū | 35. | Black Water was angry because of the women, |
| 36. | kū wãcikatē tē hà we | 36. | and he returned, indeed, |
| 37. | kū nū | 37. | and I, |
| 38. | klē yugug yòklām kòñgàg wãgzul to | 38. | beneath Hawk Mountain where many men had gathered, |
| 39. | ka nũ glè nē | 39. | there I danced. |
| 40. | nũ kulō to ka glè nē | 40. | Where the savannas were I was dancing. |
| 41. | yug tō kòza yè awañ nē | 41. | [I] was waiting for father Kòza. |
| 42. | yug tō kòza tē ēñ nu katèle | 42. | Father Kòza descended behind me. |
| 43. | yug tō kòza wãcō mã yè katèle | 43. | "Father Kòza, come hither [lit., "descend in this direction"]. |

44. huli nē klē yugug yòklām
    kòñgàg wāgzul tē mē

45. tà tē mlè wāñō kàkòl tē


46. huli nē kuñō blè wāñō kàkòl tē


47. yug tō kòza ē tō tà yè ñū

48. kū wācikatē yè cul nē ñā
49. wācikatē
50. kū wāhāl nū kè lò a tō gò
    tòg tē mē wācō kòñgàg
    kugmā
51. kū a nu a pipil we tē yè katèle


52. wāhāl nū kè lò a tō gò tòg tē
    mē wācō kòñgàg kugmā
53. kū nū a nēwi kukèg yè katèle hò


54. ke ñā
55. kòza tō wācika tà yè ñū


56. kū wācikatē tē hà we
57. kū nū
58. klē yugug yòklām kòñgàg
    wāgzul to
59. ka nū
60. kulō to ka nū glè


61. ē kòñka hà tō gòy cà yè awañ
    nū glè nē
62. gòy cà tō yahà tō cuwañ ēñ nu
    katèle
63. klē yugug yòklām kòñgàg
    wāgzul ki
64. yunke
65. gòy cà tō yahà tō cuwañ wācō
    mā yè katèle

44. Now, beneath Hawk Mountain
    where many men had gathered,

45. [they] finished getting together
    with the women [i.e., they
    married all the women].

46. Now, [they] finished getting
    together with the eligible females
    [i.e., they married all the eligible
    females ]."

47. Father Kòza was angry because of
    the women,

48. and [he] wanted to return.

49. [He] returned.

50. "Now, when you become men all
    about this land,

51. I will descend behind you in order
    to reduce your numbers [lit., "turn
    you into few"].

52. Now, when you become men all
    about this land,

53. I will descend in order to destroy
    your lives,"

54. [so he] was saying.

55. Kòza was angry because of the
    women,

56. and he returned, indeed,

57. and I,

58. beneath Hawk Mountain where
    many men had gathered,

59. there I,

60. where the savannas were, I
    danced.

61. [I] was dancing waiting for my
    relative Black Water.

62. Cuwañ Yahà Black Water
    descended behind me.

63. Beneath Hawk Mountain where
    many men had gathered,

64. [he] arrived [lit., "came out"].

65. "Cuwañ Yahà Black Water, come
    hither [lit., "descend in this
    direction"].

66. huli nĕ klĕ yugug yòklām
    kòñgàg wāgzul mĕ nĕ

67. tà tĕ mlè wāñõ kàkòl ñā

68. huli nĕ kuñõ blè wāñõ kàkòl ñā

69. gòy cà tō yahà tō cuwañ ĕ tō tà
    yè ñū

70. tĕ cul nĕ ñā

71. wāci ĕ tĕ

72. kū wāhāl nū kè lò a tō gò tòg
    tĕ mĕ wācō kòñgàg kugmā

73. kū a nu a pipil tĕ yè katèle

74. wāhāl nū kè lò a tō gò tòg tĕ
    mĕ wācō kòñgàg kugmā

75. kū a nĕwi kukèg yè katèle

76. gòy cà tō yahà tō cuwañ tĕ
    wācikatĕ tĕ hà we

77. kū nū

78. klĕ yugug yòklām kòñgàg
    wāgzul to

79. ka nū

80. kulõ to ka nū glè nĕ

81. ĕ kòñka hà tō gòy cà yè
    awañ nĕ

82. gòy cà tō yahà ĕñ nu katèle

83. klĕ yugug yòklām kòñgàg
    wāgzul ki

84. yunke

85. gòy cà tō yahà wācō mā yè
    katèle

86. huli nĕ klĕ yugug yòklām
    kòñgàg wāgzul mĕ nĕ

---

66. Now, beneath Hawk Mountain
    where many men were gathering
    all about,

67. [they] finished getting together
    with the women [i.e., they
    married all the women].

68. Now, [they] finished getting
    together with the eligible females
    [i.e., they married all the eligible
    females]."

69. Cuwañ Yahà Black Water was
    angry because of the women,

70. and [he] wanted to go.

71. [He] went back.

72. "Now, when you become men all
    about this land,

73. I will descend behind you in order
    to reduce your numbers [lit., "turn
    you into few"].

74. Now, when you become men all
    about this land,

75. I will descend in order to destroy
    your lives."

76. Cuwañ Yahà Black Water wanted
    to return, indeed,

77. and I,

78. beneath Hawk Mountain where
    many men had gathered,

79. there I,

80. where the savannas were, I was
    dancing.

81. [I] was waiting for my relative
    Black Water.

82. Yahà Black Water descended
    behind me.

83. Beneath Hawk Mountain where
    many men had gathered,

84. [he] arrived [lit., "came out"].

85. "Yahà Black Water, come hither
    [lit., "descend in this direction"].

86. Now, beneath Hawk Mountain
    where many men were gathering
    all about,

87. tà tẽ mlè wãñõ kàkòl ñã

87. [they] finished getting together with the women [i.e., they married all the women].

88. huli nẽ kuñõ blè wãñõ kàkòl ñã

88. Now, [they] finished getting together with the eligible females [i.e., they married all the eligible females]."

89. kũ ẽñ cõ wãñgèy a yè awañ nẽ wã

89. "I am waiting for you in order to go to war.

90. wãñgèy tõ ñã wã

90. It is war, indeed.

91. kòñgàg hã wũ amẽ pã lò kale yè mũ

91. They went along the path of others in order to descend in this direction.

92. tõ kòñgàg lò yè wãcu ẽ yòmẽ pã yi

92. Had they been true men, they would have made their own paths by themselves,

93. kũ lò le yè mũ

93. and [they would] descend there,

94. kũ ẽñ cõ wãñgèy a yè awañ nẽ wã

94. and I am waiting for you in order to go to war."

95. gòy cà tõ yahà tõ cuwañ ẽ tõ tà yè ñũ

95. Cuwañ Yahà Black Water was angry because of the women,

96. wãñgèy cul nẽ ñã

96. and [he] wanted to go to war.

97. klẽ yugug yòklãm kòñgàg wãgzul

97. Beneath Hawk Mountain where many men had gathered,

98. pipil we tẽ yè cul nẽ ñã

98. [he] wanted to reduce [their] numbers [lit., "turn them into few"].

99. klẽ yugug yòklãm kòñgàg wãgzul to

99. Beneath Hawk Mountain where many men had gathered,

100. ka cale yò nẽm yè cul nẽ ñã

100. [I] wanted to leave the place where [they] had fought.

101. klẽ yugug yòklãm kòñgàg wãgzul to

101. Beneath Hawk Mountain where many men had gathered,

102. ka nũ cale yò nẽm

102. I left the place where [they] had fought.

103. kòñgàg tẽ pipil we tẽ mũ

103. The numbers of men were reduced [lit., "the men were turned into few"].

104. ẽñ kòñka hà tõ gòy cà tẽ yò wèg tũ

104. [I] did not see where my relative Black Water went,

105. kũ zòklãl ki la mũ

105. and [I] entered the forest.

106. zòklãl ki la

106. When I entered the forest,

107. kũ ẽñ glè nẽ

107. I was dancing.

108. cuwañ ẽñ nu tã katèle

109. tã glè yò ki kala mũ

110. cuwañ wãcõ mã yè katèle

111. huli nẽ gòy cà tẽ nẽ

112. klẽ yugug yòklãm kòñgàg
wãgzul

113. pipil we tẽ tẽ

114. wãkey ẽñ cõ ẽñ kòñka hà tõ
gòy cà tẽ yò wèg

115. lò gò tòg tẽ mẽ ẽñ yè kòtï tẽ

116. gòy cà tõ

117. klẽ yugug yòklãm kòñgàg
wãgzul

118. pipil we tẽ ya hã wã

119. klẽ yugug tã ti yòklãm wã ti
ka nẽ

120. kũ ẽñ cõ ẽñ kòñka hà tẽ yò
wèg tũ

121. kũ ẽñ cõ zòklãl ki la yò

122. ẽñ glè ñã hã wũ ki ñã

123. wãkey ẽñ cõ ẽñ kòñka hà tẽ yò
wèg

124. lò yè gò tòg tẽ mẽ ẽñ yè kòtï
tẽ yè

125. wãkey ẽñ cõ wãgyò tẽ yò wèg

126. lò yè gò tòg tẽ mẽ ẽñ yè kòtï
tẽ yè

127. wãkey ẽñ cõ gòy cà tõ yahà tẽ
yò wèg

128. lò gò tòg tẽ mẽ ẽñ yè kòtï tẽ yè

129. wãkey ẽñ cõ ẽñ kòñka hà tẽ yò
wèg

130. lò gò tòg tẽ mẽ ẽñ yè kòtï tẽ yè

108. Cuwañ descended behind me.

109. He arrived at my dance plaza.

110. "Cuwañ, come hither [lit.,
"descend in this direction"].

111. Now, Black Water was there.

112. Beneath Hawk Mountain where
many men had gathered,

113. [he] reduced [their] numbers.

114. Had I seen where my relative
Black Water went,

115. I would not be here all about this
land.

116. Black Water,

117. beneath Hawk Mountain where
many men had gathered,

118. really reduced their numbers,
indeed.

119. Beneath Hawk Mountain he was,

120. and I did not see where my
relative went,

121. and, where I entered the forest,

122. I have been dancing until now.

123. Had I seen where my relative
went,

124. I would not be here all about this
land.

125. Had I seen where the person
went,

126. I would not be here all about this
land.

127. Had I seen where Yahà Black
Water went,

128. I would not be here all about this
land.

129. Had I seen where my relative
went,

130. I would not be here all about this
land."

Perhaps you can sense that this narrative, like the song discussed earlier, is significant for its formal poetic and even musical qualities, in addition to its content. In certain contexts, such as ceremonial performances, these qualities actually overshadow the story line. The repetition of the sentence "beneath Hawk Mountain where many men had gathered" cuts what Feld and Keil (1994) call a "groove" — into which one settles. It keeps the beat for the narrative as music. However, you can break down the "musical" structure further. The longer narrative consists in two parts: the buildup to the war, and the war's aftermath. The dividing line is somewhere between line 90 — "it is war, indeed" — and line 100 — "[I] wanted to leave the place where [they] had fought."

You will see that the first part consists in a succession of parallel units, with a number of lines repeated verbatim in each case. The parallelism actually manifests itself as sound — that is, cadences and rhythms and voice qualities — as well as grammar — that is, segmentable words and sentences. There are four principal units, the first beginning at about line 7 and running through line 25, the second from 26 through 42, the third from 43 to 64, and the fourth from 65 through 82. You might draw the boundaries differently, but you would nevertheless come up with the same quadripartite structure.

As regards content, each unit concerns an arrival and a conversation — the main speaker informs the one who arrives that all of the eligible women have been married off. In each case, the arriving person expresses his anger.

Line 85 begins an apparently identical fifth episode, but this turns out to be the pivotal episode in which the fight occurs. Line 85 directly parallels lines 7, 26, 43, and 65. But the parallelism breaks down in line 89, where the narrator avers that he is waiting to go to war. By line 100, the war has occurred. It goes by so quickly — without gory embellishment — that you hardly notice it.

A last episode begins around line 108; it involves a final arrival. Line 110 is parallel to lines 7, 26, 43, 65, and 85. But this last episode involves the expression of loss that the main speaker feels. The key refrain is in lines 114 and 115:

| | |
|---|---|
| 114. wãkey ēñ cō ēñ kòñka hà tō gòy cà tē yò wèg | 114. Had I seen where my relative Black Water went, |
| 115. lò gò tòg tē mē ēñ yè kòtï tē | 115. I would not be here all about this land. |

It is repeated in a quick succession of variants in lines 123–124, 125–126, 127–128, and 129–130. In other words, just as there were four parallel episodes in the first part, so there are four repeated line pairs in the second. The end resembles the beginning, but in condensed form. Moreover, in each case, a fifth repetition occurs, but this forms part of the pivotal portion of the narrative concerning the fight.

From an emotional point of view, the movement is from the recounting of anger — anger because all the eligible women have been married off — to regret at the loss of contact with important others. The emotional message, which is made prominent through the structure of repetitions, is interwoven with the groove describing the great gathering, the group assembly. You cannot help but associate the gathering with the buildup of anger, on the one side, and the expression of regret and loss, on the other. The narrative plays up anger and foreboding, then finishes it off with separation and nostalgia.

Note the association between group assembly and marriage. The men seem to have assembled first for the purpose of marriage. The result, however, is anger and, eventually, the destruction of community. Marriage is associated with an anticommunitarian theme. If you examine the matter closely, however, the problem is not with affinity as a metaphor for community, since elsewhere in the origin myth marriage does result in community, in solidaristic relations between individuals:

> "Now we are in-laws,
> and let [us] lie together,
> and [let us] put our fires in front of one
> another,"

The problem is rather with group assemblage. If you compare this narrative with that of the animals' festival, you see that the marriage metaphor is not present there at all, yet you still find the buildup of anger, and you still find that anger results in fighting and dispersal, as in the present instance.

What is going on here? I think I am now, finally, in a position to answer that question. My answer is that the horrible consequences of group assembly are nevertheless good for culture, understood as circulating discourse. Discourse manages to have it both ways. If group assembly goes smoothly, then discourse gets out of it opportunities for circulation, for replication, for spread. If group assembly gets rough, however — if fights break out, if dispersion takes place, if disaster strikes — discourse still wins. It extracts from social catastrophe something that ensures its own propulsion, its own circulation. This is the interest that people have in fighting, in social calamity. By virtue of its referential powers, discourse salvages from the debris of catastrophe human interest; it extracts the interest and transports it into other contexts. Discourse whose topic is personal tragedy or social disaster taps into a primal fascination — witness the role of tragedy in Western culture. By incorporating accounts of calamity into its referential content, the origin myth ensures people's interest in it; it makes them want to hear it, to pass it on. Calamity makes for good discourse circulation, and hence for cultural sharing, just as tabloids feed on their daily diet of murder and rape and villainy.

I have already pointed out that the reverse is also true. Far from discouraging people from attending collective ceremonies, the image painted in discourse — of danger, of iniquity, of all that your mother warned you against — actually entices people. It appeals to the dark side of our nature, to something that our rational selves cannot comprehend. Culture as brain tells you one thing, but culture as belly understands another.

From the perspective of classic theories of culture, this argument makes no sense. If you think that culture is a single thing, that the referential portion of discourse simply reflects experience, that you can pass effortlessly from intelligibility to sensibility, then the P. I. Ibirama facts seem baffling. Why would culture purvey such a bad image of ceremony if ceremony were its ally? Why would ceremonies persist if they were so destructive to social integration, and hence to the circulation of culture? Won't people enact the horrible deeds they learn from narrative, and therefore destroy society? The problem presents itself as unsolvable, like the Eleatic philosopher's paradox — if the arrow flies each time halfway closer to its target, how does it get there? Experience undermines ideas. How can culture reach its goals if it fights against itself?

The answer is that sensibility and intelligibility are not so straightforwardly interconnected. In fact, social integration and social harmony are useful to culture only insofar as they provide opportunities for discourse circulation, occasions on which transmission *can* take place. But disharmony and disintegration are also in their own way good — hard as it may be for us to believe! They furnish the material, the topics, in which people are interested. Even if you have occasion for circulation, you must also have interest. Opportunity alone is not enough. Discourse appeals to the brain, but it must also appeal to the belly. Human catastrophe is, sadly, an appealing topic. People want to hear about it. It is part of our fascination with the dark side of existence. It therefore furnishes topics that induce telephone-game-like circulation, that appeal to our baser selves, not to the better angels of our nature.

# *Chapter 7.* Rocks That Talk

*with Patricia Kent, M.D.*

Who would think to compare ceremonies to dreams? After all, they are of different orders of existence, like armadillos and myths, or araucaria pines and phonemes. Yet something leads us ineluctably to speculate on their ties. Whereas ceremonies are not talked about or interpreted at P. I. Ibirama, dreams are incessantly discussed. Whereas ceremonies are publicly accessible to the senses, dreams are only privately accessible. Dreams and ceremonies are opposed, but in their opposition they are linked. Why?

The answer may lie in the epistemological field mapped out by discourse. In the case of physical space, you will recall that what is patent to the senses goes unspoken. At least, it is not a topic of culturally standardized narratives; there is no publicly accepted interpretation of the visible, audible, tactile, and olfactory world. What becomes a topic of conversation, what becomes the subject of publicly circulating discourses, is what lies beyond the senses — the land above the sky, the world of the dead, the other side of the diaphane. However, the world that is publicly accessible to the senses eludes conscious attention. It is not the subject of interpretation through the referential aspect of discourse. Ceremonies, indeed, participate in this opposition. They resist interpretation by referential discourse. From the mysterious goings-on — the piercing of lips, the tossing back and forth of fiber bags called "father," "mother," and "child" — participants must extract their own individual meanings.

Now this suggests that dreams are not accessible to the senses, that they are not public in the same way as ceremonies, that, on the contrary, they are like the land above the sky or the world of the dead. What are we then to make of their epistemological status? Does this seeming nonaccessibility to the senses deny their status as real? According to the argument of Chapter 1, the public interest in dreams confirms the dream experience, vouchsafes that it does indeed tap into a reality that is of significance to the commonweal. But now the opposition of dreams to ceremonies seems to suggest that dreams are not public, at least not in the same way. What to make of this?

The peculiarity of dreams is that, while they are accessible to the senses of an individual, as much so as ceremonies, they are not *publicly* accessible to the senses. Two individuals cannot intuitively appreciate that they are sharing the same sensory input. This is the "do you see what I see" problem. At P. I. Ibirama, you implicitly assume that the answer is no for dreams, but yes for ceremonies. Therefore, the access you have to the world through dreams resembles the access you have to the land above the sky or the land of dead. In neither case can the group respond in unison, "I see what you see." In each case, individuals "see," but their empirical knowledge — their "seeing" — can be shared with others only thanks to the referential properties of discourse.

The role of individuals in accessing nonpublic sensory experiences is itself acknowledged in discourse. Recall, from Chapter 3, that it was one Klañmàg who ascended to retrieve his brother's bones, after the brother had been snatched away by a giant falcon. On July 4, 1975, Wãñpõ commented that "it was Klañmàg who told of what it is like in [the world above this one]." Similarly, on January 1, 1975, he remarked that it was because of Goes Living "that we know things about [the land of the dead]." The public has access to these parts of the world, but only through the senses of one individual. Everyone else gains access through the discourse of that individual. Discourse becomes a door through which parts of reality, otherwise closed to the public, can be opened.

We do not deny that the world as accessed through this discourse is real. In some sense, the dreamt and mythologized worlds are more "real" than the immediately experienced one. They are talked about, interpreted, agreed upon. We are reminded here — much more so than in the case of ceremonies — of Western-based modes of knowledge, including science. But an ingredient lacking in the P. I. Ibirama case is, seemingly, replicability. As regards dreams, there appears to be no way that you can experience what another has experienced.

We propose to show, however, that in the P. I. Ibirama community there is a kind of replicability, at least insofar as dream experience is concerned. Even if you cannot experience the precise dream another individual has had, you can gain access to the same kind of reality that another has experienced. In the case of waking experiences, two individuals do not have access to precisely the same experience unless they happen to be in precisely the same place at the same time. Here, of course, one thinks of the central role of propinquity in ceremonies. By virtue of their co-presence in the same place at the same time, individuals are ensured equal access to the phenomena of ceremonies. As regards other experiences, however, if one individual reports an experience, another individual cannot precisely duplicate it. But the individual can have access to a phenomenon that is similar to the original one, that reveals the "same" reality, even if not precisely the same experience.

It is ironic that dreams should give rise to shared, sciencelike, conscious understandings of reality. After all, dreams seem to average Westerners to be private, individual matters. How can they lead to shared understanding? That question is the central challenge of the present chapter. Our observation is that dreams are made known to the public through *dream narratives*, and that the latter form themselves into culturally standardized types. The key to knowledge at P. I. Ibirama is the narrativization of experience. Narratives, as part of the circulating discourse within the broader holding environment of the community, are influenced and shaped by other discourse. The narratives of one individual interact with the narratives of another. The modeling of one narrative on another leads to the formation of recognizable cultural types, which can be metadiscursively remarked. Such remarking of regularities among narratives is what constitutes interpretation of the world.

However, dream narratives are presumably distinct from the *dream experiences* that give rise to them. Are dream experiences also culturally and historically specific products of community discourse patterns? In other words, is the experience of reality through dreams itself culturally conditioned? The suspicion we articulate here is that it is. Rather than the "royal road" to the unconscious that Freud supposed, to something inside the individual, dreams — at P. I. Ibirama, at least — appear to be a road to collective consciousness, a consciousness shaped by circulating discourse.

To investigate how dream narratives become culturally standardized, we study their social circulation — their tellings and retellings. You will see that social circulation is impelled, in part at least, by normative statements about the efficacy of circulation, that is, by a circulating metadiscourse. In the course of tellings and retellings, interpretations are added onto narratives, and some of these interpretations take the shape of an implicit theory. The interpretations link and order different dream narratives, and the dream narratives so linked and ordered form a culture-specific dream narrative type.

This culturally specific type parallels other widely circulating discourse. We are referring to mythologized accounts of shamanic experiences of reality. The shamanic narratives themselves are, in all probability, historically recent, having entered into circulation within the last 100 to 150 years. This suggests that dream narratives (and possibly even the dream experiences on which they are based) originate from a culturally and historically specific system of discourse, as it confronts a reality revealed through dreamt experience.

In classical psychoanalysis, the dream is a subjective experience that is remembered. Perhaps in that remembering, or, if not, then subsequently, it is encoded in discourse, as it is communicated to the analyst. The goal of the analyst is to attach to the discourse an interpretation — that is, a piece of metadiscourse — which makes the original discourse understandable to both patient and analyst. The dream circulation may end there, or it may continue as the analyst incorporates the dream into a case presentation, where the discourse is discussed and further metadiscursive materials are attached to it. However, there is an implicit assumption in Western European/American culture that dreams do not circulate socially outside this restricted context. That assumption does not hold for at least some other cultures, in which, indeed, social circulation is so intense as to lead us to conceptualize them as "dream cultures."[1]

During our research in the Ibirama community, we began collecting a corpus of dreams from Wãñẽki[2] — one of our neighbors. The first dream was recorded on November 21, 1974, but a more intensive period of dream narrativizing began in March of 1975. Between March 28 and September 26, a period of almost exactly six months, thirty-four dreams were recorded. In reviewing these dreams recently, it became apparent that not all of them were actually dreamt by Wãñẽki. In addition to his own dreams, he was telling dreams that had been told to him by others. This was true of fully ten (or 30 percent) of the dreams.

Startlingly, the reported dreams were not just secondhand, but could be thirdhand or more. One dream, for example, was imputed to an old woman. How did it get to Wãñẽki? According to Wãñẽki, the dream was told first to another woman, Wãkra. From there we are unable to trace it, but quite likely it was told by Wãkra to Wãñẽki's wife Cãtag, with perhaps some additional intervening steps. Cãtag then told the dream to Wãñẽki. So there were, in all probability, at least four separate narrations involved:

Ãglò > Wãkra > . . . > Cãtag > Wãñẽki > Anthropologist

We have evidence not only of previous circulation, but also of intent to circulate dreams in the future. On September 15, 1975, Wãñẽki recounted a dream he had had, noting that he had already told it to his wife, but also that he was "going to tell this dream to Wãñpõ [his brother-in-law, who figured in the dream]."

Other cases are similar, disclosing a pattern of dream tellings and retellings. Indeed, at P. I. Ibirama, we find an intense interest in dreams as narratives — an interest on the part of both men and women. Not only do people tell and retell their own dreams and those of others, they also comment on them. In many cases, the comments interpret the dream experience. Here again we see that dreams and ceremony are opposed: Ceremonial symbolism is never interpreted.

Classical psychoanalysis includes metadiscursive statements that recommend the recounting of dreams. This is true also at P. I. Ibirama, although the "metapsychology" in which P. I. Ibirama statements are encoded is distinct. On September 11 of 1975, for example, Wãñĕkï remarked:

> It is always best to tell one's bad dreams,
> so nothing bad will happen.
> If one doesn't tell them,
> one will keep on having them every night.
> If one tells [them],
> one will only have them every once in a while.

Other commentary indicates that there is more to it than not wanting to have bad dreams. Dreams indicate that you may be coming into contact with spirits (*gàyun*) and thus may be poised to become a shaman. Here are the notes on Wãñĕkï's April 11, 1975, comments:

> Cãtag [Wãñĕkï's wife] told him
> that perhaps he was becoming a *kuyà* [shaman],
> and that maybe he shouldn't tell anybody his dreams;
> because he was always seeing dead people in his dreams.
> If he didn't tell anybody about his dreams,
> then he would start dreaming more,
> and eventually, when he was alone in the forest,
> he would meet up with the *gàyun* [spirit] of some animal. . . .
> He doesn't want to be a shaman, though,
> because if he didn't do everything correctly,
> the *gàyun* might kill him.
> So he continues telling about his dreams,
> so that he won't dream anymore,
> and won't become a shaman.[3]

A significant theme here and elsewhere is danger. In dreams, you encounter the spirits of animals and also the ghosts of dead kinsmen. You yourself are in danger of dying. Telling the dream is your way of avoiding this fate, of dispelling the fear that accrues to dreaming. Not all dreams are dangerous, but some of them are, and telling dissipates danger.

Why should telling result in dissipation? That question is not explicitly addressed in the natively circulating metadiscourse. It is addressed in classical metapsychology, where the interpretation of a telling derives its therapeutic efficacy from the bringing to consciousness of repressed materials. If the fear is grounded in neurotic anxiety, bringing the source of the anxiety to consciousness can dissipate the fear.

However, it is interesting that telling is also a way of making public, of sharing with others.[4] There is a warmth in community interaction, a sense that you are not alone in your danger, that it is not you as an isolated individual, but rather the group — as a greater, more powerful entity — that confronts the terrifying unknown of the spirit world. Moreover, the unknown is itself rendered somewhat knowable through the experiences of others, with which your own experiences can be compared. Sociability and fear are opposed because the fear is linked in part to isolation, to disconnectedness.

However, there is another culturally sanctioned route for individuals. You can confront the fear on your own, and in doing so you gain power within the community. But the power achieved through isolated mastery is double-edged. By separating yourself from the group, you earn respect, but the respect is colored with fear. If you have insufficient political support, you can become the scapegoat for other problems. For example, you might become the explanation for otherwise unexplained deaths. Traditionally, your life in such instances might truly be in jeopardy.[5] The metadiscourse therefore contains a truth. Telling dispels fear; not telling, the precondition for individual mastery, takes you into socially (as well as spiritually) dangerous terrain.

We are careful here to distinguish the fear associated with dreaming generally from the fear reported in dream narratives and, presumably, actually present in dream experiences. We are referring only to the former, to fear associated with dreaming more generally. Later you will see that at least one class of must-tell dreams — those concerning encounters with spirits — does itself invariably involve fear. The dispelling of fear in the latter case, however, may be similarly accomplished, that is, by telling others about it.

In psychoanalysis, the interpretation by the analyst of the dream narrative is designed to render the dream more understandable. It can be argued that the same procedure is at work at P. I. Ibirama. Understandability means fitting the dream into broader patterns of discourse. We show this through a specific example of interpretation. In a dream — recorded on September 15, 1975, and already considered in Chapter 1 — Wañēkï describes a hunt in which he, together with two other men, kills a tapir. The men proceed to cut it up, but the animal seems to Wañēkï to be still alive. The narrative proceeds as follows:

> They took out all of the innards except for the heart,
> which was still beating.
> At each beat of the heart,
> the tapir's head would move to one side

and then back again at the next beat.
Wãñẽkï again said that they should leave this animal and go on,
because it was going to harm them.
but Kañã'ï said that his wife was waiting for him
and would want some meat.
Wãñpõ said that tapir meat was even better than pork.
Then Wãñẽkï was looking at the tapir's heart,
which was the only organ left inside the body,
when it all of a sudden appeared as though the heart had looked up at him
    and then down again.
Wãñẽkï became afraid,
and told the others.
Wãñpõ said that he didn't even want to hear about that stuff,
and cut himself a piece of meat to take home,
as did Kañã'ï.
Wãñẽkï didn't want any, though.
They all started walking away,
and Wãñẽkï turned around to look at the tapir,
which was standing up,
and shaking its head at him.
The others also turned to look,
but didn't say anything.

The notebook entry continues, with an indication[6] that Wãñẽkï's experiences upon awakening are now being recounted:

> [Then he woke up.
> He told his wife about this dream;
> she said that it was a bad dream,
> and it was a good thing that he had told her about it.
> It was a bad dream,
> because the animal never died,
> it must not have been a tapir,
> but something else,
> maybe an *gàyun* (spirit).
> He is also going to tell this dream to Wãñpõ].

The raw discourse of the dream has been rendered culturally understandable. Wãñẽkï's wife—whose father was the great shaman Kàmlẽn (see Plate 5), and who was therefore herself regarded as knowledgeable about the spirit world—interprets the dream as concerning not a flesh-and-blood tapir, but rather the "spirit" (*gàyun*) of the tapir. She explicitly cites the fact that "the animal never died," but her interpretation probably stems in part also from the humanlike behavior of the tapir's heart—"all of a sudden [it] appeared as though the heart had looked up at him." The theme of spirits assuming human form is repeated in metadiscourse and played out in mythology, as we discuss later.

In another dream—this one retold by Wãñẽkï based on an original narrative by Uglõ—the dreamer herself furnishes the interpretation. In the dream she had been interacting with a young woman. She had thought the woman was her daughter, but the daughter was acting strangely. The interpretation follows:

> Uglõ decided that it must have been a *gàyun* (spirit)
> in her dream
> instead of Wañka [her daughter],
> one who was similar in appearance to her.

Still another dream: Wãñẽkï was out hunting with someone he did not know, someone who "never looked at Wãñẽkï, but talked half turned away. He said that his people lived down below the earth . . ." According to the interpretation in the field notes, "Wãñẽkï thinks that it [the hunting companion] might have been a *gàyun*, because he didn't look at him."

Not all interpretations involve spirits. In a few instances, dreams are understood as premonitions of future events. Wãñẽkï's wife dreamt of heavy rains and winds. After recounting the dream, she and her husband concluded "that it must be going to rain sometime soon." While not all interpretations refer to spirits, most do. There is operative at P. I. Ibirama a kind of implicit theory of dreams—dreams are conceptualized in the metadiscourse as concerning contacts with a spirit world. The term for spirit (*gàyun*) refers to a being that cannot be directly apprehended by the senses of ordinary persons in waking (nondream) experience. Shamans do interact with *gàyun*, and any person can encounter one in dreams. Ghosts of dead people are referred to by the term *kuplèg*, but they too are sometimes called *gàyun*, though the reverse is not true; the term *kuplèg* never applies to supernatural beings other than human ghosts.

The implicit theory of dreams may be rendered as follows: In the course of dreaming, one's own spirit wanders about. It encounters other spirits, both human and nonhuman. The nonhuman spirits present themselves in a variety of guises, both animal and human. Not all dreams involve encounters with nonhuman spirits or ghosts, but some of them—indeed, almost all that socially circulate—do. The art of interpretation consists in identifying a dream figure as a disguised spirit.

Dream narratives that elicit the most intense interest, and that circulate most widely, concern either recently deceased kin or spirits or both. In this regard, we note that tapping into dreams via the socially circulating dream narratives undoubtedly distorts the sampling of dreams. People at P. I. Ibirama probably have many more dreams than they feel compelled to tell. In-depth psychoanalysis would pull up dreams considerably different from those the community pays attention to. It would undoubtedly bring to light sexual dreams. This is consistent with the view that dream narratives correlate with waking discourse about dreams.

At the same time, it is significant that the P. I. Ibirama community focuses on dreams at all, that they talk about the dreams as important, and that importance is defined relative to metadiscursive commentary, based on an implicit theory. The tendency to produce a culture-specific dream type or types is thus in part a function of selection. Only some of the dreams are of special interest to the community.

You should note the formal similarity between dream theory and descent and marriage rules. Both are metadiscursive. Both involve statements about other narratives. In the case of marriage and descent rules, however, the purport is stipulative. The rules tell you how to behave, or, more precisely, how to narrativize your behavior, as well as that of others. Dream theory seems to be nonstipulative. It merely interprets what is already given in the dream narrative. As we propose, however, the effect of interpretations is indeed stipulative. You are "required"—if we can stretch the sense of that term—to produce dream narratives interpretable by means of the theory.

In the above examples, interpretations are not actually part of the original contiguous dream narrative. They are tacked on after the fact by the dream narrator or someone else whom the narrator quotes. In our field notes, these added interpretations are clearly marked as additions. However, there are cases in which interpretations form part of the dream narratives themselves. A figure in the dream is identified as a spirit (*gàyun*) in the course of the dream narrative itself. Here is a fragment from one of Wãñẽki's dream narratives:

> He was working in his garden,
> and had picked up a large rock,
> to roll down the hill,
> to get it out of the way.
> The rock spoke up,
> saying that he shouldn't remove him from his bed,
> why was he tearing apart his house?
> When the rock first spoke,
> it looked like the same rock,
> but then it appeared just like a person.
> (It was a *gàyun* of the rock) . . .

Our field notes include parentheses around the sentence "It was a *gàyun* of the rock." Possibly this indicates that the phrase was an explication for our benefit. However, it is seamlessly embedded within the larger narrative, not tacked on afterward like other interpretations; and it is stated as fact, not as interpretation, as if it were evident to Wãñĕkï in the dream itself. It is neither hypothetical nor qualified. Compare this occurrence with that in the tapir dream above, where Wãñĕkï speculates, "it must not have been a tapir, but something else, maybe a *gàyun* (spirit)." In the present dream, there is no doubt. The dream simply, factually concerned the spirit of the rock.

In another case, the discourse process of interpretation is one of the events of the dream narrative. In one dream, Wãñĕkï encounters a monkey that behaves strangely, like a human. Afterward:

> . . . they returned
> to where they had left Ayu and Cãtag [Wãñĕkï's
>    wife],
> and told them what had happened.
> Cãtag told him [Wãñĕkï]
> that he shouldn't have tried to kill the howler monkey,
> because it was her father.

Note that this passage is part of the dream narrative. The interaction closely resembles actual waking behaviors, in which Wãñĕkï's wife interprets his dreams, but this interpretation occurs within the dream.

From such evidence, we conclude that dream interpretation itself can become part of dream narratives, circulating along with the other dreamt events. Furthermore — and here we speculate — it may be that the interpretation, which in some cases is tacked on as a supplement to the dream narrative, in other cases is incorporated not only into the dream narrative, but also into the experience itself. We are referring not only to the act of interpretation, as in the last example above, but also to its content. In other words, the dreamer's dream may be structured in accord with the implicit theory embedded in the metadiscourse of dream interpretation. This would be a second mechanism by which culturally and historically specific dream narrative types are produced. On the one hand, the community is interested in and selects and circulates those dream narratives that conform to its implicit theory. On the other hand, the implicit theory works its way into and structures the original dream narrative and, possibly, even the dream experience.

The two tendencies may be termed *dream selection* and *dream suggestion*, respectively. Through them, culturally specific dream types take shape. The type investigated most thoroughly here concerns spirit beings, who manifest themselves in dreams through animals or inanimate objects. We have given two examples: the dream of the spirit that appeared in the tapir's heart and the dream of the rock spirit. Both concern an object — an animal in one, a rock in the other — that assumes human characteristics. In the case of the tapir, the characteristics are minimal. In the description "it all of a sudden appeared as though the heart had looked up at him and then down again," a humanlike interaction occurs. This is reinforced by the dead tapir's "standing up, and shaking its head at him [Wãñĕkï]." The rock, however, exhibits fully linguistic speech behavior, which is followed by its transformation into human form: "The rock spoke up, saying that he shouldn't remove him from his bed, why was he tearing apart his house? When the rock first spoke, it looked like the same rock, but then it appeared just like a person."

The cultural specificity of this dream narrative type can be readily appreciated if you ask yourself in how many of your own dreams you have experienced this kind of interaction. Have you encountered an animal or an inanimate object that takes on human characteristics and even talks to you? In Wãñĕkï's dreams, excluding the dreams of others that he has retold, one of every six (17 percent) matches this type.

Two additional dream narratives show close parallels to those already discussed:

> Ayu and Patè[7] came up
> and asked [where] they [Wãñĕkï and his wife, Cãtag] had come from.
> "Listen," they said,
> and a howler monkey started calling.
> Wãñĕkï went with Patè to hunt them.
> There were five monkeys.
> Patè said that they should each kill one
> and leave the rest.
> Wãñĕkï raised his gun,
> but the howler monkey motioned him to stop,
> saying "s-s-s-t,"
> and did this again.
> Then this one howler monkey became tiny,
> and started rolling back and forth on the branch.
> The other monkeys had left.
> Patè said that they had better leave
> and not kill that monkey,
> because he might kill them in turn.
> So they returned
> to where they had left Ayu and Cãtag,
> and told them what had happened.
> Cãtag told him

that he shouldn't have tried to kill the howler monkey,
because it was her father.

Here the humanlike behavior is again implicit, the howler monkey (see Plate 13) motioning Wãñĕkï to stop, then saying, " s-s-s-t," not a fully linguistic utterance.

In a final example, the transformation of an animal (again a howler monkey) into human form is patent:

He [Wãñĕkï], Nil Januário, Wãñpõ Maneta, and Kañã'ï João all went hunting.
Wãñpõ said
that there must be howler monkeys over there.
They stopped,
and heard the call of the howler monkey.
Wãñĕkï went ahead,
and saw that there were some monkeys
in the top of a *canela* tree.
Nil said
that he was going to shoot one,
and raised his shotgun,
but the monkey shouted not to kill him.
They all started running away from fright,
but Wãñĕkï stopped
and shouted to Wãñpõ to stop
and talk to the monkey,
because it must be his father.
But the others all ran away,
so he went back to talk with him himself.
The howler monkey said to him,
"Why didn't you talk to me,
instead of trying to shoot me?"
He climbed down out of the tree,
and he then looked like Kàmlẽn [Wãñpõ's and Cãtag's deceased father, Plate 5],
with a white cloth tied around his chest.
He had his lost arm back, though,
and it was stuck into the cloth.

You should remember the real world in which Wãñĕkï grew up. Hunting was the key male activity. Dream interactions with animals are not, therefore, something unusual, even though Wãñĕkï had not recently engaged in much hunting, owing to his advanced age and to the transformation of subsistence practices on the small reserve. At the same time, daily experience with animals (farm animals or pets, for example) does not in itself

*Plate 13.* Photograph of Brazilian howler monkey (*Alouatta fusca*). This is an exemplar of the species whose spirit the great shaman Kàmlēn (Plate 5) summoned in curing, and that Wāñēkï encountered in his dream — though the image proved to be a disguise assumed by Kàmlēn's spirit. Photo courtesy of L. C. Marigo.

produce this highly specific dream type, with animals taking on human characteristics and interacting with the dreamer. Furthermore, in the rock dream, it becomes obvious that not only animals but even inanimate objects assume human form. We can only explain this as the result of selection pressures or of suggestions arising from metadiscursive interpretation or both.

Another component of these dreams is fear. In the tapir dream narrative, you see the statement, "Wāñēkï became afraid, and told the others." In the first howler monkey dream, fear is suggested by the threat to the dreamer's life: "Patè said that they had better leave and not kill that howler monkey, because he might kill them in turn." In the second howler monkey dream — the one in which the monkey assumes full human form — you find "they all started running away from fright." In this latter case, however, Wāñēkï masters his fear. Fear is present even in the rock dream: "Wāñēkï was afraid that these *gàyun* were going to kill him, because they seemed to be angry with him."

If you compare these dream narratives — whose contemporaneity we emphasize, since each dream occurred in 1975 — with other circulating discourse, and especially with widely disseminated, quasi-mythologized accounts of past shamanic experience, you find striking parallels. Consider a story told by Wāñpō, the brother-in-law of Wāñēkï, and son of the great shaman Kàmlēn. The story is about another shaman named Cu. Cu had been the teacher of Kàmlēn. He died before the turn of the century, and Kàmlēn himself died in the 1920s:

> Cu heard the tapir come tramping through the dry bamboo.
> It arrived
> and looked around,
> but was really [a *gàyun*].
> He looked like a tapir,
> but then began to talk:
> "Father, what are you doing?"
> Cu was afraid
> and so he said:
> "I am waiting for tapirs here."
> The *gàyun* replied,
> "Well, they will not come today.
> But there will be a deer coming."
> A little while later the deer came,
> and Cu killed it.
> The *gàyun* now looked the same as a human.

Now look at the dream fragment in which Wāñēkï encounters Kàmlēn's spirit in the form of the howler monkey:

> Nil said
> that he was going to shoot one [howler    monkey],
> and raised his shotgun,
> but the howler monkey shouted not to kill him.
> They all started running away from fright,
> but Wāñēkï stopped
> and shouted to Wāñpō to stop
> and talk to the monkey,
> because it must be his father.
> But the others all ran away,
> so he went back to talk with him himself.
> The howler monkey said to him,
> "Why didn't you talk to me,

instead of trying to shoot me?"
He climbed down out of the tree,
and he then looked like Kàmlēn.

In each case, the animal in question takes on a key human attribute — the power of speech. In both cases, additionally, the animal subsequently assumes human form. Finally, both myth and dream contain an element of fear, which invariably permeates encounters between humans and spirits, whether in dreams or in shamanic experience.

Lest you imagine that the quasi-mythologized story of Cu, excerpted above, is atypical, here is another example, this one dealing with a man named Yòkàg. It was narrated by Wāñpō on March 18, 1975:

He [Yòkàg] arrived in the forest
and found a monkey knocking pine nuts out of an araucaria tree,
even though it was not the season.
The monkey was up in the tree,
and Yòkàg was about to kill him.
Suddenly, the monkey turned and said,
"You don't need to kill me."
When the monkey descended,
it was clear that he was a person (i.e., *gàyun*).
The *gàyun* told the other monkeys
to get pine nuts for Yòkàg.
They did so,
and these nuts were big.
He also gave a little monkey to him,
which Yòkàg raised,
and in the time of the pine nuts
the monkey helped get them out of the trees.

This fragment includes transformation into human form and fully linguistic speech, but it lacks the element of fear.

The parallelism between the widely disseminated stories and the dream narratives is not confined to the motif of encountering a spirit. Consider this brief narrative[8] by Wāñpō regarding, again, the great shaman Cu:

When there were no animals to eat,
Cu's family sent him out to get wild pig.
So he took his arrows,
went off into the forest
to notify the *gàyun* of the wild pigs
to send pigs,

and then returned that afternoon.
The wild pig *gàyun* is just like a farmer.
If you go to the farmer
and ask him to release his pigs,
he will do so.
The same with the wild pigs' *gàyun*.
So the *gàyun* let some pigs go.
The pig *gàyun* is a human,
and he has all of the pigs penned up,
releasing them at varying intervals.

Compare that story with the following dream, originally told by Kañã'ï to Wãñēkï, and then retold by Wãñēkï on July 14, 1975: [9]

He [Kañã'ï] saw Kowi (dead),
who told him,
"Didn't you see those wild pigs
that I sent you to eat?"
Kañã'ï said yes,
that he had killed one.
There had been a lot of wild pigs in a garden a year ago,
and the Indians had killed a lot of them.
Kowi was telling him
that in his land
there were huge pens,
with wild pigs, *cateto* [a kind of wild pig], and other animals.
Kowi told the other *gàyun*
that they should let some of the animals out,
so the Indians back on the reserve could have some meat.
Kowi went to another *gàyun* named Pedro (also an Indian),
who was the owner of one wild pig.
Kowi asked him whether he couldn't let one loose,
and Pedro said yes,
just pick one.
So he let one go.
He told Kañã'ï
that he had let it go for Wãñpō Maneta and Wãñpō Patè —
but others had killed the wild pigs
and not given any of the meat to these men.
He said
that they could have given them a piece each,
but it didn't matter,
because he would let out some more animals

and that these two Wãñpõs [i.e., Wãñpõ Maneta and
Wãñpõ Patè] should get some.

In both dream narrative and story there is an account — reflected also in
metadiscursive interpretation — of wild animals as controlled by humanlike
spirits. These spirits keep animals in pens and let them out periodically for
the humans to hunt. Perhaps you will agree with us that the parallel is too
close to be due to chance.

You even see in these widely disseminated, quasi-mythologized accounts
a reflection of native metapsychological theory — not telling your dreams
leads you down the path of shamanism. Here is an excerpt from the story
of Cu as a young man, about to become a shaman:

> Cu was sleeping
> and talking to *gàyun*.
> His mother then woke him up,
> but he said not to bother him . . .
> "Mother, I'm going to sleep."
> So he slept again
> and began talking in his sleep.
> Then his mother woke him up again.
> The howler monkey must have shown to him his medicine . . .
> He then woke up
> and his mother asked him
> with whom he had been speaking.
> He said nothing.

Other stories as well illustrate the danger of becoming a shaman, with the
person who sees the spirit dying as a result.

Obviously, we are dealing with commonalities among a wide range of
discourses. Dream narratives are not isolated from other narratives. Rather,
they commingle with them. They influence them and are influenced by
them. They are part of the same discursive field. No wonder culturally distinct types of dream narrative emerge! They develop out of publicly circulating discourse, and not just the discourse of contemporary dreams, but
also the discourse of ancient stories, handed down across the generations.
Dream narratives are the product, in short, of culture. However, this is not
culture in the classical sense of uniformly shared meanings; rather, it is culture in the sense of circulating, publicly accessible discourse.

How wrong it would be, however, to imagine that the interaction is one-
way, that mythology — part of primordial culture — unilaterally determines
dream narratives. Dream experiences are a font of creativity and generativ-
ity, contributing to the repertoire of narratives in the community. They can

become shapers of culture, construed as circulating discourse. You find also that the seemingly primordial stories are not actually all that primordial. Some of them can be dated, by genealogical reckoning, to the latter nineteenth century. Stories about Cu—whom we can locate on our genealogies—are of this recent historical vintage. Cu lived just two generations before Wãñpõ, Nil, and Wãñĕkï. Wãñpõ's father was Kàmlēn, who, as noted earlier, died in the 1920s. He was an elderly man when he died, and he had known Cu in his youth. Indeed, Cu was not only Kàmlēn's father's brother, he was also Kàmlēn's mentor—the one from whom Kàmlēn learned shamanic secrets.

Here is Kàmlēn's story, as narrated by his son, Wãñpõ, on March 20, 1975:

> Kàmlēn said
> that when he was small,
> he went around with Cu, his father's brother.
> He must have been 10 or 15 years old,
> and he went alone with him.
> They would follow after the others along the path.
> There was a tall tree along the path,
> and Cu was looking up at the top.
> But Kàmlēn was not,
> because he did not know.
> When he did look up,
> he saw a large howler monkey.
> He thought that it was just a howler monkey,
> but it was really a *gàyun* [spirit].
> So he asked Cu,
> "Is that a howler monkey?"
> and Cu said no,
> "It is a man,
> it is a spirit."
> Kàmlēn grew fearful
> and said,
> "Father, I am afraid."
> Cu responded,
> "You don't have to be afraid,
> he is not angry with you."
> So they left.
> Cu told him not to tell anything to the others.
> When Cu died,
> the howler monkey began to talk with my father,

but before then never.
First, Cu taught my father.
When the others left camp,
Cu stayed behind with Kàmlēn.
Cu couldn't get on by himself
because he was so old,
and Kàmlēn always cared for him.
At these times Cu would teach
and show everything to Kàmlēn.
The two went together on the trail of the others.
They saw the howler monkey *gàyun*
and a little while later Kàmlēn said
that he had a headache.
But that night he slept
and saw the howler monkey spirit.
The howler monkey said
that he had given the headache to him.
He wanted to know
whether my father would remember him.
Next day Kàmlēn told Cu everything about his dream,
and what the *gàyun* had said to him.
The howler monkey said
that first he had helped Cu
and that now he would help him,
that he didn't have anything to worry about,
because he was not going to die.

You have a sense of the immediacy of the narrative to the narrator; this is a story about his own father. The story of Cu is different. Wāñpō never knew Cu, never interacted with him as a real person. Cu was already a quasi-mythical figure, someone who lived in a distant, albeit not fully ancient, past. Kàmlēn, however, was the man who raised Wāñpō. He was a flesh-and-blood human being, someone whose own experiences — and here you see that the narrated experiences include dreams — he narrated to his son. This fragment of discourse stands at a crucial juncture between contemporary dream narrative and historical tale or even myth.

For Wāñpō's children and grandchildren, the story of Kàmlēn is already part of lore. Kàmlēn stands to them in the relation that Cu did to Wāñpō — an ancestor whom they did not know firsthand and never experienced as a flesh-and-blood individual, an ancestor both mysterious and magically powerful. From a discourse point of view, the question is, Will the stories about Kàmlēn continue to circulate? In fact, Kàmlēn has already entered into lore. According to the 1974 P. I. Ibirama chief, Ali Krire,[10] who had no close kin ties to Kàmlĕn:

> Before old Kàmlĕn died,
> he said
> that he would walk "around above."
> He therefore became a *rapina* [Port., "bird of prey, falcon"].
> Every time someone sees [one of these falcons]
> he says:
> "Take care of me."
> They have to say this
> so that he won't do bad things.

The fear continues. How typical it is in narratives of shamanism and of encounters with the spirit world, and here you see it in another guise. Kàmlĕn overcame his fear of spirits and acquired the status of great shaman in his own lifetime. That status brought with it a respect from other members of the community, based at least in part on fear. Because of his supernatural power, Kàmlĕn might do something to harm people. The fear persists even after his death. It has occasioned this seemingly odd discourse usage — individuals uttering "take care of me" every time they see a falcon.

Evidently, the kind of culture that is carried in discourse is not primordial but historical and malleable. Kàmlĕn and his dream narratives have reshaped discourse practice in the P. I. Ibirama community. If you think about the influence of culture on dreams, therefore, it is obvious in this case that the past is not so ancient. The discourse has taken shape in relatively recent historical times, between 50 and 150 years ago.

Discourse is malleable. One source of its change is the dreamwork, in whose crucible new images are fashioned. These new images interact with existing ones, and they undergo interpretation though a loose network of metadiscursive statements, but the images, nevertheless, are not merely identical to those that have come before them. A bi-directional process is at work here. Prior discourse influences dream narratives and, possibly, even dream experiences. However, novel, freshly constructed dream narratives also recalibrate and reshape prior discourse.

In a paper entitled "The Occurrence in Dreams of Material from Fairy Tales," Freud remarked that "elements and situations derived from fairy tales are also frequently to be found in dreams" (1913: 281). He remarked further that "in interpreting the passages in question the patient will produce the significant fairy tale as an association." Here Freud seems to make an observation similar to that developed in the present chapter. However, his purpose is distinct. While the fairy tale provides imagery used by the dreamwork, the compatibility is found in the fact that fairy tale and dream alike have a common origin — basic psychic structures and wishes stemming from the human unconscious. Dreams were for Freud the "royal road" to the unconscious. He moved from them inward, so to speak, into the psyche of the individual. His concern was not with the differences between collectivities as regards the dream narratives, but rather with the commonalities underlying them.

We do not mean to criticize his method, but rather to clarify our own. The position we are articulating is that at least some of the dreams in a community are culture-specific phenomena. They are culture-specific because they exhibit intracultural similarities as regards dream narrative types. The method of demonstrating intracommunity similarities coupled with intercommunity differences is crucial to our purposes. Freud did not employ this method. Dream narratives for him were defined at a different plane, that is, with regard to the latent or underlying (rather than manifest) content. You find no awareness in Freud of culture-specific narrative types. Indeed, explanation of such types — that is, of variability — is beyond the scope of the Freudian project.

You see this, for example, in Spiro's (1979) rejection of Lévi-Strauss. While his concern is with myths, not dream types, the quest for universal explanation of the particular is apparent. Spiro asserts that the central Brazilian myths of the origin of cooking fire are expressions of the Oedipus complex. His concern is with similarity, not difference. He wants to explain the particular in terms of the universal. While such concerns are important, can we not also acknowledge the problem of variability — that myths differ from society to society?

In his work on the Trobriand matrilineal complex, Bronislaw Malinowski (1953 [1927]) attempted to address the problem of variability. He argued that socially specific family patterns create differences in underlying psychic structure, which Freud had posited as universal. Malinowski, who published his ideas originally in 1924, was taken to task by Ernest Jones (1925),[11] who reasserted the universality of the Oedipus complex. What has gotten lost in the shuffle, however, is the question of cultural variability in *manifest content*, or in what we might call *natively interpreted content*, even if latent content is everywhere the same.

Our approach accounts for the possibility of culturally specific dream types, such as those concerning the transformation of animals or rocks into human form. On the one side, received discourses influence dream narratives. Two mechanisms are involved — the selection of dream narratives and the suggestion of materials for the dream narrative or dream experience. On the other side, novel dream narratives affect received discourse. The dreamwork is creative. It produces, under the pressure of selection and suggestion, a new dream narrative, distinct from those that have come before it. The new narrative interacts with received narratives, supplementing the repertoire and potentially altering patterns.

None of this, however, accounts for the specific character of the narratives in the P. I. Ibirama case. Why do animals and rocks take on human form, speaking and interacting with the dreamer? Why does dream interpretation focus on the spirit world? While we propose no definitive answer, you cannot help but see that dreaming bears the imprint of the broader discourse processes operative at P. I. Ibirama. What is talked about is what cannot be immediately seen, heard, tasted, touched, or smelled. If people interpreted dreams simply as alternative contacts with the ordinary everyday world — "I dreamt about that rock over there" — what more would there be to say? Everyone would yawn and go about their business. However, if people dreamt about what they could not otherwise see, then everyone would stand up and take note. The interpretation of dreams as about an otherwise inaccessible reality imparts momentum to dream narratives, propelling them through physical space.

The transformation of an object — a rock or a howler monkey, for instance — into human form, therefore, is not just a dreamt experience. It is a trope of the inaccessibility of reality more generally. How better to communicate the idea that there is something out there other than what we see? Behind the surface of perception lurks something strange, something imperceptible (in everyday, waking life), and yet simultaneously knowable. Dreamt objects are closer to noumena — that is, "true" entities — than are immediately experienced ones. Dreams in which ordinary things don human shapes confirm the implicit epistemology.

Let us return to our original question: What is the relationship between dreams and ceremonies? We can now articulate an answer. In each case, the central problem is publicness. In ceremony, everyone must be in the same place at the same time. They must assemble. This enables them to jointly experience the phenomena of the ceremony, thereby implicitly answering in the affirmative the question "Do you see what I see?" At the same time, because the question is never explicitly formulated in referential discourse, the joint experience of reality makes room for heterogeneity as regards individual inferences. Importantly, publicness here is a matter of phenomenal accessibility and sensibility. The issue is joint sensory access to the world, and ceremony provides joint access, countering the skepticism that individuals have in regard to the referential content of circulating discourse. From a politico-epistemological perspective, ceremony is leveling. Everyone is on more or less equal footing.

In dreams, publicness does not involve joint sensory access to phenomena. There is no "you were there too" confirmation. You gain access to other people's experiences only through the referential content of the discourse they utter. Direct sensory sharing is minimal here; the centrifugal pull of the dreamwork, with its endless capacity for creativity and invention, makes it impossible for dream experience to be perfectly replicated. In ceremonies, those present at one time can experience the same phenomena. It is in order to make momentaneous phenomena endure that people strive for precise replication of the sensible behaviors and contextual characteristics.

If ceremony at P. I. Ibirama is inherently egalitarian, allowing everyone to form their own interpretations, dreaming is inegalitarian, asymmetrical. Only one individual at a time has sensory access to the world through dreams. Other individuals rely upon that one individual's report. The world, so to speak, does not open itself equally to all in dreams, as it does in ceremony. Rather, selected individuals have privileged access. Others are dependent on them. A privileged individual knows something about the world that the others learn only indirectly.

It is this indirectness that makes dreaming such an intriguing social process. Here, you see discourse achieve an ascendancy over individuals. At issue is not only what people want to say about their dreams, but also what other people want to hear. As we have argued, the latter is in part a function of interpretive patterns built up gradually over time — interpretive patterns that are themselves carried along in circulating discourse, transmitted through discussions people have about each other's dreams. The issue is not simply the creativity of dreamwork. A novel dream narrative has no impact if it has no circulation. The question is, Is the dream narrative one that people want to hear, to pass on? No matter how novel, if no one is interested, the dream narrative languishes.

If you compare dreaming with ceremonies, you see that in both cases a crucial dimension of publicness is replicability. In ceremonies, it is repeating the same behaviors, creating the same contexts. In this way, new individuals can be introduced to a sensorily or phenomenally defined public. In dreaming, however, replication consists in repeating the same narrative — and here we mean sameness as regards referential content. Replication allows an individual's original experience to socially circulate.

Unlike ceremony, narrative replication does not depend on group assemblage. Narratives can be told by one person to another in sequential, telephone-game-like fashion. The mechanism of circulation is independent of large-scale gathering. The notion of publicness here is distinct. Intelligibility or conscious knowledge of the world through referential discourse takes over from direct sensory awareness. While in ceremony the world is sensible, in dreams it becomes intelligible — a function of the semantic content of discourse.

Circulation checks the creativity and individuality of the dreamwork. Not only is there selective pressure, which filters out some narratives; there is suggestive pressure. If an individual is to participate in the circulation of dream narratives within a community, that individual must produce narratives conforming to the canons of narrative production. Individuals are pressured to harness the creativity of the dreamwork, to shape narratives after the image the community desires. Indeed, the evidence implies that through suggestive pressure, circulating discourse actually works its way into, and in some measure takes control of, the dreamwork.

This is a matter of power of collectivities over individuals. In this process, the reservoir of discourse in a community takes control of individual experience, shaping it and organizing its expression, making it conform to broader community patterns. Telling one's dreams in accord with community standards for dream narratives implicates the individual in a relationship of subordination to the broader community, as manifested in circulating discourse.

You can now appreciate why the theory, lodged in community-wide interpretive patterns, stresses a reality that is distinct from, and not directly accessible to, the senses. Because of the nonimmediacy of the world, because of reality's inaccessibility to waking everyday perception, referential discourse gains power over individuals. Discourse reveals to them what they cannot directly see or smell or touch or taste. Individuals know that beneath the veneer of normalcy is a world of strange goings-on, of human-like spirits (*gàyun*) who, unnoticed, control daily life. You may be looking at a rock, unaware — were it not for your acquaintance with referential discourse — that the rock is not a rock at all. It is a spirit, capable of talking to you. Indeed, it may even have power over your life and death.

Whereas Durkheim argued that the collectivity controlled individuals — that its power was manifested equally in group assemblage and in talk — we argue that two distinct processes are at work. At P. I. Ibirama, group assemblage does not involve control over individual consciousness. Ceremonies are uninterpreted, behaviors uncontrolled by words. People want to replicate behaviors so as to replicate experiences. However, neither the experiences nor the phenomena are interpreted for them. Rather, people make of ceremonial phenomena what they will. They rely on the tacit assumption, "you see what I see, because you are here where I am, looking at what I am looking at." Individuals have access to the same experiences. No accepted, community-wide discourse tells them how to understand or make sense of those experiences.

In dreaming, however, individuals are not left to their own devices. When novel dream narratives enter into public circulation, they undergo interpretation through an already circulating discourse. That circulating discourse seizes control over the novel dream narrative. In seizing control of the dream narrative, it simultaneously seizes control of knowledge. You can know what another individual has experienced only through their narrative of it. You have no possibility of independently "seeing what they see."

If power originates in control by circulating discourse over novel dream narratives, you can resist the power by not telling your dreams. This is precisely what a shaman does. When individuals tell their dreams, those dreams — and with them the inner, creative experiences of the individuals — are laid bare for community inspection. The private access you have to reality, to the world, is made public; it is fit to accepted understandings. This is comforting to you, but it is also a source of domination over you by the accepted, circulating discourse. If you do not tell your dreams, you keep your private experiences private. You accumulate knowledge. Should it become known that you are intentionally withholding your dreams, others will assume that you have some special knowledge about the world. In that knowledge is power.

If the referential component of discourse is to circulate, people must have a reason for circulating it; people must be interested in the message it carries. An excellent way for discourse to propel itself is to construct a reality that can only be accessed through itself, a world that is not publicly available through the senses. Additionally, the reality must not be simply out there — invisible wraiths wandering through campsites. The imperceptible reality must have power over individuals' lives. A discourse that attributes power to invisible spirits, therefore, ensures its own circulation. People need to know about the reality if it is going to affect them. If the only way they can know it is through discourse, then they must pay attention to that discourse. The discourse acquires a propulsive force. If the noumenal world hidden behind the surface of perception were inconsequential, if it made no difference to individuals in their daily lives, the discourse reporting that world would also be inconsequential. People would not be compelled to circulate it. But, because the spirit world is consequential, the discourse about it moves through space and across time.

The power created by discourse as a means of perpetuating itself can also be used by shamans to achieve their personal goals. Discourse power becomes a source of individual power. When shamans withhold dreams, they keep the knowledge of the world they have acquired to themselves. Because that knowledge is consequential, because the hidden world affects you, for that reason you are interested in it. It has a potential impact on your life. Shamans thus harness the power lodged in circulating discourse for their own ends. Through it, they win respect in the community's eyes. Those who resist selective and suggestive pressures transform the impersonal power of discourse into personal power. Circulating discourse, in gaining power for itself, simultaneously introduces asymmetrical relations among individuals into the community.

Shamans resist the power of discourse in much the way ordinary people do in ceremonies. Part of what shamans do involves nonverbal behavior analogous to that found in ceremony. Kàmlēn, who had seen the howler monkey spirit, performed cures in which he imitated the howler monkey's call — "hu' hu' hu' hu' hu' hu' "[12] — uttered in a deep pitch, with a breathy quality to the [u], beginning with a rhythmical pulsing of the syllables that gradually increases in tempo, with Kàmlēn rocking back and forth on his haunches. As in collective ceremonies, he did not tell anyone what he was doing. They were left to infer for themselves that he was summoning the howler monkey spirit, or, perhaps, that his body was taken over by the spirit.

Shamans do not only resist the power of discourse; they also bolster and augment it. In refusing to narrate their own dream experiences, they confirm the circulating theory — dreaming allows one access to spirits not otherwise perceptible. Indeed, the shaman's behavior instantiates the theory, making palpable the existence of otherwise ethereal spirits. By imitating the howler monkey's objective behavior, Kàmlēn made its spirit accessible not only to the intellect, but also to the senses. Shamanic behavior makes perceptible what is otherwise only intelligible. The behavior is there for all to see. By coming to resemble noumena, phenomena confirm them. Discourse, as a creator of noumena, is thereby also corroborated.

# *Chapter 8.* Between Myth and Dream

The circulation of physical things — this is what Malinowski (1961 [1922]: 81–104, *passim*) so brilliantly documented in his *Argonauts of the Western Pacific*. There were red spondylus shell necklaces known as *soulava*, and white *Conus millepunctatus* "arm shells" known as *mwali* — physical things, bits of culture. They traversed literally hundreds of miles of open sea. Over "opaque, greenish" sea and "intensely blue, clear" sea, they sailed from island to island, spending little time with any one owner. The *soulava* necklaces moved in huge clockwise circles, and the *mwali* arm shells moved in huge counterclockwise circles, the flow forming the so-called "kula ring" of eastern Papuo-Melanesia.

You can compare this curvilinear circulation of things in space to the circulation of Euro-American heirlooms, which change hands but infrequently. Heirlooms often lodge themselves in the same physical place, yet nevertheless descend down across the generations, in rectilinear motion, like a point projected into a line along one axis of a four-dimensional space.

In both cases, culture consists in physical things. Its circulation is seemingly independent of replication. For a dream or a myth to circulate at P. I. Ibirama, however, it must undergo replication. Someone must have had prior perceptual access to a thing — analogous to the text artifact in Plate 1 with which this book began, but consisting in transient sounds. From the outward physical characteristics, the copier imagines an abstract form or idea that he or she reproduces. The form sallies forth into the physical world of things, where, unlike a spondylus shell, it resides only fleetingly. A listener in this second telling imagines another abstract form, presumed to be related to the earlier form, although about this we can only guess.[1] The listener reproduces it in a third telling, and so forth. Public circulation occurs through this copying or replication process.

I submit that what falls under the rubric of culture is touched by replication.[2] It is linked to an abstract form or entity that is periodically reproduced, like the strands of DNA underlying biological life. I note that, as in discourse, what is important in DNA is not only the concrete specificities of the individual strand, but also the form, the abstract entity that the strand represents. As in culture, similarities are what give rise to the idea of distinctive populations, capable of perpetuating themselves across time.

In the case of discourse, the public life of the thing is short. At least this is true of discourse unmediated by technology, such as printing or tape recording. Think of the word "cool," which circulated so fashionably in the United States in the late 1980s and early 1990s. Circulation depends upon the precise replication of phonetic detail — [kʰuUl] or even [kʰuʌl], with a pronounced diphthong, the first half stressed and higher pitched, the second half relatively unstressed and lower pitched. How many times have you heard it from the mouths of students and even colleagues! Yet each instance lasts typically less than a second. Now you hear it; now it's gone.

Other aspects of culture, like dance movements and gestures, are similarly short-lived. But consider Amerindian ceramic pots, so many now locked up behind display cases in somber, high-ceilinged museum halls. Individual pots can last for a long time, and they can move through space. However, what makes them cultural is that they are similar to other specimens, that they reflect cultural types. The shapes, materials, colors, and designs are distinctive. They are characteristic of specific peoples over specific historical periods. Each pot is a copy or replica of others that have gone before it, but it is a replica that is comparatively long-lived.

Let's look in more detail at short-lived replicas — dream narratives and myths at P. I. Ibirama. What differentiates dream narratives from myths is the frequency of replication, and the relative rate of decay and disappearance of the discourse over time. Dream narratives are analogous to news; indeed, they may be news, reports of experiences people have recently had. They spread rapidly throughout a community, going from household to household, as you recall from the last chapter. However, they typically have a shallow time depth, a short half-life.

In contrast to dreams, myths have a rather sluggish lateral circulation. Their principal movement is across the generations. However, correspondingly, the half-life of mythical narratives is long.

You can think of myths and dreams as two poles of cultural circulation, corresponding to two kinds of culture. Dreams belong on the side of creativity and innovation — "news," as I have dubbed it. Myths belong to the side of continuity and tradition. Myths represent inertial as opposed to accelerative culture. You might think of them as an example of Newton's first law of motion, as continuing to move through time unless specifically counteracted by an external force, such as an opposed discourse — for example, one moving into the community from the outside, as in culture contact.

The contrast is far from perfect. Myths do change during replication. And, as I have tried to show, dream narratives tend — through the forces of selection and suggestion — to conform to community-wide standards, becoming more mythlike. Nevertheless, there is a tendency for dreams and myths to circulate differently at P. I. Ibirama. What you probably wonder is whether there are corresponding differences in the replication processes.

If you look closely at the processes, you discern that, as regards the continuum between referential meaning and physical form of the discourse, dream narrative — being maximally newslike — is most closely bound up with pure referential meaning. As with other kinds of news, people have the most interest in knowing what the dreamer actually experienced. They are less likely to be interested, immediately at least, in the rhetorical architecture of the narrative itself. They want to know what "happened" — dream narratives are the avenue of public access to private experiences of reality that individuals have had. Dream narratives are, for this reason, crucial to building up a public image of the real.

The public's interest in referential content versus rhetorical form is, of course, a matter of degree. A rhetorically well-constructed narrative will more likely be retold. Indeed, you can think of dream experiences themselves as situated along a continuum of narrativizability, with which, perhaps, all of us are familiar. Some dream experiences, so luminous while you are having them, nevertheless vanish upon waking, collapsing into a puff of inarticulate experience when you endeavor to tell them to someone else — like those delicate French pastries, so seemingly substantial, that nevertheless disintegrate in your mouth upon chewing, hardly satisfying your desire. Other dreams, however, are more readily told as stories. The stories obey a logic sufficiently similar to that of other narratives.

If you compare dreams to myths, it is apparent that, in overall terms, the interest people have in dreams pertains more to their content, to the referential pole, to what the dreams are about. When people initially tell a dream they want others to grasp something of the experience they had. The dream narrative, before all else, consists in putting into words an experience, an encounter with reality. The narrative later undergoes change, as it circulates. However, its social life begins in an attempt to communicate something about an experience, about an encounter with the world. It is for this reason that reference is so important, at least initially, in the area of dream narrative.

What does it mean to replicate the referential or semantic content of a narrative? On one extreme, replication of referential meaning occurs when the actual physical shape of the utterance — the sound or graphic form in which that meaning is carried — is itself replicated. Suppose, for example, that the original narrative included the following:

zazan        tõ    gàyun  hã    wã
armadillo  erg.  spirit  focus  stative
"It was the spirit of the armadillo!"

One way to replicate referential content is to produce a copy of this original that is similar or identical to it in physical form. Hence, the replica might look like this: *zazan tõ gàyun hã wã*. The graphic shapes show perceptible similarity to the original. To replicate the physical shape or form is to make replication, and hence circulation, dependent on embodiment and sensibility.

The other extreme, which you can think of as closer to the pole of pure referential replication, is paraphrase. In paraphrase, you put into *other* words what you found in the original. Here replication is dependent on intelligibility. The limiting case of the paraphrase is the gloss, or definition, where one word is replicated by a combination of other words; the combination does not include the glossed word. Take, for example, the word *armadillo* in English, which *Webster's Third International Dictionary* renders as

> any of several burrowing chiefly nocturnal mammals having body and head encased in an armor of small bony plates in which many of them can curl up into a ball presenting the armor on all sides when attacked, being widely distributed in warmer parts of the Americas and in some areas esteemed as food.

This latter type of largely disembodied, purely referential replication defines the limit of the pole of news. Retellings of news are relatively more paraphrase-like.

In this regard, dream narratives stand in opposition to the origin myth, which is itself at the outer limit of myth. The goal in replicating the origin myth at P. I. Ibirama is not only, perhaps not even primarily, to transmit referential or semantic content. It is instead to transmit the actual physical sound in as much detail as possible — to make it seem like the physical circulation of things in the kula ring. Most myths at P. I. Ibirama fall somewhere between this extreme and that of the paraphrase-like replication of dream narratives. In the origin myth, the physical form not only of the words, but also of the intonation contours, rhythmic patterns, and other paralinguistic devices must be duplicated. The referential content is carried along, piggy-backed, so to speak, on the embodied material form.

The intriguing correlation is that the more mythlike the circulation of a cultural unit — whether that unit be discursive (myths) or partially discursive (songs) or nondiscursive (dance styles) — the more likely it is to be built up from internal repetitions of lines or other units. You need think only of the refrain from the origin myth, "Beneath Hawk Mountain where many men had gathered," repeated over and over and over again.

Why is this? I believe that repetition serves as a sign. To repeat a sound sequence or a movement as part of an extended performance demonstrates to you, as well as to others, that you have mastered the unit. If you can repeat it, then surely you can replicate it at some later date. Internal repetition makes the fact of replicability public.

As discourse migrates from one pole to another, from news (dream narrative, in this instance) to myth, the replication of its physical and rhetorical characteristics assumes greater and greater importance. The cultural unit imperceptibly metamorphoses. It shifts from referential meaning to material substance, from noumenal understanding to phenomenon, from idea to thing.

Yet the life-cyclic trajectory is an odd one. For it is not referential meaning that becomes material — unlike the Nike of Samothrace, whose ethereal and ephemeral life as story character solidified into marble, passing down through more than two thousand years of history! Rather, it is the carriers of referential meanings, the sign vehicles, that come to the fore, undergoing a process of fixation. They become less paraphrase-like — depending upon a complex calculus of equivalences — and more repetition-like. Intelligible meanings, expressed through different but presumedly equivalent fragments of discourse, congeal as sensible sounds, capable of replication in telling after telling.

Nike-esque, meaning-into-flesh transformation also occurs at P. I. Ibirama — in Kàmlẽn's "hu' hu' hu' hu' hu' hu' " that recalls the howler monkey, whose spirit he summoned. However, this is a different process. Like an alchemical transmutation of base metals into gold, an object of the intellect here becomes an object of the senses.

As you recall, relatively direct experience of the material world — in this case, of sound substance — is characteristic of ceremonies. The metamorphic process is thus nothing other than the process of ceremonialization, discussed earlier. It is here that "culture," in the classical sense, is created; the cycling or migration from the pole of news to the pole of myth results in replicable, transmittable entities that get passed down across the generations.

The pole of news is the contact point between culture — understood as circulating discourse — and the physical world in which it is situated. To be made public, individual experience must undergo conversion into referential meanings. In other words, it must be attached to material forms through which people can perceptually access it. Because of the possibilities of paraphrase, however, different members of the public may encounter different material forms of expression, all the while assuming (rightly or wrongly) that these communicate the same referential meanings across tellings.

At P. I. Ibirama, dreaming is quintessential news. Here culture encounters private experience. You share your experience by telling someone about it, encoding it in a dream narrative. This is culture's "hot" pole — the pole of creativity, novelty, change, adaptation. What you share with others is meanings about the world. You share truths, your personal access to noumena, your understanding of a reality that shows faintly through the surface of perception.

However, crucially, at this pole — where culture comes into contact with the external world — there is no public access to the experience as phenomenal. Only when people are assembled in the same place at the same time does the community have shared public access to phenomena. When they do have this shared access, the world need not be interpreted through discourse. Implicitly, people can answer yes to the question "Do you see what I see?" Whether you label this collective experience "sacred," as do Lawrence Sullivan, Mircea Eliade, and other historians of religion, you appreciate that it is the ground of culture. It is the elemental form of publicness — collective perceptual access to replicable human expressive form. You share an experience with another by sensorily beholding the world with that other, in the same place, at the same time.

Dream experiences and other news, however, depend on something more. They depend on reference — the ability of discourse to encode information about the world. However, that ability, which we associate with "language," is part of the same process. Language is itself arrayed between the poles of dream and myth, news and ceremony. It depends upon the fixation of expressive forms, repeated over and over again. Most obviously aligned with this ceremonial/mythic pole are phonology and the lexicon. However, language also allows the formation of novel combinations, new signs never before articulated. Closest to this end is syntax, which fades imperceptibly into discourse, much of the fixity of syntax deriving from the fixity of discourse — in the P. I. Ibirama case, especially, the origin myth.

The pole of experience being "hot," in the sense of creativity and change, fixed material forms are never perfectly adequate to express experience. Otherwise, what you would have would not be news, but simply more of the same. So the material forms of larger expressive units, sentences and whole narratives, are more likely to be novel as they proceed outward from this "hot" pole.

Correspondingly, as the material forms undergo replication, as they circulate publicly, they themselves tend to become fixed. The noumenal understandings, to make their way to the colder pole of tradition, myth, and ceremony, must undergo replication, replication, and more replication. In the course of that replication, the material of expression tends to become fixed. While the material substance — sound and rhetorical form, in the P. I. Ibirama case — continues to encode noumenal understandings, gradually the understandings become publicly accessible also as phenomena. In a rather strange way, therefore, original phenomenal experience, mediated by noumenal understanding, cycles back into the world of experience. The vehicles of expression themselves tend, in the course of replication, to become fixed, thinglike.

The formation of dream narrative types is my best example of the cycling process. Dream narratives take shape out of "hot," nonrepeatable, one-of-a-kind experiences. As they are told and retold — circulating like the spondylus shell necklaces and arm shells of Papuo-Melanesia — they are fit into narrative types. Gradually, they migrate in the direction of myth, the vast majority, however, dying out before they reach this pole. Some of the experiences of great shamans, however, live on. Those of Cu and Kàmlẽn may be among them. Indeed, the Cu stories, in considerable measure, have already been mythologized. In the 1970s and early 1980s, when I spent time sitting around campfires, these stories were being told.[3]

At the same time, the eldest stratum in society still knew Cu's genealogical affiliations. His stories had not yet become fully mythologized, detached from contemporary experience. However, two stories considered earlier in this book — those of the land above the sky and the land of the dead — may already have completed the migration, cycling out of the pole of dreams, into that of myth. None of the characters in those stories has a traceable genealogical connection to anyone presently alive, yet the myths bear striking resemblances to dream narratives. Members of the P. I. Ibirama community, indeed, still treat the stories as reports of actual individual experiences. Recall Wãñpõ's July 4, 1975, remark: "It was Klañmàg who told of what it is like in [the world above this one]." You have the unmistakable sense that these narratives are but once removed from shamanic stories, which, in turn, are but a few generations removed from Wãñẽkĩ's 1975 dream narratives. The full journey between poles in this community, from hot news to cold myth, may take only a few centuries.

You will want to know whether meaning is public. The answer I offer you is no, but also yes. Meaning is not directly public, but something like publicness is achieved. When meanings circulate via paraphrase, especially near the hot pole of dreaming, different sensible signs, different narratives, encode what you take to be the "same story," the "same dream." You impute an underlying similarity to the two tellings. This underlying similarity or equivalence may or may not be the same as what someone else imputes. The theory of culture as shared meaning insists on equivalence here, but a discourse-centered theory of culture is more flexible. Meanings are in some measure recalcitrantly private.

Recognizing the problems with paraphrase and its complex calculus of equivalences, human beings endeavor to ensure meaningful equivalence by holding constant the material form of expression. This leads to one of the two great conversion principles operative at the interface between discourse and social life. Discourse becomes ceremonialized by rendering the sound (or other) material in which it is encoded repeatable, replicable. However, replicability of perceptible substance cannot guarantee equivalence of meaning. You cannot be assured that the meaning you attribute to a stretch of sound is the same as that your neighbor does. Even the idea of replication itself leads you to recognize that what circulates is not substance per se, but the form of substance, the image of sound, in the case of spoken discourse. This is as true of DNA as it is of culture.

Finally, you can attempt to fix the meaning, to make it clear, pellucid, by means of interpretation or metadiscourse. You use other words to assert the similarity in meaning between two sets of words. This is the process of "exegesis." David Hilbert's metamathematical project from the 1920s and 1930s (see Kleene 1967: 53–59, *passim*) was of such a metadiscursive, assurance-giving type. He wished to demonstrate, by metamathematical means, the true character of classical mathematics, in other words, that you could prove the consistency and completeness of classical mathematical systems. You know the result. Working within this paradigm, the mathematician Kurt Gödel (1931) proved the opposite, that mathematical systems, sufficiently rich to contain elementary arithmetic, could *not* be shown to be simultaneously consistent and complete (see Kleene 1967: 204 ff.). If there was no absolute ground of publicness in metamathematics, neither is there in metadiscourse generally. Exegetical processes only displace the problem of meaningful publicness to the level of the metadiscourse. They fail to solve it.

Even if meaning is not public, but only privately inferred from signs that are themselves public, there is nevertheless something profoundly immaterial that circulates along with material substance. This immaterial, ethereal stuff may be the very *raison d'être* of circulation. I might as well call it meaning, although, because of the baggage of fixity and publicness the word carries, I have preferred the clumsier expression "noumenal understanding."

What is circulated along with replicable discourse is a consciousness of the world as real. The reality is not always perceptible. You—if you are a member of the P. I. Ibirama community—appreciate this, for example, even in a rock. You behold the rock perceptually, its rounded and pocked surfaces, its colorations and shading, all the while thinking that it might really be a spirit, a *gàyun*. It might be capable of talking to you. It might hold the power of life and death over you. This is a consciousness you have of the world, and your consciousness is a product of socially circulating discourse. However, it is a product not just of perceptible sound, but also of meaning carried by perceptible sound. You have been influenced, in your thinking, by the circulating discourse.

You may be wondering if the author has not strayed far afield from the classical problems of social organization he professes to address. I confess to leading you down a circuitous route, hacking my way through the terra incognita of discourse. Yet I submit that our destination is near. Over the next hill, you see familiar ground, but now from a new perspective. You are looking at social organization, but not as neat, "on-the-ground" groupings. Instead what you see are individuals — like Wāñpō and Wāñēkï and Nil and Kūñēpā — unique individuals, each interesting in his or her own right. You see that culture circulates among them, as spondylus shells circulate in Papuo-Melanesia.

The circulation of discourse (and also of nondiscursive signals) is an objective fact. It traces the lineaments of social configuration. As in the kula ring, it etches patterns in physical space, organizes relationships among individuals. But how can this objective circulation give rise to social configuration? What power do replicated sounds or other discursive signals have that can effect this organization? My answer is that the circulating discourse contains meanings, and that those meanings provide the effective (and affective) force.

Meanings bring about social order by virtue of their Nike-esque transmutation into things or events. This concretization is the counterpart of ceremonialization. Referential meanings are enacted or performed, made palpable to the senses. Recall Āglò's enactment of the "Goes Living" myth from Chapter 3. Here is meaning — what the myth is about — transformed into describable practice. However, not all women whose husbands die dramatize the myth in their behavior. They could do so, but probably most don't. At least, few claim to have visited the land of the dead. Transmutation of meaning into action is usually more subtle.

Transmutation occurs along a continuum between disembodied meaning and embodiment, noumenal understanding and phenomenal practice. In kinship, this is most evident in the discourse expectations surrounding kin terms. When deployed in narrative contexts, kin terms trigger expectations about the action that is to unfold. The expectations are violable, to be sure, especially for dramatic effect, but they are expectations nonetheless. You cannot say that they are fully conscious, not the way your thought about the rock as spirit is. They are rather part of a rhetorical unconscious or preconscious. They can be made conscious by explicit formulation as "roles" — as in Sir Henry Maine's *universitas juris*, or bundle of rights and duties. But they need not be so formulated.

The expectations operate on your narrativization of your own (past, pres-

ent, and future) conduct, as well as the conduct of others. However unaware of it you may be, you struggle to fit describable conduct into the
rhetorical mold of kin term usage. You also struggle to conduct yourself
such that your behavior will fit. By means of this mechanism, meaning becomes practice; spirit, so to speak, becomes flesh.

If kin terms operate in the rhetorical unconscious, descent groups and
exogamy operate consciously. They are grounded in explicitly formulated
ideas about community. However, if I am correct, exogamous descent
groups are not simply "out there," prior to and independent of the discourse in which they are inscribed. Rather, they are themselves products of
concretization. They represent ideas taking shape as behavior, just as objects solidify out of darkness at dawn.

The efficacy of the meanings — the extent to which they produce a community in which discourse can circulate — is directly correlated with the
rhetorical persuasiveness of the discourse in which they are carried. The
discourse can be taken metaphorically, playfully, as at P. I. Ibirama, or it can
be taken seriously, as (apparently) among the Ashanti. The important point
is that talk about social organization is first and foremost *talk*. The talk
circulates insofar as it is appealing or convincing — good words about sociability. Probably, the more serious the talk is, the more likely it is to be lived
in actual behavior. However, the very act of circulation sutures society.

From this point of view, social organization is far from fixed, hardly an
independent precondition for discourse circulation. Just the opposite, social integration is effected by the circulation of discourse whose topic is
social organization. That discourse is no more fixed than other discourse
circulating within the community. Because circulation involves the cycling
process whereby new meanings are introduced at the hot pole of experience, social organization itself is constantly in flux. Meaning produces (or
at least shapes) behavior, which is in turn experienced. The experience can
confirm the already circulating discourse of community, or, like dreaming,
it can lead to narratives that change the circulating discourse. Even in the
case of social organization, there is a process of cycling between novel discourse, at the contact point with experience, and traditional discourse, itself
part of received culture.

If you look at this process dispassionately, you might be puzzled: Why
should discourse endeavor to construe community in the first place? What
is in it for discourse? My answer relies upon what I believe is a fundamental
principle of culture, viz., discourse tends to shape itself in such a way as to
maximize its circulation. The discourse of community, of social organization, is bootstrapping in this regard. It gives people a satisfying idea that
there is community, that they have reason to interact. In the course of interaction, not only the discourse of community but also other discourse as

well, circulates. The discourse of community is a discourse that perpetuates itself, that survives.

You have seen the processes of selection and suggestion in dream narratives. Selection puts into circulation dream narratives that resemble the types already in circulation. Suggestion actually engenders experiences that give rise to dream narratives conforming to those types. I am proposing that the same process is at work in social organization. If you think about selection and suggestion, they are the means by which discursive patterns perpetuate themselves, persist over time, circulate in space.

The precondition for community-wide circulation is a community of interacting individuals. This is the sine qua non of culture. Circulation beyond the family depends upon fashioning a discourse that makes sense of the community, one after whose image a community can be constructed. The key to discourse circulation is the construction of a noumenal understanding of the phenomenal world in terms of community. Competitive pressure forces discourse to fashion itself in such a way that it creates the conditions for its own circulation. If it does not do so, it is replaced by other discourse, cycling out of the hot pole of experience. The discourse of community that is successful survives. By virtue of its circulation, it establishes and maintains community. By virtue of its meaning, it defines for consciousness the nature and operation of that community.

It has been so hard for order-seeking social anthropologists to account for periods of revolutionary breakdown. This is because meaning and experience, intelligibility and sensibility, noumena and phenomena have been understood as unified. Their crucial disjuncture goes unrecognized. From the perspective of discourse cycling, breakdown makes sense. We are at the contact point between culture and the world. The traditional discourse of community fails to assimilate the novel narratives arising from emergent, unpredictable experience. A new discourse of community arises out of the ashes of the old one, accounting for the breakdown, but itself vulnerable to the vagaries of unsocialized phenomena.

Descent group and exogamy discourses draw their images from the family. However, they are not the only possibilities. They have analogues in modern Western culture. Marketplace and public sphere discourses struggle to make sense out of community not in terms of family relations, but in terms of human nature — "We hold these truths to be self-evident, that all men are created equal, that they are endowed by their Creator with certain unalienable Rights, that among these are Life, Liberty, and the pursuit of Happiness."[4] The ability to rationally calculate, the ability to formulate positions in debates — these abilities are within everyone's realm of possibility. They are not based on particularistic criteria. A discourse of community grounded in them has universal appeal. To be a member of this community, it matters not what your lineage is, nor whether you are properly married. What counts is that you speak and reason, that you can live by your wits.

Looking at the presuppositions of this discourse, anthropologists cannot help but see culture-specific understandings. At the same time, the cultural character of the discourse does not deny its persuasiveness. If the discourse creates the conditions for a broader circulation, is this not precisely because it seems so convincing to so many? Although they are cultural inventions, discourses of marketplace and public sphere are compelling. They circulate because they are compelling. The question is, Are they so compelling that they will ultimately obliterate family-based discourses of community, such as those that have flourished at P. I. Ibirama?

How skeptical we all are of the referential content of discourse. Especially if it is news, emanating from the hot pole of experience, and if it fails to conform to existing patterns, a fragment of discourse is readily dismissed. Not just any talk or writing achieves broad circulation. To do so, discourse must possess certain properties. One is that it must show similarity, especially physical similarity, to prior circulating discourse. This is its ground of acceptance. A new stretch of discourse — first understood only as referential content, and hence replicated by paraphrase — tends toward fixity in its form of expression. The form, in its substantive incarnations, becomes an object of shared experience, such shared sensible experience being the ground of culture.

To secure a wider circulation, discourses must also have the capacity to concretize in the sensible world the noumenal reality they depict. For society-building discourses — those in which kinship terms or images of community circulate — this is especially true. Not all discourses are created equal. Classical research on social organization demonstrates that, in small-scale societies, community is generally talked about in terms of family. This is not a matter of chance. Rather, it is proof that family-based conceptualizations of community are effective, at least in small-scale situations. Were it otherwise, the discourse of family would not circulate.

Nor are all family-based community-building discourses the same. They construe community through the idiom of family, but they do not all construe it the same way. Possibilities for nuance abound. Even among ethnographically attested instances — where we know the discourse has stuck — some discourses may work better than others, some may prove more tenaciously adapted than others. Less effective discourses are filtered out or modified over time; they prove less efficient at sustaining community. Selection occurs through the perpetual operation of cycling or traditionalization. Though discourse creates the conditions for its own circulation, it cannot create them just as it pleases. Some discourses are better than others at maintaining and expanding their circulation.

Discourses not only create conditions; they also encounter a world outside of themselves. In some measure, they must be accountable to that sensible world. After all, if skepticism toward referential meaning abounds, experiences confirm or deny. Does a discourse describe the phenomenal world the senses behold? Does what I see or taste or touch or smell belie what I have been told?

Discourse cycling principles, viewed differently, are ways of bringing about a rapprochement between meaning and the senses. One principle at work here is the fixing of the form of expression of the referential content that is generated through experiential encounter. Another is concretization—noumenal understandings are enacted in the world; enactments in turn are objects of the senses.

Talk encounters a world that is perceptually accessible, and it must somehow make its peace with that world (or worlds). Geertz (1973: 93–94) two decades ago articulated a similar idea in his insight regarding "models of" and "models for." Culture, like DNA strands, is a repository of information about the phenomenal world in which it finds itself. It also creates or modifies part of the world it represents. Presumably, it facilitates adaptation. Discourse is a key site of adaptation. It is discourse that is held accountable, put on the executioner's block, if it lies. It is discourse whose circulation and continued existence depend upon an accommodation with the senses, for otherwise it will surely die.

In Western science, the experiment is the contact point with the hot pole of experience. Scientific experimental description is the analogue to the P. I. Ibirama dream narrative. A similar selection procedure is at work. Novel experiences—reports of experimental findings—are fit to preexisting discourse molds. At the hot pole of experience, circulation through paraphrase takes precedence over circulation through formal replication. Discourse cycling takes effect subsequently, as novel findings are traditionalized. At the cold pole of tradition, numerous crystalline icons of science appear, which children acquire in elementary or secondary school: "$E=mc^2$," "to every action there is an equal and opposite reaction," "loss of electrons means oxidation, gain of electrons means reduction," "the survival of the fittest." Scientific and dream discourses are far from identical. Nevertheless, both participate in cycling. Both ground noumena in phenomena, the intelligible in the sensible.

Why, if that is the case, do we find discourses about disembodied spirits? Why do some discourses develop a conception of God—an ultimate noumenon that is not phenomenal? At P. I. Ibirama, people do have experiential access to spirits through dreams. Implicitly, dream experience is understood as an experience of reality, of the external world. It is of intense interest to the commonweal, because it taps into an otherwise inaccessible reality. Metadiscursive theory at P. I. Ibirama interprets some dream experiences as encounters with spirits — spirits not normally visible in waking life. These spirits lie concealed behind the surface of phenomena, beneath the veneer of perceptibility, coming out, so to speak, only at night. They control events in the world, and those events are accessible to the senses, but the spirits lead an occult life. At P. I. Ibirama, the discourse of spirits is grounded in experience. It is linked to the sensible. It is just that the perceptual object is elusive, never confirmable by two or more people at once operating in the do-you-see-what-I-see mode.

High Western discourses have undergone a curious evolution — dreams have severed their connection with external reality. They no longer capture the fancy of the public, no longer, seemingly, tap into what affects the commonweal. Instead, they are relegated to an inner, subjective realm, which in turn is irrelevant, or only indirectly relevant, to the workaday world. A major chunk of the hot pole of experience has broken off or disintegrated. It no longer infuses publicly circulating discourse of the real with new information.

At the same time, deactivation has not eliminated discourses positing abstruse, rarefied noumenal beings, hidden from waking sensibility but affecting the perceptible world. The most salient of these in Western discourses is "God," but a recent, rapidly spreading discourse, in North America as well as other parts of the world, has focused on aliens from other planets, contact with whom is often through dreams.[5] The alien dream discourse is similar to the discourse circulating at the P. I. Ibirama community. Perhaps this is testimony to the persuasive power of the idea, which validates itself by reference to the experiential pole of dreaming. The idea is, evidently, a tenacious one, maintaining and expanding its circulation, even in the face of the hostile counterdiscourses emanating from natural science.

The discourse of God takes the problematic of imperceptibility one step further. God is a being whose existence is refractory to confirmation through the senses. To be sure, reports of miracles, in which God is made tangible through transmutation, continue to circulate. A rash of miracles has recently unsettled the area in and around the south Texas city of Brownsville. In the town of Elsa, for example, an image of the Virgin Mary miraculously appeared on the "driver's side rear fender of Dario Mendoza's 1981 maroon Chevrolet Camaro" (Ortega 1993: B1)[6]:

> "The image first showed up on a warm evening . . . as Mr. Mendoza was chatting with a few relatives outside his house," says his nephew, Santiago Quintero, Jr.
>
> Mr. Quintero, who was also present, says the miracle so impressed the family that he and his mother, sister and uncle all slept outside next to the image that night.

The next day, Mr. Mendoza, apparently struck by a surge of skepticism, washed the car. But the image remained, and actually grew larger, Mr. Quintero says.

" . . . That night," say residents, "more than 100 people, including a maria-chi band and two other *conjuntos,* or musical groups, showed up for a fiesta in honor of 'La Virgencita'."

As at P. I. Ibirama, here you see the concretization of noumenality, the otherwise imperceptible made known through the senses. Official Catholic church discourse professes neutrality on, or actually denies, such miracles, but rumors of them nevertheless continue to circulate.

At the same time, there are those who, while rejecting miracles, still participate in the circulation of discourse about "God." What significance can we attribute to this?

In *The Elementary Forms of the Religious Life*, Durkheim offered the view that talk about God was really talk about society, encrypted talk, to be sure, but talk all the same. "God" stood for society, for the collectivity. It represented the power of the collectivity over its individual members. The parallels are great, Durkheim suggested. Like society, God existed before any of us, and, like society, God will continue to exist long after we have gone: "The believer is not deceived when he believes in the existence of a moral power upon which he depends and from which he receives all that is best in himself: this power exists, it is society" (Durkheim 1969 [1912]: 257).

Having looked at culture as circulating discourse, you might be inclined to sharpen this insight. The idea of God is made possible by circulating discourse. It does not linger near the hot pole of experience, but represents an interpretation of all possible narratives of experience — a metadiscourse whose object is all other discourses. The interpretation circulates because it makes sense, or seems to make sense, of those discourses. Though it posits no directly experienceable, seeable, touchable entity, yet it is satisfying as a way of interpreting narrativizations of experience. How can this be?

People are inherently skeptical of the referential content of discourse. "Show me" is the common refrain. At the same time, a radical insistence upon groundedness in experience — a radical empiricism — denies the existence of a reality that is not sensible but nevertheless knowable, a reality manifested through circulation in the public arena. Strange as it may seem, such a reality exists. It is the reality of meaning, of noumenal understandings carried by discourse.

As pure intellectual objects, pure noumena, God and meaning are closely intertwined. It is only through referential meanings, circulating in discourse, percolating through space and across time, that God achieves a public life. The idea diffuses, though it lacks empirical foundation in any single experience. The idea of God is like the idea of the tapir, present in ghostlike fashion in the textual artifact photographed in Plate 1. Yet unlike the "tapir" in Plate 1, there is no counterpart in the experienceable world analogous to the tapir of Plate 2.

Every single one of us, whether or not we believe in God, knows that there is something out there—something that cannot be seen, touched, tasted, felt, or smelled, and, yet, that is real. That something is meaning. The idea of God focuses our attention on it. Referential or semantic meanings are relevant to a broader public. They are also efficacious—they can get people to do things. Yet they are ghostlike, circulating along piggy-backed on discourse forms, but themselves intangible, unseen.

Even the hardest-headed skeptics among us must agree that there is something God-like about referential meanings. Discourses modify them-selves so as to maintain or increase their circulation. But by what agency do they do so? You can say that the agents are individuals. Individuals modify and manipulate discourses as they circulate. They are the bedrock source of change. Yet, at least insofar as the cold pole of tradition is concerned, individuals only modify what has diffused to them from others, what has seeped down over time. Circulating discourses are the end result of innu-merable revisions and tinkerings and refinements. Only at the hot pole of experience can they be thought of as individual products, and even there the suggestive power of prior discourse is at work. To say something new, one must use old expressive forms, which have crystallized at the cold pole of tradition.

In the course of circulation, discourse undergoes replication. Actual physical forms are replicated—sound patterns that encode nonreferential as well as referential meanings. This is crystallization at the cold pole of tradition. However, people also replicate meanings, and, in some cases, with little attention to the replication of form. This is truer the closer to the hot pole of experience you get. Paraphrase seeks to preserve referential meanings without preserving the physical forms in which they are encoded. Yet even the precise replication of form can result in the carrying over of something that is wholly different in kind from the form itself.

What travels around with discourse is thus, in part, something that is not directly perceptible, not sensible, and yet seemingly real. Those referential meanings endure over time, though they are subject to decay. And they exist apart from this or that particular individual. If any one single member of the P. I. Ibirama community thought up the spirits-manifest-themselves-in-dreams theory, that individual is long forgotten, long gone. The dis-course has taken on a life of its own. And with it, meanings have taken on a life of their own. Meaning is truly God-like—not perceptible and yet real, not the product of any one individual and yet known to individuals.

There is danger here! We should not wander too far into this land of noumena, lest we forget the phenomenal counterparts. Like some poststructuralists, in grappling with the independent life of noumena, we may fail to situate these noumena within a phenomenal world. After all, it is only because of that phenomenal world that circulation is possible in the first place. The hot pole of experience is reportable because of the cold, relatively fixed forms of expression, such as words. Without the existence of phenomenal replication, there could be no circulation, no transportation, of noumena.

Curiously, indeed, noumenal understanding — so mysterious from the point of view of theory, so refractory to the senses — becomes a humdrum of daily life. It is the accepted backdrop of experience. Moreover, it comes to exercise a kind of tyranny from which individuals seek relief. At P. I. Ibirama, recall, contact with phenomena, unmediated by referential meanings, becomes the counterforce to the dominance of reference. It becomes the basis for a public constituted out of shared experience of the sensible world. Such shared experience, in some measure, resists the tyranny of reference. Its reasserts a wonder at a world uncluttered by interpretation, a world opening itself to individuals through the senses. How curious that it should be associated with the sacred, with experiences that seem to reveal the otherwise hidden existence of divinity.

And so, empiricism, you must cede your throne. No longer can you deny to noumenal understanding its proper place of prominence. While sensibility may be foundational, yet there is mystery out there. In the replication of discourse, just as in the replication of genetic material, you must acknowledge the presence of something immaterial — the abstracted form behind both original and copy. Material replication perpetuates that form, but it is the form that carries over. In spoken sound, most conspicuously, but even in the Amerindian pot and the Papuo-Melanesian spondylus shell necklace, the fleeting material thing is not what is preserved. It is rather its form that lingers on.

Though you have ceded your throne, however, yet there is life in you. For no matter how abstract the meaning, if it is to circulate — if it is to become part of public processes — it must manifest itself through material expressions such as sounds. And it is only by beholding material expressions that we tap into the public life and circulation of meaning. We need you back. Not only is there life in you, but we cannot do without you. As the great pendulum of intellectual life nears its point of maximum displacement and is about to turn, we can expect that the rampant rejection of the world reflected in your denial will be reversed. This may even be your season of renewal.

# Notes

## Preface

1. Benjamin Lee (n.d.) provides a masterfully detailed discussion of the history of twentieth-century philosophy as it impinges upon the anthropological problems of knowledge in his manuscript *Talking Heads: Languages, Meta-Languages, and the Semiotics of Subjectivity*.

## 1. A Tapir's Heart

1. From George W. Stocking's (1968: 145) essay "From Physics to Ethnology," which, however, argues that the contribution of the sea water observations to the later formulations, contrary to popular interpretation, was at best indirect.

2. P. I. stands for Posto Indígena, or "Indigenous Post." It is one of the posts established by the Brazilian government Indian agency known as FUNAI, or Fundação Nacional do Índio (National Indian Foundation), for the support of indigenous peoples.

3. Since the term "public" has become popular these days, perhaps I should indicate early on what I mean by it, as well as what I don't mean by it. I mean by it something like intersubjectively accessible. I think this is the sense that Geertz (1973: 12) had in mind when he wrote that "culture is public because meaning is." I'll hasten to add, however, that I disagree with the latter proposition, or at least wish to qualify it. My idea is that culture is made public when it is made accessible to the senses of another, for example, in visible body movements or in audible sounds emitted when one talks. Both of our usages, however, are linked to the Kantian notion of public (*veröffentlich*).

The latter forms the basis also for Habermas's (1989 [1962]) usage, but his notions of the "public sphere" and of "a public" are much more specific refractions. His public sphere is an arena between the domestic sphere and the state (regarding this version, see also Calhoun [1992], Graham [1993], Taylor [1990], and Warner [1991]). As I use it, the term "public" can apply to the domestic sphere as well. Culture circulates and is made "public," for example, when stories are told around the campfire.

4. *Seu* is a Portuguese term of respectful address or reference, analogous to

"Mister" in English, but it is used with the Christian name, rather than with the surname. "Seu Eduardo" thus means "Mr. Edward," or, in effect, "Mr. Hoerhan."

5. *Dona* is the analogue to *Seu*, but affixed to a female rather than a male Christian name.

6. We surveyed seventy-seven households in 1975. A number of these contained descendants of the Kaingang who had come in 1914 to help with the "pacification" project. Most of those Kaingang had married Brazilians, creating a sizable *mestizo* population on the reserve. A few of the houses were unoccupied. The average number of persons per household was between six and seven.

7. However, there is a growing body of literature in linguistic anthropology, which, either explicitly or implicitly, draws upon this kind of distinction and weaves an ethnographic account around it. Joel Sherzer's (1990) *Verbal Art in San Blas*, for example, has the subtitle *Kuna Culture through Its Discourse*; Ellen Basso's (1990) collection is called *Native Latin American Cultures through Their Discourse*; and John Bowen's new (1993) book is entitled *Muslims through Discourse*. In all three cases, discourse — understood as sensible form as well as referential content — is viewed as critical to understanding culture.

And this is true in a range of other works where the question of culture as (or as reflected in) discourse is raised. Among them are Joel Kuipers's (1990) *Power in Performance* concerning Indonesia, John Bowen's (1991) earlier book *Sumatran Politics and Poetics*, Joe Errington's (1988) *Structure and Style in Javanese*, Marina Roseman's (1991) ethnomusicological study *Healing Sounds from the Malaysian Rainforest*, Steve Feld's (1990 [1982]) *Sound and Sentiment* on New Guinea, Alessandro Duranti's (1994) *From Grammar to Politics* about Samoa, Laura Graham's (1995) *Performing Dreams* about the Xavante of Central Brazil, Ellen Basso's (1985, 1987) books on the Kalapalo Indians of Central Brazil, Anthony Seeger's (1987) *Why Suyá Sing*, Janet Wall Hendricks's (1993) *To Drink of Death: The Narrative of a Shuar Warrior*, Jonathan D. Hill's (1993) *Keepers of the Sacred Chants* about the Wakuénai of the Northwest Amazon, Joel Sherzer's (1983) earlier book *Kuna Ways of Speaking*, Steve Caton's (1990) *"Peaks of Yemen I Summon"* on Bedouin poetry, Corinne Kratz's (1994) *Affecting Performance* on initiation rites in Kenya, and Richard Bauman's (1986) *Story, Performance, and Event* on West Texas, as well as in the collections by Brenneis and Myers (1984) and Sherzer and Urban (1986). Aaron Fox's (1992) work on honky-tonk bars in Texas should be mentioned here as well. The problematic of language and discourse as linked to sensible context, which in turn seems to necessitate looking at linguistic elements (such as pronouns and deictics) and other aspects of discourse as themselves sensible, is to be found in the work of William Hanks (1990) and in the recent collection by Duranti and Goodwin (1992). The whole point of view has antecedents in the ethnography of speaking, especially in Dell Hymes's (1981) *"In Vain I Tried to Tell You"* and Dennis Tedlock's (1983) *The Spoken Word and the Work of Interpretation*, and in the semiotic approach developed by Michael Silverstein (1976).

8. They used the term to refer to a specific class of lexical items and grammatical forms wherein reference depends upon indexicality, for example, the first and second person pronouns or tense. The general characterization, however, is applicable to discourse as conceptualized here.

9. Parsons makes the distinctions in various works, although what students at

the time called the "biological system" he preferred to call the "behavioral organism." See, for example, Parsons (1966: 28). For the University of Chicago Department of Anthropology history, see Stocking (1979: 45).

## 2. We the Living

1. The original name of Posto Indígena (or Indigenous Post) Ibirama was P. I. Duque de Caxias. That name was bestowed by Eduardo de Lima e Silva Hoerhan, who named the post after the famous nineteenth-century duke, said to be among his relatives.

2. SPI stands for Serviço de Proteção aos Indios, or Indian Protection Service. Founded in 1910, in part in response to the situation in Santa Catarina, its name was changed in 1967 to FUNAI (Fundação Nacional do Indio), or National Indian Foundation (see Souza Lima 1991).

3. For the flip side of this problematic, see James Clifford's (1988: 277–346) "Identity in Mashpee" in his book *The Predicament of Culture*. Clifford follows the court case surrounding a 1976 suit filed by a group who claimed land based on their indigenous identity as "Mashpee." To put the matter in present terms, groupness had for them (or so they represented in court) a noumenal reality. The jury, however, found against them, apparently concluding that the noumenon had no phenomenal counterpart, and hence was no noumenon at all, but rather a false representation.

4. Taunay (1918: 573, n. 1) claims that "Bugre" is a shortened form of Bulgarian ("Bulgario," in Portuguese), and that the reference of the term originally was to gypsies.

5. See Briggs's (1986) illuminating discussion of the distortions and illusions inherent in the social science interview.

6. The initial *x* in Xocrens, following Portuguese orthography, is pronounced like *sh* in English or *sch* in German.

7. For those interested in phonology, the phoneme /w/ in the language of the P. I. Ibirama community is realized phonetically as a voiced labiodental fricative or a labiodental nasal. The palatal nasal /ñ/ in syllable final position is realized as an [i] glide. The /g/ following a nasal vowel appears as a lightly articulated velar nasal, which could easily be missed. Hence, the word *wãñkòmãg* would sound something like [vãikòmã], with stress on the final syllable. This is quite close to what would be the German pronunciation of *aweikoma*.

8. This is a slightly modified version of actual discourse from the P. I. Ibirama community, which I will discuss subsequently. The original does not contain the "we."

9. Actually, in this instance the "he" (*ti*) is anaphorically deleted. It does, however, appear in full form in an only slightly modified version of this sentence by a different speaker in a 1982 telling:

| ti kòñkahà | tõ | zàgpope | tõ | patè | ti | no | katèle |
|---|---|---|---|---|---|---|---|
| relative | erg. | name | erg. | name | he | in front of | arrive descending |

"Relative Zàgpope Patè arrived in front of him."

10. For a discussion of the contrast between internal and external ethnicity, see R. N. Adams (1989).

11. For a discussion of that literature, see Singer (1989: 247–255). Fernandez (1986: 70, n. 29) offers an intriguing formulation of "pronominalism," which posits "that any general account of society and culture must begin with the motives and relations of particular pronouns, for they point directly to the essential reality of social life and in their 'taking of the other' are both the creators and the repositories of culture."

12. I omit a portion of the narrative here in which Wãñpõ explains that Eduardo had already learned Kaingang, and indicates from whom he had learned it.

13. Paul Mullen worked with the Summer Institute of Linguistics (SIL) through the Assembly of God church on the reserve. The text is presented in a work entitled *Históras e Mitos Na Língua Xokleng*, an experimental edition that carries no date or place of publication, though the introduction indicates that it resulted from work carried out between 1983 and 1985. It was probably produced at SIL headquarters in Brasília. The authors are listed as Kãnnhãhá Nãnbla, Kuzug Gaklã, Olímpio Zetxa Pripré, and an anonymous author. The transcription is by Nãnbla Gaklã, Jules Henry, and Paul Mullen. I have modified the transcription to conform to the orthography of the remainder of this book.

## 3. The Hole in the Sky

1. See, again, Briggs (1986) for an appraisal of the interview as a communicative event.

2. From field notes made on July 4, 1975.

3. For more technical discussions of authority and evidence in discourse, see the recent collection of essays by Hill and Irvine (1993).

4. Thomas Buckley (1984) describes an intriguing refraction of the problematic of space in the traditional culture of the California Yurok. He proposes that they traditionally had two registers of speech, a secular and a sacred register. In the secular register, for example, there are separate terms for "sky" and "earth." In the sacred register, the terms are collapsed into one, whose meaning is something like "that which exists."

5. Such bodily characteristics are part of what Bourdieu (1984 [1975]) aptly calls the "habitus." They are inscribed in the body and socially transmitted. They are cultural, in this sense, regardless of whether they become the subject of reflection.

6. The grammatically correct traditional form ought to be *ãgkàñka*, where the plural is indicated by a vowel change. The nontraditionality underscores its emergent quality, as argued in the previous chapter.

7. It is interesting to compare this situation with that among the Weyewa of Indonesia as described by Kuipers (1990). There ritual speech assumes greater power in proportion as it is abstracted from the referential here and now. Something similar may be going on with the cline of certainty and authority attributed to different kinds of speech among the Seneca of western New York State, as described by Chafe (1993). Similar themes can be detected in other essays in Hill and Irvine (1993).

8. For another example, see Keith Basso's (1988) "'Speaking with Names': Language and Landscape among the Western Apache."

### 4. A Lock of Hair in a Ball of Wax

1. Half a century after Morgan, a different kind of elicitation procedure developed. W. H. R. Rivers, in his classic "The Genealogical Method of Anthropological Inquiry," says: "My procedure is to ask my informant the terms which he would apply to the different members of his pedigree, and reciprocally the terms which they would apply to him" (reprinted with Rivers 1968 [1914]: 100). As a discourse process, this kind of elicitation was distinct, but it too depended ultimately upon the equation of a complex kin term expression with a simple one, only here mediated also by proper names and stretched out into numerous anaphorically related clauses. The researcher led the informant through complex expressions (e.g., mother's brother's son) by using a series of intermediate questions, such as "What is your mother's name?" "What is her brother's name?" "By what term do you call him?" "What is his son's name?" "By what term do you refer to him?" The assumption underlying the researcher's questioning, of course, is the same. The kin terms can be brought into systematic interrelation with one another through complex kin term expressions built up out of elementary terms. The difference is that, in this case, a circuitous rather than direct route is followed.

2. I was unable to ascertain the meaning of *ponkan*. Presumably, this is some method of preparing meat.

3. According to von Ihering (1968: 700–702), the *traíra* (Port.) is a fish of the *Caracideo* family, subfamily *Eritrinineo*, several species of which are found in Brazilian fresh waters. The fish reaches two feet in length, and weighs six to seven pounds. It is noted for eating smaller fish, in this case, the *piava* (Port.). The latter itself, however — of the same family as the *traíra*, but of the subfamily *Anostomatineo*, according to von Ihering (1968: 537) — actually can reach a length of twenty inches.

### 5. The Jaguar's Spots

1. Again, the Mashpee (Clifford 1988) example is relevant here. The P. I. Ibirama "descent" groups are a bit like the Mashpee as portrayed in the trial — more a precipitate of talk than of action.

2. In public discourse, the word *mētōpam* is used for the disk design. I found no evidence of the term *kanêm*, though I have no doubt that Henry elicited it.

3. The kind of "agreement" I am referring to here is implicit, not necessarily the product of argumentation. I do not mean only consensus arrived at through discussion and debate. I mean by "agreement" simply that the terminology and rules of descent circulate throughout the community. Implicit agreement is thus related to Habermas's (1984, 1987) notion of the "lifeworld," a set of background or tacit assumptions that are not argued over. Not every aspect of the terminology need be shared, so that, in this sense, there is room for some measure of implicit disagreement. However, even if some aspects of the discourse are explicitly argued over, with explicit disagreements expressed, the very act of arguing can result in the cir-

culation of other aspects of the discourse which are not argued about, and which come to be, thereby, implicitly agreed upon. The key notion is thus, really, circulation, not agreement.

4. I have phonemicized Henry's largely phonetic spellings. The enclitic *mē* is the distributive ("all about"). In naturally occurring discourse, the words *win* and *kuñkēn* occur sometimes with and sometimes without it.

5. I analyze the microdiscursive similarities and differences among episodes in *A Discourse-Centered Approach to Culture*. There, however, my interest is primarily in the formal properties of the poetic structure. Here the episodes interest me from the point of view of models of community.

6. This type of dancing with a maize dance ornament was shown to me. It consists in standing with one's arms at one's side, then bending the arms at the elbows, raising and lowering the forearms to the sides of the body in unison. However, such dancing was not practiced in recent memory. The exemplification seems to be part of a textual exegesis that has been passed down across the generations with the myth itself.

7. Evidently a different Kïy.

8. The clothing referred to is a blanket made of *ortiga* fiber wrapped around the waist, as in Plate 8. The blanket, however, has a specific decoration on it, which I was unable to identify. It is called *kul co*, which my informants could not translate. It is distinct from the "red" and "white" blankets of the subsequent episodes.

## 6. This Is Your Making

1. The image of a "chaotic, swirling cauldron of social encounter" from the last chapter was, as you see, not arbitrarily chosen. The animals here have been physically placed in a large vat, made from a hollowed-out log. Reading this story, you get a sense of the circulating understanding of encounter as chaotic, murky, unpredictable.

2. This portion of the narrative is sung, and the song does not make full semantic sense, there being many vocables. I have set off the line numbers of the sung portions of the text by means of alphabetic letters following the first line on which the song begins. These sung portions are also indented.

3. I knew the participants in this particular lip piercing, all of whom were alive at the time of my first field stint in 1974–1976. By 1981, the father of the child whose lip was pierced had died. So also had the child himself, who was by then a full-grown man. The mother was still alive.

4. It also dominates in the second of the four narratives, these two forming the bulk of the myth. It has no presence in the shorter third and fourth narratives.

5. The final [u] in the phonetic representation of /wāgzul/ is an unstressed, nonphonemic echo vowel.

## 7. Rocks That Talk

1. For related studies, see the essays in B. Tedlock's (1987) *Dreaming: Anthropological and Psychological Interpretations*. Tedlock's own introduction gives an excellent

overview of recent issues pertaining to dreaming and culture. For other Amerindian cases, see the review article by Price-Williams and Degarrod (1989), and the closely related work by Graham (1994). An earlier standard work on the broader subject is *The Dream and Human Societies*, edited by G. E. von Grunebaum and Roger Caillois (1966).

2. Affectionately known as Wãñĕkï Tèy, "long Wãñĕkï," because of his stature (over six feet tall and slender).

3. Throughout this chapter, field notes and dreams are put into the same line structure as transcribed and translated narratives, even though the field notes and dreams were recorded directly in English (from conversations in Portuguese or the native language). Nevertheless, the notes, while usually in the third person, have the feel of the original discourse. It therefore seemed reasonable to represent them, typographically, in the same way.

4. A similar argument can be found in Herdt (1987) and also in Graham (1994).

5. This is indicated in a statement made on September 5, 1974, by Wãñpõ: "The chief is generally afraid of the *kuyà* [shaman] and sometimes has him murdered because of this fear. If the *kuyà* kills someone, and everyone will know that he has because he brags about it, they may have him murdered with *kalà* lances."

6. The postdream material is put into brackets after the dream.

7. His actual name is Wãñĕkï, son of Patè, but we call him Patè to avoid confusion.

8. From March 18, 1975.

9. Note that neither of these was the narrator of the brief story above, and, furthermore, that the story had been told some four months earlier.

10. In remarks made on September 5, 1974.

11. For a review of the debate, see Anne Parsons (1969).

12. The ['] here is used to represent a glottal stop.

## 8. Between Myth and Dream

1. Some anthropologists, like David Schneider, assumed that the two were identical. Geertz's idea that meaning is public seems to suggest this as well. In calling for empirical studies of replication, however, I am not discounting the possibility that the underlying similarity exists. On the contrary, as you will see, I believe that in some measure it must exist.

2. Some elements of culture purport not to participate in the copying process. In modern Western art, for instance, each object is regarded as unique, not as a replica. Even if you do not see it as copying other fashions or styles, as instantiating a type, you would still find that the discourse surrounding it is subject to replication.

3. Laura Graham (1995) reports a much more rapid cycling of dreams into ceremony among the Xavante of central Brazil. There young men "dream" songs, then immediately teach the songs to their age mates, who in turn publicly perform them. What we do not know here, however, is whether dream narratives other than songs socially circulate, and, if so, what their life cycles are like.

4. From the American Declaration of Independence.

5. My source of information is Susan Lepselter's (1994) thus far unpublished

Master's thesis in the Department of Anthropology at the University of Texas at Austin.

6. About a month earlier, a three-foot-tall image of the Virgin Mary miraculously appeared about nine feet up from the base of a tree across the street from the Texas Commerce Bank building in downtown Brownsville. According to one observer: "This is a natural phenomenon, it's not the work of any artist. . . . It must be the work of God" (Gonzalez 1993: B3).

# References

Adams, Richard N.
   1989   Internal and external ethnicity: With special reference to Central America.
          In *Estado, democratización y desarrollo en Centroamérica y Panamá*, 475–
          497. Guatemala: Asociación Centroamericano de Sociología.
Aldinger
   1913   Zur Ehrenrettung der Botokuden. *Süd-und-Mittelamerika* 6: 39–41.
          Berlin.
Amaral, C. M. do
   1902   Memoria sôbre usos e costumes de Indios Guaranys, Caiuás e Botocudos.
          *Revista do Instituto Histórico e Geográfico Brasileiro* 63 (2): 263–273. Rio de
          Janeiro.
Anderson, Benedict
   1983   *Imagined Communities: Reflections on the Origin and Spread of Nationalism.*
          London: Verso.
Augustine, Saint, Bishop of Hippo
   1993   *The City of God.* Trans. Marcus Dods. New York: Modern Library.
Baldus, Herbert
   1952   Terminologia de parentesco Kaingang. *Sociologia* 14: 76–79. São Paulo.
   1955   Das Dualsystem der Kaingang-Indianer. *Acts of the International Congress
          of Anthropological and Ethnological Sciences* 4 (2): 376–378.
Basso, Ellen B.
   1985   *A Musical View of the Universe: Kalapalo Myth and Ritual Performances.*
          Philadelphia: University of Pennsylvania Press.
   1987   *In Favor of Deceit: A Study of Tricksters in an Amazonian Society.* Tucson:
          University of Arizona Press.
Basso, Ellen B. (ed.)
   1990   *Native Latin American Cultures through Their Discourse.* Bloomington,
          Ind.: Folklore Institute, Indiana University.
Basso, Keith
   1988   "Speaking with names": Language and landscape among the Western
          Apache. *Cultural Anthropology* 3 (2): 99–130.
Bauman, Richard
   1986   *Story, Performance, and Event: Contextual Studies of Oral Narrative.* Cam-
          bridge: Cambridge University Press.

Bleyer, Hrn. Dr.
    1904    Die wilden Waldindianer Santa Catharinas: die 'Schokléng'. *Zeitschrift für Ethnologie* 36: 830–844.
Blumensohn, Jules Henry
    1936    A preliminary sketch of the kinship and social organization of the Botocudo Indians of the Rio Plate in the Municipality of Blumenau, Santa Catarina, Brazil. *Boletim do Museu Nacional* 12: 49–58.
Borba, Telemaco Morosini
    1908    *Actualidade Indígena*. Coritiba, Brazil: Typ. Impressora Paranaense.
Bourdieu, Pierre
    1984    [1975] *Distinction: A Social Critique of the Judgement of Taste*. Trans. R. Nice. Cambridge, Mass.: Harvard University Press.
Bowen, John R.
    1991    *Sumatran Politics and Poetics: Gayo History, 1900–1989*. New Haven: Yale University Press.
    1993    *Muslims through Discourse: Religion and Ritual in Gayo Society*. Princeton: Princeton University Press.
Brenneis, Donald, and Fred R. Meyers (eds.)
    1984    *Dangerous Words: Language and Politics in the Pacific*. New York: New York University Press.
Briggs, Charles L.
    1986    *Learning How to Ask: A Sociolinguistic Appraisal of the Role of the Interview in Social Science Research*. Cambridge: Cambridge University Press.
    1993    Personal sentiments and polyphonic voices in Warao women's ritual wailing: Music and poetics in a critical and collective discourse. *American Anthropologist* 95 (4): 929–957.
Buckley, Thomas
    1984    Yurok speech registers and ontology. *Language in Society* 13: 467–488.
Calhoun, Craig (ed.)
    1992    *Habermas and the Public Sphere*. Cambridge, Mass.: MIT Press.
Caton, Steven C.
    1990    *"Peaks of Yemen I Summon": Poetry as Cultural Practice in a North Yemeni Tribe*. Berkeley: University of California Press.
Chafe, Wallace
    1993    Seneca speaking styles and the location of authority. In *Responsibility and Evidence in Oral Discourse*, ed. J. H. Hill and J. T. Irvine, 72–87. Cambridge: Cambridge University Press.
Chagas Lima, Francisco das
    1842    Memória sobre o descobrimento e colonia de Guarapuáva. *Revista do Instituto Histórico e Geográfico Brasileiro* 4: 43–64. Rio de Janeiro.
Chagnon, Napoleon
    1968    *Yanomamö: The Fierce People*. New York: Holt, Rinehart and Winston.
Clastres, Pierre
    1977    [1974] *Society Against the State: The Leader as Servant and the Humane Uses of Power Among the Indians of the Americas*. Trans. R. Hurley. New York: Urizen Books.

Clifford, James
   1988   *The Predicament of Culture: Twentieth-Century Ethnography, Literature, and Art.* Cambridge, Mass.: Harvard University Press.
Cortázar, Julio
   1973   Julio Cortázar. In *Seven Voices: Seven Latin American Writers Talk to Rita Guibert*, ed. R. Guibert, trans. F. Partridge. New York: Knopf.
Crocker, William H.
   1990   *The Canela (Eastern Timbira), I: An Ethnographic Introduction.* Smithsonian Contributions to Anthropology, no. 33. Washington, D.C.: Smithsonian Institution Press.
Cunha, Manuela Carneiro da
   1978   *Os Mortos e os Outros: Uma Análise do Sistema Funerário e da Noção de Pessoa entre os Índios Krahó.* São Paulo: Editora Hucitec.
Cunningham, Clark E.
   1964   Order in the Atoni house. *Bijdragen tot de Taal-, Land- en Volkenkunde* 120: 34–68.
Da Matta, Roberto
   1976   *Um Mundo Dividido: A Estrutura Social dos Índios Apinayé.* Petrópolis, Brazil: Editora Vozes.
Duranti, Alessandro
   1994   *From Grammar to Politics: Linguistic Anthropology in a Western Samoan Village.* Berkeley: University of California Press.
Duranti, Alessandro, and Charles Goodwin (eds.)
   1992   *Rethinking Context: Language as an Interactive Phenomenon.* Cambridge: Cambridge University Press.
Durkheim, Emile
   1969   |1912| *The Elementary Forms of the Religious Life.* Trans. J. W. Swain. New York: The Free Press.
Durkheim, Emile, and Marcel Mauss
   1963   [1903] *Primitive Classification.* Trans. R. Needham. Chicago: The University of Chicago Press.
Eliade, Mircea
   1963   *Patterns in Comparative Religion.* Trans. R. Sheed. New York: World.
Errington, J. Joseph
   1988   *Structure and Style in Javanese: A Semiotic View of Linguistic Etiquette.* Philadelphia: University of Pennsylvania Press.
Feld, Steven
   1990   [1982] *Sound and Sentiment: Birds, Weeping, Poetics, and Song in Kaluli Expression.* Philadelphia: University of Pennsylvania Press.
   n.d.   Waterfalls of song: The sensuality of place resounding in Bosavi, Papua New Guinea. To appear in *Place, Expression, and Experience*, ed. K. Basso and S. Feld.
Feld, Steven, and Charles Keil
   1994   *Music Grooves.* Chicago: University of Chicago Press.
Fernandez, James W.
   1986   *Persuasions and Performances: The Play of Tropes in Culture.* Bloomington, Ind.: Indiana University Press.

Fortes, Meyer
    1953    The structure of unilineal descent groups. *American Anthropologist* 55: 25–39.
Foucault, Michel
    1972    [1969] *The Archaeology of Knowledge*. Trans. A. M. S. Smith. New York: Pantheon Books.
Fox, Aaron
    1992    The jukebox of history: Narratives of loss and desire in the discourse of country music. *Popular Music* 11 (1): 53–82.
Freud, Sigmund
    1913    The occurrence in dreams of material from fairy tales. In Volume 12 of *The Standard Edition of the Complete Psychological Works of Sigmund Freud*, ed. J. Strachey, 280–287. London: Hogarth, 1953–1974.
Geertz, Clifford
    1973    *The Interpretation of Cultures: Selected Essays*. New York: Basic Books.
    1984    Anti anti-relativism. *American Anthropologist* 86: 263–278.
Gensch, Hugo
    1908    Wörterverzeichnis der Bugres von Santa Catharina. Mit Vorbemerkung von Ed. Seler. *Zeitschrift für Ethnologie* 40: 744–759.
Gödel, Kurt
    1931    Über formal unentscheidbare Sätze der Principia Mathematica und verwandter Systeme I. *Monatshefte für Mathematik und Physik* 37: 349–360.
Gonzalez, Patricia A.
    1993    Hundreds visit Brownsville to see image of Mary on tree. *Austin American-Statesman*, Tuesday, August 10, 1993, p. B3.
Goodenough, Ward H.
    1956    Componential analysis and the study of meaning. Language 32 (1): 195–216.
Graham, Laura
    1984    Semanticity and melody: Parameters of contrast in Shavante vocal expression. *Latin American Music Review* 5: 161–185.
    1986    Three modes of Shavante vocal expression: Wailing, collective singing, and political oratory. In *Native South American Discourse*, ed. J. Sherzer and G. Urban, 83–118. Berlin: Mouton de Gruyter.
    1993    A public sphere in Amazonia? *American Ethnologist* 40 (4): 717–741.
    1994    Dialogic dreams: Creative selves coming into life in the flow of time. *American Ethnologist* 21 (4): 723–745.
    1995    *Performing Dreams: The Discourse of Immortality among the Xavante of Central Brazil*. Austin: University of Texas Press.
Guérios, Rosário Farani Mansur
    1944    O Xocrén é idioma Caingangue. *Arquivos do Museu Paranaense* 4: 301–331. Curitiba, Brazil.
    1945    O Xocrén é idioma Caingangue. *Boletim Bibliografico* 6: 60–68. São Paulo.
Habermas, Jürgen
    1984    *Reason and the Rationalization of Society*. Vol. 1 of *The Theory of Communicative Action*, trans. T. McCarthy. Boston: Beacon Press.
    1987    *Lifeworld and System: A Critique of Functionalist Reasoning*. Vol. 2 of *The*

*Theory of Communicative Action*, trans. T. McCarthy. Boston: Beacon Press.

1989   [1962] *The Structural Transformation of the Public Sphere: An Inquiry into a Category of Bourgeois Society*. Trans. T. Burger. Cambridge, Mass.: MIT Press.

Hanks, William F.

1990   *Referential Practice: Language and Lived Space among the Maya*. Chicago: University of Chicago Press.

Hendricks, Janet Wall

1993   *To Drink of Death: The Narrative of a Shuar Warrior*. Tucson: University of Arizona Press.

Henry, Jules

1935   A Kaingang text. *International Journal of American Linguistics* 8: 172–218.

1936a  The linguistic expression of emotion. *American Anthropologist* n.s. 38: 250–256.

1936b  The personality of the Kaingang Indians. *Character and Personality* 5: 113–123.

1940   A method for learning to talk primitive languages. *American Anthropologist* n.s. 42: 635–641.

1942   The Kaingang Indians of Santa Catarina, Brasil. *América Indígena* 2 (1): 75–79.

1948   The Kaingang language. *International Journal of American Linguistics* 14: 194–204.

1964   [1941] *Jungle People: A Kaingáng Tribe of the Highlands of Brazil*. New York: Vintage Books.

Herdt, Gilbert

1987   Selfhood and discourse in Sombra dream sharing. In *Dreaming: Anthropological and Psychological Interpretations*, ed. B. Tedlock, 105–131. Cambridge: Cambridge University Press.

Hicks, David

1966a  The Kaingang and the Aweikoma: A cultural contrast. *Anthropos* 61: 839–846.

1966b  A structural analysis of Aweikoma symbolism. *Ethnos* 31: 96–111.

1971a  A comparative analysis of the Kaingang and Aweikoma relationship terminologies (Brazil). *Anthropos* 66: 931–935.

1971b  A structural model of Aweikoma society. In *The Translation of Culture: Essays to E. E. Evans-Pritchard*, ed. T. O. Beidelman, 141–159. London: Tavistock.

Hill, Jane H., and Judith T. Irvine (eds.)

1993   *Responsibility and Evidence in Oral Discourse*. Cambridge: Cambridge University Press.

Hill, Jonathan D.

1993   *Keepers of the Sacred Chants: The Poetics of Ritual Power in an Amazonian Society*. Tucson: University of Arizona Press.

Hugh-Jones, Christine

1979   *From the Milk River: Spatial and Temporal Processes in Northwest Amazonia*. Cambridge: Cambridge University Press.

Hymes, Dell
    1981    *"In vain I tried to tell you": Essays in Native American Ethnopoetics.* Philadelphia: University of Pennsylvania Press.
Jakobson, Roman
    1957    *Shifters, Verbal Categories, and the Russian Verb.* Cambridge, Mass.: Harvard University Russian Language Project.
Jones, Ernest
    1925    Mother-right and the sexual ignorance of savages. *International Journal of Psycho-Analysis* 6 (2): 109–130.
Joyce, James
    1989    [1896?] *James Joyce: The Critical Writings.* Ed. E. Mason and R. Ellmann. Ithaca: Cornell University Press.
Kana, N. L.
    1980    The order and significance of the Savunese house. In *The Flow of Life: Essays on Eastern Indonesia,* ed. J. J. Fox, 221–230. Cambridge, Mass.: Harvard University Press.
Keane, Webb
    1995    The spoken house: Text, act, and object in Eastern Indonesia. *American Ethnologist* 22 (1): 102–124.
Kleene, Stephen Cole
    1967    *Introduction to Metamathematics.* Princeton, N.J.: D. Van Nostrand.
Koenigswald, Gustav von
    1908    Die Botokuden in Südbrasilien. *Globus* 93: 37–43. Braunschweig.
Kratz, Corinne A.
    1994    *Affecting Performance: Meaning, Movement, and Experience in Okiek Women's Initiation.* Washington, D.C.: Smithsonian Institution Press.
Kroeber, Alfred L.
    1909    Classificatory systems of relationship. *Journal of the Royal Anthropological Institute* 39: 77–84.
Kühne, Heinz
    1979    Der Bodenbau der Kaingáng-und Lakranó-Indianer: ihre Stellung im Rahmen der Gê-Völker: Der Bodenbau in Wechselwirkung zum geistigen Leben, zur Gesellung und zur Umwelt. *Archiv für Völkerkunde* 33: 61–84.
    1980    Sammelwirtschaft, Fischfang und Tierhaltung der Kaingáng-und Lakranó-Indianer: ihre Stellung im Rahmen der Gê-Völker. *Archiv für Völkerkunde* 34: 101–122.
Kuipers, Joel C.
    1990    *Power in Performance: The Creation of Textual Authority in Weyewa Ritual Speech.* Philadelphia: University of Pennsylvania Press.
Lave, Jean Carter
    1979    Cycles and trends in Krĩkatí naming practices. In *Dialectical Societies: The Gê and Bororo of Central Brazil,* ed. D. Maybury-Lewis, 16–44. Cambridge, Mass.: Harvard University Press.
Lee, Benjamin
    n.d.    Talking heads: Languages, meta-languages, and the semiotics of subjectivity. Manuscript in preparation for publication.

Lepselter, Susan
 1994 UFO stories: The poetics of uncanny encounters in a counterpublic discourse. Master's thesis, Department of Anthropology, University of Texas
at Austin.

Lévi-Strauss, Claude
 1967 [1952] Social structures of Central and Eastern Brazil. In *Structural Anthropology*, trans. C. Jacobson and B. B. Schoepf, 116–127. Garden City, N.Y.:
Anchor.
 1968 [1955] *Tristes Tropiques: An Anthropological Study of Primitive Societies in Brazil*. Trans. J. Russell. New York: Atheneum.
 1969a [1949] *The Elementary Structures of Kinship*. Trans. J. H. Bell and J. R. von
Sturmer. Boston: Beacon Press.
 1969b [1964] *The Raw and the Cooked*. Introduction to a Science of Mythology,
vol. I. Trans. J. and D. Weightman. New York: Harper & Row.

Lissauer, A.
 1904a Schädel eines Bugre aus Blumenau. *Zeitschrift für Ethnologie* 36: 847–852.
 1904b Schädel eines Schokleng. *Zeitschrift für Ethnologie* 36: 844–847.

Lopes da Silva, Araçy
 1986 *Nomes e Amigos: Da Prática Xavante a uma Reflexão sobre os Jê*. São Paulo:
Universidade de São Paulo.

Lounsbury, Floyd G.
 1964 The structural analysis of kinship semantics. In *Proceedings of the 9th International Congress of Linguistics*, ed. H. G. Hunt, 1073–1092. The Hague:
Mouton.

Maine, Sir Henry
 1965 [1861] *Ancient Law*. New York: Dutton.

Malinowski, Bronislaw
 1953 [1927] *Sex and Repression in Savage Society*. London: Routledge and Kegan
Paul.
 1961 [1922] *Argonauts of the Western Pacific: An Account of Native Enterprise and
Adventure in the Archipelagoes of Melanesian New Guinea*. New York: E. P.
Dutton & Co.

Mason, J. Alden
 1950 The languages of South American Indians. In *Handbook of South American
Indians* 6: 157–317. Washington, D.C.: U.S. Government Printing Office.

Maybury-Lewis, David
 1965 *The Savage and the Innocent*. London: Evans Brothers.
 1967 *Akwē-Shavante Society*. Oxford: Oxford University Press.

Maybury-Lewis, David (ed.)
 1979 *Dialectical Societies: The Gê and Bororo of Central Brazil*. Cambridge, Mass.:
Harvard University Press.

Melatti, Julio Cezar
 1978 *Ritos de uma Tribo Timbira*. São Paulo: Editora Ática.

Merton, Robert K.
 1968 *Social Theory and Social Structure*. New York: The Free Press.

Métraux, Alfred
  1946   The Caingang. In *Handbook of South American Indians* 1: 445–475. Washington, D.C.: U.S. Government Printing Office.
Meyer, H.
  1896   Über die Bugres. *Verhandlungen der Gesellschaft für Erdkunde zu Berlin* 23: 257–266.
Morgan, Lewis Henry
  1871   *Systems of Consanguinity and Affinity of the Human Family.* Smithsonian Contributions to Knowledge, vol. 17. Washington, D.C.: The Smithsonian Institution.
Nãnbla, Kãnnhãhá, Kuzug Gaklã, Olímpio Zetxa Pripré, and Anonymous
  n.d.   *Histórias e Mitos na Língua Xokleng.* [No place or publisher given, but probably was produced in Brasília by SIL.]
Newton, Isaac
  1934   [1686] *Principia: Sir Isaac Newton's Mathematical Principles of Natural Philosophy and His System of the World.* Vol. 1, *The Motion of Bodies*, trans. F. Cajori. Berkeley: University of California Press.
Nimuendajú, Curt
  1946   *The Eastern Timbira.* Ed. and trans. R. H. Lowie. University of California Publications in Archaeology and Ethnology 41. Berkeley: University of California Press.
  1967   *The Apinayé.* Ed. R. H. Lowie and J. M. Cooper, trans. R. H. Lowie. Netherlands: Oosterhout N. B.
Nimuendajú, Curt, and R. F. M. Guérios
  1948   Cartas etno-lingüísticas. *Revista do Museu Paulista*, n.s. 2: 207–241. São Paulo.
Nowak, Ronald M., and John L. Paradiso (eds.)
  1983   *Walker's Mammals of the World.* 4th ed. Baltimore: The Johns Hopkins University Press.
Ortega, Bob
  1993   A tiny town in Texas is flooded with pilgrims seeking a miracle. *The Wall Street Journal*, Wednesday, September 29, 1993, p. B1.
Parsons, Anne
  1969   Is the Oedipus complex universal? The Jones-Malinowski debate revisited. Chapter 1 in *Belief, Magic, and Anomie: Essays in Psychosocial Anthropology*, 3–66. New York: The Free Press.
Parsons, Talcott
  1951   *The Social System.* New York: The Free Press.
  1966   *Societies: Evolutionary and Comparative Perspectives.* Engelwood Cliffs, N.J.: Prentice-Hall.
Price-Williams, Douglass, and Lydia Nakashima Degarrod
  1989   Communication, context, and use of dreams in Amerindian societies. *Journal of Latin American Lore* 51 (2): 195–209.
Reichel-Dolmatoff, Gerardo
  1971   *Amazonian Cosmos: The Sexual and Religious Symbolism of the Tukano Indians.* Chicago: The University of Chicago Press.

Rivers, W. H. R.

1968 [1914] *Kinship and Social Organization*. London School of Economics Monographs on Social Anthropology, no. 34. New York: Humanities Press.

Roseman, Marina

1991 *Healing Sounds from the Malaysian Rainforest: Temiar Music and Medicine*. Berkeley: University of California Press.

Santos, Sílvio Coelho dos

1973 *Indios e Brancos no Sul do Brasil: A Dramática Experiência dos Xokleng*. Florianópolis, Santa Catarina, Brazil: Edeme.

Schaden, Egon

1937 Einiges über die Schokleng von Santa Catharina. *Pindorama* 1 (2–3): 24–28. São Paulo.

Schaden, Francisco S. G.

1949 Apontamentos bibliograficos para o estudo dos Indios Xokleng. *Boletim Bibliografico* 12: 113–119. São Paulo.

1953 A pacificação e aculturação dos Xokleng. *Revista de Antropologia* 1: 136–139. São Paulo.

1957 Xokleng und Kaingang in Südbrasilien. *Staden-Jahrbuch* 5: 265–272. São Paulo.

1958 Xokleng e Kaingang. *Revista de Antropologia* 6: 105–112. São Paulo.

Seeger, Anthony

1981 *Nature and Society in Central Brazil. The Suyá Indians of Mato Grosso*. Cambridge, Mass.: Harvard University Press.

1987 *Why Suyá Sing: A Musical Anthropology of an Amazonian People*. Cambridge: Cambridge University Press.

Sherzer, Joel

1983 *Kuna Ways of Speaking: An Ethnographic Perspective*. Austin: University of Texas Press.

1990 *Verbal Art in San Blas: Kuna Culture through Its Discourse*. Cambridge: Cambridge University Press.

Sherzer, Joel, and Greg Urban (eds.)

1986 *Native South American Discourse*. Berlin: Mouton de Gruyter.

Silverstein, Michael

1976 Shifters, linguistic categories, and cultural description. In *Meaning in Anthropology*, ed. K. Basso and H. Selby, 11–55. Albuquerque: University of New Mexico Press.

Singer, Milton

1989 Pronouns, persons, and the semiotic self. In *Semiotics, Self, and Society*, ed. B. Lee and G. Urban, 229–296. Berlin: Mouton de Gruyter.

Souza Lima, Antonio Carlos de

1991 On indigenism and nationality in Brazil. In *Nation-States and Indians in Latin America*, ed. G. Urban and J. Sherzer, 236–258. Austin: University of Texas Press.

Spencer, Baldwin, and Francis James Gillen

1968 [1899] *The Native Tribes of Central Australia*. New York: Dover Publications.

Spiro, Melford E.
  1979    Whatever happened to the Id? *American Anthropologist* 81 (1): 5–13.
Stocking, George W., Jr.
  1968    *Race, Culture, and Evolution: Essays in the History of Anthropology*. New York: The Free Press.
  1979    *Anthropology at Chicago*. Chicago: The University of Chicago Library.
Sullivan, Lawrence E.
  1988    *Icanchu's Drum: An Orientation to Meaning in South American Religion*. New York: MacMillan.
Taunay, Alfredo d'Escragnolle
  1918    Os Indios Kaingángs. *Revista do Museu Paulista* 10: 569–628. São Paulo.
Taylor, Charles
  1990    Invoking civil society. In *Working Papers and Proceedings of the Center for Psychosocial Studies*, no. 31, 17 pp. Chicago: Center for Psychosocial Studies.
Tedlock, Barbara (ed.)
  1987    *Dreaming: Anthropological and Psychological Interpretations*. Cambridge: Cambridge University Press.
Tedlock, Dennis
  1983    *The Spoken Word and the Work of Interpretation*. Philadelphia: University of Pennsylvania Press.
Turner, Terrence S.
  1979    Kinship, household, and community structure among the Kayapó. In *Dialectical Societies: The Gê and Bororo of Central Brazil*, ed. D. Maybury-Lewis, 179–214. Cambridge, Mass.: Harvard University Press.
Turner, Victor
  1967    *The Forest of Symbols: Aspects of Ndembu Ritual*. Ithaca, N.Y.: Cornell University Press.
Tylor, Edward B.
  1889    On a method of investigating the development of institutions; applied to laws of marriage and descent. *Journal of the Royal Anthropological Institute* 18: 245–269.
Urban, Greg
  1988    Ritual wailing in Amerindian Brazil. *American Anthropologist* 90 (2): 385–400.
  1991    *A Discourse-Centered Approach to Culture: Native South American Myths and Rituals*. Austin: University of Texas Press.
Vidal, Lux Boelitz
  1977    *Morte e Vida de uma Sociedade Indígena Brasileira*. São Paulo: Editora Hucitec.
Vocabulario da língua Bugre
  1888    [1852] *Revista do Instituto Histórico e Geográfico Brasileiro* 15: 60–75. Rio de Janeiro.
von Grunebaum, Gustave Edmund, and Roger Caillois (eds.)
  1966    *The Dream and Human Societies*. Berkeley: University of California Press.
von Ihering, Rodolpho
  1968    *Dicionário dos Animais do Brasil*. São Paulo: Editôra Universidade de Brasília.

Warner, Michael
  1991   *Letters of the Republic*. Cambridge, Mass.: Harvard University Press.
Wheatley, Paul
  1971   *The Pivot of the Four Quarters: A Preliminary Enquiry into the Origins and Character of the Ancient Chinese City*. Chicago: Aldine.
Wiesemann, Ursula
  1972   *Die phonologische und Grammatische Struktur der Kaingáng-Sprache*. Janua Linguarum, Serie Practica, no. 90. The Hague: Mouton.
  1978   Os dialetos da língua Kaingang e o Xokleng. *Arquivos de Anatomia e Antropologia* 3: 199–217. Rio de Janeiro.
Wissler, Clark
  1938   *The American Indian: An Introduction to the Anthropology of the New World*. 3d ed. Oxford: Oxford University Press.

# Index

Adams, R. N., 262n.10
advertisement, 176
aesthetics, 9, 141–143, 147, 184, 200, 203
agency, 29, 45, 47
*ãglan* (lip-piercing) ceremony: and communal imagery, 172, 188, 191–192; in narrative, 178–183; and pain, 195–196; and referential aspect of discourse; 174–175, 187; singing at, 200, 202
Ãglò, 96–98, 123, 218, 249
*ãgyïn* (reintegrating widow) ceremony: and communal imagery, 83–84, 188–192; described, 15, 138–139, 172; in narrative, 183; and origin myth, 187, 203; and referential aspect of discourse, 174
Aldinger, 33
aliens from outer space, 254
Ali Krire, 234
alliance theory, 134, 169, 190, 192
Amaral, C. M. do, 33
Ãmẽno, 181–182
anaphoric deletion, 53, 261n.9
ancestors: opposed to the living, 46, 48–51, 56, 59–63; and paint designs, 141; Jê, 150
Anderson, Benedict, 51
Apinayé, 14, 81, 193
armadillo, 178, 180–181, 184, 244
art, 123
Ashanti, 142, 144, 146, 149, 250

Assembly of God church, 172, 190, 262n.13
Augustine, 65
Australia, 87–88, 98, 173
autodenomination, 30–44
Aweikoma, 12, 41–43, 58, 261n.7. *See also* Shokleng
*axis mundi*, 70–71, 75, 85, 87, 98
Ayu, 224–225

bag-tossing game, 175, 191–192
Bahía, 33
Bakhtin, Mikhail, 134–135
Baldus, Herbert, 14, 101–103, 105, 124
Bamberger, Joan, 14
Barasana, 86
Basso, Ellen, 260n.7
Basso, Keith, 263n.8
Bastide, Roger, 134
Bauman, Richard, 260n.7
Bavaresco, Isaac, 13
Bavaresco, Tina, 13
Berkeley, Bishop, 21, 110
big bang theory, 74
Black Water, 198, 207–208, 210–212
Bleyer, 38
Blumenau, 17, 32–33
Blumensohn, J. H., 39
Boas, Franz, 1, 44
Borba, Telemaco Morosini, 40
Bororo, 81–82, 127
Botocudo, 12, 28, 33, 35–40, 42–45, 58. *See also* Shokleng

boundedness, 29, 47–48
Bourdieu, Pierre, 85, 262n.5
Bowen, John, 260n.7
Brazil: Amerindian, 36, 60, 104, 126, 175; anthropological research in, 14–15; central Indian, 81, 84, 193–194; coastal, 153; description, 11–12
Brenneis, Donald, 260n.7
Briggs, Charles, 153, 261n.5, 262n.1
Buckley, Thomas, 262n.4
Buenos Aires, 42
*bugreiros* (Indian hunters), 14
Bugres, 12, 28, 32–33, 35–37, 39, 43, 45, 261n.4. *See also* Shokleng

Caillois, Roger, 265n.1
Cairjós, 36
Calhoun, Craig, 149, 259n.3
Cames, 40
Campos, 37
Cãtag, 218–219, 224–225
Caton, Steve, 260n.7
ceremonial parents, 102, 105–106, 174–175, 179, 191–192, 196
ceremonies for the dead, 125
ceremony, 23, 172–177, 185–189, 193–194, 197, 200, 203–204, 211, 214, 240, 245, 249; compared with dreams, 215–219, 236–239; interpretation of, 186–187; replication of action in, 177, 237; sensibility of, 236–237
Chafe, Wallace, 262n.7
Chagas Lima, Francisco das, 37, 40
Chagnon, Napoleon, 67, 69
Cimitille, Luiz de, 40
clans, 25, 138
Clastres, Pierre, 134
Clifford, James, 261n.3, 263n.1
coatimundi, 182
Cocteau, Jean, 15, 94
commands, 120, 123, 129, 196–197
community, 125; family as trope for, 137, 169–170, 188–191, 193, 204, 213, 251–252; metaphors of, 137, 149, 156, 158, 168–169, 188; parental bond as

trope for, 192–194, 196; spousal bond as trope for, 194. *See also* discourse, community-building
componential analysis, 100
Congress of Americanists, 42
consciousness: and ceremony, 184; community, 56, 58, 60, 62, 64, 148, 161, 217; of culture, 49, 59; degrees of, 56, 161, 163, 168; of discourse, 133; language-based, 203–204, 248; and narrative, 72; and other forms of spatial experience, 67; and reality, 152, 248; of repressed material, 220; of self, 52
co-reference, 106, 108
Coroados. *See* Shokleng
Crocker, William, 193
cross cousins, 100, 103
Cu, 228–229, 231–233, 247
culturalism, 11, 66, 100
culture, 27, 29, 45, 60–63, 75, 187–188, 204, 214; as adaptive mechanism, 24; Amerindian, 15; Brazilian, 18; as circulating discourse, 2, 65, 172–173, 177–178, 186, 213, 231–234, 245, 247, 252, 253, 255, 259n.3; consciousness and embodiment of, 49–50; continuity of, 76; diffusionists' model of, 66; ethnicization of, 47–48, 52; Geertz's model of, 10, 259n.3; learnability of, 120; material, 106, 241–242; principles of, 24; shared, 69, 173, 247; storytelling and, 72; theory, 23, 25; as tradition, 172; traditional anthropological models of, 59, 100, 123, 148–149, 214, 245; transmission of, 21, 64, 66, 138, 204, 214, 241–242; two kinds of, 86; western, 136, 176, 187, 218, 251
Cunha, Manuela Carneiro da, 194
Cunningham, Clark, 81
Curitiba, 20, 40
Cuwañ, 88, 206, 208–211

dance, 15, 91, 126, 163–167, 185, 188–190, 197, 203, 244, 264n.6

dance plaza, 83–84, 86, 125, 128, 155, 163–166, 168, 188–189, 191, 204, 211

Dante Alighieri, 91

Davidson, Donald, 10

death, 45–47, 80, 85, 91, 183, 189

deer, 178–180, 183–184, 228

Degarrod, Lydia, 265n.1

dehumanization, 36

Derrida, Jacques, 134

descent theory, 134–135, 137, 140–142, 144, 146, 148–150, 152, 169

dirt, as food, 15, 69, 92–94

discourse: community-building, 135, 137, 142, 146–151, 155, 170–171, 250–251; documentary, 7–8; in ethnography, 22, 30, 66–67, 74, 108; expectations, 109–110, 116, 120–123, 129–130, 132–133, 154, 159, 249; expectations violated, 123, 129, 130, 160; household, 176–178, 182, 184, 187, 198, 203; interpretation of, 133, 248; naturally occurring, 106, 108, 129, 131, 190; not addressing the noumenal, 80–81, 87, 93, 96, 173; political, 52, 55–60, 64, 197; as representation of behavior, 109; rhythms, 153, 158, 161, 205, 212, 244; sensibility and intelligibility of, 23–24, 69, 71–72, 74

— — —, circulation of, 6, 249–253, 256, 263n.3; among elders, 61, 79; of catastrophe, 213–214; and ceremony, 187; and distance from subjectivity, 48–49, 55; and dream narrative, 237–239, 251; and exchange, 162–163, 167–168; intelligibility of, 93–96; and kin classification, 79, 81, 99, 133; as linear and sequential, 172; and narrativization of everyday life, 123; and social organization, 63, 135, 137–138, 170–171

— — —, creating its own conditions of circulation, 27, 29; through aesthetics, 143; through attributing power to the noumenal, 239; through conception of community, 148, 251–252;

through conception of noumenal space, 87, 98; through exchange, 167; through residence rules, 80–81; through social organization, 59, 64, 67, 138, 152

— — —, material nature of, 10, 71, 74, 174, 182, 247, 257, 260n.7; continuum with referential meaning, 243, 245, 256; foregrounded in ceremony, 185, 204; in myth, 244; and publicness, 197; and ritualizability, 178

— — —, referential aspect of: and *āglan*, 174–175, 187; and *āgyin*, 174; and catastrophe, 213–214; and ceremony and dream, 215–216, 236–239; consciousness and, 168, 184–185; and culture, 177–178; and emotion, 195–196; replication of, 243–244; and self-consciousness, 52; skepticism toward, 252, 255; and social organization, 194; and temporality, 76

— — —, replication of: 24–25, 137, 150, 152, 256–257; and ceremonialization of, 248; fixation through, 246–247; likelihood of, 55; and modification, 133; and rhythm, 205; and social encounter, 186, 213; unconscious, 162

Dival, 20

DNA, 24, 241–242, 248, 253

Dorins, 40

dream narratives: 3–9, 22–23, 217–225, 234–240, 243; compared with myth, 243–247; compared with mythologized shamanic experience, 228–231, 233, 239–240; replication and circulation of, 241–245, 251

dreams: compared with ceremony, 215–219, 236–239, 265n.3; as contact with spirit world, 80, 89, 222, 226–227, 253–254; as culture-specific phenomena, 235–236; and fear, 220, 227, 229; and intelligibility, 237; interpretation of, 218, 221–224, 227, 231, 236–237, 253; psychic origin of, 235; psychoanalytic view of, 218, 254; replication of, 216–217, 235–237; selection, 224, 235–236, 251; as source of cultural change, 234, 246; suggestion, 224, 235–236, 251

Duque de Caxias, P. I., 261n.1

Duranti, Alessandro, 260n.7

Durkheim, Emile: on collectivity, 29, 47–48, 64, 173, 177, 189, 195, 204, 238; on collectivity as God, 255; on image of natural world, 156; on social classification, 1, 25, 134, 148

eagle, 178, 180, 183

Eastern Timbira, 15, 81, 193

Einstein, Albert, 74

Eliade, Mircea, 71, 246

emotion, 175–176, 187–191, 194–196, 204, 212–214

empiricism, 1–3, 5, 7–10, 89, 257

enactment, 24–25, 29, 70–71, 97, 249, 253; fixation of, 25

Errington, Joe, 260n.7

Espírito Santo, 33

essentialization, 58–62

ethnicity, 35, 45, 47–49, 52, 59–62, 64, 137–138, 153; external and internal, 262n.10

ethnosemantics, 124, 129

exchange, 162–163, 167–168, 170–171

fairy tales, 234–235

falcon, 70, 72, 89–90, 119, 216, 234

fantasy, 8, 9

Feld, Steven, 87, 212, 260n.7

Fernandez, James, 262n.11

fiction, 6, 9

field, as narrative space, 11

Firth, Raymond, 11

Florianópolis, 12, 14, 159

Fortes, Meyer, 11, 25, 134–135, 140–142, 144, 146, 149

Foucault, Michel, 22–23, 134

Fox, Aaron, 260n.7

Freud, Sigmund, 13, 175, 184, 217, 234–235

FUNAI, 13, 15–20, 52, 103, 159, 259n.2, 261n.2

Gaklã, Kuzug, 262n.13

Gaklã, Nãnbla, 262n.13

Geertz, Clifford, 10, 253, 259n.3, 265n.1

gender, 53–56; inversion, 130; segregation, 189–190

genealogies, 14, 70, 78

genetic code. *See* DNA

Gensch, Hugo, 32, 41–42

Geographical Society of Berlin, 32

Gillen, Francis James, 87

globalization, 10, 25

glossing, 104–105, 124, 130, 244

God, 73, 253–256, 266n.6

Gödel, Kurt, 248

Goes Living, 69, 71, 91, 94–97, 123–124, 182–183, 216, 249

*gòlõ* (wildcat), 180–181

Goodenough, Ward, 100, 124

Goodwin, Charles, 260n.7

Graham, Laura, 18, 153, 259n.3, 260n.7, 265nn.3, 4

grammar, 5–6, 53, 106, 130, 199–200, 203, 260n.8

Gramsci, Antonio, 134–135

grief, expression of, 175–176

"groove," 212–213

groupness, 147–149, 152, 189

Grunebaum, Gustave von, 265n.1

Guarapuava, 37, 40

Guérios, R. F. M., 35, 38, 41–42

Habermas, Jürgen, 149, 259n.3, 263n.3

habitus, 85, 262n.5

Hanks, William, 260n.7

Harvard Central Brazil Project, 14

Hawk Mountain, 88, 205–212, 245

"he" (third person singular masculine pronoun), 49, 261n.9

hegemony, 137

Hendricks, Janet Wall, 260n.7

Henry, Jules, 14, 262n.13; on *ãglan*, 191, 195–196; on body painting, 139, 143, 168–169, 263n.2; on campsite shapes, 82, 84; on kinship terminology, 102–103, 124, 140–142, 144; lack of reference to definite spatial locations, 89;

and P. I. Ibirama group designation, 39, 41–42; on procedures surrounding death, 189; view of P. I. Ibirama culture as disintegrated, 48
Herdt, Gilbert, 265n.4
Hicks, David, 41–42
Hilbert, David, 248
Hill, Jane, 262nn.3, 7
Hill, Jonathan D., 260n.7
Hoerhan, Eduardo de Lima e Silva: on body painting, 143; elder's recollection of, 198; and establishment of contact with P. I. Ibirama group, 12–14, 28–35, 38–39, 42, 47, 61, 63–64, 81, 117, 262n.12; in narrative, 56–57; on P. I. Ibirama's lack of nucleus, 83; on P. I. Ibirama's original name, 261n.1
hole in the sky, 15, 69–71, 74, 80, 90
honey, 69, 92–96
howler monkey, 24, 181, 224–229, 231–233, 240, 245
Hugh Jones, Christine, 88
Hymes, Dell, 260n.7

"I" (first person singular pronoun), 49–50
Ibirama, 12
Ibirama, P. I.: community, 14, 29, 40, 69; native terms for group at, 32–33, 35, 37–41, 44
Ihering, H. von, 42, 263n.3
Indonesia, 81, 86–87, 98, 260n.7, 262n.7
intelligibility, 5, 10, 15, 21–27, 89, 152, 160, 197, 204, 214; language and, 5, 10; of objects cross-culturally, 44; and pronoun usage, 50; and replication, 244–245; of reported experience, 91; in song, 202–203; of spirit world, 71, 73
interconversion: principles of, 24, 26, 146, 248; between sensibility and intelligibility, 63, 65, 73, 93–98, 137, 151, 170
interviews, 66, 68, 72–73, 124, 129, 177, 262n.1

Iroquois, 99–101, 104
Irvine, Judith, 262nn.3, 7
Itajaí River and Valley, 12, 28, 82–83
Ivahy, 38

jaguar, 28, 65, 156–157; in narrative about animals' festival, 178–180, 183–184, 198; in origin myth, 143, 155, 157, 171, 204–205; as spirit, 15, 19, 94; as spirit, described by Wãñpõ, 69, 95
jaguarterica, 178–180
Jakobson, Roman, 23
Jê linguistic group, 12, 14, 42, 50
Jones, Ernest, 235
Joyce, James, 80

Kaingang, 14–15, 32, 36–43, 101–103, 105, 131–132, 169, 260n.6; of Ivaí, 16; of Santa Catarina, 12, 39
Kaklozàl, 106–108, 110, 114–116, 120
Kaluli, 87
Kãmlẽn: Wãñpõ's father, 34, 103, 193, 221, 232–234, 240, 245, 247; Wãñpõ's father, disguised as howler monkey in Wãñẽki's dreams, 226–229; Wãñpõ's son, 68, 76
Kana, N. L., 81
Kãñã'ĩ, 76, 78, 106, 118, 138, 230; in Wãñẽki's dreams, 3–4, 7, 221, 226
Kãñle, 147–148
Kant, Immanuel, 8, 10, 123
Kapil, 47
Kayapó, 15, 193
Kàyèta, 139, 142, 147
Keane, Webb, 81
Keil, Charles, 212
kinship, 26, 64; classificatory, 26, 99–104, 123; descriptive, 99; intelligibility of, 78–79; terminology, 77, 99–110, 115–125, 128–133, 168–169, 249–250; 263n.1; trope of, 115
Kïy, 128, 163–165, 264n.7
Klañmàg, 69–71, 89–90, 119, 216, 247
Kleno, 144, 148, 165
Koenigswald, Gustav von, 33
Kowi, 29, 32, 35, 56, 145, 230

Kòza, 207–208
Kòziklã, 42
Krahó, 14, 194
Kratz, Corinne, 260n.7
Krĩkatí, 14
Kroeber, A. L., 26, 100, 106, 108, 124, 132
Kühne, Heinz, 43
Kuipers, Joel, 260n.7, 262n.7
Kũkũ, 181
kula ring, 241, 247, 249
*kumēn* (plant), 182
Kũñẽpã, 136, 144, 146–147, 249
Kuyankàg, 70, 89, 119–120
Kuzug, 76, 118, 138, 144, 147

Lakranó, 43. *See also* Shokleng
land above the sky, 15, 69–70, 73, 89–90, 129, 247
land of the dead, 15, 69, 83–85, 91, 94–97, 189, 247, 249
language, 5, 133, 246; "Bugre," 32; English, 5, 39, 105; German, 39, 42; *langue*, 124, 128; *parole*, 128; of P. I. Ibirama, 38–41, 205; Portuguese, 15, 18, 32–33, 35, 39–41, 104, 261n.4; Tupi, 36
Laranjinha, 38
Lave, Jean Carter, 14, 150
Lee, Benjamin, 259n.1
Lẽl Tẽ. *See* Goes Living
Lepselter, Susan, 265n.5
Lévi-Strauss, Claude, 13–14, 134–135; on bird-nester theme, 126–127; on Bororo village space, 81–82; on marriage systems, 25, 162, 190; Spiro's criticism of, 235
line, 185, 200, 202, 206, 212
lineages, 25, 138, 149, 171
lip-plugs, 15, 28, 33–37, 39, 52, 75, 172, 191; description of insertion, 195–196; intelligibility of, 37
Lissauer, A., 32, 38
Lopes da Silva, Araçy, 150
Lounsbury, Floyd, 101–102, 104, 124, 132

Maine, Sir Henry, 109, 140, 249
Malinowski, Bronislaw, 235, 241
manifest content, 235
Manoel Ribas, P. I., 16, 103–104, 131–132
Marxism, 11
Mason, J. Alden, 41
matrilocality, 79
Matta, Roberto da, 14, 150
Mauss, Marcel, 134, 148, 156
Maybury-Lewis, David, 14, 81, 83, 193
meaning, 85–86; cultural, 1–2, 26, 65; and discourse, 197, 249–251, 253; and discourse, reality of, 255–257; and embodied practice, 147; and enactment, 25; ethnographers', 2; Geertzian, 259n.3, 265n.1; metadiscourse of, 104–106, 248; nonreferential, 183–184, 188, 197, 256; pragmatic, 183; privateness of, 247–248; and proper names, 76; referential or semantic, 36, 39, 118, 170, 176, 183, 185–187, 195–200, 204, 243, 245–246, 249, 253, 255–257; ritual, 174, 177; shared, 58; subjectivity and objectivity of, 6; in text, 5; Turner's two poles of, 194–195
media, 25
Melatti, Julio Cezar, 14, 193–194
Melsius, 73–74
Mendoza, Dario, 254–255
Merton, Robert, 109–110
metadiscourse, 10, 21–22, 24, 104–105, 168, 248; of kinship terminology, 78, 108, 133, 169; of marriage, 130–131
metadiscursive framing, 6–9
metaphor, 135–136
metapsychology, 219, 231
Métraux, Alfred, 41–42
Meyer, H., 32
Miguel, 19–20, 22
Minas Gerais, 33
miracles, 254–255
Miranda, Carmen, 11
Mõgñã, 103
moieties, 26, 42, 81, 100–104, 124, 131, 133, 138, 147

monkey, 181. *See also* howler monkey
morality, domestic, 123, 127–128
Morgan, Lewis Henry, 25–26, 99–101, 104, 123, 132, 263n.1
Mu, 17, 68
Mullen, Paul, 61, 78, 262n.13
Myers, Fred, 260n.7
myth, 110, 122, 172, 222, 249; compared to dream narratives, 243–247; as core of culture, 48; diffusion of, 66; and kinship terminology, 125, 144, 169; lack of ethnicity in, 47; negative image of community assembly in, 173; of origin of death, 45–47, 70; place-names in, 87–88; replication of, 241–245, Spiro and Lévi-Strauss on, 235. *See also* origin myth

Nãg, 76, 78
names, 76–77, 87, 106, 141–142, 148, 150, 158
Nãnbla, Kãmlãliá, 262n.13
Nãmla, 18, 130, 198–199
narrative, 72, 106, 217; asymmetrical relation to descent discourse, 160; lack of group designation in, 144
narrativization, 122, 168; of behavior, 122–123, 249–250; of everyday life, 123; of role expectations, 120, 122; of sense experience, 22; of space, 71, 85, 90–91
nation-state, 40, 47, 62
natively interpreted content, 235
Ndembu, 174, 187, 194
New Guinea, 87, 260n.7
Nẽwo, 107, 110–117, 120, 122, 127
Newton, Delores, 14
Newton, Sir Isaac, 74, 77, 80, 86, 89, 96, 242
Nike of Samothrace, 25, 245
Nil, 232, 249; at *ãgyin*, 138; as a boy, 33; and discourse of definitions, 104, 106; discourse on paint designs, 142; early encounters with whites, 28–29; narrating origin myth, 49, 128, 154; teaching author, 18–21, 49; vil-

lage drawings, 82–83; in Wãnẽki's dreams, 226, 228
Nimuendajú, Curt, 35, 38, 41–42, 81, 193
Northern Kayapó, 14
Noto-botocudos, 36
noumena, 21, 23, 89, 118, 246, 251, 255–257; conversion into phenomena, 25, 65, 71, 73; culturally standardized talk about, 80–81; and exchange, 162; and group denomination, 29, 37, 40; Kant's usage, 8; and societies, cultures, and ethnicities, 64; and "we," 44
noumenal attachment, 152–153, 158
noumenal community, 48, 51–52, 58, 62, 162, 170
Nũklèg, 164–165

Oedipus complex, 235
Og, 181–182
origin myth: at *ãgyin*, 174, 187, 203–204; animals in, 3, 142, 156–158; and exchange, 163; fixation of through performance, 25; locus of recitation, 86; and marriage, 213; negative image of community assembly in, 173; and paint designs, 143; and place-names, 88; pronouns in, 49–51; rhythm in, 153–154, 158, 205; as set of narrations, 159; stability of, 151, 161, 244, 246; style of, 128; teaching of, 18–19, 21

Paci, 56
painting, body, 15, 135–136, 138–148, 151, 155–160, 168–169, 171, 174, 197, 263n.2
Papanduva, 57
Paraguay-Paraná river system, 12
parallel cousins, 100, 103
parallelism, 53, 94, 212
Paraná, 16, 20, 103
paraphrase, 244–245, 247–248, 252–253, 256
Parmenides, 73–74
Parsons, Anne, 265n.11

Parsons, Talcott, 26, 109, 133, 260n.9
Patè, 19
Pazi, 125–127, 155, 167
peccary, 181
Pedro (spirit), 230
phenomena: 21, 23, 251, 256–257; and
    exchange, 162; and group denomina-
    tion, 29, 32, 35, 37, 40; Kant's usage,
    8; lack of culturally standardized talk
    about, 80; noumena's conversion
    into, 25, 65, 73; and "we," 44–45, 47
phenomenal attachment, 152–153, 158,
    170–171
phenomenal community, 48, 51–52, 58,
    60, 62, 162
photographs, ethnographic, 14
Pligyug, 154–155, 162
poetics, 117, 153, 168, 170, 200, 204–
    205, 211, 264n.5
porcupine, 178–180, 184
postmodernism, 23
poststructuralism, 22–23, 197
pragmatics, 183–184
Price-Williams, Douglass, 265n.1
Pripré, Olímpio Zetxa, 262n.13
pronominalism, 262n.11
pronouns, 44–64, 80–81, 106–108,
    119, 129, 144, 260n.7
psychoanalysis, 9, 175–176, 218–220,
    223
psychology, Kroeberian, 26
public, Kantian nation of, 259n.3
public sphere, 10, 137, 149–150, 251–
    252, 259n.3

Quintero, Santiago, Jr., 254–255

Ramanujan, A. K., 185–186
reflexivity, 25
Reichel-Dolmatoff, Gerardo, 67
repetition, 117, 185, 203, 205–206, 212–
    213, 244–245
reported speech, 52, 97, 127–128
rhyme, 200
Ricouer, Paul, 10
Rio de Janeiro, 11, 13, 15, 17, 152–153
Rio Negro, 198

ritual, 14, 63; interpretation of, 174–176
Rivers, W. H. R., 26, 100, 103, 124,
    263n.1
rocks, speaking, 1, 223–225, 227, 248
roles, 109–110, 118–122, 126, 129–130,
    132
Roseman, Marina, 260n.7

Salto da Ariranha, 38
Santa Catarina, 2, 12–13, 28, 32, 33, 36,
    63, 261n.2
Santos, Sílvio Coelho dos, 14, 38
São João dos Pobres, 14
São Paulo, 17, 38, 152
Saussure, Ferdinand de, 5, 105, 124, 128
Schaden, Egon, 38
Schaden, Francisco, 38
Schneider, David, 265n.1
Seeger, Anthony, 11, 150, 193, 260n.7
Seeger, Judy, 11
semantics, 184; formal, 100
sensibility, 5, 10, 15, 21–27, 75, 89, 152,
    160, 197, 204, 214; and interpreta-
    tion, 186; and metadiscourse, 168;
    and pronoun usage, 50; and replica-
    tion, 244; of sign vehicle, 10; in
    song, 202–203
Serra do Taboleiro, 14
Serra Geral, 11–12, 28, 65
Serra Pitanga, 38
shamanism: dreams and, 80, 219, 222;
    and enactment, 24, 240; and fear,
    234; and healing, 24; mythologized,
    compared with dream narratives,
    228–231, 233, 239–240
Sherzer, Joel, 260n.7
Shokleng, 12, 28, 33, 36–43, 45, 58
signals, nonreferential, 185–188, 193,
    195–197, 203
sign vehicles, 2, 6–7, 10, 147–148, 245
Silverstein, Michael, 23, 260n.7
Singer, Milton, 262n.11
singing, 15, 18, 20–21, 174, 179–185, 198–
    203, 264n.2; and *ãglan* , 200, 202;
    rhythm, 200, 202–203; syncopation,
    202; volume modulation, 200–201
snake, 110–111, 113–117, 158

social groups: assembly into, 172–173, 176–178, 184–189, 193–194, 203–205, 213, 238; dispersal of, 173, 176, 178, 185, 204, 213–214

social integration, 134–135, 137, 148, 151, 153, 171, 214, 250

social organization, 25–30, 63–65, 129, 135, 148, 160, 170, 187–188, 249–250; natives' talk about, 137–138

Souza Lima, Antonio Carlos de, 261n.2

space, 66; ancient Greek view of, 74; anthropological attempt to ask about, 72; apparent, 74, 81, 84–85, 96; and ceremony, 188–191, 197; community, 81–87, 98; and discourse of kinship, 79, 81; and gender segregation, 189–190; household, 75, 77–78, 81, 85–87, 190; individuals and, 80; intelligibility of, 66–67, 74–76, 84–86, 96; narrativization of, 71, 85, 90–91; sensibility of, 66–67, 74, 76, 84–86, 96; true, 71, 81, 85, 96

speech, 5, 23, 25, 66

speech register, 168–169

Spencer, Baldwin, 87

SPI, 28, 36, 261n.2

spirit world, 15, 22, 24, 221–222, 234, 236, 239

Spiro, Melford, 235

Stocking, George W., 259n.1, 261n.9

structural functionalism, 11

structuralism, 11, 25

Sullivan, Lawrence, 70–71, 186, 246

Summer Institute of Linguistics, 79, 262n.13

Suyá, 193, 260n.7

syntax, 246

systems, Parsonian, 26

Tallensi, 142, 149

tape recording, 16, 18, 21, 74–75, 198

tapir, 2, 256; Âglò's husband's description of, 96; idea of, 255; in narrative about animals' festival, 178–180; in origin myth, 155–157, 204; in Wâñëki's dreams, 2–8, 23–24, 220–222, 225, 227–228

tattoos, thigh, 172, 191–192, 195

Taunay, Alfredo d'Escragnolle, 40, 261n.4

Taylor, Charles, 259n.3

Tedlock, Barbara, 264n.1

Tedlock, Dennis, 260n.7

"they" (third person plural pronoun) 47, 51, 62–63, 81, 85

time: discourse transcending, 76, 88; Newton's discussion of, 74; and P. I. Ibirama community, 46–51, 53, 56–62

Trobriand Islands, 235

Turner, Terence, 14, 150, 193

Turner, Victor, 71, 174, 194

Tylor, Edward B., 25, 100–103, 124, 131, 133

Uglõ, 222

unconscious, 175–177, 183–186, 194, 204; and dreams, 235; and kinship terminology, 250

*universitus juris*, 109, 118, 249

uxorilocality, 79

Vidal, Lux Boelitz, 150, 193

video recording, 18

Virgin Mary, 254–255, 266n.6

Votorões, 40

wailing, 153, 175

Wãkra, 218

Wakuénai, 260n.7

Wanda, 76

Wâñëki: commenting on origin myth, 154; death of, 17–18; and discourse of definitions, 104; dreams of, 2–4, 6, 23–24, 218–228, 247; early encounters with whites, 28, 56; home of, 16; on kinship terminology, 106; meeting with, 15; name of, 144, 265n.2; narrating origin of death story, 45–46; narrating story of great fire, 50; narrating story of Nêwo, 110–115; on spirit world, 69, 71, 73, 95; telling Kañâ'i's dream, 230–231; village drawings, 82–83

Wãñēkí (Ãglò's husband), 96–97
Wãñēkí Patè, 128, 225, 227
Wañka, 222
Wãñpõ: and discourse of definitions,
    104; early encounters with whites,
    28–29, 56–57, 262n.11; on fear of
    shamans, 265n.5; on giving names,
    141; giving name to author, 103;
    home of, 16, 68, 75–79, 81, 85, 153,
    190; and Kañãĩ's dream, 230–231; on
    kinship terminology, 105; and Mu,
    17; narrating Ãglò's vision, 96–97;
    narrating story about Cu, 228; nar-
    rating story about Kàmlēn, 232–233;
    narrating story about Yòkàg, 229; on
    spirit world, 69, 71, 73–74, 89, 91–
    93, 95, 216, 247; and Wãñēki's
    dreams, 3–4, 6–7, 218, 221, 226
Wãñpõ Patè, 76, 78, 230–231
Wãñtàn, 178
Warner, Michael, 259n.3
Warodi, 18
"we" (first person plural pronoun),
    44–64, 80–81, 85, 261n.8
"welcome of tears," 153

Wheatley, Paul, 67
Wiesemann, Ursula, 38, 43
wild pig, 229–230
Wissler, Clark, 66–67
Wittgenstein, Ludwig, 185
Wòmle, 29–32, 35, 38, 42, 47, 56–57, 61,
    63–64, 81, 117
world system, 25
writing, 25, 66

Xavante, 14–15, 18, 81, 83, 193, 260n.7,
    265n.3
Xetá, 36

Yanomamö, 67
Yòkàg, 229
Yòko, 19–20
Yu'o, 76, 97

Zàgpope Patè, 49, 127–128, 155–156,
    166–167, 261n.9
Zambia, 174
Zeca Olímpio, 76
Zēzē, 143, 159–160
Zughà, 165